A GUIDE TO SCREENWRITING SUCCESS

A GUIDE TO SCREENWRITING SUCCESS

Writing for Film and Television

Stephen V. Duncan

ROWMAN & LITTLEFIELD PUBLISHERS, INC.
Lanham • Boulder • New York • Toronto • Oxford

ROWMAN & LITTLEFIELD PUBLISHERS, INC.

Published in the United States of America
by Rowman & Littlefield Publishers, Inc.
A wholly owned subsidiary of The Rowman & Littlefield Publishing Group, Inc.
4501 Forbes Boulevard, Suite 200, Lanham, Maryland 20706
www.rowmanlittlefield.com

P.O. Box 317, Oxford OX2 9RU, UK

British Library Cataloguing in Publication Information Available

Library of Congress Cataloging-in-Publication Data

Duncan, Stephen V., 1949–
A guide to screenwriting success : writing for film and television / Stephen V. Duncan.
p. cm.
Includes bibliographical references and index.
ISBN-13: 978-0-7425-5300-2 (cloth : alk. paper)
ISBN-10: 0-7425-5300-0 (cloth : alk. paper)
ISBN-13: 978-0-7425-5301-9 (pbk. : alk. paper)
ISBN-10: 0-7425-5301-9 (pbk. : alk. paper)
1. Motion picture authorship. 2. Television authorship. I. Title.
PN1996.D84 2006
808.2'3—dc22

2005023911

Printed in the United States of America

⊗™The paper used in this publication meets the minimum requirements of American National Standard for Information Sciences—Permanence of Paper for Printed Library Materials, ANSI/NISO Z39.48-1992.

Contents

PART III

Writing for Television

Appendix

Figures

Introduction

The art of screenwriting is *deceptively* difficult. I really hate to start on a sour note, but it has to be said right now while you're still bright-eyed, full of enthusiasm, and can take a good punch on the chin. I want you to go into this adventure sober and with the right point of reference and not to expect this endeavor to be *a piece of cake*. Upon first glance, the actual script does look *breezy* because it contains far, far, far fewer words than a novel. It's this simplicity that is the very evil that ends up possessing most novices. And it's a quick understanding of this insidious trap that, in the end, is your very salvation.

There's little doubt in my mind that many careers have been launched based on the movie-going experience of walking out of a bad film and groaning "I can write a better movie than that!" Then a few folks put their money where their mouths are, sit down, and begin to turn their million-dollar idea into a 120-page screenplay. That's when the panic begins to set in. Most people panic because of one simple reason—they don't know a thing about the *process* of writing a screenplay. Perhaps, some of you have already experienced this feeling. Most of you have an idea in the back of your mind for a screenplay. A few of you may have no clue of what you want to write about. And now, you are reading this book for help. Well, you've come to the right place.

Let me begin by saying that screenwriting is 50 percent *craft*, 40 percent *creativity*, and 10 percent *artistry*. Where do I get these numbers? I made them up, of course. But they're based on my experience and gut instincts, many sessions of working with novice screenwriters, and a bunch of long hours toiling over a hot computer. The good news is you'll learn *craft* from this book. But when it comes to the *creativity* and *artistry* stuff, you're on your own, but not forsaken.

Believe it or not, your *natural instincts* can take you a *very* long way in the aesthetic department. It's the lack of *craft*—the how-to-do-it part—that usually thwarts *consistent* success in any field of endeavor. Your *creative* and *artistic* instincts simply need access to a complete *box of tools*. Bear in mind that you'll have to learn how to *use* the tools well. And before you begin to *build a screenplay*, you're also going to need a well-planned *blueprint*. As you embark on your screenwriting experience, it's important that you also begin to *think like a screenwriter.* Train yourself to see, hear, smell, and touch the world in a way that'll feed visual images and auditory impressions into your brain . . . images and impressions from which you can match well-chosen words. Unlike the stalwart playwright, the screenwriter has the entire *world* for a stage. And if what we see doesn't inspire us, well, we simply *invent* a new world.

Exposing yourself to the entertainment industry will help you to think more like a screenwriter. By reading the "trades" on a regular basis, such as the *Daily Variety* and the *Hollywood Reporter*, you'll see what types of films are being written and produced; who's doing them; the stars, writers, directors, and producers involved; and which of the films are successful or clunkers. But don't let the *business* lead you down the wrong path or distract you too much from the *passion* for your story. Information about what's going on should be used to feed your instincts, not to tell you what kind of script to write. By the time you finish your screenplay about time travel, romantic comedies will be the next "hot" genre. Don't chase the next hot genre, *set the pace for one.*

Which leads me to the next point: expect to be on an *emotional roller-coaster* while you're developing and writing your screenplay. Whether you like it or not, you'll be making a big emotional investment in what you write. It's terribly hard to escape that. Our emotions are a very important part of *who* we are as human beings. Some days, you're going to be absolutely in love with your work. Other days, you're going to want to spit on it. The ticket to enduring this up-and-down ride is to understand that writing is a *process—the act of going through a series of creative doors.* Few of us can simply sit down with a vague idea and start banging out page after page until we have 120 of them and then never have to go back and change a single word. Even if we could, the moment the screenplay is sold, the studio will ask for a rewrite, and, if we refuse, it'll hire another writer who will do it. That's reality. So your "first draft" is your only true opportunity to write the story *you* want to tell. The important thing to remember is that the journey of screenwriting begins with a single sentence and ends with about 120 pages of narrative and dialogue. To be sure, there are mysterious incantations along the way. By using a step-by-step process to develop and write a screenplay, you give yourself the capacity to endure the inevitable plethora of emotions. The passage of *time* is an important element to this writing process. Time gives you the opportunity to *reflect* on what you're doing. A natural phenomenon happens inside your brain once you start writing a story: it automatically begins to seek out information that'll help you to fully realize what you're writing about. This process is called *cognitive dissonance,* but I promise I won't spend too much time on arcane theories like this in this book. I will focus on the writing process, first and foremost.

Patience and persistence are two very important Ps for the screenwriter to develop no matter the level of experience. *Believe* that you're doing the best you can and don't give up no matter how frustrating or hard the process of writing seems to get. Simply know that, at some point, everything will be fine. The role of *talent* in writing is, of course, an important one. How do you know if you have the talent for screenwriting? It's a difficult question that every writer has to face when they look in the mirror. The simple truth is you won't know unless you try. After writing several screenplays, you'll know—deep down inside—the answer to the question, *Do I have talent?* An important first step is to develop the *craft.* Then let the *talent* kick in on its own. Either it will or it won't. But trust me; lack of talent has never stopped a screenwriter from being successful. But the lack of *patience* and *persistence* has certainly tripped up a lot of them.

As in most things, there are many ways to approach the screenwriting process. Nowadays, it seems *everybody* has a theory about how to write a good screenplay. Many of these so-called gurus and script doctors know their stuff. They've mastered the theory of craft and totally believe in their own instincts about what's good when it comes to someone else's work. Most, if not all, of these mavens have never had one of their own screenplays produced. And most don't experience the daily delight and distress of being a screenwriter. The bottom line is this: it's hard to stare at an empty monitor and to fill it up with the right words in the right order that'll give birth to a highly collaborative process. This process involves thousands of other people (some creative, some who have no clue, most who are technical) who bring to life a piece of work that'll be seen by millions (cross your fingers) on the big and small screen. I promise you'll never hear someone say, "I'm going home to curl up to a good screenplay." Screenplays are the beginning of the long process of filmmaking.

This book consists of three sections. Each section is designed to be used as a stand-alone guide to writing and rewriting feature films and television writing. I explore the tried-and-true techniques used by many successful screenwriters, including myself. Key screenwriting terminology is bold-faced (such as "**spec**," below) and can be found in the glossary. I've attempted to stay practical as much as possible. My goal is to bring you as close to the "real" experience of screenwriting as I possibly can by walking you through a writing process that works. In doing so, I strive to offer the nuts and bolts with useful tools such as templates and to provide you with actual examples using my "**spec**" screenplay (a screenplay written on speculation for no pay) *Blood Ties* also known as *Motherland* and *Thesis*. These examples are the actual working documents as they were originally written (of course, I cleaned them up a bit). They reflect the *change* and *progress* that I made over the course of developing and writing my screenplay. In fact, I've taken the material a step further and adapted it into a novel. It was published as *Presumed Dead* in September of 2000. You'll find that this book strongly embraces what is generally called the "Hollywood" formula. I don't particularly care for this phrase because many writers take this to heart too strongly. But I focus on what the studios are most interested in for a simple, non-altruistic reason—*Hollywood films make money.* If making money offends you . . . well, that's something I can't help you with. Of course, this doesn't mean you shouldn't write film scripts for altruistic or artistic reasons. I believe you've got to know the rules before you can effectively break them. And, of course, the *formula* doesn't stop you from being artistic anyway. I've actually heard it said that the art form for the new century is the film. I suppose that's a typical attitude that conveniently supports today's "superhighway" mentality. After all, people are actually learning to write screenplays on the Internet. Whether film will take its place in social history as the art form of the new century is something, I believe, for future generations to decide. Hindsight is always twenty-twenty.

In the meantime, I hope you do write with the urgency and desire of contributing something of value to our world's society and its artistic legacy. So, while your enthusiasm and eagerness are at full throttle, let's get started . . .

PART I

Writing the Feature Film

CHAPTER 1

Develop a Solid Premise

WHERE DO I START?

It's easier than you think.

It seems that the hardest thing about writing is figuring out *what* to write. But once you understand the process, you'll see it's not that difficult. There are a few ways you can approach making this important decision.

The first approach is called *what if?* Using this method, you can start with an interesting character or an intriguing situation and simply ask yourself the question. Here are a couple of examples.

What if . . . a preteen boy who badly wants to be a grown man makes the wish to become so and it comes true? Of course, this notion focuses on a *character* and could have been the germ that gave birth to the screenplay for *Big* starring Tom Hanks.

What if . . . a scientist discovers a way to have dinosaurs walk the earth again? This notion focuses on a *situation* and could have been the origin of Michael Crichton's novel *Jurassic Park*, which went on to become one of director Steven Spielberg's biggest movie box office successes.

Another approach is to *write what you know*. This could include using something from your profession as the basis of a story. Or a vacation you took to Cleveland. Or it could be about an interesting friend. Or even about an eccentric family member.

The *research* approach is really a variation of *what you know*. If you read and learn about something, then you know about it. So, find a subject, or person, that interests you, learn everything you can about it and start developing your premise around that information.

The *what's hot and what's not* approach means you look at the kinds of movies that are being successfully produced and write a story that fits into the mold. But here's the rub: by the time you write the screenplay that's in the *hot* genre, the industry could have moved on to the next genre. So, perhaps it's better to discover what's successful today and then chose something that's not being produced at all. If a Western hasn't been successfully produced in a while, and you like this genre, it might be a good idea to write one. The Western genre was considered dead until *Dances with Wolves* came along. Clint Eastwood had a Western script he had been trying to make for nearly ten years called *Unforgiven*, but nobody really wanted to touch it . . . until Kevin Costner's hit. Then Eastwood's little movie about a retired gunman went on to win the coveted Oscar. That same year, studio vaults around Hollywood were desperately scavenged for Western screenplays already under an option and agents deluged development executives and producers with their clients' Western scripts.

But don't limit your imagination to what has been done in the past. A few years ago, a screenplay was optioned because it was a story set in the Old West but aliens landed. Another recent example of how to spin classic storytelling into something fresh and unique appeared at the 2005 Sundance Film Festival. The screenplay entitled *Brick* takes elements of classic film noir and reinvents the genre by using tough guy dialogue and plot devices from the 1940s in a contemporary high school teen murder mystery. The writer went the extra step by producing the film himself.

WHAT MAKES A GOOD PREMISE FOR A SCREEN STORY?

IT'S NOT THE WHOLE STORY.

Ideally, it's one sentence that serves to spark both interest and curiosity in the reader. I say "reader" because a screenplay's first audience is someone who reads it. Agents, professional readers, studio executives, story editors, producers, directors, and actors—are your first industry audience. Of course, your significant other, your mother, and your best friend have to give their nod of approval before that happens. The premise should clearly state *what the story is about*. It should be concise. At the end of a very long letter to a friend, Ernest Hemingway quotes French mathematician Blaise Pascal, *"Sorry, I would have written a shorter letter if I had had more time."* Boiling a story down to one sentence is, indeed, a challenge but well worth the effort.

Some call the premise the *one-liner.* Agents like to hear one-liners. So do studio executives and producers in pitch meetings. But pitching is another chapter. I prefer to call the premise the screenwriter's *only beacon of light in the dark abyss of rewrites.* Quite often the writer can get lost in the details of the writing process. A strong premise can keep you on track in the morass of detail and help you focus all those inevitable notes from experts who seem to be necessary to the development of a *salable* screenplay.

The *problem* presented in the basic premise needs to have a difficulty factor sufficient enough to carry the main character—the protagonist—through a two-hour odyssey of pursuing a solution. If I had to boil down what absolutely makes a movie premise a solid one, it would have to be this: *One person with a problem that gets bigger and more complicated as he or she tries to solve it through other people.*

The key word for a strong premise is *problem*.

High Concept Premises

Many of today's popular films are **high concept**.

But what does that mean exactly? Basically, it's a screenplay based on a *situation* or *setting* that's patently *more important* to the story than the characters themselves. Here are a few examples of what one might consider high concept films:

Splash—A man finally meets the girl of his dreams and she turns out to be a fish.

Liar, Liar—A lawyer has to tell the truth for one day.

Wayne's World—Two guys find success with their cable-access television show in the basement of their suburban home.

The Sixth Sense—A boy sees dead people.

The Terminator—A ruthless killer robot from the future comes back in time to kill the woman who is destined to give birth to the leader of the future's revolution.
Back to the Future—A young man takes a trip back into his parent's past in a Delorian car and has to get them together before he ceases to exist.
Big—A boy gets his wish to be a man.
Die Hard—While trying to make amends with his wife, a burned-out cop is trapped in a building by terrorists.
Jaws—A giant killer shark terrorizes a beach community at the height of tourist season.
The Matrix—The real world is really a virtual world controlled by a giant computer.

There are certainly many others. Statistically, most high concept films are unsuccessful . . . but not necessarily for the screenwriter. Many of these scripts are written on "spec" and find themselves at the center of furious bidding wars among movie studios. Some of the scripts get sold for a lot of money. But many of these high-priced screenplays never make it to the screen because they don't survive the rewriting process that's critical to attracting important actors and directors to the material. When a studio pays a lot of money for a screenplay, the pressure for it to succeed is enormous.

While a high concept story *can* work for the unseasoned writer—many have made fine films—there are a few pitfalls associated with developing and writing such a script. One pitfall is the inherent shallowness of the concept itself. No matter how interesting or intriguing, the situation or character *usually* has little depth. There's generally very little to sink your teeth into and the specter of repetition looms heavily over the development of a story that must engage an audience for two hours.

So the screenwriter should add dramatic elements to the high concept that'll give it more dimensions. In most cases, what the screenwriter should add is a good old-fashioned *love story*. Other elements commonly added to flesh out a high concept include *running gags* and one or two emotion-based subplots that *distract* the protagonist from the high concept itself.

A misnomer is that high concept premises must be big-budget films, nowadays called *tent pole* movies. This can't be further from the truth. Budget has nothing to do with it. For example, the premise for the drama *Good Will Hunting* can be considered high concept not because of its budget but because the story's *situation* is more important than the characters. However, since this film is a drama and not a popular genre, the term **lo-high concept** can be applied here.

Bottom line, writing a screenplay based on a high concept premise is among the top ways to get attention in the entertainment industry.

INDEPENDENT FILMS AND THE HOLLYWOOD FORMULA

This is an uneasy alliance.

For the Academy of Motion Picture Arts and Sciences, 1996 became the Year of the Independents. All five films nominated for Best Picture were independently financed and produced. *The English Patient* won the statuette and its budget was only $30 million—large for an independent—but it stars mostly high-profile Hollywood actors. The screenplay defies the Hollywood formula and yet became very successful. However, one must bear in mind that the screenplay is based on a popular novel. That certainly helps.

Jerry Maguire, produced and distributed by the major studio Sony, cost a lot of money to make but it also *made* a lot of money. Ironically, *Jerry Maguire* was written and directed by independent filmmaker Cameron Crowe. In one way, this film defies the Hollywood formula by including two fully developed subplots. It's this that prompted critics to ask, "What does this film want to be about?" It doesn't matter, the film works. I think Tom Cruise and Cuba Gooding Jr. had a lot to do with that.

Shine is no doubt the film that least embraces the Hollywood formula. It's based on a true story, and the film developed out of a documentary that took ten years to realize.

If one had to guess which film was the biggest surprise of 1996, I would have to vote *Sling Blade*, which did not receive an academy nomination for Best Picture. While it was made for about $1 million, the screenplay embraces the Hollywood formula with both arms. Though the script was well written—it won the **Writers Guild of America (WGA)** Award for Best Screenplay Based on Material Previously Produced or Published—there's no doubt what captivates audiences the most is actor-writer-director Billy Bob Thornton's creation of the mentally challenged and oddly lovable murdering hero Karl.

Fargo was also a surprise film. This was the first film for which its writers—Ethan and Joel Coen—had wholly embraced the Hollywood formula albeit with some caution. They break or stretch a lot of the "rules" and the screenplay works. This was the WGA winner for Best Screenplay Written Directly for the Screen in 1997.

The 1996 Academy of Motion Picture Arts and Sciences Award nominee, *Secrets & Lies*, interestingly, did not begin with a screenplay. The director, Mike Leigh, had the story's scenario firmly etched into his mind and allowed the actors to improvise each scene's dialogue. I suspect that a lot of screenwriters did not appreciate this film being nominated for best original screenplay since the actors themselves did most of the writing. But there is no doubt, the screenplay's structure is *not* the usual Hollywood formula . . . and, it too, works extremely well.

In the first decade of the twenty-first century, it seems that the meaning of independent filmmaking is increasingly being defined by years of struggling than by the type of material produced. The subject matter (themes), the screenwriters, the directors, and the actors are all crossing the line. The curious thing about independent filmmakers today is that they have struck an uneasy alliance with Hollywood studios, and it's proving to be more and more financially and critically beneficial to both sides.

As a screenwriter, I think it comes down to one important thing these days—the budget. Do I write a "small" movie or a "big" one with blockbuster potential? Just remember this: in 1996, for every film nominated for Best Picture, the director either wrote it or had a major hand in the screenwriting.

Then, just when the independent film industry was going like gangbusters, along came *Titanic*, which cost in the neighborhood of $200 million to make and reached $1 billion in worldwide box office gross revenue in less than six months.

In the first decade of the new millennium, independent filmmakers and studios are very much in business with one another. Major studios have purchased many of the smaller companies that had focused on making independent films. Most have been left alone to do what they do best, and the studios bring in their marketing muscle once films are produced.

Major studios, talent agencies, and producers are more often searching film festivals for the next hot screenwriter or director. Big stars are even bypassing big paydays to do smaller films and work with new directors. Many of these stars are developing films through their own production companies, especially small dramas.

The 2004 Oscar race has been dubbed Year of the Biopic. Of the five nominated films, three are stories about famous individuals: *The Aviator, Finding Neverland*, and *Ray*. The other two, *Million Dollar Baby* and *Sideways* (winner of the WGA Award and Oscar for adaptation; the WGA and academy awarded *Eternal Sunshine of the Spotless Mind* the best original screenplay) are considered "small" films. In fact, only one of these nominated films is a big-budget Hollywood film. And the academy gave the Oscar to *Million Dollar Baby*. So, perhaps it's safe to say that this uneasy alliance between independent filmmakers and multinational entertainment corporations is here to stay. In fact, one might even say, the alliance is becoming comfortable.

ELEMENTS OF A SOLID PREMISE

KEEP IT SIMPLE.

The following are the basic ingredients.

1. *A problem*. In *The Fugitive*, Dr. Kimble has been wrongfully convicted of killing his wife and sent to death row—big problem.
2. *An interesting theme*. Kimble's wife is killed because of corporate greed.
3. *A protagonist with a strong goal*. Kimble needs to find the one-armed man to clear his name if he doesn't want to be executed.
4. *Unrelenting antagonist with a strong need* to stop the protagonist from reaching his or her goal. Lieutenant Sam Gerard stays on Kimble's trail with the fervor of an untamed pit bull.
5. *An interesting setting*. The setting for *The Fugitive* is the world of high-tech medicine.

Put these elements together and you get the following solid premise: A prominent doctor is wrongfully convicted of murdering his wife, escapes prison, and is unrelentingly pursued by a U.S. marshal as he sets out to find the guilty one-armed man.

A weak premise tends to be vague. For example: a young man finds college life is not for him. While this may not patently be a bad premise, it's certainly incomplete, passive, and lacking a specific story theme and setting. How would I fix it? Here's one way among many others: *A frustrated law student unwittingly represents a buddy in a small-claims case and finds himself implicated in the murder of the opposing party and on the run from the actual killer.*

I took out the vagueness by inferring personal conflict with the words *unwittingly* and *frustrated*. I added a concrete *problem*—implicated in the murder of the opposing party. By making the young man a law student, there's a more specific *theme and setting*—the law and its training ground. And I provided an *antagonist (villain)*—the real murderer.

One key thing to remember about this technique is this: Your idea will come to you as one or more of these elements; all you have to do is to figure out the missing element and you're home free.

FILM GENRES

TO LAUGH, TO CRY, TO BLOW THINGS UP.

Next you need to decide the **genre** in which you wish to develop your premise. This is an important decision since a premise could conceivably be executed in more than one genre. There are many types of films—or genres—in which you can write. Here are a few popular staples:

Drama	Comedy	Science Fiction
Romance	Thriller	Horror
Western	Action	Fantasy

Then there are also popular hybrids of these fundamental genres:

Action Drama	Science Fiction Thriller
Action Adventure	Horror Thriller
Romantic Comedy	Horror Comedy

Which genre should you choose to write? That's a question only you can answer. But it's probably best to write the type *you* find most enjoyable to watch. Be aware that each genre has its own peculiarities and conventions. For example, *thrillers* tend to be *plot driven*. In fact, most thrillers—or *murder mysteries*—actually contain *two different plots*. For example, the first is called *the apparent plot*. This reveals the surface of the story—what you, the audience, *believe* is really going on. The second is called *the real plot*. This is the *truth* of the matter. In general, the protagonist of a thriller finds him or herself being victimized by a situation that has been going on for some time. The protagonist usually unwittingly gets involved in the situation. This "victimization" usually lasts for the first half of the story, and then the protagonist turns the tables, refusing to be a victim any longer. The two plots converge at the story's midpoint and—written properly—take the audience on a "thrilling" roller-coaster ride to the very end.

The *romantic comedy* genre has its rules as well. For example, despite the couple's conflicts there's always a happy ending. For some reason, new screenwriters dislike the idea of happy endings. But the new writer would be prudent to consider the fact that the majority of moviegoers love it when the boy and girl end up together and in love in the end. Why? I think it's because romance does not work so wonderfully in real life and people go to the movies to escape reality.

In 1999, the film *The Sixth Sense* turned the combining of different genres on its ear. While the film was marketed as a *supernatural thriller*, it's in fact more like a *horror thriller family drama*. The point is that it's a good idea to watch a lot of films in the genre you wish to write your story. Read the screenplays as well. In most cases, they are available at websites. Get a good feel for what kinds of stories have already been told in a particular genre over the last five or ten years. You can do this by checking the box office tally and by reading entertainment trades magazines to learn what films are being developed for the future. Study the storytelling conventions used in the particular genre. And pay close attention to time and history. There's nothing worse than hearing today's language in a film that takes place in the Old West or portraying a historical event incorrectly. Of course, you may want to use contemporary language in a historical setting as part of your approach to writing the screenplay. However, be aware this will give a humorous tone to the material, which can be used to advantage. Director-actor Mel Brooks uses this technique in many of his films. His most famous is his parody called *Young Frankenstein*.

Also, stories of one genre could be adapted to other genres to create a fresh new approach. For example, *Star Trek* has been referred to as *Wagon Train in Space*. And the Japanese classic *Seven Samurai* has been transmuted into many different types of movie genres, the most famous being the Western *The Magnificent Seven*.

Use the sample premises as guides to help you develop your own screenplay premise. Note that I've included the key *dramatic roles* (the characters) and their goals in the story. I will address the concept of dramatic roles in the next chapter.

SAMPLE FILM PREMISES

The Fugitive. A prominent doctor is wrongfully convicted of murdering his wife, escapes prison, and is unrelentingly pursued by a U.S. marshal as he sets out to find the guilty one-armed man. Protagonist: Doctor on the run; Goal: find the one-armed man and clear his name; Antagonist: U.S. Marshal; Goal: catch Doctor on the run; Villain: Cooked Doctor; Goal: kill Doctor on the run.

The Firm. A young lawyer takes a dream position in a Memphis firm only to discover it's a front for the Mafia and he can never quit. Protagonist: Idealistic Young Lawyer; Goal: help the FBI uncover evidence so he can leave the firm; Antagonist (becomes co-protagonist): Lawyer's Wife; Goal: get her husband back; Villain: President of the firm; Goal: kill the Young Lawyer before incriminating evidence is released.

Witness. A self-righteous cop takes refuge from his fellow officers in a nonviolent Amish commune in order to protect himself and the young boy who witnessed a murder by dirty cops. Protagonist: Self-righteous Cop; Goal: protect the boy while uncovering the dirty cops; Antagonist (becomes co-protagonist): Amish Woman; Goal: protect her son; Villain: Dirty Police Commissioner; Goal: kill the Witness and Self-righteous Cop.

Die Hard. While on vacation, a N.Y. cop visits his estranged wife in Los Angeles to make amends on their rocky marriage and unwittingly gets trapped by terrorists who have taken over the entire office building. Protagonist: N.Y. Cop; Goal: stop the terrorist from killing his wife; Antagonist (becomes co-protagonist): N.Y. Cop's Wife; Goal: keep husband's identity secret and stay alive; Villain: the Robber-Terrorist Leader; Goal: steal stocks and bonds from the company.

Unforgiven. A violent gunslinger turned pig farmer comes out of retirement in order to collect a large bounty. Protagonist: Retired Gunslinger; Goal: collect the bounty; Antagonist: Violent Sheriff; Goal: stop the Retired Gunslinger from collecting the bounty.

A Few Good Men. The son of a famous jurist now in the Navy is assigned a murder case and must come to grips with the fact that he may lose his first court trial. Protagonist: Young JAG (Judge Advocate General) Lawyer; Goal: win his first trial; Antagonist (becomes co-protagonist): Senior Female JAG Lawyer; Goal: free the two marines; Villain: U.S. Marine Corps JAG Lawyer; Goal: Convict the two marines.

Sleepless in Seattle. While looking for love on a late night Seattle radio talk show, a grieving widower with a young son discovers his dead wife "reincarnated" in a beautiful but engaged Baltimore woman. Protagonist: Seattle Widower; Goal: find and marry a new wife and mother for his son; Antagonist: the Beautiful Baltimore Woman; Goal: marry the right man.

Big. A boy gets his wish to be a man but dislikes the responsibility of adulthood and wants to be a kid again. Protagonist: Boy Turned Man; Goal: find the magic game to become a kid again; Antagonist: New Adult Girlfriend; Goal: develop a relationship with Boy Turned Man.

Fatal Attraction. A man has a weekend fling with a woman and she becomes obsessed with him and his family life. Protagonist: Cheating Husband; Goal: stop the Obsessed Woman from ruining his life; Antagonist: Obsessed Woman; Goal: destroy the man, his wife, and child.

Midnight Run. In order to collect a big payday, a bounty hunter has only twenty-four hours to find and escort across country a Mafia accountant turned state's witness who has jumped bail. Protagonist: Burned-out Bounty Hunter; Goal: deliver the Bail Jumper by midnight; Antagonist: Bail Jumping Mafia Accountant; Goal: stay free; Villain: Mafia Don; Goal: kill Bail Jumper and Bounty Hunter.

Thelma & Louise. Two women on a vacation from their respective husband and boyfriend find themselves on the run to Mexico in order to escape the law after one of them kills a man who tries to rape the other. Co-protagonists: Thelma and Louise; Goal: get to Mexico before being caught; Antagonist: Hometown Cop; Goal: catch the two women.

Tootsie. An unemployable actor who masquerades as a woman to raise money to put on his roommate's play unwittingly becomes a big star on a popular daytime soap opera. Protagonist: Cross-dressing Actor; Goal: raise money to produce his roommate's play; Antagonist: Fading Soap Queen he falls in love with; Goal: rediscover her self-esteem.

Jerry Maguire. A successful sports agent gets an attack of good conscious, which gets him fired and he strikes out on his own to compete with his former employer—the largest sports management agency in the world. Protagonist: Idealistic Sports Agent; Goal: get clients through honesty; Co-antagonist (becomes co-protagonist #1): Young Female Accountant who becomes his partner and falls in love; Goal: marry the Idealistic Sports Agent; Co-antagonist (becomes co-protagonist #2): Aging Wide Receiver who is Idealistic Sports Agent's only client; Goal: get a $10-million contract; Villain: Dishonest Sports Agent; Goal: keep Idealistic Sports Agent from stealing clients from large agency that fired him.

Sling Blade. A mildly retarded man just released from a mental hospital after twenty-five years for murdering his mother befriends a boy whose single mother is involved in an abusive relationship. Protagonist: Mildly Retarded Man; Goal: save the Boy from the abusive relationship; Antagonist (becomes co-protagonist): Boy; Goal: prevent his Mother from being hurt by her Abusive Boyfriend; Villain: Abusive Boyfriend; Goal: move in and control the Mother and Boy's life.

YOUR ASSIGNMENT

Develop a solid premise for the screenplay that you want to write. Be sure to include the five essential elements and try to keep it to a single sentence. If, at first, you can't write the premise in one sentence then no sweat. Write it as best as you can the first time out of the box. Then rewrite it.

Rewrite it again.

Rewrite it some more.

Rewrite it yet again.

Rewrite it as many times as necessary until you have one hard-hitting sentence that says exactly what your story is about. Remember, you don't need to explain the story or solve anything in the premise, just stick to the fundamental elements.

Consider your premise a *beacon of light* and move to the next step . . .

CHAPTER 2

Invent Interesting Characters

WE ARE ALL CHARACTERS

THEY ARE EVERYWHERE.

Each of us has certain needs, desires, and goals that are peculiar to our personalities and our life situations. The difference between the characters and us in a story is twofold: **point of view** and **motivation**.

Real people like you and me see the world through diverse prisms of a myriad of conflicting goals and emotions. We don't always have the luxury to simply concentrate on one problem until it's completely solved. We have to juggle everything—everyday—and deal with endless challenges that constantly confront us.

> "A studio thinks you need to give a character clever things to say. A writer is more concerned about the choices a character makes. Your job as a writer is to make tough choices. That's how you find out who the characters are." To make his point, (screenwriter) Billy Ray (*Suspect Zero, Volcano, Hart's War*) describes the ending to *Broadcast News* when Holly Hunter's character has a defining moment when she decides whether or not to get on the plane with William Hurt's character.[1]

However, the lives of your characters need to be much more concentrated than real life. In effect, characters must exist in a *heightened reality.* The characters in your story need to have *one major problem* to solve. While there may be other problems, they must deal with in the story, those problems *must* somehow relate to the major problem at hand. And it's *how* they go about solving this one major problem that makes them interesting to the audience and gives the story *focus*.

Of course, their physical attributes, emotional status, sense of humor, profession, and so on also help to make characters interesting to the audience. In other words, a "full" character is more interesting than a "cardboard" character. Much of what makes a character full or real is inside the writer's mind and rarely makes it to the screenplay in any one specific way. For example, the fact that a male character didn't get along with his father may never be actually *talked* about in the story. But this character will *act* a certain way in certain situations because he disliked his father. The character may replicate the same behavior perfected in the childhood relationship with his son or be an opposite exaggeration of the adolescent experience. How this fits into the ***context*** of the story is the important thing to consider and to master.

In real life, our *motivation* to live our lives a certain way has a multitude of rationalizations. In the screen story, your characters should have motivation for one reason and one reason only: to solve the one major problem before them.

How well we understand the characters we write helps us to decide how they talk, how they react in certain situations, what kind of clothes they wear, what their homes look like, how they treat their friends and family, and so on. This understanding also helps us to decide how the characters will go about solving their problems in the story.

The screenwriter must answer three very important questions about each major character in the story before proceeding to develop them.

1. Exactly what does this particular character want?
2. What is this particular character willing to do to get it?
3. How will the audience *feel* about this character?

The answers to these questions should have the overall effect of *counterpointing* each character to the others in the story—putting them on opposite sides of the problem. This in effect gives them "dramatic roles" within the context of the screen story. These dramatic roles are traditionally referred to as protagonist, antagonist, true antagonist (or villain), and pivotal character (sometimes referred to as a supporting character).

DRAMATIC ROLES

It's more than real life.

It's important for the writer to see his or her characters as real people. But there must be more than reality involved in character development. Your characters must have purpose and a clear function in the story. Therefore, look at each character as playing a specific *role* in your storytelling.

The Protagonist

The **protagonist** is sometimes called the *Good Guy.*

Plain and simple, the protagonist is whom the story is about. The story is told from the protagonist's point of view. The major problem in the story belongs to this character, and this character must drive the story forward. And, of course, he or she isn't necessarily the good guy in the story.

The most effective protagonist *acts* instead of *reacts* in the story. He or she makes things happen instead of waiting for things to happen to him or her. When he or she reacts, it's to something out of his or her control. And his or her immediate goal becomes gaining control.

The best protagonist has strength. This attribute can be physical or moral. This strength is gauged, in part, by the strength of the antagonist and villain (if there's one) in the story. Often, the protagonist is larger than life. And it's for this very reason that he or she should have at least one major blemish. One of the reasons for the success of *Spider-Man 2* is the fact that the story makes a serious exploration of the human side of a superhero.

By giving the protagonist what's called a **fatal flaw**, you make him or her likable and human. This flaw is the universal trait that allows the audience to identify with the character's plight.

This flaw can manifest itself in a physical way such as being short or blind or simple-minded. The flaw can be moral in nature. For example, it could be the love of money, the addiction to love, blind ambition, or even blind loyalty. This fatal flaw helps to give the audience access to the larger-than-life hero or heroine on the big screen. The audience identifies with the character's weakness.

A 1990s phenomenon that continues into the twenty-first century is the practice of exploring the dark side of the protagonist. This has been a fresh way of pushing the envelope on the Hollywood approach to telling a story about one person. Though it's not particularly apparent, some films in the last few years have taken its hero or heroine and showed the audience his or her dark side. This is, by the way, different from the anti-hero approach where the story is essentially a "study of evil." This "new" approach, I believe, is an attempt by screenwriters to update the past image of a *hero of near perfection* with a distinct idea of what is right and wrong to blurring the line between these choices in a more morally complicated and corrupt contemporary society.

I believe this can be seen in Paul Newman's character in the film *Nobody's Fool*. He's a likable guy with a decidedly unlikable side that's not above cheating, lying, and stealing. And then there's Karl who, in *Sling Blade*, is also likable but a cold-blooded murderer.

Co-protagonists

This is the stuff of "Buddy Movies."

Simply stated, this is a same-sex love story. Co-protagonists don't always start out in cahoots. When we meet them in the story, they are usually introduced in a protagonist-antagonist relationship. Somewhere along the way, they join forces when they realize they share the same goal. But the *antagonistic relationship* continues even though the two characters now agree on the identical pursuit in the story. This continuing emotional relationship is often the driving force in the story's subplot.

The Antagonist

The **antagonist** is sometimes called the *Bad Guy*.

However, women can be bad too. Relying on a *bad person persona* is not always a precise way to develop the antagonist. This character does not have to be "bad" in the truest sense of the word. In a love story, the relationship is definitely protagonist-antagonist. But nobody's "bad" in the way we usually think of the concept. The antagonist is more accurately *in opposition* to the protagonist in terms of how they are to reach his or her goal.

This, in effect, provides the story with *counterpoint*. A more precise word would be **conflict**—which is what drama is all about. For example, if the protagonist believes in God, the antagonist should be an atheist. If the protagonist wants to go to New York on vacation, the antagonist should want to go to the Amazon rain forest. If the protagonist wants to uphold the law, the antagonist should want to break it. If the protagonist likes the color red, the antagonist should like green or any color other than red. The list can go on forever . . .

A **villain** is an important ingredient in buddy movies because it's essential to have someone step up and take the role of the *true antagonist* in the story. This gives co-protagonists a focused opposition while they pursue their joint goal.

There are different brands of antagonists, and they are sometimes the most interesting characters. Even though a screenplay is usually about one person, the protagonist, the audience is sometimes attracted to the "evil" force in the story. Movies in the 1990s made excellent use of this fascination with the bad guy. Antagonist and villains have made strong careers for many actors and actresses. Here is a list that covers most of the types:

Fortuitous. This type of antagonist will say "I never meant for things to end up like this . . ." A classic example can be found in Shakespeare's *Macbeth*. Popular films that showcase this type of antagonist are *Fatal Attraction, Basic Instinct*, and *Four Weddings and a Funeral*.

Scapegoat. Generally a portrait of an evil person. Almost always, this type of antagonist is more interesting than the protagonist. He or she is sometimes called the *antagonist who would be a protagonist* or *anti-hero*. In most cases, this type of antagonist must receive a comeuppance at the end of the story to satisfy the audience's need for justice. Excellent examples can be found in the films *Falling Down* and *Pulp Fiction*. However, some films break this tradition by letting the bad guy get away with it. Good examples of this are in the films *The Silence of the Lambs* and *True Romance*.

Innocent. The audience is often caught saying to themselves "Oh, he did it!" This type of antagonist is the staple of murder mysteries and whodunits.

Off the Wall. These over-exaggerated weirdo antagonists became more and more popular in the cynical 1990s. Films such as *Speed, Natural Born Killers*, and the *Batman* movies have effectively employed this type of antagonist to the audience's delight.

Prosaic. The toughest type of antagonist to write yet the most common one found in screenplays. This type of antagonist is not colorful, has little originality, does not repent, and offers the audience no big surprises. They are, simply stated, *realistic*. You can find this type of antagonist in *The Caine Mutiny, Ed Wood, Forrest Gump, The Shawshank Redemption, Quiz Show*, and *Jerry Maguire*.

Pivotal Characters

Pivotal characters are sometimes called *supporting characters*.

This character's main role in the story is to prevent the protagonist from walking away from the problem. You've all seen it when the hero just gives up and rushes to the airport to leave town and a pivotal character arrives just in time to stop him. Pivotal characters often force the action in the story. Pivotal characters who support the antagonist not only *force* the action but also most often carry out the bidding of the antagonist or villain.

The second function of the pivotal character is to bring a different point of view to the story's problem. This helps to give the story's theme a more universal appeal.

We sometimes call pivotal characters *sidekicks* and *henchmen*. This brand of character also serves to bring a variety of viewpoints to a story and its theme. If you were to look at a story as if it were war, your protagonist and antagonist would be opposing lieutenants. Their soldiers would be the pivotal characters. So each side has its own platoon.

The more complicated the story's plot, the more pivotal characters are needed and the more important they become. For example, the film *Clear and Present Danger* was littered with both good and bad pivotal characters who all did the bidding of either the protagonist or the antagonist. Even the villain in this story had strong pivotal characters to put on the battlefield. And within each of these circles, the characters shared a *triangular* relationship. This complex character design was absolutely necessary to the telling of a story whose very nature depended on showcasing a highly sophisticated government organization—the Central Intelligence Agency—and how it conducts clandestine operations.

CHARACTER TRIANGLES

A CHARACTER TRIANGLE IS *THE* DRIVING FORCE OF DRAMA.

This is not as complicated as it may seem at first glance. In fact, the idea is simple: contrasting characters are connected in threes. Within this triangle are relationships that are defined by protagonist, antagonist, and pivotal character roles. These roles may even evolve or rotate depending on the specific triangle in which a particular character is traveling.

The story's protagonist shares two different triangles and is the focus of the primary and secondary stories, **main plot** and **subplot** respectively. Each of the two other sides of the two triangles has antagonist and pivotal character *relationships*. These two major types of relationships form the story's *central conflict*. And it is in these relationships that the protagonist learns how to solve the story's main problem.

FIGURE 2.1 Character Triangles Development Template

(insert your character names in the blank spaces)

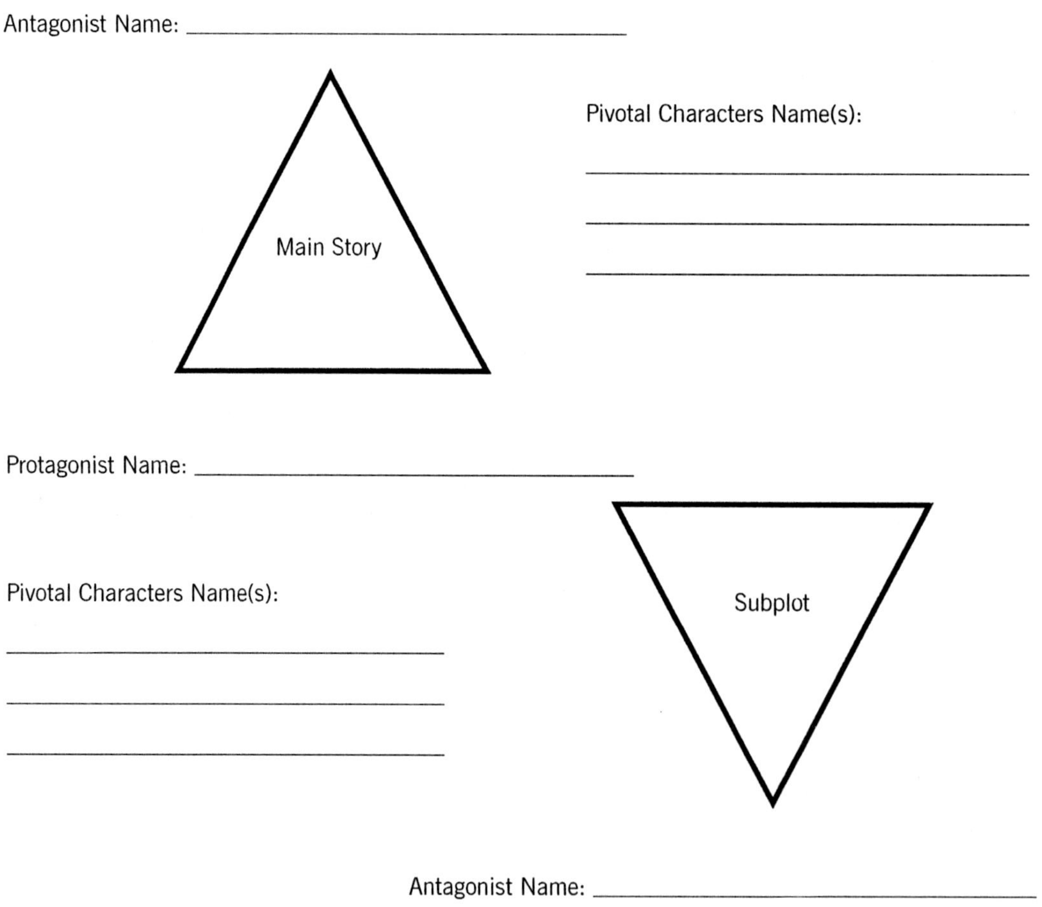

Antagonist Name: ______________________

Main Story

Pivotal Characters Name(s):

____

____

____

Protagonist Name: ______________________

Pivotal Characters Name(s):

____

____

____

Subplot

Antagonist Name: ______________________

FISH OUT OF WATER

FISH OUT OF WATER MEANS A STRANGER IN A STRANGE LAND.

The **fish out of water** concept is a popular and effective way to make a character *interesting* in a story. This is an entertaining means to force a character to use strongly defined skills in a situation where they normally don't apply.

The character of Forrest Gump is the ultimate fish out of water. Everywhere he goes in life he's out of place. An innocent banker sent to prison for life in *The Shawshank Redemption* is another example. In *The Godfather,* the youngest son, Michael—played brilliantly by Al Pacino—is a fish out of water. In *Jerry Maguire,* the title role character has never had to play by the rules until now.

There are many other examples of stories that force characters to survive in unfamiliar situations. It's a very effective way to create interesting characters.

UNITY OF OPPOSITES

IT'S NOT ENOUGH TO SUCCEED, OTHERS MUST FAIL.

This is a very important concept to apply when counterpointing a protagonist and antagonist in a story. Essentially, this idea is at its best when the protagonist and antagonist *want the exact same thing* in the story. I call this perfect **unity of opposites**.

For example, in *Romancing the Stone,* the protagonist, antagonist, and villain all wanted the same precious emerald. Indiana Jones and the Nazi colonel both wanted the ark in *Raiders of the Lost Ark.* The most perfect character triangle is two people wanting the same person as the object of love . . .

So, this idea of *unity of opposites* is the thing that ties the protagonist and antagonist together. If you invent this correctly, it prevents one or the other from simply winning and walking away from the story because neither can win without the other losing.

THE NATURE OF CHARACTERS

PROTAGONIST RARELY CHANGE, THEY *GROW.*

He or she may change their point of view, but the best protagonist always remains true to himself or herself. Even at the end of the film *The Fugitive,* when Lt. Sam Gerard knew that Dr. Kimble was innocent, he *still* took him back to jail. The evidence of his growth was to remove the handcuffs and give Kimble an ice pack. It was Gerard's *true nature* to bring in his man. Some screenwriters see their stories as being character driven. That is, the writer starts with character rather than plot.

Some protagonists are more active in stories than others. Passive protagonists are usually the stuff of thrillers. But even they turn the tables at some point in the story and fend for themselves. They learn how to be strong enough to reach their goal. They *grow* as a result of the events of the story. This is sometimes referred to as *character arc.* And it's considered to be the most important ingredient in the story—how different is the protagonist at the end of the story from when he or she was at the start of it.

Because of the visual nature of screenwriting, growth is more effectively illustrated through a protagonist's *behavior* rather than through speeches and dialogue. It's behavior—the doing of something—that, more often than not, reveals a person's true beliefs. And beliefs are dictated by the value system that you or a character have perfected over the years. This rationale is at the heart of character development and the key to inventing interesting and consistently behaving characters.

When we speak of a character "changing," it's usually in relation to growth over a long period of time. We generally call stories where characters actually change *sagas*.

Character Arc

There are basically five points of "arc" possible for a protagonist to attain. These levels are based on Abraham Maslow's *Hierarchy Theory of Human Needs and Motivation* sociology model. They are as follows:

First Point: *Self*. The protagonist is only concerned with himself or herself . . . *looking out for number one!*

Second Point: *Bonding*. The protagonist develops a one-on-one relationship with someone: a lover, a buddy, a sister, a brother, a mother, a father, and so on. He or she is no longer just looking out for number one.

Third Point: *Family*. Having now developed a relationship, the protagonist is very interested in folding it into a small group setting: a clan, team, gang, company, and so on. There is a need to belong.

Fourth Point: *Community*. Once the protagonist is a member of an organized small group, he or she wants to become a part of a larger organized group . . . such as a neighborhood or corporation.

Fifth Point: *Humanity*. Having achieved comfort and love, the protagonist wants to seek a higher calling . . . to be *self-actualized* as Maslow calls it. This takes the protagonist to a "spiritual" existence, perhaps putting him or her into the same company as Martin Luther King Jr., Ghandi, and Mother Teresa.

In film, some good examples of these various arcs are as follows:

Ratzo Rizzo—played by Dustin Hoffman in *Midnight Cowboy*—he goes from Point One to Point Two in the story and stops.

Rick's character in *Casablanca*—he goes from Point One to Point Four—teetering on the edge of going to Point Five at Fade Out.

Scrooge in *A Christmas Carol* and George Bailey in *It's a Wonderful Life* both evolve from Point One to Point Five.

Michael Corleone in *The Godfather* offers an interesting twist on his arc. He starts out at Point Three at the beginning of the story (having just served his country as a soldier fighting the Nazi's at Point Four) and descends to Point One by the end of the story.

The bottom line in most stories is to leave the audience knowing that the protagonist at least realizes he or she is better off (or worse off) for the experiences of the story and is on the road to changing and becoming a better (or worse) person as a result.

TYPES OF ENDING FOR THE PROTAGONIST

The outcome of a story is very important. The following is a summary of all of the possible plot outcomes:

The Hero Wins

This is your Hollywood staple happy ending to a story. The best execution of this age-old approach is to somehow get the audience to care a lot about what the protagonist wants in the story . . . and make the audience daydream about reaching the same goal in their own drab, routine lives.

The Hero Loses

This is your basic bummer ending. Bottom line, nobody likes a loser. And most moviegoers want to escape this emotion. However, if your ending is a bummer, then at least give some sort of upbeat twist to make up for it.

The Hero Wins by Losing

This is an excellent technique for turning a bummer into an uplifting story.

The Hero Loses by Winning

This is the antithesis of the above story ending. Again, you have a bummer and you send the audience home feeling down.

The Hero Wins but Loses

This is the stuff of dark comedies and satire.

CHARACTER BIOGRAPHIES

A CHARACTER BIOGRAPHY IS THE SUM TOTAL OF A CHARACTER'S LIFE.

It's important to explore your protagonist, antagonist and key pivotal characters in depth. This will make the storytelling a bit easier. It's very important for you to determine how the characters have (or have not) related to each other right up until the time the story begins.

A *thumbnail* is a short summary of the areas included in the *Character Development Template*. But you—the writer—must possess an in-depth understanding of all of your major characters inside and outside of the story you're writing. To help make your characters come alive in your own mind, think of them as real people. Give them birthdays, zodiac signs, favorite quotes, poems, and books. Know how they will react or respond in situations that have absolutely nothing to do with your story. Know how they will relate to others in the real world. To assist you, use the template included in this book to begin crafting full, well-rounded people who will populate the key dramatic roles in your movie script. You might even think of specific actors who would be perfect to portray your characters.

CHARACTER DEVELOPMENT TEMPLATE[2]

Full Name:

Dramatic Role (protagonist, antagonist, pivotal character):

Physiology Profile:

Sex

Age

General Appearance
General Health
Abnormalities (defects if any)

Sociology Profile:
Race and Religion
Class Status
Home Life—past and present and the influence of it
Education
Occupation and Abilities
Key Relationships
Politics—where he or she stands on current important issues
Hobbies

Psychology Profile:
Sex Life
Ethics, Values, Moral Standards
Drive and Ambition
Frustrations, Disappointments
Temperament
IQ
General Attitude toward Life
Complexes (if any)
Qualities Important to the Story
How Will the Audience Feel about This Character?

THE AUDIENCE AS CHARACTER

THEY'RE THE MOST IMPORTANT PARTICIPANT.

To thoroughly engage all those strangers—the audience—sitting in the dark theater, you must make sure they identify in some way with the problems, emotions, and struggle of the protagonist. As such, all the characters must be believable so the audience feels as if they're a part of the story.

An important way to accomplish this is to *never* insult the intelligence of the audience. That is not to say you should keep them in the dark, no pun intended. While being mindful of good storytelling techniques and the role of suspense, always assume your audience has been around the block once or twice.

Taking the basic statistical bell curve to heart, there will always be a handful of individuals in the audience who are one step ahead of the story. But most of the viewers will be thoroughly engaged if you do your job well. And, of course, no matter what you write, there will be a few folks who walk out of the theater scratching their heads. It's that middle group at which you want to set your aim.

To help avoid creating unbelievable characters, it's a good idea to start developing your characters *before* exploring the full details of your story. The reason is simple: this will mitigate the tendency to *contrive* the plot and inventing events and situations that make the story *conveniently* work instead of it working owing to the character's natural behavior to pursue his or her *beliefs* and *values*. If your characters are born in a vacuum, there's a better chance of them telling you what *they want to do* when presented with problems from the story's premise. Remember, all of your characters had lives *before* the problem in the story began.

YOUR ASSIGNMENT

Character affects the story profoundly. In fact, most screenwriting gurus agree that character *is* story. Start by filling out the *Character Development Template*. If you like, you can expand this basic information into narrative form by writing in the conscious mind using the template as an outline. This includes the protagonist, antagonist, villain, and important pivotal characters—especially the ones who will be supporting your protagonist. But to be honest, you don't need a lot of detail to create three-dimensional characters. In fact, by using words and short phrases, you can successfully complete the *Character Development Template* in one single-spaced page for each main character and be most effective. The key is not how much you write but how well you know your characters in these major areas of their lives.

Also, use the *Character Triangles Development Template* (Figure 2.1) to make sure your dramatic roles are designed for maximum storytelling.

Don't forget to explore each character right up to the beginning of the story . . .

NOTES

1. Lajos Egri, *The Art of Dramatic Writing*, rev. ed. (New York: Simon & Schuster, 1960), 36.
2. Rachel Wimberly, "Starting From Zero," September 11, 2004, at Scriptmag.com.

CHAPTER 3

Craft a Strong Story

Films are not much more than short stories. While much is said and written about structure, the art of storytelling is a chief component of a screenplay. A well-told story can mitigate many other flaws in a script. Up to this point, all the creative work you've done must now contribute to forming this important ingredient.

SUSPENSION OF DISBELIEF

TELL THE TRUTH WITH LIES.

Suspension of disbelief simply means that the characters and the world you create for them must somehow make the audience forget *truth* and totally accept your *false reality* for two or more hours.

THE BASIC STORY

THIS IS THE *CHASSIS* OF A SCREENPLAY.

I went to the dictionary and looked up the word **story**. Here's what I found: (1) a narrative, either true or fictitious, in prose or verse; (2) the **plot** or succession of incidents of a novel, poem, drama, etc. I assume screenplay falls under the *etc.* category in the second definition. A strong story must have a clear *beginning*: usually one person with a problem; a *middle*: the problem escalates because another person is in the way of achieving a solution; and an *ending*: the problem is solved only after defeating its opposing force(s). And the most satisfying stories have happy endings.

While it's absolutely necessary for a screen story to have a beginning, a middle, and an end, it must also contain certain other elements that serve to thoroughly engage and entertain an audience.

When asked what elements he is hoping to identify and develop when he's trying to come up with a story arc, screenwriter Steven Zaillian (*Schindler's List*, *The Interpreter*, *Gangs of New York*) comments: "It changes with each story. I purposely don't want to know because I want to approach everything as if it's the only thing I've ever done so it'll be new to me. Sometimes it's a character. Sometimes it's a plot. Sometimes it's a theme."[1]

Each writer begins at a different place when it comes to story development. But there are certain elements that are necessary in creating a story that engages the audience.

WHAT THE AUDIENCE EXPECTS.

The best-written screen story is sure about what it is. The audience should almost be immediately aware of what they're in for. If you're writing a comedy, then your story should begin and end with funny stuff. If your story opens with a ten-minute car chase **sequence**, then you should deliver an action story to the audience. If you are writing a love story, then the entire story should be about two people falling in love.

THE CLASSIC LOVE STORY

THIS IS THE MOST UNIVERSAL THEME.

It's pretty hard to go wrong when you write a good love story. In fact, most screenplays have one as either the main story or as a subplot. It's a surefire way to tap into every single audience member—regardless of race, creed, color, or religion. Over the years, Hollywood has taken full advantage of this appealing theme. I've put into a template the basic approach commonly used in developing and writing most love stories for the screen.

1. Boy meets Girl.
2. Boy is confronted by a "problem" with Girl, ends up falling in love with her.
3. Boy loses Girl—his own fault.
4. Boy gets Girl back.
5. Boy loses Girl again—her doing, looks like forever.
6. Boy gets Girl back.
7. Boy loses Girl once again—this time by no fault of his own (an outside force).
8. Boy gets Girl back.
9. Boy, having learned his lesson, confronts and eliminates the influence of the outside force forever.
10. Boy and Girl live happily ever after.

Of course, this works for a *female protagonist*, too!

While these ten points don't constitute a *plot*, per se, they are the basic *moves* used in the storytelling from which to fashion a beginning, a middle, and an end. The important thing to understand is that this approach includes opportunities to create conflict between the protagonist and antagonist by delivering an "on now/off/on again" emotional roller-coaster ride for the audience.

Even if this approach is used in the subplot of a story, it naturally mirrors the winning and losing nature that should also exist in your main story.

STORY VERSUS PLOT

WHAT VERSUS *HOW*.

While story tells us what the tale is about, the plot tells us how the story unfolds. This is a very important distinction to grasp, especially during the developing stages of your screenplay. As you form your story, the trick is not to think of the where and how of it. At this early stage, it's more important to concentrate on the what of the story and leave the details for later. This means you should also avoid writing about what dialogue will take place between characters. Write in broad strokes and concentrate on the emotions that'll carry the story forward.

So, you might say that *story* concerns itself more with the protagonist's wants, needs, desires, and feelings—these are often competing perceptions. *Plot* concerns itself with the *events* that are generated from the protagonist pursuing (acting upon) his or her wants, needs, desires, and feelings. You're probably saying to yourself, this is too simple . . . but it really is this simple.

BACKDROP OR SETTING

This is the world that's being explored.

In writing the story, first place your well-developed characters into an interesting environment. This **setting** should be fresh or unfamiliar to the general audience and relate to the overall theme of the story. Ideally, you want to take the audience "behind closed doors." If it's a familiar setting, then you should strive to show an unfamiliar dimension of it. Many successful films accomplish this very effectively:

Big—the world of creating and manufacturing toys.

Broadcast News—the process of network news gathering.

Casablanca—the intrigue of the French underground resistance.

The Godfather—the underbelly of an organized crime family.

Rain Man—the secret realm of autism.

Tootsie—the inner workings of producing a daytime drama.

Witness—the uncomplicated lifestyle of the Amish.

Jurassic Park—what it was like when dinosaurs walked the earth.

Crimson Tide—the daily at-sea routine on an Intercontinental Ballistic Missile submarine.

The American President—the daily routine of the U.S. president.

Jerry Maguire—the pressure to succeed as a high-powered sports agent.

American Beauty—fly-on-the-wall glimpse at upper-middle-class suburban lifestyles in the San Fernando Valley of Los Angeles.

Selecting an interesting and intriguing setting is very important to the storytelling because this decision presents the characters with an important dramatic choice: When in Rome, do as the Romans? or When in Rome, just be myself? No matter the protagonist's decision, trouble should follow it.

THEME AND SUBTEXT

What's this story *really* about?

When you boil it all down, there are really only five general types of story conflict **themes** you can write about. They are the following:

1. Man versus Man
2. Man versus Nature

3. Man versus Self
4. Man versus Society
5. Man versus Fate

Of course, one can most certainly substitute *Woman* for Man in the above themes. Every other kind of story theme is a derivative, variation, or combination of the above. The one important thing to remember about these themes is that you must "put a face" on such abstract notions as nature or society or fate. This is easily accomplished by manifesting the theme through a *person* who represents some aspect of the chosen theme.

The movie *Jaws* uses the theme *man against nature.* It has a giant shark that represents nature. But the filmmakers also use characters to represent both points of view by pitting a *shark lover* and a *shark hunter* against each other.

A film that cleverly uses the *man against self* theme is *Four Weddings and a Funeral.* The writer astutely surrounds the protagonist—a man at battle with his fears of commitment and marriage—with other characters who represent those exact fears. The *inner self* of the protagonist, in effect, comes to life through the pivotal characters in the story.

Outbreak utilizes the *man against society* theme most effectively by creating an evil army general who stops at nothing—including destroying an entire town to protect a government secret about a highly infectious virus.

In the film *Wall Street,* the character of Gordon Gecko, portrayed by Michael Douglas, personifies corporate greed.

Man against fate is probably the trickiest theme to tackle in storytelling. *Jurassic Park* offers a story utilizing this theme. I suppose, in general, many science fiction stories such as the *Star Trek* films are more suited to exploring this nebulous theme more than other genres because the writers have to virtually create a world that doesn't exist.

The next step is to find the *one word* that is the theme of your story. Then, find a cliché that best articulates your one-word theme. Here are some examples:

> ***Titanic***—Dishonesty: Thou shall not lie.
> ***Jerry Maguire***—Honesty: Honesty is the best policy.
> ***As Good As It Gets***—Trust: No man is an island.
> ***Shrek***—Tolerance: Don't judge a book by its cover.

Every single scene in these films explores the one-word theme in some way, whether it is a pure exploration, antithesis, or an unusual facet of it. Drawing on a cliché is helpful since everyone in the audience knows it; that's what makes it a cliché. This facilitates communicating the universality of your theme to the audience. This is one of those rare occasions when using a cliché in writing is actually a good thing.

Common Themes in Film

THE TEN COMMANDMENTS

1–5. These are religious, so I've omitted them.
6. Thou shalt not kill.
7. Thou shalt not commit adultery.

8. Thou shalt not steal.
9. Thou shalt not bear false witness against thy neighbor.
10. Thou shalt not covet thy neighbor's house, thou shalt not covet thy neighbor's wife, nor his manservant, nor his maidservant, nor his ox, nor his ass, nor any thing that is thy neighbor's. (Updating this one is a lot of fun.)

The Seven Deadly Sins	The Seven Heavenly Virtues
Pride	Faith
Envy	Hope
Gluttony	Charity
Lust	Fortitude
Anger	Justice
Greed	Temperance
Sloth	Prudence

THE CENTRAL QUESTION

This speaks to theme.

Theme manifests itself in two ways: *physical* and *metaphysical.*

Physical theme has to do with what the protagonist is trying to accomplish in the story—his or her goal. So, if the protagonist's problem is a serial killer on the loose, then the **physical central question** is, "Can Joe catch the serial killer before he kills again?" So, this level of theme is very much about behavior and its outcome is tangible.

The other level of theme, *metaphysical*, can be worked out in two basic formats: (1) as a question, or (2) as a hypothesis. The question format can be presented through a visual or in dialogue. For example, in the film *Witness,* the **metaphysical central question** is, Can an anti-technology, anti-violence culture co-exist in modern society? This becomes obvious within the first five minutes of the film . . . presented in a breathtaking visual that puts a horse-drawn carriage in front of an eighteen-wheeler on a major Pennsylvania highway.

You could also present the *Witness* theme as a broader hypothesis: Violence leads to violence. This thesis is tested when a self-righteous policeman, John Book, investigates a murder and his only witness is Samuel, an Amish boy. John Book finds himself in Amish country and his views of how to be cop are challenged by this culture's down-to-earth, nonviolent lifestyle. The film certainly challenges this thesis and, by its end, makes one think that perhaps *nonviolence leads to nonviolence.*

In the film *Chinatown*, the screenwriter has the protagonist, Jake Gittes, state the theme in the form of a thesis early on in dialogue: "Only a rich man can get away with murder." So, the metaphysical theme level is very much about spiritual, humanistic, universal ideas. It's most important for you to develop your theme on both levels clearly and precisely. While you don't want to hit the audience over the head with theme, you certainly want viewers to sense or feel the theme of your story. Theme gives story *meaning*.

Some films also use the *moral imperative* approach to establishing theme in the story. For example, in the opening sequence of *Gladiator,* Maximus tells his troops before they go off to battle that what they do there that day will live in eternity. This, in effect, helps to establish the story's theme since ultimately the film is about preserving democracy in Rome, thus for civilization in general.

THE ACT ONE METAPHOR

THIS SHOULD BE A CLEVER DEVICE.

As you know, a **metaphor** is a representation or symbol for something else. Every good screenplay has one of these. In *Witness*, the **Act One metaphor** is cleverly combined with the **central question** in a visual way: a series of shots showing the horse-drawn buggy causing a traffic jam on a major interstate highway . . . then ironically stopping to heed a traffic light at a busy intersection in town.

Other clever ways of creating this concept can include using objects from a character's past or present. Once the audience understands the emotional value of an object—a medallion, a dog-eared photo, or even an old pair of shoes—it can be used as dramatic shorthand to evoke emotional reactions from both the character involved and the audience.

You can also use a particular *situation* to exploit theme. For example, in *Jerry Maguire*, a group of disgruntled divorcees' regular support meeting serves as an excellent visual metaphor for Jerry's conflict with his young assistant. Sometimes, characters are used to represent theme. In *Jerry Maguire*, the young boy represents honesty as he always tells the truth; in *As Good As It Gets*, the dog represents ultimate trust—unconditional love. There are many other examples, look for them when you watch your favorite films.

On a more artsy level, a piece of plastic caught up in a whirlwind on a sidewalk serves as a metaphor for the lives of the characters in *American Beauty.*

STORY VISUAL MOTIFS

IT'S BETTER TO VISUALLY SHOW, NOT TELL THROUGH DIALOGUE, THE SYMBOLS OF THEME.

This can be very tricky. Samuel Goldwyn of the early MGM Studio once said: "Every film must have its subtleties but they must be obvious." This really says it all about using thematic symbols in a screen story. A celebrated example of how to effectively use **visual motifs** can be found throughout the entire film *Witness.* The use of hand tools and the wheat and flour images scattered through the scenes serve to subtly remind the audience of how far modern society has come in terms of how it interprets its own value system. Such symbolic visuals as the waving field of grain, the bullets in the flour jar, the handmade toy for young Samuel, the communal barn raising—all serve as story visual motifs in this Oscar-winning film.

In a way, this technique gives the story visual metaphors in which to cloak its theme.

BACK STORY IN THE FORWARD DRIVE

AVOID "STAGE WAITS."

Exposition should work *for* the story not against it. It's awfully tempting to take all the stuff you write about characters in their biographies and deliver it to the audience in the form of dialogue. Even more tragic would be to show this background information in the form of **flashbacks**. (The flashback as a structure approach is discussed in chapter 4.) I know you took the time, effort, and creativity to come up with all this **back story**, so why not use it in the story? Well, in fact, you should—but in a way that helps the story, not hinders it.

Putting back story into the "forward drive" simply means *showing the effects* of the past on today's situations—*not telling* the audience about what happened in the past through verbal dialogue.

Here are a few examples:

1. If one of your characters was an excellent high school athlete, then show us his love of sports as the story unfolds *today*. Place scenes in sports oriented locations. Perhaps he grabs lunch at the YMCA during a pickup basketball game with his coworkers instead of a fancy restaurant. His office might contain sports memorabilia or trophies from his days of glory, not diplomas or academic awards.
2. If one of your characters had a drug abuse problem in the past, constantly tempt that character with drugs and alcohol *today* and show how he or she handles it as the story unfolds. It need not have a thing to do with the screenplay's story.
3. If a character didn't get along with his or her father as a child, show the difficulty that the character has dealing with his or her own children *today* as the story unfolds. He might repeat his father's behavior. Or he might do just the opposite by spoiling his son.

The bottom line: the audience is not so much interested in what characters *did* in the past as much as what they are *doing* to solve the problems before them from scene to scene. The magic phrase is, *as the story unfolds . . .*

Remember, like us, characters are best judged by their behavior rather than by what they say. What they do and what they say will either be consistent or inconsistent. And the audience will get it.

VISUAL STORYTELLING

Pictures speak louder than words.

It is essential that you find ways to tell your story visually rather than depend on dialogue (more on dialogue in a later chapter). Here are some hints to help you use what the audience sees more than what they hear from the mouths of characters:

Use behavior. You know what they say: action speaks louder than words. What the audience sees can be more important than what they say. For example, instead of a guy saying, "I love you," he would simply touch a woman's hand and smile.

Use location. Where a scene takes place can speak volumes. Putting a scene in a morgue versus an office can make a big difference.

Use time of day. If a character wakes up someone at 3:00 a.m. versus paying a visit to them at their office during work hours brings a different tone to the scene.

Contrast what a character says by behavior. This gives the audience a certain feeling about the character's values and morals.

Use sounds. The brain processes sounds in such a way it creates a visual. You can put two characters in a pitch black room with a single candle. This can be romantic . . . if the audience hears a nearby ocean lapping at the shoreline, or it can be spooky if it's thundering outside.

Never forget that film is essentially a visual medium and, as such, the story should be *shown* more than *talked about*.

THE TICKING CLOCK

This creates a sense of urgency.

This technique quite often shows up in action films as detonators ticking away before setting off the bomb that'll kill the hero or a loved one. Though this is an effective way to get the audience on the edge of their seats, it's not a practical way to create a **sense of urgency** in screen stories outside the action or action-adventure genres.

So, a most universal approach to creating a "ticking clock" for most protagonists in most genres is to invent important deadlines. In sports stories, it's usually the big championship game; in love stories, it could be the girl has set a date to marry the other guy; in a murder mystery, it could be to catch the murderer before he kills again.

Whatever the specific device, it should be tied to time and present the protagonist with an important deadline or series of deadlines if he or she is to succeed in reaching his or her goal in the story. In the blockbuster film *Seven*, starring Morgan Freeman and Brad Pitt, the co-protagonists realized they had seven murders to solve and found themselves working against time to prevent two after realizing that five of them had already been committed. Of course, the big twist is one of the protagonists is tricked into committing the seventh sin himself.

Here are other examples of how the screenwriter creates a sense of urgency in a story:

> *Jerry Maguire*—He must get the multimillion dollar contract for his only client *before* the season starts . . .
> *Sling Blade*—Karl must do something *before* his little buddy and mother are killed by the abusive boyfriend . . .
> *Star Wars*—Luke must act to destroy the death star *before* it destroys the home planet.
> *Witness*—John Book must uncover dirty cops *before* they find and kill the only witness to the murder they committed—an innocent Amish boy.
> *Gladiator*—The gladiator must stop Caesar's ruthless son *before* he turns Rome into a brutal dictatorship . . .
> *Thirteen Days*—President Kennedy has *only thirteen days* to get Russia to remove missiles from Cuba or there will be a nuclear war . . .

DRAMATIC ACTION

It's all about stimulus response.

Characters *act* and *react* not only to events but to one another. At first thought, action is sometimes expected to come in the form of a car chase, fistfight, or train wreck. And it does. But **dramatic action** has more to do with the characters and how they deal with the incidents of the story. So, one could define dramatic action as:

Something Happens . . . . *Choice*
Something Must Be Done . . . . *Decision*
Something Is Done . . . . *Change*
Something Else Happens . . . . *Another Choice*
Something Must Be Done . . . . *Another Decision*

Something Else Must Be Done . . . *Another Choice*
Repeat until the story ends.

Important to this *formula* is the fact that all of the above refers directly to the protagonist in the story and infers being *proactive*. It also infers a *process* of decision making. Dramatic action is what propels the protagonist through the story and is one of the most important elements of storytelling necessary to creating the structure of the screenplay. I address structure in detail in the next chapter.

CREATING CONFLICT

IT'S ABOUT CHOICES AND DECISIONS.

Ideally, the antagonist creates the choices and forces the protagonist to make a decision. Decision making is an important ingredient to creating conflict in a story. The basis of it lies in presenting the characters—especially the protagonist—with *constant choices*. Each new decision should *raise the stakes* (see Rising Action below) for both the protagonist and antagonist.

Often in real life, the choice *not taken* simply goes away. However, in storytelling, it should always come back to haunt the characters, especially the protagonist. Whether it's a jilted lover or a henchman who is allowed to escape, this is the very essence of how to escalate the difficulty of each obstacle to come for the protagonist and antagonist in a story. Conflict is the essence of drama. Without it, the story is boring.

STORY LOGIC

IT HAS TO MAKE SENSE.

Sound reasoning is extremely important in storytelling. It goes hand in glove with the concept of "suspending disbelief." But the most important thing to remember about logic in storytelling is that it applies to the story itself, not necessarily to the real world we live in. What happens in a story must make sense for the world or setting you've created. What's logical for one character versus another has more to do with their relationships than with anything in the real world.

Logic in storytelling is "inference" at its best. A film that did a superb job of creating logic through inference is Arnold Schwarzenegger's *Junior*. The screenwriter took great pains to lay the groundwork that—within the context of the story—make it possible for a man to get pregnant and have a baby. This is sometimes called *movie logic*.

STORY GENERATES PLOT

IT'S THE *DOING* THAT COUNTS.

We call the basic "spine" of the story *plot*. While it would be wonderful to come up with a plot that no one has ever seen before on screen, it's simply impossible. It's all been done before. Sorry. The following is a pretty good summary of most of the basic plot structures being used by all types of writers.

The Hunt. Plain and simple, we're talking the staple chase story. The protagonist is after someone or running away from someone. If your screenplay is in this category, you should try to invent fresh ways to show the action of the chase. This is probably the most used plot structure in Hollywood films today. *The Fugitive* is an excellent example. Another is *The Hunt for Red October.*

The Journey. In this plot structure, what the protagonist is looking for is not a person but a thing or a feeling. It could be a magic lamp or an ark or a precious stone. A good example of this plot structure is the film *Raiders of the Lost Ark.* Or it could be self-esteem, being loved, or a sense of what being a mother is all about as in the film *Stepmom.*

The Duel. Simply stated, this plot structure involves two characters clashing head-on. *Rocky* is one of the most popular film series to use this approach to storytelling.

Unselfish Atonement. The protagonist gives up something of great value for the good of others. Sometimes this involves making the ultimate sacrifice—giving up one's life. This fits into the category I call the "bummer" and can leave an audience depressed unless you find a way to make the sacrifice an uplifting one. A Tom Hanks film, *Joe Versus the Volcano,* utilized this plot but added a twist of fate that, in the end, left the protagonist with his life and the beautiful girl.

It's difficult to come up with an example of a film that falls strictly into this category because this plot isn't very popular with audiences. *Phenomenon,* a John Travolta film, comes close. The character makes the ultimate sacrifice—his life—in the end. I can't say it was the protagonist's choice to die, but he certainly came to terms with it. In *Gladiator,* the gladiator gives his life to save Rome. So his death is for a noble cause.

Revenge. Though not considered a virtue, it's certainly the stuff of entertaining movie plots. The protagonist starts out being abused and ends up turning the tables on the abuser. In other words, the protagonist gets even with the antagonist or villain. There's usually a price for seeking revenge and it's generally a good idea to deal with that by the end of the story. The film *The Firm* has this plot approach and departed from the John Grishman book it was based upon by redeeming the protagonist in the end so that he could continue to practice law. In the book version, the protagonist took ill-gotten earnings to drop out of life and hide from the mob and the law. Probably the most famous revenge plots can be found in the Charles Bronson *Death Wish* series of films.

Coming of Age. Generally, this is the approach where a young person learns an important lesson about adult emotions. But this can also apply to adults "growing" into emotions that have eluded them. There are lots of examples of this plot approach, such as the film version of John Grisham's *The Client, Home Alone,* and—in the adult vein—*Awakenings,* starring Robert DeNiro, and *Good Will Hunting,* starring Matt Damon. You can also find this approach in the Oscar-winning film *American Beauty.*

STORY AND RISING ACTION

It's about what's at stake.

This is the stuff of act two in a screen story. Some call **rising action** "tightening the coil" of the story. Others call it "peeling away the onion skin." But the less romantic explanation is the escalation of difficulties that the protagonist experiences while attempting to achieve his or her goal in the story. Each hurdle should get higher and more difficult to conquer. And each step should bring more jeopardy to the success or failure of the protagonist. The more the protagonist has to lose, the more suspenseful and dramatic the story will become.

STORY AND RISING ACTION: THE MORAL DILEMMA AND CONSTANT CHOICES

CLIMB THAT MOUNTAIN.

The efforts of the protagonist in the first half of act two should be mainly toward resisting change and gaining new skills. Then in the second half, the protagonist has fully accepted the change and begins to look toward new horizons by solving the problem at hand.

The best way to accomplish rising action is to give the protagonist a major **moral dilemma** and confront him or her with constant *choices*. We're back to how to create conflict in the story.

A dilemma is *deciding between two equally distasteful choices*: having to choose whether to do something that involves right and wrong makes it *moral*. For example, let's say you find out that your mother has killed someone. It may have been an accident, self-defense, or the victim deserved to die. What do you do? The right thing to do is to turn her in. But she's your mother—you can't do that! Can you? Or should you lie or run away? You have a moral dilemma.

As a result of this moral dilemma, the protagonist's decision should create a series of actions from which to choose. Each time he or she decides on one particular course of action, it creates another problem in the form of a new choice. And the one not chosen should continue to simmer and come back to live another day as a full-blown problem or conflict in the story. This constant barrage of choices and decisions that escalate the chance of losing what's at stake for the protagonist serves to create rising action in the story. Particular decisions also serve to decide the type of story to unfold. In the case of your mother's predicament, one choice can produce a taunt court drama while the other could create a cross-country chase—both generated from the same situation and both a very different style of story.

Also important is whose morality is at stake in your story. If the story is about a hero saving society from some awful consequence, then "society's morality" is most important. This applies especially to action and crime stories. This means that the protagonist needs to act in society's best interest not his own. That's what makes him a hero or her a heroine.

If you're writing a character-driven story then the protagonist's morality is most important to the story because the character will act in his or her own best interest, which may not be in the best interest of society.

It's the protagonist's *pursuit of morality* that best generates plot from story.

THE ALMIGHTY CLIMAX

THE AUDIENCE DEMANDS SATISFACTION.

This is where you want to take the audience. It's the reason for the story in the first place. It's nirvana. It's heaven. But not without a final fight! This is the place in the story where the protagonist and antagonist literally come *face-to-face* for the last time in order to solve the problem of the story. In a general sense, one could say a screen story really has two climaxes: physical and emotional.

The **physical climax** comes in the form of, guess what?—a physical struggle. It could be a fist-fight or a car chase or a simple shouting match.

The **emotional climax** has to do with the protagonist being satisfied with his or her quest for the goal. It has to do with *the moment* in the story that the protagonist has worked diligently to reach from the very beginning. It has to do with the inner self, the lessons learned from the events of the story. It has to do with metaphysical theme.

The **climax** is the final confrontation.

THE FINAL TWIST

GIVE THEM MORE THAN EXPECTED.

Even though it should be more than satisfying for the audience that the protagonist has accomplished what he or she sets out to achieve, it's even better to create an unexpected situation . . . a **twist** *beyond* what was expected by the protagonist and especially what was expected by the audience. This relates more to the emotional climax of the story. For example, in one story the hero may not just bring down the bad guy but also may get the girl he could never win before. Or a character may learn that truth is more important and satisfying then keeping a coveted, well-paying job that requires dishonesty.

In *Jerry Maguire,* the title character realizes that succeeding as an honest sports agent isn't enough . . . he needs someone to love and care for as well.

In *Sling Blade,* Karl decides to relieve his young buddy's domestic problem with the abusive boyfriend by killing him . . . and gets to go back to the mental hospital where he wants to be anyway.

These characters didn't necessarily set out to get these things but in the end earned it for doing the right thing. Look at this technique as icing on the cake for your audience.

CRIME AND PUNISHMENT

GIVE THEM THEIR JUST DESSERTS.

This is a confusing area to deal with in recent times. These days, many successful movies are about bad people getting away with doing bad things. Though they may be entertaining on a visceral level, personally, I believe that this type of ending turns off most audiences. In our hearts—deep down inside—our society wants to believe that good people get rewarded for doing good things and bad people get punished for doing bad things. If that wasn't true, I don't believe so much emphasis would be placed on putting more policemen on the streets and building more prisons. It's a booming segment of the national economy. And in the post-9/11 era, it's gone global.

In recent films, a sort of schism has been developing in this area. I call it the fascination with the "dark side of goodness." I touched on this when I talked about protagonists, but essentially, this concept is helping to create more and more stories in which the "good" guy is evil but learns his lesson and is redeemed in the end. The popularity of the film *American Beauty* is a testament to this trend.

HAPPY ENDING

NOBODY LIKES A LOSER.

Everybody loves a winner. The audience wants to identify with the protagonist of a story. We want to vicariously live the story on the screen without actually having to deal with all the problems ourselves. After all, it's hard enough living day-to-day life as it is. And many issues in our lives often don't have happy endings.

That's what movies are for, aren't they? Of course, if the protagonist must lose because it would be unrealistic to win in the particular story you're telling, then you can always use "the twist" technique to uplift the potentially downer ending.

For example, in the film *Phenomenon,* starring John Travolta, the protagonist dies. What a downer. In my opinion, the filmmakers dropped the ball on this one. They could have easily added an upbeat ending by having the antagonist (the love interest) get pregnant from her night with Travolta's character, and, at the party at the town pub, reveal everyone celebrating Travolta's character's son's (or daughter's) first birthday! For some reason, this was not done; perhaps the filmmakers thought it was too pat. I would have loved to have walked out of the theater feeling better than I did after watching this movie. But how can you argue with the film that made over $100 million?

The choice of how to end a story generally falls into the following categories:

1. *The protagonist wins.* This is the they-lived-happily-ever-after type of ending and the staple ending for many Hollywood studio films.
2. *The protagonist loses.* This is the basic bummer ending. You don't see too many films with this ending, especially produced by studios, because tragedies don't generally go over big with audiences. One film with a bummer ending that did do well at the box office is *The Perfect Storm.* But I believe the main contributing factors to its success are fabulous special effects and being based on a best-selling book, not to mention the star-laden cast.
3. *The protagonist wins but loses.* This is a variation of the bummer type ending by leaving the audience with a little hope at the end. Films such as *Leaving Las Vegas* and *Sling Blade* use this ending. Nick Cage actually succeeds in drinking himself to death but we sense that Elizabeth Shue's character will be better for having known Nick. And Karl has to kill in order to get back to the institution but that's what he wanted all along anyway.
4. *The protagonist loses by winning.* This type of ending tends to occur in satire or black comedy. An example is *Death Becomes Her* where the women get to live forever but all of their friends die.
5. *The protagonist wins by losing.* This is your basic *Rocky* ending. You can also call this the somebody-up-there-likes-me type of ending.

How you decide to end your story is very important to how the audience will feel when they leave the theater. I believe that folks pay $10 or more to go the movies to be uplifted. We want to laugh, and we want to cry. But above all, we want to walk out the theater feeling good. Not bummed out. So, in my opinion, the best stories end with the bad guy getting punished. But the bottom line is not whether the ending is happy or sad, but whether it's *satisfying* to the audience. What is exactly satisfying is sometimes an enigma. For example, the Oscar-winning film *Million Dollar Baby*—despite it having a bummer ending—has won critical and audience praise at the box office.

SUBPLOTS AND RUNNERS

THIS IS WHERE *THEME* LIVES.

This is the place to say what you—the writer—want to say to society. A subplot is a short story that's connected to the main story through the protagonist and gives the audience the opportunity to learn more about the protagonist outside the main plot's problem. This is the place to explore that fancy quote you've dug out of the Bible or *Bartlett's*. This is the ideal place to avoid preaching to the audience about some subject that gets your motor revved up. Instead, let your protagonist do it for you . . . but always, always subtly.

A **runner** is a *relationship arc* between two or more characters. A runner usually delves into feelings and ideas promoted from the characters' point of view. Sometimes, they even provide comic relief, such as in a running gag. At their best, runners—there can be more than one—provide the audience with a deeper understanding of what's going on in the story by reflecting how events in the story emotionally affect the characters involved.

Runners can also be used to develop certain qualities of the protagonist that otherwise can't be developed because of the nature of the story's plot. For example, in *The Fugitive,* runners between Lt. Gerard and his fellow U.S. marshals were used to develop a softer side of his pit bull nature. This gives us insight into Gerard so that when he eventually becomes Dr. Kimble's ally in the story we believe he has the emotional capacity to do so. Without Gerard's mentor relationship with the rookie marshal, aptly named Newman, and his wisecracking right-hand man, the audience, by and large, would have groaned when Gerard took off the handcuffs and put ice on Kimble's wrists at the end of the film.

THE STORYTELLING PROCESS

Build on what you know.

Rather than clutter your mind with precise details, descriptions, scenes, dialogue, and camera shots, it's much better to take a gradual approach to including this stuff in your story. It's all important but it stifles you from focusing on the heart of the story. I guess you can compare this approach to a baby who first learns to crawl. Later, the kid finds his feet and masters walking. Then, the kid starts to run everywhere!

The Short Synopsis

Start by crawling.

So, begin the process by keeping it simple. Stay on your hands and knees. The story itself should be no longer than one or two single-spaced pages. Write your premise (your *beacon of light*), the one-word theme and cliché, decide on the story's tone (related to genre) to help you stay on track as you form your basic story. The trick, if there's such a thing, is to keep the story's moves *broad*. Don't get too specific or you'll begin to lose focus. Remember, all you want to do at this point is to put down *what* happens in the story—not *how* it happens. For example, if your character is taking a cross-country trek in the story, write only the broad strokes like this:

> Joe drives from Los Angeles to Tucson with his girlfriend, Sally. Along the way, they pick up a hitchhiker, Chuck, who turns out to be an escaped convict. In the middle of the Arizona desert, Chuck kills Sally, leaves Joe for dead, and steals the car. Joe awakens, flags down a bus full of passengers, hijacks them, and starts to hunt down Chuck.

Notice I didn't give too many specifics of *how* Joe's girlfriend was killed or *how* the car is stolen—only *what* happens. The only thing I should be interested in developing next is *what* happens after Joe begins his chase. So, in fleshing out the story, at this point you should be more interested in what Joe wants, what Joe needs, how Joe feels rather than what Joe *does*. You should save the details for later development when you start expanding the story. Right now, all you want to do is lay out a simple *beginning*, *middle*, and *end* in synopsis form. To help you, I've included an example of the short synopsis for *Motherland* (which became *Thesis* then *Blood Ties*).

Use the *Basic Story Development Template* (see below) to help develop the criteria for your **synopsis**. These simple questions force you to think about what's needed to begin writing your story. If you don't know the answers to some of these questions, you must work hard to create them. Otherwise you'll find yourself grappling with these issues sooner or later. Do it now—you'll have more fun in the writing process.

Start with what you know and work forward or backward to figure out the things you don't know right now. Do this until all the questions are answered.

BASIC STORY DEVELOPMENT TEMPLATE

(Use the answers to the following questions to begin developing the foundation for your Basic Story Synopsis.)

Beginning (Act One)

1. What clever or interesting hook will introduce the story to the audience?
2. What does the protagonist want, and why can't he or she have it?
3. What things happen to make the protagonist's problem or predicament get worse?
4. What forces the protagonist into a new situation?

Middle (Act Two)

1. What keeps the protagonist from adjusting to the new situation in which he or she finds himself or herself involved?
2. What does the protagonist need to know, learn or do to be more successful in his or her new situation?
3. What does the protagonist finally try to do in order to solve his or her problem?
4. How does he or she fail this time for the first major setback?
5. How does the antagonist continue to hurt the protagonist after the major setback?
6. What finally makes the protagonist realize the only way to solve his or her problem is to confront the antagonist once and for all?

Ending (Act Three)

1. What is the protagonist's original goal and how does he or she recommit to it?
2. What must the protagonist do to create a final confrontation with the antagonist and try to get what he or she wants in the story once and for all?
3. What happens in the final confrontation between the protagonist and antagonist, and how does the protagonist GET or NOT GET what he or she wants in the story?
4. What unexpected gain (if any) does the protagonist realize?
5. With whom (major characters) does the protagonist need to take care of unfinished business?

THE END

Sample Short Synopsis

MOTHERLAND
(Working Title)
By Steve Duncan

Premise: This is the story of an African-American sociology professor who, upon discovering that his teaching assistant is responsible for the disappearance of three African-American youths, travels to Africa to retrieve them . . . ultimately discovering the true essence of his own past while living with an ancient African tribe.

Theme: Tradition. *Metaphysical Central Question*: What does *African* in African-American mean?

Cliché: The more things change, the more they stay the same.

Tone: Drama with humor; a coming of age journey.

The Basic Story

Story opens with the kidnapping of 13-year-old PAYNE "PEE WEE" FRAZIER, a shy, not-so-street-smart African-American boy. Then we meet KENNETH CHESTNUT, an African-American sociology professor at USC. We learn that Chestnut's graduate African student, JASON DUFFY, has conspired with SCOTT KENYATTA, one of Chestnut's former students, to provide the basis of a graduate thesis. We discover that Pee Wee is on a slow boat to Africa with two other black youths, CLARENCE "SKEETER" BANKS and TISHA "TISH" TOLIVER. Chestnut learns of the kidnapping plot when Duffy is arrested for the murder of the three children. They confess that it's only a graduate thesis, but the police don't believe them. So they turn to Chestnut and ask for his help. Chestnut sets off for Africa to retrieve the three youths.

The youths arrive in Africa and begin to discover their roots right away. They are met by an AFRICAN GUIDE who is to take them to their ultimate destination. They start out on a boat down a river; take a trek through a treacherous forest to arrive at the remote ancient tribe's village. Chestnut is not far behind but is sidetracked by an African who thinks that Chestnut is up to no good. Meanwhile at the ancient tribe's village, Pee Wee, Skeeter, and Tish are up to their elbows in culture clash. First there's the comparison between an ancient ritual dance and Skeeter doing a rap performance. In the process, Skeeter and a VILLAGE GIRL are attracted to one another. Meanwhile, Chestnut is having his own culture clash in his journey as the prisoner of the AFRICAN TRIBESMEN.

Unknown to Chestnut, a small group of WHITE TRADESMEN tag along to find the remote village of the ancient tribe. They are up to no good.

Finally, Chestnut arrives and finds himself semi-imprisoned with the three youths. Here a generation clash occurs as the four of them try to figure out how to escape the tribe. They decide they will just leave. And the VILLAGE CHIEF lets them go. But once in the thick forest, they soon find themselves lost. They also find themselves confronted by the Tradesmen who mean them no good. But Chestnut and the three youths are saved by the ancient Tribesmen and taken back to the camp.

Back at the village, Chestnut decides to take advantage of being there and starts to document their stay in the same vein as his well-intentioned student Duffy would have. The observations include the two boys going through an ancient right of passage and a hunting ritual. Tish learns much about the life of the TRIBESWOMEN. Controversy arises when Skeeter and the young African Girl seek out each other's affections. Although it's a clash of values, it's both amusing and touching.

Chestnut (somehow) gets word back to the U.S. authorities that the three youths are indeed alive and well. The four more enlightened African-Americans are guided out of the remote location and return to America.

Back home, Chestnut arranges to get Duffy out of jail. Skeeter, Tish, and Pee Wee return home new people with a deeper understanding of what being African-American really means . . .

THE END

EXPAND SYNOPSIS TO THREE ACTS

Start walking.

Now it's time to start putting a little flesh on the bones of your synopsis. Look at your one-to-two pager and divide it up like this:

Act One: Beginning—*The Setup.*

Your primary concern is to:

- Grab the audience's interest.
- Introduce the protagonist's main problem and goal.
- Introduce all the main characters.
- Present the protagonist with a moral dilemma.

Act Two: Middle—*The Confrontations.*

Your primary concern is to:

- Introduce at least three escalating major obstacles for the protagonist to overcome in pursuit of his or her overall goal in the story. Thin out act two as two halves. In the first half, the protagonist *gains ground* in the story; in the second half the protagonist *loses ground* in the story.

Act Three: Ending—*The Resolution.*

Your primary concern is to:

- Bring the protagonist and antagonist (and/or villain) face-to-face for the final confrontation with an emerging winner.

Start adding some of the details of *how* events in the story will occur. Mind you, it's still not the time to get too specific. If you feel the urge to write the *how*, instead use the word *somehow*. Try to stay away from the details of specific scenes and especially what the characters are talking about. If you feel the urge to write about what the characters are saying in dialogue, use the phrase "we learn." Concentrate on telling the story through events generated by what the protagonist wants, not through dialogue.

Start to paint a visual picture of the story in narrative form, adding juicy adjectives that'll create vivid visual images in the reader's mind's eye. This is the beginning of adding *tone* and *atmosphere* to your piece. For example, if your story is a comedy, the words should evoke a light-hearted feeling when read; if it's action-adventure, we should feel like we're on a roller-coaster ride simply through the words you've chosen; if it's a thriller, we should get goose bumps as we read the story.

There's no one way to tell you how to write your story. Look at this as a way to open some new doors of creativity as you develop your story. All you're really doing is beginning to find places to put all those jumbled ideas and images that are randomly bouncing around inside your head.

In fact, a good exercise is to simply make a list of all the stuff you want to include in your story without regard to how they will actually fit into the screenplay. Just write them down as they come to mind and in no particular order of importance. You can then use this list to help you to expand your basic story by adding a bit more detail. You'll be surprised how little you really do know about the details of your story despite all that stuff that's creating a log jam in your brain. The ultimate goal here is to plant more seeds for ideas.

Another trick for expanding the middle is to make a list of all the things that could go wrong for your protagonist in the story. Then put them in order of difficulty. Use the top four—the first three as act two obstacles and the final one for the climax. Use the other complications to fill the protagonist quest with even more conflict.

A good guideline for this story expansion step is to keep the story under ten double-spaced pages (use five single-spaced pages and help save a tree). Read the example of how I expanded *Motherland* (at this point, I had changed the title to *Thesis*). This example should give you an idea of how this approach works. My story expansion actually ended up being about twelve pages long. But that's close enough . . .

SAMPLE EXPANSION OF SYNOPSIS INTO THREE ACTS

THESIS

By Steve Duncan

Act One

Story opens with the kidnapping of 13-year-old PAYNE "PEE WEE" FRAZIER, a shy, not-so-street-smart African-American boy, by an African-American man whose face is unseen. It's late at night and they are inside the rugged bathroom at a camp in the California mountains. The boy resists more than expected—produces a Scout knife for protection. The tussle causes Pee Wee to cut his attacker and himself. From an unseen perch in the nearby woods, a frightened 13-year-old African-American WITNESS watches as Pee Wee, bound and gagged, is put into the trunk of a car and driven away.

We meet DR. KENNETH CHESTNUT, an African-American sociology professor at USC as he sits with his all-white class of students. They observe a tribal dance and Congo drum demonstration by a touring African troupe. During the performance, Chestnut has a mystical experience where he sees himself playing the Congo drums and dancing with the group, all while watching himself. When it's over, we meet Chestnut's teaching assistant, 25-year-old JASON DUFFY.

In his office, Chestnut is visited by a police DETECTIVE who is investigating the murder of Pee Wee and disappearance of two other black youths from a California summer camp program for inner-city youths. The Detective wants to talk to Duffy. The Detective has pictures of the kids as he questions Duffy with Chestnut in the room. We learn that the Detective believes that Pee Wee was murdered because of the blood stains found at the scene. During questioning, Duffy is cool and believable and we learn that Duffy had helped to organize the camp but had returned to Los Angeles the night of the crime. The Detective leaves, but he's not so convinced that Duffy is telling the truth.

At the L.A. Airport, we meet SCOTT KENYATTA, a 23-year-old African student, as he makes final arrangements to fly three crates to the Congo. The crates contain a species of monkey found in the Ituri Forest in the Congo.

At USC, during a final summer class session, Duffy is arrested by the Detective for suspicion of murder and taken away. After his lecture, Chestnut goes to the police station, asks questions. The Detective tells Chestnut that Duffy's blood type was the same blood type found at the scene of the crime. Chestnut talks to Duffy who becomes unusually evasive and belligerent. But he sticks to his innocent plea. We learn that Duffy says he's just another black man being accused of a crime he didn't commit. Chestnut knows something is very wrong.

Chestnut goes to see Pee Wee's parents with the hope of learning something. He learns that Pee Wee lives in a very nice house and is from an upper-middle-class nuclear family. The boy had just become a Boy Scout and was an all-around good kid. Pee Wee has two brothers and two sisters. He's the middle child. The parents are very upset and bitterly blame Duffy for the fate of their boy.

Now Chestnut goes to see the parents of Clarence "Skeeter" Banks. The mother, MRS. BANKS, lives in a rundown South Central Los Angeles welfare housing project. The father is not there, he's in jail for ten days. The mother is distressed because she had been depending on Skeeter to help her. But she didn't know where he was and it was not all that unusual for him to disappear for days at a time.

Chestnut visits Tisha "Tish" Toliver's home. He finds a pretty and educated divorced mother, MRS. TOLIVER, who thought Tish was with her father when she disappeared. She's angry and upset at her ex-husband and tells Chestnut to get out of her business.

Chestnut arrives at the police station. Duffy has called in a panic. Duffy is put into a lineup because the 13-year-old eyewitness has come forward. The boy identifies Duffy as the killer.

Now Chestnut finally hears the truth from Duffy. Chestnut learns that Pee Wee is not dead—it's only a graduate thesis designed to see how today's black youth react to a primitive African tribe in the bush.

He and Kenyatta, one of Chestnut's former graduate students, had conspired to send the youths to Africa to live among an ancient tribe called the Efe. We realize he wasn't worried about being convicted and felt so strongly about the thesis project that he decided to take his lumps. But with the eyewitness, he's scared. Chestnut and Duffy tell the Detective about the thesis. The Detective laughs and does not believe them. Chestnut informs Duffy that he will get a lawyer.

Through the lawyer, Chestnut learns that the current evidence is enough to bound Duffy over for a hearing. The only thing that is going to save Duffy from that fate is for the three youths to walk into the police station and prove they are alive and well. Chestnut decides to delay the start of his summer lecture engagements, go to the Congo, and bring back the three youths himself.

Act Two

Kenyatta is in the Congo. They are in a small town in the Ituri rain forest. He meets a GUIDE who is from the Lese people. Kenyatta opens the first crate. The monkey is taken away and a hidden compartment is revealed. Inside is Pee Wee. The other crates contain TISHA "TISH" TOLIVER and CLARENCE "SKEETER" BANKS. The three youths see daylight for the first time in several days. Pee Wee's cut (that he acquired during his struggle at camp) is swollen badly. Kenyatta ignores the cut, and they begin their journey into the jungle.

Chestnut arrives in the Congo. He finds a TRADESMAN who offers to take him into the Ituri Forest to find Kenyatta and the American youths. They use a Land Rover and take the dirt roads that cut through the thick forest. It's much faster than the river and more expensive for Chestnut. We get the feeling that the Tradesman is a sleazeball out for himself and only interested in making money.

Meanwhile, Kenyatta and the Lese Guide ride a boat up the Congo River with the black youths. They are filled with new wonders and bad attitudes. Kenyatta and the three black youths trek through a treacherous forest.

Chestnut arrives at a Lese village and is indeed fascinated by this new experience as he witnesses an argument between an Efe tribesman and a Lese tribesman over the Efe's young daughter whom the Lese tribesman plans to marry. Chestnut is surprised by this show of intercultural racism.

Chestnut learns that the Lese and Efe people are very much dependent upon one another for food, goods, and services.

Meanwhile Pee Wee, Skeeter, and Tish arrive at the Efe tribe's village. It's nightfall. Kenyatta seems to know the VILLAGE LEADER and pays him in machetes, clothes, and aluminum pots. The kids are taken away to their own hut.

In the Lese village, over a drink of fermented sap from the raffia plant, Chestnut learns that the tribesmen believe white people eat black people, especially women and children. He is truly taken by this new environment.

Chestnut arrives at the Efe village. He is very angry with Kenyatta, and the two men have a fist-fight right there in the middle of the village. Chestnut wins the fight and gains the respect of the Efe men. Chestnut is taken to see the three youths, tells them he's going to take them back home. That night, an Efe father sits around a campfire and tells the children a story about how the monkeys came to live in the trees. During the telling, he encourages everyone to sing. Chestnut, Skeeter, Tish, and Pee Wee are there. After the story, Skeeter does a rap song to the lively African chant. Skeeter and a teen EFE GIRL are attracted to one another.

Tish is with the Efe women. They make a fuss over her straightened hair and Western clothes. Skeeter is not getting along with an EFE TEENAGER who has an eye for the teen Efe Girl. But Skeeter is much taller than the Efe boy and successfully intimidates him. However, Pee Wee is getting along just fine with his peers—they are all the same size.

Later that night, Kenyatta tries to talk Chestnut into staying and taking part in his thesis; Chestnut refuses.

The next day in the forest, while trekking on their way to return to America, Chestnut, the three youths, and the Efe Guide come across a dead elephant. Hundreds of Efe people arrive and gather as they strip and smoke the meat from the giant animal. The Guide announces that the elephant is a "gift from the forest" and he must stop and help. The Tradesman who helped Chestnut days before lurks there with some of his gun-toting buddies. The Tradesman is very interested in the prized ivory tusks of the elephant. Chestnut notices that the elephant was shot by a powerful rifle. Chestnut decides to continue on unescorted.

Chestnut and his charges get lost in the thick jungle and nightfall traps them. Chestnut has a mystical experience while lost in the forest. Just moments from an attack by a jungle cat, the Efe Guide saves their lives and takes them back to the village.

The next morning, Kenyatta prepares to leave when Chestnut and his charges arrive. Kenyatta makes one last plea to convince Chestnut to stay for just a few weeks of observation. Chestnut says the answer is still no.

Pee Wee and Tish mix with the Efe teens before leaving. They have made friends already. Chestnut observes Skeeter's fascination with a group of Efe men who prepare poison arrows for a monkey hunt. Skeeter begs the men to let him go on the hunting trip with them, but it takes Chestnut's agreement to come along for them to agree.

Chestnut and Skeeter go on the monkey hunt with the Efe men. Along the way, Skeeter and Chestnut start a bonding process as they become a part of a wild chase through the forest after a wounded monkey that ultimately gets away. They both learn a lot about survival in the Ituri Forest through the Efe people.

Back at the village, Chestnut agrees (as a result of his experiences to date) to stay and observe the youths for a week only. But Kenyatta must go to town and send a telegram back to the L.A. Police Department. Kenyatta agrees and immediately starts his journey to town.

An Efe Tribesman on a hunt has the good fortune to find a dead monkey in the forest. He brings it back to the village and shares it with the hunter whose monkey got away the day before but never acknowledges the fact. Chestnut notes the village politics involved. Chestnut begins to make written notes, and we hear his voice-over as he writes. We begin to get his astute insight as to the comparisons and contrasts of modern life between African-Americans and the Africans of the rain forest.

Pee Wee falls very ill with a high fever from his cut. The village women take care of him. But Chestnut is afraid that Pee Wee will die and that would be very bad news for Duffy.

That night, Chestnut dreams he is running wildly through the jungle for no apparent reason.

The next morning, the Efe village Leader announces that they must break camp and move closer to the river to hunt for honey. What about Kenyatta? Chestnut asks. He will find us says the village Leader.

As they break camp, Skeeter and the Efe Girl flirt. There's a humorous moment as Skeeter teaches her ghetto slang. Chestnut is fascinated by it all as he takes copious notes.

In the rain forest, Kenyatta accidentally runs upon the Tradesman and his poaching pals trying to kill another elephant. The elephant gets away. The angry Tradesman and his pals take Kenyatta on a horrifying romp through the thick jungle before murdering him.

During camp move, more bonding takes place between Chestnut and Skeeter while Pee Wee takes a turn for the worse.

At the new campsite, the elder women take care of the very sick and feverish Pee Wee while the other women put up the new village. Tish helps as Chestnut makes notes.

That night, the Efe hunters go out to hunt for the bees' nests. Chestnut and Skeeter go along. They find a big nest and wait for morning. The next morning, the women arrive to watch the honey being retrieved. It's a festive time for the Efes because honey is considered the "ultimate gift of the forest." There's a real sense of community, togetherness, love, and happiness notes Chestnut.

At the new camp, Tish witnesses young teen girls who get their teeth chipped and have beauty scars put on their bodies. Chestnut is amused at the different reactions to the meaning of beauty.

Chestnut observes both women and men fishing using natural chemicals to put the fish to sleep. He's amazed by the intelligent, scientific way the Efe people approach the fishing process.

Meanwhile, back in Los Angeles, Duffy faces a judge at a court hearing. He is bound over for trial on the charges of murder and kidnapping.

While the Efe men smoke marijuana, Chestnut is invited to participate. But Skeeter tells him to "Just say no."

That night, Pee Wee recovers from his fever as the women perform a fertility treatment on a woman who has come from another clan. Pee Wee's going to be alright. Chestnut realizes he can stay no longer; he must get the three kids back to their parents. He again wonders what happened to Kenyatta . . . the only man who can explain everything. He must find him . . .

Act Three

But the next day, during a group antelope hunt, Chestnut and Skeeter discover Kenyatta's dead body in the forest. The men cut up the animal, give the liver to the shooter. Skeeter jokes he always hated liver. Chestnut is angry and wants to avenge Kenyatta's death.

Chestnut decides to take on the Tradesman and the poachers. He engages the help of the Efe Tribesmen. Dressing and feeling like an African warrior, Chestnut and the Efe Tribesmen hunt down the Tradesman in a very intelligent manner. They use bows and drugged arrows against guns and rifles. After subduing the Tradesman and his boys, they head for town to turn them over to the authorities.

Back at the Efe camp, Tish embarks on a short trip to a nearby Lese village to take part in a "coming out" ceremony of a Lese teenage girl who has been in seclusion for three months.

Chestnut and the Efe men arrive in town and turn the Tradesman and his sidekicks over to the authorities.

Back at the Efe camp, Skeeter makes love to the Efe Girl and angers her father.

Chestnut decides it's time to return home to America. He and the kids say their good-byes to the Efe people. At the town, the Tradesman and his poachers are free, having bribed their way out of trouble. The Tradesman tells Chestnut and the kids with a sneer that they don't belong in Africa.

Back in Los Angeles, Chestnut and the three kids make a dramatic entrance during Duffy's courtroom trial. The case is dismissed.

Chestnut escorts Tish to her home. Tish's divorced parents stop bickering and realize their daughter is a much more mature and responsible teen.

Chestnut takes Pee Wee home where he is greeted enthusiastically by his family.

And Chestnut takes Skeeter home where his father is out of jail but still using drugs. Skeeter's mother has been beaten and is pitiful. She thanks Chestnut for bringing her child back to her.

At USC, Chestnut and Duffy are back at work. Duffy is out of jail pending minor charges. The parents are happy with their children's new attitudes; they don't press serious charges against Duffy. In a surprise move, we see that Skeeter is Duffy's new assistant. Skeeter is now very Afrocentric in his dress and attitude. They all plan to go back to the Congo next summer to properly finish the thesis after Skeeter graduates from high school.

THE END

YOUR ASSIGNMENT

Start developing your story. Remember that all you're doing at this point is sketching out the *beginning, middle,* and *end* in *two steps.* Tell *what* happens in broad strokes for the basic story. That means concentrate on the protagonist's needs, wants, and desires. Leave much of the details of *how* for later. Then expand the story into three acts, use the Four Big Chunk approach—act one, act two first half, act two second half, and act three—fleshing out a bit more detail as you go.

Remember to introduce your protagonist to the problem with flair in an interesting setting. Then give the protagonist a "deadline" by which to solve the problem so the story has a sense of urgency.

Present the protagonist with constant choices that—upon making decisions—create obstacles that escalate in difficulty. Use your "list of things that can go wrong." You need at least three major complications and they should be in the *middle* of the story. Save the worse that can go wrong for the climax.

Decide what the climax and final twists are going to be. Punish the bad guy (or girl) and reward the hero (or heroine). In total, you shouldn't have more than two single-spaced pages when you're done with the basic story and around five single-spaced pages after you expand the synopsis. Here's a good length guideline:

> one page for Act One
> one page for Act Two First Half
> one page for Act Two Second Half
> one page for Act Three
> one page just in case some of the other pages go a little long.

Also, write out the essence of your subplot in no more than half a page. Focus on the theme that you're dying to explore through the protagonist's emotional relationship. Remember, you'll expand all of this material later. (Note: *Thesis* does not have a subplot written out. But the subplot involves Chestnut's relationship with Skeeter—a male love story, like big brother–little brother. I also use *runners* with Chestnut between Pee Wee and Tish to further flesh out his paternal side.)

NOTE

1. Richard Stayton, "Zaillian's List: Steven Zaillian casts his fate to the muse" (Los Angeles: Written By, March 2001).

CHAPTER 4

Frame an Engaging Story with Sound Structure

UNFOLD THE STORY

Now that you've learned to crawl and walk, it's time to start running. This last step in the process of developing your story is not much more than a technical drill. I say technical because much of what you're going to be doing at this point is *math*. But not like you normally think of it.

See, you've already come up with most of the sums to your addition problems. So, now you're going to be making up the *list of numbers* that *add up to those sums*. Structuring a story is a lot like saying "I know the total is twenty. Now, I need to figure out which seven numbers (scenes) add up to that."

CLASSIC SCREENPLAY STRUCTURE: MAKING SAUSAGES

I've often heard new writers complain that **classic structure** is a too much of a *formula*. Well, while it's certainly a system for writing a screenplay, it only becomes a formula if the writer uses it in that way. I think it's more productive to look at classic structure as you would look at making sausages. Yes, that's what I said, *sausages*. All sausages are basically made the same way—meat is ground up and stuffed into an edible sleeve then pinched off in five-, six-, or twelve-inch lengths to create individual sausages. Even though all sausages look the same, there are many types: Italian, Louisiana, Swedish, or Greek—you name it. They come as mild, hot, or very hot. They even come as pork, beef, or turkey. But they all still look alike.

Screenplays are sort of like that. The good ones follow the same basic structure theory. In this way, most screenplays are alike. But the ingredients of each screenplay—like sausages—are very, very different and unique.

I've read somewhere that the Greeks invented the three-act structure. So, it's been around for a long time. They probably decided upon three acts because they wanted to sell statuettes of the Greek landmarks and goblets of cheap wine during intermission. Besides, nobody's going to sit for three whole hours without going to the potty. But seriously, folks, over the years the three-act structure has proven itself as a solid blueprint for engaging and holding an audience's attention over a two-hour period of time. I don't know if Aristotle had the idea of intermission in his head when he wrote his *Poetics*, but it certainly worked in his favor. If he were alive today, he'd be a very rich man from all the royalties.

For the screenwriter, to *structure* a story means to *shape it* into a dramatic form that primarily focuses on the *protagonist's journey* and do it in a way that both grabs the interest of the audience and maintains that interest.

Structure offers you a tried and true way of approaching your story in terms of its main character, the protagonist. In fact, it's the protagonist who creates the structure of a screenplay. Let me repeat that—*it's the protagonist who creates the structure of a screenplay by making decisions necessary to reaching a goal or solving a problem.* By design, structure is a broad and general theory. The story detail must still come from your brain, from your creativity, and from the characters you've chosen to populate your story. Structure, by no means, is a magic formula. It's really just *guidelines* that help to keep you on the track of good storytelling. You might even say it's a way of *thinking about your story—not a way of writing it.* In fact, most of today's screenwriting theory was developed through analyzing well-written plays and screenplays that, for the most part, were written purely on instinct by the writer. So, structure, in effect, is an apotheosis of a writer's *natural instincts* for telling a good tale. The exact *what* and *how* of **story structure** must be totally justified in your mind as the screenwriter. If you can't justify your protagonist's actions, don't expect the audience to either.

A good way to start developing structure for your story is to think of a logical process that anyone would use to solve the problem that you've given to your protagonist. Then use this *logical approach* as the *basic framework* for designing the story's structure.

For example, if your story involves your protagonist dealing with a crime, his or her approach to solving the problem has a logical framework already in place—the criminal justice system. So, if your protagonist is accused of murder, there's a process in place that he must follow to solve his problem. He needs to get a lawyer. The lawyer needs to gather evidence. The lawyer goes to trial. Both sides argue their case. A jury deliberates guilt or innocence. You can use this process to mold your screenplay's overall framework. In this case, this process is well known by the audience and will feel *realistic* and *believable*. Many, many films use the criminal justice system as the framework for structure. One film that comes to mind is *Presumed Innocent* starring Harrison Ford.

If your protagonist is a quarterback on a football team and his goal is to win the Super Bowl, you have the logical process of spring training, pre-season games, regular season games, conference play-offs, then the big championship game. This is the process on which you can hang the structure of your story. You may even decide to end the story at the end of the play-offs as Oliver Stone did in *Any Given Sunday*. In that film we never see the Super Bowl game.

LINEAR VERSUS NONLINEAR STRUCTURE

A LINEAR VERSUS A NONLINEAR STRUCTURE IS IMPORTANT TO SUSPENSE.

When you start structuring your story, you've got to decide *how* you're going to *tell* the story:

A **linear story** is one that starts at the beginning and unfolds in chronological order. Events are portrayed as they happen, and the suspense and drama emerge as a result of an unrelenting buildup of these events, ultimately leading to the climax of the story. This is the most common way to approach screenplay structure.

A **nonlinear story** is one that may begin at the end of, or even the middle of, the story and tells you how the protagonist got to that point in the tale. There are many examples of movies that use this approach, but probably the most recent success is the film *Forrest Gump*. This story actually begins three quarters of the way into the story and Gump catches us up on how he came to be sitting on that bus bench at that point in time. Then the story dispenses with the nonlinear approach and shifts to linear storytelling.

A Soldier's Story is an excellent example of a movie that skillfully uses the *flashback* as a suspenseful storytelling device. A Pulitzer Prize–winning play, this film—at times—uses a flashback within a flashback within a flashback. To keep the audience from getting completely lost, the screenwriter skillfully backs out of these series of flashbacks the same way he goes into them. The result is suspense that pulls you to the edge of your seat.

American Beauty breaks the rules by having the protagonist tell us his story from his grave, using the flashback technique. *Reversal of Fortune* used the same technique, as the protagonist tells us her story while in a deep coma. The classic film noir *Sunset Boulevard* also uses this technique.

Flashbacks and Structure

This can be a friend or foe.

As I mentioned before, a perfect example of using this storytelling convention as a way to *structure* a story is found in *Forrest Gump*. The first two hours of the movie has the protagonist waiting for a bus and recounting how he got to be there through a series of flashbacks. But we don't know we've joined the film two hours into the story. The flashbacks themselves provide the story with its structure. Then the last twenty minutes of the story moves forward without the use of flashbacks or voice-over.

The use of the protagonist's voice-over is a dead giveaway that a story is being told in flashback. In the wrong hands, the use of flashbacks is hazardous to the telling of a story. To effectively use this technique, you have to think of the flashback as a *storytelling device*. That means that the flashback itself is an integral part of how the story unfolds. If it simply becomes a way to give the audience facts and events from the past, then the flashback becomes a screenwriter's "crutch."

In *The Fugitive*, the screenwriter uses flashbacks as a device to remind us of the protagonist's motivation for finding the one-armed man. The actual flashbacks don't necessarily give us new information. The story is, for the most part, an open one—we know who killed the man's wife. But, almost like clockwork, a flashback occurs in the story at key **structure milestones** in the story . . . moments when the protagonist is haunted by the reason his life has changed so drastically. We get better insight in how Dr. Kimble was involved at the actual murder and how it was so easy for him to have been convicted of the crime. The flashbacks in this film also serve to give the story a love story subplot. We get to see just how much Kimble loved his wife.

Stories where the protagonist is to face a series of life-and-death situations can be considerably weakened if told in flashback using the protagonist's voice-over. Deep down, the audience knows nothing is going to happen to the protagonist so it lessens the suspense of the danger he or she encounters throughout the story.

However, this doesn't mean that the use of voice-over in a life-and-death story cannot be used effectively. For example, writer-director Oliver Stone used the voice-over technique very realistically in his Vietnam War film *Platoon*. Despite the fact that the protagonist's life was in constant danger throughout the story, the screenwriter's aim was to tell about the horror of the *experience itself*. This approach forces the audience to ask the question "Is it better to have been killed in combat than to have to relive such experiences over and over in one's mind for the rest of one's life?"

The flashback is, technically, just one example of **parallel narrative** storytelling techniques and the most popular method used by writers. There are basic elements to pay attention to when using this particular technique.

1. There is a "triggering" crisis to the flashbacks (past story).
2. The "past" and "present" stories are on a collision course.
3. Both stories are told from the protagonist's point of view.
4. Both stories have a thematic relationship.
5. Both stories have a beginning, a middle, and an ending (the basic three acts).
6. There is a strong sense of urgency.
7. Both stories usually are told in chronological order but not necessarily.
8. There's a "quest" toward the third act climax.
9. There is a detective element to the storytelling.
10. There is a new understanding for the protagonist in the end

While, of course, these rules are not set in stone, following them will make for a much stronger screenplay structure.

Finally, you can also use the *flash-forward* convention in your storytelling. This is less a storytelling convention than a narrative technique. For example, let's say you have a character giving a speech about the future. This could be visually boring for the audience. You can use the *flash-forward* to show how what he's talking about is already happening. In effect, you put the present situation into the past by leaping forward in the story.

FORESHADOWING AND STRUCTURE

AVOID AUDIENCE GROANS.

To **foreshadow** means to plant subtle clues in a story that ultimately will serve to explain or justify future events or character actions—called a **payoff**—in the story.

A simple example of this technique can be found in *The Firm*, the film based on John Grisham's best-selling novel. Early in the story, the protagonist encounters a horse-drawn wagon full of cotton several times in the alley next to the firm's building. This innocuous confrontation between a police officer and the wagon's owner plays in the background of at least two key dramatic scenes involving the protagonist. Later, as the story builds to a climax, the protagonist is faced with only one way to escape his foes—a closed and locked window. He smashes the window with his expensive briefcase and takes a swan dive—right into the wagon full of cotton in the alley below. If this had not been foreshadowed, the entire audience would have collectively groaned.

You can use this technique in much more sophisticated applications involving character dialogue. Or foreshadowing can also be effectively accomplished through visual clues: a gun in the drawer when a character opens it to get a book of matches; a broken light bulb in a dark hallway of an apartment's basement; even a suspicious glance or an accepting smile between two characters.

Foreshadowing is an excellent way to mitigate story *contrivances*. Contrivances are events added to a story in order for it to work or make sense to the audience. The audience can see and feel a contrivance a mile away.

SUBPLOT AND STRUCTURE

THE SUBPLOT AND STRUCTURE SHOULD BE SUBTLE BUT OBVIOUS.

Although not a strict rule (few rules are in artistic endeavors), developing eight separate scenes is an excellent guideline for planning and creating your subplot. While it's true that the protagonist and antagonist within the subplot also interact during the main story, it's the problem of the main story that primarily *distracts* them from dealing with the details of the subplot. Since theme is best explored in a subplot, you should plan to weave your theme into these eight specific scenes. Also, having a strong subplot that explores the story's theme creates the screenplay's central conflict. That is, the protagonist learns what is necessary to solve the problem in the main plot *through* the conflict in the subplot relationship.

Why eight to ten scenes? you may ask. Well, the structure of a subplot usually mirrors that of the main story. Following this logic, between pages 1–10 you would incorporate subplot scene number one, which, like the main story, introduces the protagonist to the subplot's problem. Then you would introduce the conflict to be played out in the subplot between pages 11–30 (where you introduce the conflicts of the main story). Soon after your protagonist moves into his or her new territory around page 31, the subplot should also reflect a move into a new territory for the protagonist. The protagonist realizes "first growth" around page 45, so soon after—and sometimes just before—he or she should also experience first growth in the subplot. The same for page 60, point of no return; page 75, all is lost; page 90, back against the wall; and finally, the climax. These are the eight scenes that constitute your subplot. Some of these scenes actually may be included *inside* a main story scene or during transition scenes so as to keep the pace moving right along.

Transition scenes, which are necessary to storytelling, can sometimes be boring. However, these are sometimes the best opportunities to inject the subplot. For example, your protagonist and antagonist in the subplot are on the run and you need to show a passage of time to keep the audience properly oriented. So, to add to the drama, write a scene from the subplot in between the main story's night scene and the main story's next day scene. If the night scene includes a big explosion and escape, then you could call this subplot scene a "quiet moment" in the story before the next onslaught of gunshots. This is a staple technique used in action and action-adventure stories. It's also an excellent way to "cover up the cracks" of structure because it allows you to change the direction of the main story in a totally *organic* way that also embraces your theme.

But even if the genre of the story does not include physical action, a subplot scene fits well if placed soon after a major confrontation between the protagonist and the antagonist (or villain) in the main story.

The ultimate goal is, of course, to weave the subplot scenes (and the theme) into the main story in a seamless fashion. Again, this creates a sense of the central conflict. If you plan out all of this now in your story's development, it will be less murky as you begin to write the rough draft to your screenplay.

Let's look at the *Love Story Development Template* that makes up most subplots, with the structure milestones added.

FIGURE 4.1 Structure as a Roller-Coaster Ride

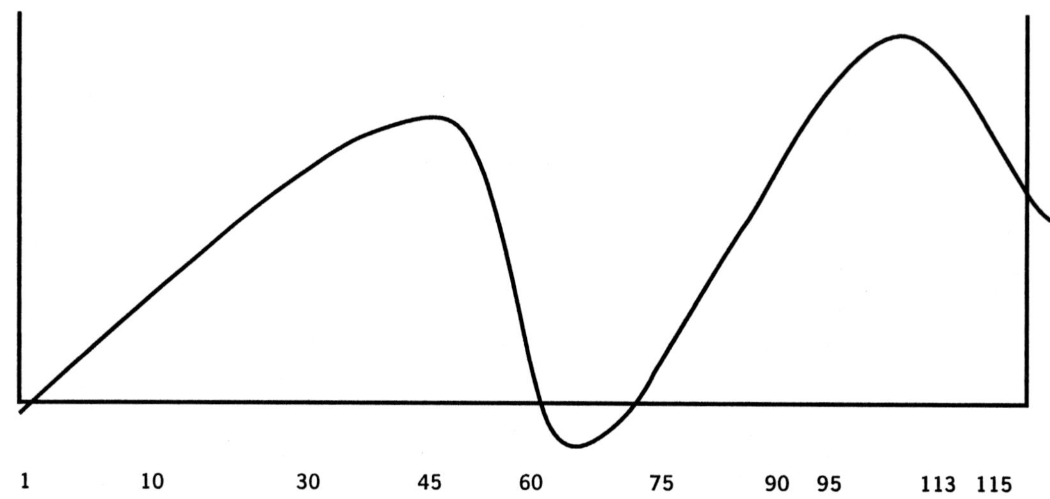

LOVE STORY DEVELOPMENT TEMPLATE—STRUCTURED

Pages 1–10: Boy meets Girl.
Pages 11–30: Boy is confronted by a problem with Girl; ends up falling in love with her.
Pages 31–45: Boy loses Girl—his own fault.
Pages 46–60: Boy gets Girl back.
Pages 61–75: Boy loses Girl again—her doing, looks like forever.
Pages 76–90: Boy gets Girl back. Boy loses Girl once again, this time by no fault of his own (an outside force).
Pages 91–95: Boy gets Girl back.
Pages 96–The End: Boy, having learned his lesson, confronts and eliminates the influence of the outside force forever. Boy and Girl live happily ever after.

This approach clearly structures how the protagonist's relationship will go as both the main plot and subplot unfold. In this illustration, I've reduced the ten love story steps to eight major scenes to create a roller-coaster ride with lots of ups and downs.

The bottom line is that the structure of a screenplay should, by its design, *take the audience on a roller-coaster ride* with the protagonist in the lead car. Your story needs to have ups, downs, and sharp turns (see Figure 4.1).

PAGE COUNT AND STRUCTURE

THIS IS A GUIDELINE NOT THE LAW.

The classic screenplay has evolved to 120 pages. At *one page per minute* average, that means a movie runs about two hours. However, more and more, the typical screenplay is around 110 pages—or one hour and fifty minutes. This is the commonly accepted length at most studios these days. The reason is pure economics.

If a finished movie runs less than two hours, theater owners can book at least one extra screening of the film per day and make more money. That means the studios also make more money. These days, the longer a movie runs past 110 minutes, the more powerful that writer, producer, or director is in Hollywood. But when one of those long films flop, even those powerful geniuses usually go back to making movies that run around 110 minutes. However, if the long movie is a smash hit . . . well, need I say more?

As a newcomer to screenwriting, it's in your best interest to stay within the more universally accepted 110- to 120-page length. Otherwise, you may be judged as a rank amateur who simply hasn't taken the time to learn the basics of screenwriting.

It bears saying here that when I write about the number of pages that define each structural milestone, I'm not talking absolutes. The idea is to have some reliable way to give the story a rhythm, if you will, in its telling, something the moviegoing audience has come to appreciate and often demand.

Look at the page count as the number of minutes of a finished film. In this way, you have a tried-and-true way to gauge how your story is unfolding totally dictated by the protagonist's desires, the decisions based on those desires, and the actions taken as a result of the decisions.

Let me repeat—*this is a guideline*. If it takes fourteen pages to write your structural Pages 1–10, then that's what it takes. However, if it takes twenty pages to write your story structure Pages 1–10, then you're probably pushing the envelope of good pacing and the audience will start to squirm in their seats if you take too long to tell them what the story is about.

There are, of course, many exceptions to this guideline that work well in films. I will point them out as we explore in more detail the concept of structure.

Finally, do not think of this page-count concept as screenplay structure. It is the *pacing* of the story's structure, not structure itself. Like novels use chapters and poems use stanzas to pace themselves, screenplays use the number-of-minutes-elapsed concept.

Act One

Act One is the setup.

This is basically the first thirty minutes of a movie. That computes into the first *thirty pages* of the screenplay. Here's what you need to structurally accomplish in act one:

Pages 1–10

What's the story about?

From pages 1–3, open the story big or with a scene that grabs the audience's attention. This is sometimes referred to as the **hook** or **opening sequence**. Orient the audience to the *setting*—where the story takes place and the *world* the story will explore. Establish the *tone* of the story—drama, comedy, action-adventure, horror, science fiction, and so on. Introduce *theme* using a thematic device or the metaphysical central question to be answered in the story. A thematic device should be subtle and often is only fully devised *after* completing the rough draft of the screenplay. So don't fret about this at this point in the writing process. You can come back and insert this later during the rewriting process if you already haven't instinctively written it in.

FIGURE 4.2 Classic Screenplay Structure by the Clock: The First Hour

Think of the pacing of a film by how much time elapses as the story unfolds . . .

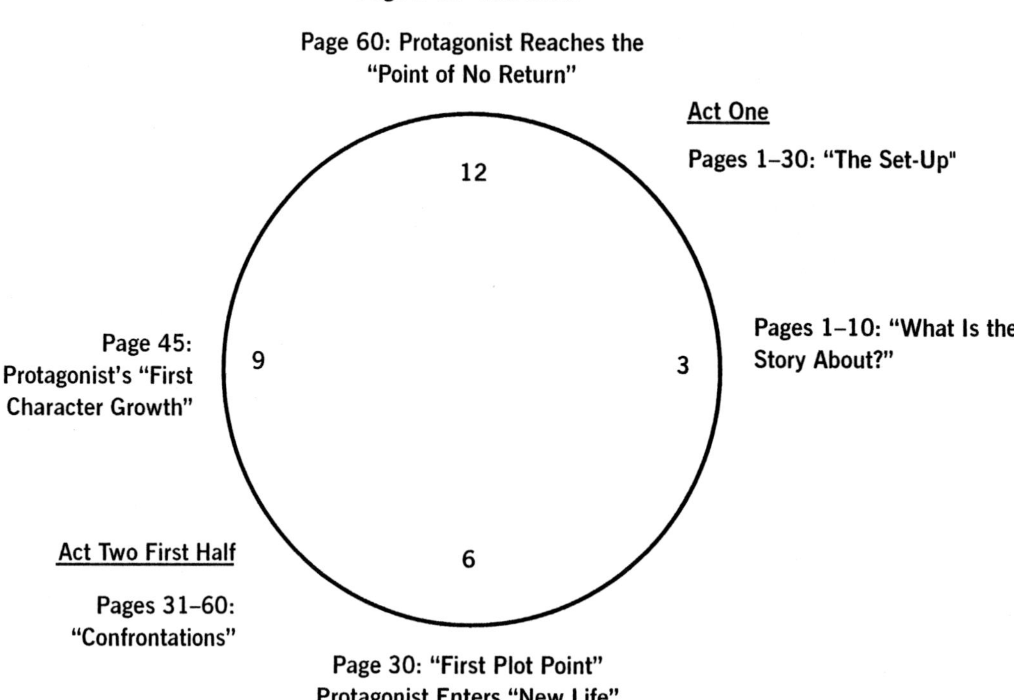

For example, a device could be a tattered teddy bear coveted by a young woman with a troubled childhood. Or, the metaphysical central question can actually be cloaked in dialogue as in the film *Chinatown*, when Jake Gittes says in effect, "only rich people can get away with murder."

At a minimum, *introduce the protagonist*. You can also introduce the antagonist and the villain (if there's one). Remember to introduce your protagonist—and all characters for that matter—with flair and style comparable to their dramatic roles in the story.

The story begins when the problem begins for the protagonist, so generally we should meet him or her at that point. This is sometimes called the **point of attack** or the **inciting incident** of the story. The inciting incident does not necessarily have to take place at the start of the film. It can happen before the story begins or after the story starts. If the inciting incident begins before the story begins, then it's *back story*. Put the back story in the *forward drive* as the story unfolds. In *Raiders of the Lost Ark*, the inciting incident takes place long before the story begins—the Nazi's decide to find and use the ark to win World War II. We only find this out when Army intelligence recruits Indiana Jones to help find the ark before the Nazis.

If the inciting incident takes place after the story begins, don't take too long to get it out or your audience may get bored. In *Witness*, the inciting incident takes place when Samuel witnesses a brutal murder in a Philadelphia bus station. This happens about ten minutes into the story. That's about as long as you want to wait to introduce the inciting incident of any story.

Bottom line, by page ten (or so) we should know *what the story is about.* And that should center on the protagonist's *problem* and serve to generate the protagonist's *initial goal.* I say initial goal because, as the problem escalates, the quest to reach the overall goal will be interrupted by bouts with short-term efforts to overcome more immediate obstacles in the story.

Pages 11 to 30

Where will the complications emerge?

In these twenty pages (or so), you should introduce every major character and the conflict they will bring to the story. In fact, your main goal here is to *make the problem get worse* for the protagonist. Don't try to solve anything at this point, just show how each major character will create conflict for the protagonist. If you didn't introduce the antagonist or villain in the first ten pages, now is the time to do so. In fact, you should endeavor to introduce all major characters of the story in act one. When you introduce them, each should somehow make the protagonist's problem get worse. Each new character's dramatic role should be crystal clear to the audience when we first meet each. And by page 30, the protagonist should be *pushed* or *forced* into an unfamiliar situation—*new territory*—created by the initial problem in the story.

This *new territory* or *new life* is commonly called the **first plot point** in a screenplay. There are only two plot points. The second occurs at the end of act two. This first is the *turning point* for the protagonist because he or she now has to set out to solve the problem or pursue a goal or get out of a predicament. It's at this point that he or she can no longer ignore the problem because it's generating too much trouble to be disregarded. In fact, the problem must get so bad the protagonist must act to solve it. Of course, he or she doesn't really want to do this because the "old life" is much more comfortable. The most effective dramatic technique to propel the protagonist into new territory is to present him or her with a *moral dilemma.* He or she should be staring unavoidable change right in the eye. And it's scary. And they can't avoid it any longer.

Entering a "new life" really refers to the protagonist's move into new territory in the story. In the best stories, this new territory indeed foreshadows a new life for the protagonist . . . having him or her soon realize life will never be the same again.

Act Two

Confrontations!

This is the middle sixty minutes of a movie. That computes into *sixty pages* of the screenplay. I like to call this part of the screenplay the *black hole of storytelling* because this is where most stories can easily get *lost in space.*

Probably the best way to look at this sixty-page challenge is to think of it in smaller segments—two thirty-minute halves. Then slice those halves into quarters. You end up with four fifteen-minute **mini-dramas** that interlink and build toward the climax. This is a much more manageable approach to laying out the story in a structured format.

If you've formed your story correctly, you already know what the major obstacles in act two are going to be. And you have an idea about the solutions. Now it's time to figure out the numbers that add up to each solution.

Here's what you need to structurally accomplish in act two:

ACT TWO: FIRST HALF

Protagonist's gaining ground.

In this part of the story, think of the protagonist as being stronger than the antagonist. This part of the story consists of two fifteen-minute *mini-dramas*. Each of these mini-dramas has to do with the protagonist *grappling with change* that's taking place in his or her life and learning to cope in an unfamiliar situation. The protagonist is forced to act on the story's problem, and the decision takes him or her into a new situation (a "new life") where he or she has no choice but to try to operate in a new environment.

It's very important to look at this first half of act two as a way to get the audience behind the protagonist. You want the audience to root for the protagonist to succeed in his or her quest. Since nobody likes a loser, this thirty minutes should both challenge the protagonist and have him or her progress—*gain ground*—in the story.

Accomplish this in two mini-dramas . . .

PAGES 31–45

It's a brave New World.

Think about it: when you are confronted with change and find yourself in a new situation, the first thing you do is to rely on the knowledge, skills, and resources you already have at your disposal. In a general sense, that's exactly what your protagonist is going to do in these fifteen minutes of the story.

It's natural to *resist change* when one arrives in a new situation. We all have an aversion to change. So your protagonist should be no different. We all have *trouble adjusting to change* and so should your protagonist. This natural behavior helps to provide an emotional dimension to the story. As storytellers, it's our job to also provide a plot as the vehicle to explore the protagonist's emotional turmoil.

So, give the protagonist a **mini-goal**. This should be a short-term goal that fits into the overall *logical process for solving the problem* at hand. When the protagonist sets out to accomplish something, it should activate the antagonist to spring into opposition. This, of course, creates conflict. And this *confrontation* leads to a *mini-climax* in the first mini-drama. So, what you've done here is to have the protagonist encounter *the first major* **obstacle** in the story. The protagonist should *overcome* this first major obstacle to chalk up a *first win*. The defining scene of this first mini-drama is called **first character growth**. What that means, in theory, is that it's now clear to the protagonist (and the audience) that accomplishing the overall goal in the story is *not going to be so easy*.

Remember, the subplot relationship should also reflect this first character growth in this mini-drama.

PAGES 46–60

Solving the problem ain't going to be that easy.

Now the protagonist realizes he or she needs new skills and knowledge in order to succeed. However, their old ways continue to nag at them. It's not that easy to change or grow as a human being. So the protagonist sets out to accomplish another *mini-goal* in the logical process of solving the problem, he or she encounters *a second major obstacle* from the antagonist or villain. But this time it's a much larger and more difficult hurdle to jump.

So, this fifteen-minute *mini-drama* consists of the struggle to learn a new way to deal with a new situation. Essentially, the protagonist must *gain new skills*. These new abilities often provide the

FIGURE 4.3 Classic Screenplay Structure by the Clock: The Second Hour

Think of the pacing of a film by how much time elapses as the story unfolds . . .

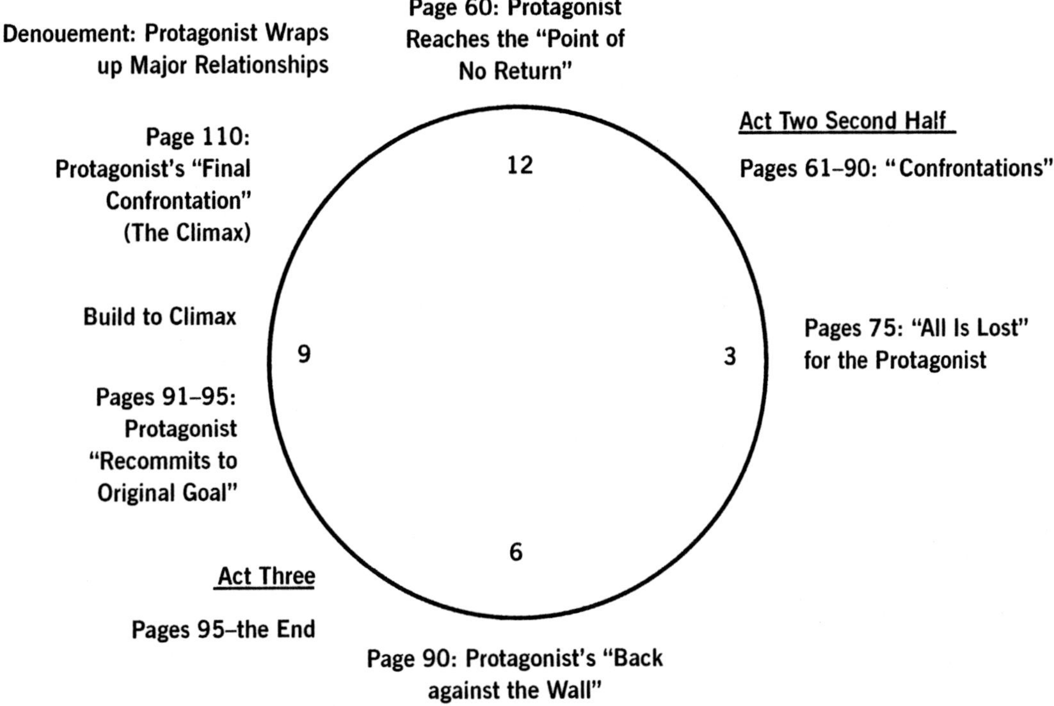

protagonist with his or her *second win.* Now—armed with better skills—the protagonist *accepts the change* in his or her new life. Now the protagonist reaches the **point of no return** in the story.

In this mini-drama's defining scene, it should become very clear to the protagonist (and the audience) that he or she can never go back to the way things were before. Life, as it was known, can not exactly exist for the protagonist. It's clearly the time to take the bull by the horns and set out once and for all to solve the main problem at hand. Do this by having the antagonist present a moral dilemma to the protagonist (it could be someone on the antagonist's side) to create a **midpoint crisis.**

Again, the subplot scene should also reflect this same idea of point of no return in the emotional relationship.

Act Two: The Second Half

Protagonist is losing ground.

Simply put, in this part of the story, think of the protagonist as weaker than the antagonist. Despite the conflict and frustration up to this point, overall, the protagonist should have come to terms with the new situation. He or she fully understands it's necessary to face the music head-on in order to survive and win. The protagonist commits to using newfound knowledge, skills, and resources—even though he or she doesn't like it—in order to solve the problem and reach the goal that's now much more complicated than he or she ever dreamed it could become.

So, the second half of act two is about the protagonist *losing a lot of the ground* gained in the first half of act two. Look at this like you would a baseball score—protagonist 2, antagonist 0. The antagonist wants to score, catch up, and pass the protagonist to win the game. So the antagonist is really pumped up at this point in the story. He or she wants to win badly.

But the protagonist wants to end the game too, while he or she's ahead. These clashing needs are what provide the substance of the second half of act two . . .

PAGES 61–75

Is there light at the end of the tunnel?

Still a little apprehensive, the protagonist decides on a course of action based upon previous experience since entering this so-called *new life*. He or she now sets out to solve the problem *once and for all* and *encounters the third major obstacle* from the antagonist or villain in the story and it's a whopper! Why? Because the antagonist or villain wants to win badly. They're throwing everything they have at the protagonist at this point. The protagonist—with the audience rooting and firmly behind him or her—now fails for the first time.

The defining scene in this third *mini-drama* should give the protagonist (and the audience) a sense that **all is lost**. The best way to create this feeling is to take away from the protagonist the obvious solution to his or her problem in the story. This could be a key witness to the murder disappearing or the computer disk that contains all the damning evidence is erased or destroyed.

Now the score is 2 to 1. The antagonist or villain has cut the lead and now want to move in to tie the score. At this point in the story, all the wind has been taken out of the protagonist's sail. He or she wants to quit—walk away from the story. But it's just not going to be that easy—too much water under the bridge with other characters. They simply won't let the protagonist walk away from the unsolved problem. They, in effect, are on an unrelenting mission of their own. It's *do-or-die* time for the protagonist.

The subplot scene should also reflect this same idea of "all is lost" in the love story relationship.

PAGES 75–90

I can't take this anymore.

Along the way, the protagonist should have developed a key relationship with a *likable pivotal character*. We often call this person the **tragic character**. At this point in the story, we want to get the protagonist to the lowest point possible. And we want the audience to feel the pain too. So, we create what's sometimes referred to as the story's **dark moment**. We do this by killing the likable pivotal character. Think of Goose in *Top Gun*. When Goose died, the audience felt the same pain as Tom Cruise. Of course, if you're writing a comedy, you don't want to litter your story with dead corpses. That's not funny. So, you should create the dark moment by taking away from the protagonist a key emotional relationship of a likable pivotal character. In the film *Mrs. Doubtfire*, the judge would no longer allow Robin Williams to see his children. This amounted to a spiritual death for the protagonist. What you're really doing is *kicking the protagonist when he or she is down*.

So, now—at the very lowest point of the story—the protagonist definitely wants to quit. But the antagonist or villain has amassed large quantities of strength and influence, while the protagonist has lost the same. So now the antagonist puts the protagonist *on the run* and scrambling—pressing, pushing, forcing a resolution that'll be in his or her favor—not that of the protagonist.

Of course being on the run is not limited to physical action. It also applies to an emotional state of being.

Logically, the protagonist should simply walk away from the situation. Hang up his spurs and go on vacation. But the concept of *unity of opposites*—neither character can win unless the other loses—should be strong enough to keep this from happening. If it's not, then the protagonist's motivation to have a rematch with the antagonist becomes a contrived one.

During this scrambling, the protagonist should discover—wittingly or unwittingly—a **key thing**. This could be a way to finally solve the problem, something he or she needed all along to win. The key thing should also have thematic value. While it may be discovering a physical solution to the problem, it should also provide an emotional truth. And this emotional truth should underline the metaphysical theme of the story. In *Cast Away*, two sides of an outdoor toilet wash ashore the island that Tom Hanks has been trapped on for four years. He doesn't know what to do with it. So, he stares at it for days. Then he realizes this will serve as his "sail" to help get him off the island. This is his key thing in the story.

When the antagonist or villain realizes that the protagonist has discovered a way to win, he or she redoubles efforts to defeat the protagonist. This, in effect, is what pushes the protagonist's **back against the wall**. This is the **second plot point** in the story because now, more than ever before, the protagonist realizes exactly what it's going to take to reach the goal. The protagonist, in effect, now discovers there's really only one choice now: face the antagonist or villain for one final battle. We call that *final confrontation* the story's climax.

The subplot should also reflect the same idea that the protagonist has his or her *back against the wall* in the emotional relationship.

Act Three

Protagonist takes care of business.

This is the place in the story when the pressure cooker is about to explode. The protagonist has taken the most reasonable courses of action to solve the problem, and now it's time to fix things once and for all.

PAGES 91–95

How did I get here in the first place?

But before the protagonist embarks on this ambitious final confrontation, he or she must **recommit to original goal** in the story. This is sometimes called the *quiet moment* of the story. Quiet not on the basis of noise but on the basis of reflection. It also sometimes embraces a *moment of truth* for the protagonist . . . *the look in the mirror* . . .

The protagonist, however, has learned a lot since entering this new life, and it's at this point that he or she takes stock. The screenwriter would do well to go back and revisit the first plot point when the protagonist faced a tough moral dilemma. In a creative way, have the protagonist reflect on what happened there. By bringing that reflection to this point of the story and shading it into a lesson learned, you give the story a stronger sense of *symmetry*.

The lesson doesn't have to be something new. It could be something that was always known by the protagonist but not faced. For example, in the film *Witness*, John Book—played convincingly by Harrison Ford—faces his *moment of truth* when a band of rowdy drunks harasses a group of Amish.

They assume Book is an honest to goodness nonviolent member of the sect because he is dressed like them. John Book has been wrestling with the idea of being less violent himself since coming to live among this group of people. But when squarely faced with the helplessness of being badgered by selfish drunks, he realizes his way is the only way for him—so he bashes in the rowdy's face. Of course, he later uses what he has learned about nonviolence while living among the Amish during the story's climax by refusing to use it any longer against the villain.

Probably one of the most creative sequences of a protagonist recommitting to his original goal can be found in the film *Forrest Gump*. When Gump's back is against the wall, he does what Jenny always told him to do—"run, Forrest, run." So, Forrest runs from coast to coast, not once but twice, to reflect on his life. When he realizes that Jenny is the focus of his life, he stops running. But along the way, he influences people who create pop culture icons, among them the smiley face.

This approach ultimately makes for a more satisfying conclusion to the story. Remember that your subplot should mirror this same structure. The protagonist should *recommit to original goal* in his emotional relationship in the story.

Pages 96–The End

Go for it!

Now the plan is set into action for the final confrontation. Lines are drawn in the sand and the two sides—the protagonist and antagonist (or villain)—begin their quests—each to win in their own way. Finally the confrontation occurs and the protagonist emerges as either the *winner* or the *loser*.

This is the *climax*—the story's resolution. You can look at the climax in two ways: physical and emotional:

The *physical climax* is just that—a battle of strength, explosions, gunplay, fistfights, and car chases—in order to come to terms with the protagonist's outer conflict.

The *emotional climax* involves the protagonist coming to terms with his or her inner conflict. I like to call this *the moment* in the story. Every word, sentence, scene, and sequence that has been written should all come to this moment in the story. The film *American Beauty* has a very clever way of creating this important beat in the story. It's not until the trigger is pulled and the bullet is on its way into Kevin Spacey's head that he has this moment of clarity (classic Shakespearean tragedy)—his life is worth living. That he's a good person after all. Then he dies.

In *The Fugitive,* Lt. Gerard faces Dr. Kimble once the villain, Dr. Nichols, has been captured. They look at each other and know the chase is over. Kimble says he didn't kill his wife. Gerard replies he knows.

In *Witness*, the *moment* doesn't have one line of dialogue as John Book faces Rachel at her door. They look into each other's eyes and volumes of thoughts race wildly. But not one word is exchanged. Then John Book leaves.

This point should be the most powerful moment in the screenplay.

There can also be what's called a *double climax*. You find this mostly in science fiction and thrillers. In *E.T.*, the first climax occurs when the little alien appears to die. Then he comes back to life and the chase is on to get the alien to his spaceship before it leaves without him. In *Alien,* the lone survivor of the blown-up spaceship prepares for the long trip home when suddenly, the Alien pops out of hiding, having gotten on the shuttle at the last minute, too. There's a final struggle and the Alien ends up getting jettisoned into space.

There's one other device you can use in the climax. It's called the **unlikely hero** (or heroine). This pivotal character is generally unlikable (as opposed to likable with the *tragic character*). The reason this character is unlikable is to throw off the audience from guessing that he or she will save the day in the end. Usually, this character disappears from the story somewhere around midpoint. This is done so that the audience will be glad to see the unsympathetic character disappear and not suspect he or she may be redeemed in the end. The unlikely hero shows up at the very last moment to save the protagonist from sure defeat. Sometimes he or she wins. Other times, he or she must give up life to save the protagonist.

In *Independence Day*, the unlikely hero is a despicable, shamed jet pilot who mistreats his kids and drinks too much. It's he who saves Will Smith and Jeff Goldblum who are trapped on the alien's mother ship. In this case, the unlikely hero gives his life to save the world.

In French, **denouement** means untying the knot but when used in a storytelling context, it means to *wrap up all loose ends*. This means that any significant relationships formed during the story must be resolved in a satisfactory way. There can be surprises here. And sometimes the resolution is no resolution. But you should show this to the audience, not leave them in confusion. Don't spend too much time doing this or it will feel anticlimactic. In a way, this is the American way of untying the knot. And wrapping up relationships need not be a long and complicated process. In *Clear and Present Danger*, Jack Ryan wraps up his feelings with all the major antagonists in the story with little more than one line of dialogue and a glare. Then he goes and testifies before Congress as the credits roll.

Be sure to wrap up your subplot, too.

SOUND STRUCTURE BASED ON AN ACTIVE PROTAGONIST

CHARACTER IS STRUCTURE.

Story structure is part and parcel to what the characters do in a story—especially the protagonist's behavior. It's very important to keep the protagonist at the center of the story. It's the protagonist who's constantly faced with choices. It's the protagonist who must make decisions. And it's the protagonist who experiences the results of those decisions—both good and bad.

This is called telling your story through the protagonist's **point of view**. Your protagonist should be in just about every scene of the screenplay. Of course, there will be scenes when this isn't practical in order to tell the story in a suspenseful manner. But if you find you have four or five scenes in a row that don't include the protagonist, the solution is simple—put him or her right in the middle of the scenes and see what happens. It should produce both interesting and challenging ripples in the story.

STORY STRUCTURE DEVELOPMENT TEMPLATE

PAGES 1–10: Introduce tone, place, time, and what the story is about. Cleverly introduce the central question that gives a clue as to the theme to be explored throughout the story.

PAGES 11–30: Set up all conflicts for the main characters in the main story and subplot. Solutions will come as the story progresses. The protagonist's problem gets worse.

PAGES 31–45: Protagonist moves into new territory by committing to pursuing a new goal. Build

to protagonist first character growth, that is, the first true realization that his or her life is changing. Protagonist encounters and overcomes first major obstacle while resisting change.
PAGES 46–60: Protagonist starts to get into big trouble. The protagonist now leaves behind the old situation, starts to gain new skills, and becomes committed to the new situation. Protagonist encounters second major obstacle bigger, more serious than the first and overcomes it. By page 60, he reaches the point of no return in pursuit of goal.
PAGES 61–75: The protagonist sets out to solve the problem, and it looks as if all is lost when the protagonist fails to get over this third obstacle. A new, larger obstacle looms. The protagonist wants to give up but the antagonist, now stronger than ever, won't allow it.
PAGES 76–90: The protagonist is literally and spiritually on the run and scrambling in the story. By page 90, back is against the wall. Along the way, discovers the missing element needed to defeat the antagonist or villain. Protagonist has no choice but to go for broke.
PAGES 91–95: Protagonist starts the journey to getting the golden ring. Restate the central question of the story, and protagonist recommits to the new life. Revisit what happened between pages 31–45 to give the story symmetry.
PAGES 96–Climax: Build to the climax of the main story: The protagonist gets the golden ring, but it's not exactly what was expected, it's something else entirely . . . and more than expected (the twist).
PAGES 114–115: Wrap up main story illustrating the protagonist's growth. Hint: People don't change, they grow. Tie up loose ends.

Note: Classic screenplays are 120 pages. However, today, most screenplays average about 115 pages.

SAMPLE COMPLETED STORY STRUCTURE DEVELOPMENT TEMPLATE

WORKING TITLE: THESIS

Act One

PAGES 1–10: Introduce tone, place, time, and what the story is about. Cleverly introduce the central question that gives a clue as to the theme to be explored throughout the story.

Story opens with the kidnapping of 13-year-old PAYNE "PEE WEE" FRAZIER, a shy, not-so-street-smart African-American boy, by an African-American man whose face is unseen. It's late at night and they are inside the rugged bathroom at a camp in the California mountains. The boy resists more than expected and produces a Scout knife for protection. The tussle causes Pee Wee to cut his attacker and himself. From an unseen perch in the nearby woods, a frightened 13-year-old African-American WITNESS watches as Pee Wee, bound and gagged, is put into the trunk of a car and driven away.

We meet DR. KENNETH CHESTNUT, a sociology professor at USC, as he sits with his all-white class of students. They observe a tribal dance and Congo drum demonstration by a touring African troupe. During the performance, Chestnut has a mystical experience where he sees himself playing the Congo drums and dancing with the group, all while watching himself. When it's over, we meet Dr. Chestnut's Teaching Assistant, 25-year-old JASON DUFFY.

In his office, Chestnut is visited by a police DETECTIVE who is investigating the murder of Payne "Pee Wee" Frazier and disappearance of two other black youths from a California summer camp program for inner-city youths. The Detective wants to talk to Duffy. The Detective has pictures of the kids as he questions Duffy with Chestnut in the room. The Detective says he believes that Pee Wee was murdered because of the blood stains found at the scene. During questioning, Duffy is cool and believable and we learn that Duffy had helped to organize the camp but had returned to Los Angeles the night of the crime. The Detective leaves, but he's not so convinced that Duffy is telling the truth.

PAGES 11–30: Set up all conflicts for the main characters in the main story and subplot. Solutions are to come as the story progresses. The protagonist's problem gets worse.

At the L.A. Airport, we meet SCOTT KENYATTA, a 23-year-old African student, as he makes final arrangements to fly three crates to the Congo. The crates contain a species of monkey found in the Ituri rain forest in the Congo.

At USC, during a final summer class session, Duffy is arrested by the Detective for suspicion of murder and taken away. After his lecture, Chestnut goes to the police station, asks questions. The Detective tells Chestnut that Duffy's blood type was the same blood type found at the scene of the crime. Chestnut talks to Duffy who becomes unusually evasive and belligerent; he sticks to his innocent plea. Duffy says he's just another black man being accused of a crime he didn't commit. Chestnut knows something is very wrong.

Chestnut goes to see Pee Wee's parents with the hope of learning something. He learns that Pee Wee lives in a very nice house and is from an upper-middle-class nuclear family. The boy had just become a Boy Scout and was an all-around good kid. Pee Wee has two brothers and two sisters. He's the middle child. The parents are very upset and bitterly blame Duffy for the fate of their boy.

Now Chestnut goes to see the parents of Clarence "Skeeter" Banks. The mother lives in a rundown South Central Los Angeles welfare housing project. The father is not there, he's in jail for ten days. The mother is distressed because she had been depending on Skeeter to help her. But she didn't know where he was and it was not all that unusual for him to disappear for days at a time.

Chestnut visits Tisha "Tish" Toliver's home. He finds a pretty and educated divorced mother who thought Tish was with her father when she disappeared. She's angry and upset at her ex-husband and tells Chestnut to get out of her business.

Chestnut arrives at the police station. Duffy has called in a panic. Duffy is put into a lineup because the 13-year-old eyewitness has come forward. The boy identifies Duffy as the killer.

Now Chestnut finally hears the truth from Duffy. He tells Chestnut that Pee Wee is not dead—it's only a graduate thesis designed to see how today's black youth would react to a primitive African tribe in the bush.

He and Kenyatta, one of Chestnut's former graduate students, had conspired to send the youths to Africa to live among an ancient tribe called the Efe. He says he wasn't worried about being convicted and feels so strongly about the thesis project that he decided to take his lumps. But with the eyewitness, he's scared. Chestnut and Duffy tell the Detective about the thesis. The Detective laughs and does not believe them. Chestnut tells Duffy that he will get a lawyer.

The lawyer tells Chestnut that the current evidence is enough to bound Duffy over for a hearing. He says the only thing that's going to save Duffy from that fate is for the three youths to walk into the police station and prove they are alive and well. Chestnut decides to delay the start of his summer lecture engagements, go to the Congo, and bring back the three youths himself.

Act Two

PAGES 31–45: Protagonist moves into new territory by committing to pursuing a new goal. Build to protagonist first character growth that is the first true realization that his or her life is changing. Protagonist encounters and overcomes first major obstacle while resisting change.

Kenyatta is in Africa. They are in a small town in the Ituri rain forest. He meets a GUIDE who is from the Lese people. Kenyatta opens the first crate. The monkey is taken away and a hidden compartment is revealed. Inside is Pee Wee. The other crates contain TISHA "TISH" TOLIVER and CLARENCE "SKEETER" BANKS. The three youths see daylight for the first time in several days. Pee Wee's cut (that he acquired during his struggle at camp) is swollen badly. Kenyatta ignores the cut and they begin their journey into the jungle.

Chestnut arrives in the Congo. He finds a TRADESMAN who offers to take him into the Ituri Forest to find Kenyatta and the American youths. They use a Land Rover and take the dirt roads that cut through the thick forest. It's much faster than the river and more expensive for Chestnut. We get the feeling that the Tradesman is a sleazeball out for himself and only interested in making money.

Meanwhile, Kenyatta and the Lese Guide ride a boat up the Congo River with the black youths. They are filled with new wonders and bad attitudes. Kenyatta and the Three Black Youths trek through a treacherous forest.

Chestnut arrives at a Lese village and is indeed fascinated by this new experience as he witnesses an argument between an Efe tribesman and Lese tribesman over the Efe's young daughter whom the Lese tribesman plans to marry. Chestnut is surprised by this show of intercultural racism.

Chestnut learns that the Lese and Efe people are very much dependent upon one another for food, goods, and services.

Meanwhile Pee Wee, Skeeter, and Tish arrive at the Efe tribe's village. It's nightfall. Kenyatta seems to know the EFE VILLAGE LEADER and pays him in machetes, clothes, and aluminum pots. The kids are taken away to their own hut.

In the Lese village, over a drink of fermented sap from the raffia plant, Chestnut learns that the tribesmen believe white people eat black people, especially women and children. He is truly taken by this new environment.

PAGES 46–60: Protagonist starts to get into big trouble. The protagonist now leaves behind the old situation, starts to gain new skills, and becomes committed to the new situation. Protagonist encounters second major obstacle, bigger, more serious than the first, and overcomes it. By page 60, reaches the point of no return in pursuit of goal.

Chestnut arrives at the Efe village. He is very angry at Kenyatta and the two men have a fistfight right there in the middle of the village. Chestnut wins the fight and gains the respect of the Efe men. Chestnut is taken to see the three youths, tells them he's going to take them back home.

That night, an Efe father sits around a campfire and tells the children a story about how the monkeys came to live in the trees. During the telling, he encourages everyone to sing. Chestnut, Skeeter, Tish, and Pee Wee are there. After the story, Skeeter does a rap song to the lively African chant. Skeeter and a teen EFE GIRL are attracted to one another.

Tish is with the Efe women. They make a fuss over her straightened hair and Western clothes. Skeeter is not getting along with an EFE TEENAGER who has an eye for the teen Efe Girl. But Skeeter is much taller than the Efe boy and successfully intimidates him. However, Pee Wee is getting along just fine with his peers—they are all the same size.

Later that night, Kenyatta tries to talk Chestnut into staying and taking part in his thesis; Chestnut refuses.

The next day in the forest, while trekking on their way to return to America, Chestnut, the three youths and the Efe Guide come across a dead elephant. Hundreds of Efe people arrive and gather as they strip and smoke the meat from the giant animal. The Guide says the elephant is a "gift from the forest" and he must stop and help. The Tradesman who helped Chestnut days before lurks there with some of his gun-toting buddies. The Tradesman is very interested in the prized ivory tusks of the elephant. Chestnut notices that the elephant was shot with a powerful rifle. Chestnut decides to continue on unescorted.

Chestnut and his charges get lost in the thick jungle and nightfall traps them. Chestnut has a mystical experience while lost in the forest. Just moments from an attack by a jungle cat, the Efe Guide saves their lives and takes them back to the village.

The next morning, Kenyatta prepares to leave when Chestnut and his charges arrive. Kenyatta makes one last plea to convince Chestnut to stay for just a few weeks of observation. Chestnut says the answer is still no.

Pee Wee and Tish mix with the Efe teens before leaving. They have made friends already. Chestnut observes Skeeter's fascination with a group of Efe men who prepare poison arrows for a monkey hunt. Skeeter begs the men to let him go on the hunting trip with them, but it takes Chestnut's agreement to come along for them to agree.

Chestnut and Skeeter go on the monkey hunt with the Efe men. Along the way, Skeeter and Chestnut start a bonding process as they become a part of a wild chase through the forest after a wounded monkey that ultimately gets away.

They both learn a lot about survival in the Ituri Forest by the Efe people.

Back at the village, Chestnut agrees (as a result of his experiences to date) to stay and observe the youths for a week only. But Kenyatta must go to town and send a telegram back to the L.A. Police Department. Kenyatta agrees and immediately starts his journey to town.

PAGES 61–75: The protagonist sets out to solve the problem (seeking truth) and by page 75, things become unbearable for protagonist as a new, larger obstacle looms. It looks as if all is lost when the protagonist fails to overcome this third obstacle. The protagonist wants to give up but the antagonist, now stronger than ever, won't allow it.

An Efe Tribesman on a hunt has the good fortune to find a dead monkey in the forest. He brings it back to the village and shares it with the hunter whose monkey got away the day before but never acknowledges the fact. Chestnut notes the village politics involved. Chestnut begins to make written notes, and we hear his voice-over as he writes. We begin to get his astute insight as to the comparisons and contrasts between modern life for African-Americans and the Africans of the rain forest.

Pee Wee falls very ill with a high fever from his cut. The village women take care of him. But Chestnut is afraid that Pee Wee will die and that would be very bad news for Duffy.

That night, Chestnut dreams and sees himself running wildly through the jungle for no apparent reason.

The next morning, the Efe Village Leader announces that they must break camp and move closer to the river to hunt for honey. What about Kenyatta? Chestnut asks. He will find us says the Village Leader.

As they break camp, Skeeter and the Efe Girl flirt. There's a humorous moment as Skeeter teaches her ghetto slang. Chestnut is fascinated by it all as he takes copious notes.

In the rain forest, Kenyatta accidentally runs upon the Tradesman and his poaching pals trying to kill another elephant. The elephant gets away. The angry Tradesman and his pals take Kenyatta on a horrifying romp through the thick jungle before murdering him.

During camp move, more bonding takes place between Chestnut and Skeeter while Pee Wee takes a turn for the worse.

At the new campsite, the elder women take care of the very sick and feverish Pee Wee while the other women put up the new village. Tish helps as Chestnut makes notes.

That night, the Efe Hunters go out to hunt for the bees' nests. Chestnut and Skeeter go along. They find a big nest and wait for morning.

The next morning, the women arrive to watch the honey being retrieved. It's a festive time for the Efes because honey is considered the ultimate gift of the forest. There's a real sense of community, togetherness, love, and happiness notes Chestnut.

PAGES 76–90: The protagonist is literally and spiritually "on the run" and "scrambling" in the story. By page 90, back is against the wall. Along the way, discovers the missing element needed to defeat the antagonist or villain. Protagonist has no choice but to go for broke.

At the new camp, Tish witnesses young teen girls who get their teeth chipped and have beauty scars put on their bodies. Chestnut is amused at the different reactions to the meaning of beauty.

Chestnut observes both women and men fishing using natural chemicals to put the fish to sleep. He's amazed by the intelligent, scientific way the Efe people approach the fishing process.

Meanwhile, back in Los Angeles, Duffy faces a judge at a court hearing. He is bound over for trial on the charge of murder and kidnapping.

While the Efe men smoke marijuana, Chestnut is invited to participate. But Skeeter tells him to "Just say no."

That night, Pee Wee recovers from his fever as the women perform a fertility treatment on a woman who has come from another clan. Pee Wee is going to be alright. Chestnut realizes he can stay no longer; he must get the three kids back to their parents. He again wonders what happened to Kenyatta.

Act Three

PAGES 91–95: Protagonist starts the journey to getting the golden ring. Restate the central question of the story and protagonist recommits to the new life; wrap up subplot while building to climax. Revisit what happened between pages 31–45 to give story symmetry.

But the next day, during a group antelope hunt, Chestnut and Skeeter discover Kenyatta's dead body in the forest. The men cut up the animal, give the liver to the shooter. Skeeter jokes he always hated liver. Chestnut is angry and wants to avenge Kenyatta's death.

PAGES 96–Climax: Build to the climax of the main story: The protagonist gets the golden ring, but it's not exactly what was expected. It's something else entirely . . . and more than expected (the "twist").

Chestnut decides to take on the Tradesman and the poachers. He engages the help of the Efe Tribesmen. Dressing and feeling like an African warrior, Chestnut and the Efe Tribesmen hunt down the Tradesman in a very intelligent manner. They use bows and drugged arrows against guns and rifles. After subduing the Tradesman and his boys, they head for town to turn them over to the authorities.

Back at the Efe camp, Tish embarks on a short trip to a nearby Lese village to take part in a "coming out" ceremony of a Lese teenage girl who has been in seclusion for three months.

Chestnut and the Efe men arrive in town, turn the Tradesman and his sidekicks over to the authorities.

Back at the Efe camp, Skeeter makes love to the Efe Girl, angers her father.

Chestnut decides it's time to return home to America. He and the kids say their good-byes to the Efe people.

At the town, the Tradesman and his poachers are free, having bribed their way out of trouble. The Tradesman tells Chestnut and the kids with a sneer that they don't belong in Africa.

Back in Los Angeles, Chestnut and the three kids make a dramatic entrance during Duffy's courtroom trial. The case is dismissed.

PAGES 114–115: Wrap up the main story and illustrate the protagonist's growth. Hint: People don't change, they grow. Tie up loose ends.

Chestnut escorts Tish to her home. Tish's divorced parents stop bickering and realize their daughter is a much more mature and responsible teen.

Chestnut takes Pee Wee home where he is greeted enthusiastically by his family.

And Chestnut takes Skeeter home where his father is out of jail, but still using drugs. Skeeter's mother has been beaten and is pitiful. She thanks Chestnut for bringing her child back to her.

At USC, Chestnut and Duffy are back at work. Duffy is out of jail pending minor charges. The parents are so happy with their children's new attitudes; they don't press serious charges against Duffy. In a surprise move, we see that Skeeter is Duffy's new assistant. Skeeter is now very Afro-centric in his dress and attitude. They all plan to go back to the Congo next summer to properly finish the thesis after Skeeter graduates from high school.

THE END

Story Structure Analysis of an Oscar-Nominated Film

THE FUGITIVE

PAGES 1–10: Introduction of DR. KIMBLE (protagonist) and his WIFE, the murder, Kimble's arrest for killing his wife. Introduction of storytelling convention of flashbacks as Kimble goes to trial. He's convicted.

PAGES 11–30: En route to jail, the bus is overtaken by other inmates. Big train crash! Kimble escapes, a new life. Introduction of GERARD (antagonist) as he discovers Kimble has escaped, officially declares Kimble "a fugitive."

PAGES 31–45: Kimble goes to local hospital, shaves, and shows his fatal flaw when he can't resist diagnosing the injured guard from the bus while stealing an ambulance. Kimble escapes a vigorous chase from Gerard, still thinking he can get his old life back. He's confronted by Gerard in the dam's tunnel. Kimble tells him I DIDN'T DO IT. Gerard says I DON'T CARE. Kimble "peter pans" into the dam . . . escapes. Gerard shows unrelenting nature by refusing to stop the chase after the jump. Kimble has FLASHBACK of his wife's murder and the one-arm man.

PAGES 46–60: A dramatic mislead occurs when the black escapee is trapped by Gerard who firmly establishes him as a formidable foe after he ruthlessly kills the escapee. Kimble contacts his attorney; the call is traced by the U.S. marshal's office. Gerard wants Kimble to re-enter his old life. Kimble obliges by going to his old hospital to seek out information to prove his innocence. He reaches the POINT OF NO RETURN when he breaks his honor code and steals an ID badge from an unwitting janitor. Kimble makes his own fake ID. Flashback to actual murder. Dramatic mislead: the arrest of the Russian kid who later identifies Kimble.

PAGES 61–75: Kimble leaves the apartment, masquerades as a janitor with his new ID. He breaks into the hospital's computer for a list of names—still seeking out the one-arm man. He runs into a hostile female doctor, saves a kid's life (fatal flaw). The ALL IS LOST moment comes when Kimble goes to jail to visit his best one-arm suspect on the list—but it's not the guy! Then he and Gerard collide in the hospital culminating in a shoot-out at bulletproof door and a chase during a St. Patrick's Day parade. Kimble gets away again.

PAGES 76–90: Kimble goes to the one-arm man's apartment (on the computer list). He breaks in and discovers photos and other key evidence. He calls Gerard and leaves the phone off the hook so the call can be traced. The one-arm man is confronted by Gerard. Gerard knows he's dirty and becomes a co-protagonist when he orders an investigation of the one-arm man. Kimble calls Dr. Nichols (co-villain) and unwittingly tells him he knows everything. Gerard now starts to care because he knows the villain is lying. Gerard maintains his antagonist role in the story—it's his job. Gerard checks out the high-tech company. The one-arm man sneaks out of his apartment to get Kimble himself. Kimble goes to an ex-coworker for help and discovers that Dr. Lentz was probably killed by Nichols so he can make millions. Kimble's BACK IS AGAINST THE WALL.

PAGES 91–95: The one-arm man attacks Kimble on a metro train, shoots cop. Kimble escapes, handcuffing the real killer and hides the evidence in a mail drop box.

PAGES 96–Climax: Kimble confronts co-villain Dr. Nichols (now the true antagonist) at his speaking engagement. This is the face-to-face FINAL CONFRONTATION. A short chase and fistfight, there's action on the rooftop—where Nichols and Kimble fall through a skylight. There's a big chase and climactic confrontation in hotel laundry room. Gerard screams he's on Kimble's side. The big shoot-out kills the true antagonist, Nichols.

DENOUEMENT . . . Gerard stays true to his character and takes Kimble in . . . But not before taking off the handcuffs. It appears all will end as well as it possibly can . . .

EXPAND STRUCTURED SYNOPSIS INTO SCENE OUTLINE

THIS IS THE PLOT.

The last step is to literally start to number the scenes inside your structured story template. The purpose of this step is to *plot* the story—to work out the how of the story. Each new scene should build on the previous one. Decide the when and where of each new scene. This establishes the time line for the entire story and helps you to decide on scene-to-scene transitions as well. You may (and probably will) discover gaps in story logic and need to add new events to the story. You may even find you have to eliminate some events.

Screenwriter Gary Ross commented on his process while writing the screenplay *Seabiscuit*:

> I outlined the thing in about a month and a half. Outlining is usually a big part of the process for me. Everybody's different, but for me much of the most creative work happens in the outline . . . Obviously, outlining is a nonlinear process. I feel like I have to hop back and forth and sort of assemble it—shuffle the cards and be able to see the middle at the same time I see the end, at the same time I see the beginning—for it to make sense as a whole. Then, as details begin to fill in and begin to make more sense, hopefully they become more cohesive.[1]

FIGURE 4.4 Elements of Classic Screenplay Structure

Act One		Act Two				Act Three				
[The Setup		] [Confrontations				] [Solution				]
Page 1	10	30	45	60	75	90	95	Climax	Denouement	The End
		[Grapple with Change		] [Accept Change—Seeking Truth][			] [	] [		]
Hook Tone Time Setting Theme Metaphor Central Question	Introduce All Major Characters and Their Conflict	Resisting Change	Gaining New Skills	Attempt to Solve Problem but Fail	On the Run	Reflect on Journey		The Final Confrontation		

What Story Is About	Problem Gets Worse		First Obstacle	A Bigger Second Obstacle		An Even Bigger Third Obstacle		Discover Missing Key Thing		Formulate New Plan	Build to Climax	Biggest Obstacle Yet	Wrap Up Loose Ends	
|	| S1	| S2		| S3		| S4	| S5		|S6	| S7		| S8	|	|
Page 1	10	30		45		60	75		90	95		Climax	Denouement	The End
		New Territory	First Character Growth		Point of No Return		All Is Lost		Back against the Wall	Recommit to Goal		Win or Lose	Unexpected Gain	
		First Plot Point							Second Plot Point					

NOTE: S1 = Subplot Scene 1; S2 = Subplot Scene 2, etc.

New doors should open for you as you go through this last step prior to actually bringing the characters and story to life in screenplay format. This step is equivalent to putting the final touches on your screenplay's *blueprint*. It's the plan from which you'll construct the screenplay. It's not, as such, the *reality* of writing the screenplay. That's a whole other set of challenges.

SAMPLE SCENE OUTLINE

THESIS

By Steve Duncan

Act One

1. CALIFORNIA MOUNTAIN CAMP. NIGHT. 13-year-old PAYNE "PEE WEE" FRAZIER, a shy, not-so-street smart African-American boy, is attacked by an African-American man whose face is unseen. It's late and they are inside the rugged bathroom at a summer camp. Pee Wee resists more than expected, produces a Scout knife for protection. The tussle causes Pee Wee to cut his attacker and himself. From an unseen perch in the nearby woods, a frightened 13-year-old African-American WITNESS watches as Pee Wee, bound and gagged, is put into the trunk of a rented car and driven away.

2. UNIVERSITY OF SOUTHERN CALIFORNIA. DAY. We meet DR. KENNETH CHESTNUT, a sociology and anthropology professor as he sits with his all-white class of students. They observe a tribal dance and Congo drum demonstration by a touring African troupe. During the performance, Chestnut has a mystical experience where he sees images of himself playing the Congo drums, then dancing with the group—all while watching himself. At the end of the performance, we meet Dr. Chestnut's Teaching Assistant, 25-year-old JASON DUFFY.

3. CHESTNUT'S USC OFFICE. DAY. He is visited by a police DETECTIVE who is investigating the suspected murder of Payne "Pee Wee" Frazier and disappearance of two other black youths from a California summer camp program for inner-city youths. The Detective wants to talk to Jason Duffy. The Detective has pictures of the kids as he questions Duffy with Chestnut in the room. The Detective says he believes that Pee Wee was murdered because of the blood stains found at the scene. During questioning, Duffy is cool, believable and we learn that Duffy had helped to organize the camp but had returned to Los Angeles the night of the crime. The Detective leaves, but he's not so convinced that Duffy is telling the truth.

4. USC TENNIS COURTS. DAY. Chestnut and Duffy finish a match. As they are toweling off, Chestnut notices a fresh knife cut on Duffy's arm. Duffy says he accidentally cut himself while cooking. But Chestnut knows Duffy is lying.

5. USC CLASSROOM. DAY. At USC, during a final summer class session, the Detective returns, notices Duffy trying to hide his cut. The Detective questions Duffy again about an inconsistency in Duffy's story, then takes Duffy into custody for further questioning.

6. DETECTIVE'S OFFICE. POLICE STATION. DAY. Chestnut arrives, asks questions. The Detective tells Chestnut that Duffy's blood type has matched the blood type found at the scene of the crime and that Duffy has a fresh wound. It's circumstantial evidence that can't be ignored.

7. VISITING ROOM. POLICE STATION. DAY. Chestnut talks to Duffy privately. Duffy confesses that he helped one of Chestnut's African exchange students named Scott Kenyatta, to apprehend Pee Wee for his thesis. He explains that the thesis was to involve the observation

of how a city kid would react and survive in the wilds of the Angeles National Forest. The study was to take place nearby and last for only several days. Then the boy was to be returned to the camp unharmed, told that he had been a part of an experiment, and so on. But he had a struggle with the feisty kid and both of them got cut. Duffy says he delivered the boy to Kenyatta alive. Duffy pleads for help from Chestnut.

8. APARTMENT BUILDING. NIGHT. Chestnut arrives. No one answers Kenyatta's door bell. Chestnut questions the Landlord who says he has not seen Kenyatta in several days and that his rent is paid in full to the end of the month. Chestnut takes a look into the window of the apartment and discovers that it's empty.

9. FRAZIER'S HOME. NIGHT. Chestnut goes to see Pee Wee's parents with the hope of learning something more. He sees that Pee Wee lives in a very nice house and is from an upper-middle-class nuclear family. The boy had just become a Boy Scout and was an all-around good kid. Pee Wee has two brothers and two sisters. He's the middle child. The parents are very upset and bitterly blame Duffy for the fate of their boy because it was Duffy who talked them into letting their son go on the trip.

10. BANKS'S HOME. DAY. The next day. Chestnut goes to see the parents of Clarence "Skeeter" Banks. The mother lives in a run-down South Central Los Angeles welfare housing project. The father is not there, he's in jail for ten days. The mother is distressed because she had been depending on Skeeter to help her. But she didn't know where he was and it was not all that unusual for him to disappear for days at a time.

11. TOLIVER'S HOME. NIGHT. Chestnut visits Tisha Toliver's home. He finds a pretty and educated divorced mother, MRS. TOLIVER, who thought Tish was with her father when she disappeared. They look at pictures, and she tells Chestnut that Tish is a neat girl and a good student with a wonderful sense of humor. The Mother's deep bitterness toward her ex-husband and the failure of her marriage comes out strong.

12. POLICE STATION. DAY. Duffy is put into a lineup because the 13-year-old Witness has come forward. The boy positively identifies Duffy as the man he saw carrying Pee Wee to the car. The Witness also identifies the rented car that Duffy drove in a photo. Blood was found in the trunk of the car. It doesn't look good for Duffy.

13. LOS ANGELES AIRPORT. DAY. Meanwhile, Chestnut learns that Kenyatta was a passenger on a flight to Africa, and that he was escorting three valuable chimps back to the Ituri Forest for the L.A. Zoo.

14. LOS ANGELES ZOO. DAY. Chestnut learns that the Zoo did send back three chimps but not escorted by a man named Scott Kenyatta.

15. VISITING ROOM. POLICE STATION. DAY. Chestnut tells Duffy he thinks he's been used. Chestnut tells Duffy that the missing youths fit into a classic sociological model, and he believes that Kenyatta may have taken the three youths out of the country, leaving Duffy holding the bag.

16. DETECTIVE'S OFFICE. DAY. Chestnut tells the Detective about his theory. Chestnut believes his friend and assistant, Duffy, is only guilty of stupidity. The Detective is amused and doesn't buy the story. Until other evidence indicates differently, Duffy will stay behind bars under the suspicion of murder and kidnapping.

17. LAWYER'S OFFICE. DAY. Chestnut hires a LAWYER for Duffy. The Lawyer says, based on the current evidence, Duffy will probably be charged and bound over for a hearing. The Lawyer tells Chestnut that the only thing that's going to save Duffy from that fate is for the three youths to walk into the police station and prove they are alive and well . . .

Act Two

1. STANLEYVILLE, THE CONGO, AFRICA. DAY. Establish the beauty of the rain forest. SCOTT KENYATTA is there. The only outpost of civilization for hundreds of miles, it's a small town located in the Ituri rain forest on the banks of the Congo River. Kenyatta meets a LESE GUIDE, a dark African tribesman. Kenyatta unloads the crates from the boat. The first monkey is taken away and a hidden compartment is revealed. Inside is Pee Wee. The other crates contain TISHA "TISH" TOLIVER (pretty, prissy, anal retentive in L.A. hip-hop clothes) and CLARENCE "SKEETER" BANKS (tough, street-smart in wanna-be gangbanger garb). The three youths see daylight for the first time in several days. They are hungry, thirsty, and pissed-off. Pee Wee's cut (that he acquired during his struggle at camp) is swollen badly. Kenyatta ignores the cut and they begin their journey on the Congo River.

2. STANLEYVILLE, THE CONGO, AFRICA. NIGHT. It's a beautiful sunset as Chestnut arrives in time to witness an argument between an Efe tribesman and Lese tribesman over the Efe's young daughter whom the Lese tribesman plans to marry. Chestnut is surprised by this show of intercultural racism. The angry Lese tribesman sends Chestnut to a white TRADESMAN to arrange for a trip into the Ituri Forest to find Kenyatta and the American youths. To save time, they can take a Land Rover on the dirt roads that cut through the thick forest. Of course, it's more expensive than waiting for the boat to return. We get the clear feeling that the Tradesman is a sleazeball out for himself and only interested in making money. Over a drink of fermented sap from the raffia plant, Chestnut learns that the tribesmen believe white people eat black people, especially women and children. Chestnut is truly taken by this new environment and wary of the Tradesman's offer. But he has no choice but to accept it.

3. BOAT ON THE CONGO RIVER. DAY. Kenyatta and the Lese Guide ride a boat up the Congo River with the black youths. They are filled with new wonders and bad attitudes. INTERCUT: Chestnut and the Tradesman on their journey.

4. ITURI RAIN FOREST. DAY. Establish the beauty of the rain forest and it's wild inhabitants. Kenyatta and the Three Black Youths trek through a tortuous forest. INTERCUT: Chestnut and the Tradesman on their journey.

5. EFE VILLAGE. NIGHT. Pee Wee, Skeeter, and Tish arrive. Kenyatta is well acquainted with the Village Chief and makes him a generous present of machetes, clothes, and aluminum pots. The kids are taken to their own hut.

6. EFE VILLAGE. DAY. The next day. Chestnut arrives. He is very angry at Kenyatta, and the two men have a fistfight right there in the middle of the village. Chestnut wins, instantly gaining the respect of the Efe men.

7. BLACK YOUTHS' HUT. EFE VILLAGE. DAY. Chestnut introduces himself to the three youths and gets their different reactions and attitudes loud and clear. It's obvious that Skeeter will be a handful. They complain about their accommodations, the food (smoked termites), and so on. Chestnut tells them that they will leave for home the following morning.

8. EFE VILLAGE. NIGHT. An Efe father sits around a campfire and tells the Efe children a story about how the monkeys came to live in the trees. During the telling, he encourages everyone to sing. Chestnut, Skeeter, Tish, and Pee Wee are there. After the story, Skeeter breaks into a rap song to the lively African chant. Skeeter and a teen EFE GIRL are attracted to one another, Tish notices the attraction. She is a bit jealous—not because she likes Skeeter—but because of her own "racism."

9. EFE VILLAGE. NIGHT. Later, Tish is with the Efe women. They make a fuss over her straightened hair (a permanent) and clothes. Skeeter is not getting along with an Efe teenager who has an eye for the teen Efe Girl. But Skeeter is much taller than the Efe boy and successfully intimidates him. However, Pee Wee is getting along just fine with his peers—they are all the same size.
10. CHESTNUT'S HUT. EFE VILLAGE. NIGHT. Later that night, Kenyatta tries to talk Chestnut into staying and taking part in his thesis. He shows Chestnut all of his paperwork and supporting materials—it's quite impressive. Chestnut learns that Kenyatta never intended to return to the United States, figuring Duffy would not get into much trouble. From his African perspective, Kenyatta's expounds his own impressions of the little value placed on black youth in America. For Chestnut, it's a stinging, but soberly true commentary. But Chestnut is still angry with Kenyatta's deed and sticks to his refusal to cooperate with the study.
11. ITURI FOREST. DAY. The next day, while trekking on their way to return to America, Chestnut, the three youths, and the Efe Guide come across a dead elephant. Hundreds of Efe people arrive and gather to strip and smoke the meat from the giant mammal. The Efe Guide says the elephant is a "gift from the forest" and he must stop and help. The Tradesman, who helped Chestnut days before, lurks there with some of his gun-toting buddies. The Tradesman is very interested in the prized ivory tusks of the elephant. And Chestnut notices that the elephant was shot with a powerful hunting rifle. Chestnut decides to continue—unescorted—on to Stanleyville with the kids.
12. ITURI FOREST. NIGHT. Chestnut and his charges get hopelessly lost in the thick jungle as nightfall traps them. Although Pee Wee is an excellent Boy Scout, his skills cannot help them here. Chestnut has a mystical experience while lost in the forest: he sees himself as an African Warrior and unwittingly baits himself and the youths into an attack by a large jungle cat. But moments before death, the Efe Guide saves their lives.
13. EFE VILLAGE. DAY. The next morning, Kenyatta prepares to leave just as Chestnut and his three charges return. Kenyatta makes one last plea to convince Chestnut to stay for just a few weeks of observation. Chestnut says the answer is still no as Pee Wee and Tish mix with the Efe teens to say good-bye. Each have already made friends. Chestnut observes Skeeter's fascination with a group of Efe men who prepare poison arrows for a monkey hunt. Skeeter begs the men to let him go on the hunting trip with them. Chestnut's not sure if that's a good idea.
14. ITURI FOREST. DAY. Chestnut and Skeeter on the monkey hunt with the Efe men. Along the way, Skeeter and Chestnut start a bonding process and they become a part of a wild chase through the forest after a wounded monkey that ultimately gets away. They both observe the plight of survival by the Efe people in the Ituri Forest as Skeeter's street smarts draws a telling parallel between the hunt and life in the inner city. On their return to the village, Chestnut observes both Efe Women and Men fishing using natural chemicals to put the fish to sleep. He's amazed by the intelligent, scientific way the Efe people approach the fishing process.
15. EFE VILLAGE. DAY. Back at the village, Chestnut goes to Kenyatta and agrees (as a result of his experiences to date) to allow the youths a one-week stay only. The caveat is that Kenyatta must go to Stanleyville and dispatch a telegram back to the States concerning Duffy and the kids. Kenyatta agrees and immediately strikes out for town.
16. EFE VILLAGE. NIGHT. An Efe Tribesman returns from a hunt with good fortune—he found a dead monkey in the forest. He shares it with the hunter whose monkey got away the day before but never acknowledges the fact. Chestnut notes the village politics involved. Chestnut

begins to make written notes and we hear his voice-over as he writes. We begin to get his astute insight as to the comparisons and contrasts between modern life for African-Americans and the Africans of the rain forest.

17. HUT. EFE VILLAGE. NIGHT. Shared by Pee Wee, Skeeter, Tish, and Chestnut. Pee Wee falls ill with a high fever from his cut. The village women take him away to care for him. Chestnut is afraid that Pee Wee will die. That would be very bad news for Duffy. Chestnut falls asleep, sees himself running wildly through the jungle for no apparent reason.

18. EFE VILLAGE. DAY. The next morning, the Efe Village Chief announces that they must break camp and move closer to the river to hunt for honey. What about Kenyatta? asks Chestnut. "He will find us," says the Village Chief. As they break camp, Skeeter and the Efe Girl flirt. There's a humorous moment as Skeeter teaches her ghetto slang. Chestnut is fascinated by it all.

19. ITURI FOREST. DAY. In the rain forest, Kenyatta accidentally runs upon the Tradesman and his poaching pals trying to kill a frightened elephant. Kenyatta's distraction helps the elephant to get away. The angry Tradesman and his pals take Kenyatta on a horrifying romp through the thick jungle before murdering him.

20. EFE CAMPSITE. DAY. At the new campsite, the elder Efe women take care of Pee Wee who has taken a turn for the worse. The other Efe women begin constructing new huts for the new village as Tish helps. Chestnut observes, makes astute notes. The men go off to hunt for honey nests.

21. ITURI FOREST. DAY. Chestnut and the Efe women arrive to watch as the honey is retrieved from a tall tree. It's a festive time for the Efe because honey is considered the ultimate gift of the forest. There's a real sense of community, togetherness, love, and humor notes Chestnut.

22. LOS ANGELES COURTROOM. DAY. Duffy faces a judge at a court hearing. He is bound over for trial on the charge of murder and kidnapping.

23. EFE CAMPSITE. DAY. A Lese Tribesman sells the Efe a mixture of marijuana and tobacco. Skeeter observes the drug deal going down. While the Efe men smoke marijuana, Chestnut is invited to participate. But Skeeter tells him to "Just say no." Meanwhile, Tish witnesses young teen girls who get their teeth chipped and have beauty scars put on their bodies. Chestnut is amused at the different reactions to the meaning of beauty.

24. EFE CAMPSITE. NIGHT. Pee Wee's fever finally breaks as an Elder Efe Woman performs a fertility treatment on another woman. Pee Wee's going to be alright, but he needs a few days to recover before traveling. Upon wondering about what happened to Kenyatta, Chestnut realizes they can stay no longer. He must get the three kids back to their parents and clear Duffy's name.

25. ITURI FOREST. DAY. The next day. During a group antelope hunt, Chestnut and Skeeter discover Kenyatta's dead body in the forest. The men cut up the antelope, give the prized liver to the hunter who first shot the animal. Skeeter jokes he always hated liver. But Chestnut is consumed with anger over Kenyatta's obvious murder. He knows who did it and wants justice.

Act Three

1. EFE CAMPSITE. DAY. Chestnut engages the help of the Efe Tribesmen to take on the Tradesman and the poachers.

2. ITURI FOREST. DAY. Dressing and feeling like an African warrior, Chestnut and the Efe Tribesmen hunt down the Tradesman in a very intelligent manner. He begins to feel like "brethren"

as they use bows and drugged arrows against guns and rifles. After subduing the Tradesman and his boys, they head for town to turn them over to the authorities.

3. EFE CAMPSITE. DAY. Tish embarks on a short trip to a nearby Lese village to take part in a "coming out" ceremony of a Lese teenage girl who has been in seclusion for three months.

4. STANLEYVILLE. DAY. Chestnut and Efe men arrive in town, turn the Tradesman and his side-kicks over to the authorities.

5. EFE CAMPSITE. NIGHT. Skeeter makes love to the Efe Girl, angers her father. Chestnut returns to the father's fury, decides it's really time to return to America.

6. EFE CAMPSITE. DAY. As the Efe break the campsite to head back to their village, Chestnut and the three youths say their good-byes. Parting gifts from the Efe create touching moments and tears.

7. STANLEYVILLE. DAY. The Tradesman and his poachers are free, having bribed their way out of trouble as Chestnut and his charges arrive. The Tradesman tells Chestnut sarcastically that he and the kids don't belong in Africa, a statement that Chestnut finds ironic coming from a white man.

8. POLICE STATION. L.A. DAY. The kids' parents descend on the station. The emotions cover the full spectrum of anger to happiness. Skeeter's mother doesn't show up, she called, couldn't get off from work. Even though the kids are all right, Pee Wee's and Tish's parents file criminal charges against Duffy. Duffy remains in jail as the Fraziers and Tolivers take their kids home. Skeeter is all alone. Chestnut offers to give him a ride home.

9. BANKS'S HOME. DAY. Chestnut takes Skeeter home where his father is out of jail, but high on drugs and hostile toward Chestnut. It's an ugly scene, and Skeeter—now a changed person—is highly embarrassed and deeply hurt.

10. COUNTY JAIL. VISITING ROOM. DAY. Chestnut and the Lawyer visit with Duffy. Duffy learns he will probably be convicted of kidnapping and will go to prison.

11. LOS ANGELES COURTROOM. DAY. Skeeter, Pee Wee, and Tish take the witness stand. We see they are changed individuals: more focused, more mature, and more worldly.

12. CHESTNUT'S USC OFFICE. DAY. Chestnut has called a meeting of the Tolivers and Fraziers without each knowing that the other will be there. He describes to them a young man who sounds very much like their children . . . and that young man turns out to be Duffy. Chestnut tries to convince the parents to drop the charges before they ruin Duffy's life over the one bad judgment he's made in his entire life.

13. LOS ANGELES COURTROOM. DAY. The Prosecutor asks the court for a dismissal. The parents have changed their minds: they no longer wish to press charges against Duffy.

14. CHESTNUT'S USC OFFICE. DAY. Chestnut and Duffy are back at work. Duffy is out of jail. In a surprise move, we see that Skeeter is Duffy's new assistant. Skeeter is now very Afro-centric in his dress and attitude. They all plan to go back to the Congo next summer to properly finish the thesis after Skeeter graduates from high school.

THE END

ALTERNATIVE SCREENPLAY STRUCTURE

There are, of course, films that don't use classic screenplay structure. Some partially use the classic approach. Some are simply free form. If you want to write a free-form or experimental screenplay,

FIGURE 4.5 Screenplay Structure Comparisons by Type of Screenplay

Here is a comparison of feature film story goals and pacing to other forms of screenwriting:

Classic Structure	Story Goals	Feature (pages)	TV Movie (pages)	Hour Drama (pages)	Half-Hour (pages)	Sitcom (pages)
Act One	Establish Tone	1–3	1–25	1–15	1–15	1–25
	Time/Place	1–3				
	Introduce all Major Characters	1–30				
	Protagonist enters New Life	31				
Act Two (First Half)	Protagonist First Character Growth	31–45	26–39 (Act 2)	16–30 (Act 2)	16–30 (Act 2)	26–50 (Act 2)
	Protagonist Point of No Return	46–60	40–53 (Act 3)			
Act Two (Second Half)	All Is Lost for Protagonist	61–75	54–67 (Act 4)	31–45 (Act 3)		
	Protagonist Back against Wall	76–90	68–81 (Act 5)			
Act Three	Climax	91–115	82–95 (Act 6)	46–60 (Act 4)		
	Denouement	115–120	96–109 (Act 7)			

then you just need to sit down and do it. There's no right or wrong way to structure in this case. It's whatever you want it to be. However, you do want to pay attention to the basic rules of dramatic writing, such as character and dialogue. And you must put this approach into its proper perspective if you decide you want to sell it or even produce it yourself. David Lynch's *Blue Velvet* and *Mulholland Drive*, David Cronenberg's *Naked Lunch*, and John Waters's *Pink Flamingos* avoid all classic film structure.

Generally, *Hollywood* is not attracted to alternatively structured screenplays. So, don't expect agents, producers, or executives to be screaming to read your screenplay. Even if you produce it yourself as an independent filmmaker, major distributors tend to shy away from a film that will not garner a large enough audience to make a profit. The ideal venue for alternatively structured screenplays and films is the film festival. There are many of them held worldwide and year round.

However, as the twenty-first century unfolds, a hybrid screenplay that uses nontraditional storytelling married to the basic three-act structure is increasingly emerging into the mainstream. The film *Go* takes three stories and follows each separately. Each smaller story has a three-act structure (beginning, middle, and ending). In this case, the three stories share both the same beginning and they all come together in the ending. It's a very entertaining and cleverly written film.

Another popular film, *Pulp Fiction,* does the same thing. But instead of following each story separately, Quentin Tarantino, its cowriter-director, chose to interweave the three stories in a way that, when combined, creates a three-act structure. The German-made film *Run Lola Run* ingeniously takes the same thirty-minute three-act structured short story and replays it three times; each new replay changes decisions made by the characters, thus altering each version's ending using the same characters and locations. The film *Memento* takes the three-act structure and plays it backwards: the ending is the beginning, the middle is the middle, and the beginning is the ending; it's very clever, has garnered critical acclaim, but failed to create significant box office returns. The film *Million Dollar Baby* breaks some big classic structure rules yet succeeded both critically and financially. Nobody wanted Mel Gibson's *The Passion of the Christ* which, because of its subject and theme, completely fell outside of Hollywood's idea of a successful screenplay or film; yet, it found a very large audience. Because alternative approaches that somehow utilize classic structure are achieving some audience appeal, these types of screenplays are being produced because they do offer the investor and distributor a better chance of turning a profit.

YOUR ASSIGNMENT

Take your expanded story and place it within the bounds of the *Story Structure Development Template*. You can also refine the narrative as you do so to make sure the story's structure is sound.

Then finish plotting by turning the structured expanded story into a *scene outline*.

Once you have finished the scene outline, you're ready to start writing the screenplay.

NOTE

1. Richard Slayton, "Gary & Callie," Callie Khouri and Gary Ross converse about adapting *Seabiscuit*, writing *Thelma & Louise*, and the art of directing your own script (Los Angeles: Written By, December 2003).

CHAPTER 5

Visual Descriptions and Dialogue

BY SIGHT AND BY SOUND

This is where the magic begins. Much of what you've done up to this point has been "blueprint" work. Even though it took creativity and imagination to get to this point, you've been using a lot of "craft" to develop your characters and story.

Before you begin breathing life into your characters, there are some important technical rules you must first master. This is important because your first audience is generally an agent, manager, or professional reader before it's read by a producer, director, star, or studio executive. You want to make a good impression. What your screenplay looks like is analogous to what you look like when you interview for a job. First impressions do count.

PAGE FORMAT

Does it look like a screenplay?

Format is *very* important. To a large degree, what a screenplay looks like is what makes it so unique. The page is designed for practical production reasons and has very little to do with the writing process. In fact, the format—at times—makes it *more* difficult to be creative.

But once you learn how to lay out the pages of a screenplay, then you've got it made. You're then *totally free* to work within the confines of the fairly exacting format.

The first cardinal rule is to *always use Courier or Courier New 12-point font. Never break this rule!* Using any other font is an absolute no-no. Why? Without a standard, the screenplay would not have a consistent pace. What if someone decides to use a 14-point font? That means the number of pages and ultimate length of the finished film would be different from someone who decides to use a 10-point font.

Again—never break this rule!

The next cardinal rule—which is more a tradition—is to always begin a screenplay with "FADE IN:" and end the screenplay with "FADE OUT."

SCREENPLAY PAGE FORMAT SPECIFICATIONS

Margins

Top	1 inch
Right	1 inch
Bottom	1 inch
Left	1.5 inches

Indents (start from left margin)

Scene Heading	None
Action	None
Mini-slugline	None
Character Dialogue Name	2 inches
Parenthetical	1.5 inches
Start Dialogue	1 inch
Dialogue Width	4 inches
Transition	5 inches

SCENE HEADINGS

SCENE HEADINGS INDICATE THE WHERE AND WHEN.

Line producers, unit production managers, and assistant directors need **scene headings** in order to do their jobs. Plain and simple, the scene heading or **slugline** helps them to budget and schedule the filming of the scenes in your screenplay. Here is a sample of a scene heading from *Blood Ties:*

```
EXT. THE CONGO RIVER - AFRICA - TO ESTABLISH - DAY
```

This tells everyone that the scene takes place outside on the Congo River in Africa during daylight hours. *EXT. means Exterior*. This scene heading also indicates this particular shot is simply to establish the location. Of course, the scene may actually be photographed in Mexico or South America instead of Africa but that's what movie magic is all about.

```
INT. YAWL - CONGO RIVER - AFRICA - DAY
```

On the other hand, this scene heading indicates the scene takes place inside a boat on the Congo River in Africa during daylight hours. *INT. means Interior.* Of course, with today's sophisticated computer graphics capabilities, it's entirely possible to photograph the scene on a soundstage in Hollywood against a green backdrop and digitally insert the river and background forest during post-production.

As a screenwriter, the key thing to remember about scene headings is that they orient the reader as to where we are *physically* in the story. Here are a few basic rules for writing scene headings:

1. Always indicate interior like this:

   ```
   INT.
   ```

   And exterior like this:

   ```
   EXT.
   ```

2. There are really only four time designations that the camera can realistically record: `DAY, NIGHT, SUNRISE,` or `SUNSET.` All others are variations. It's less confusing to line producers if you confine the designation to one of these. If it's important that the scene takes place at a time in between, indicate that in the **action-description** by staging the scene in a way that matches the time of day. For example, if it's early morning (after sunrise), show rush hour or the newspaper being delivered to a sleeping neighborhood. You may even write: Early Morning in the action-description.
3. When designating scene locations, it's clearer to go from *specific* to *general*. For example, a scene inside Joe's home needs to be in a specific place in the home. Let's say the scene takes place in the living room. Write it like this:

   ```
   INT. LIVING ROOM - JOE'S HOME - DAY
   ```

   Notice I start with the specific location: living room, then indicate the general location, Joe's home.
4. An establishing shot can be indicated in the scene heading or in the action-description.
5. It's good form to always write an action-description after a scene heading, especially when there are characters talking in the scene. It's better to establish for the reader what we *see on the screen*, then to go directly into dialogue.

Of course, these aren't hard and fast rules. Surveys of existing screenplays—produced and unproduced—will quickly prove that these rules are bent and broken all the time. However, these simple guidelines do help the reader to get the most out of the story and make it easier for the producers and directors to execute their jobs.

ACTION-DESCRIPTIONS

WHAT WE SEE ON THE SCREEN.

In addition to telling the reader what we see on the screen, the *action-description* also provides us with a sense of *tone* and *atmosphere*. Here's an example of what I mean by that:

```
EXT. THE CONGO RIVER - AFRICA - TO ESTABLISH - DAY

A long stretch of the murky brown water flows against the lush green
jungle on both sides.

In the distance, the yawl chugs steadily, its engine belches black
smoke into the pristine blue sky.
```

```
INT. YAWL - CONGO RIVER - AFRICA - DAY

Alone, the Lese Tribesman lounges on the front of the boat, stares
out at the passing jungle.

Pee Wee, Skeeter and Tish, in the rear of the boat, are soaking in
their own sweat.

Tish and Skeeter have shed most of their stylish hip-hop outfits,
while Pee Wee has rolled up the pant legs and sleeves of his colorful
pajamas.
```

The above action-description not only orients the reader as to the visuals on the screen but also attempts to instill a certain *feeling* about the scenes, the characters, thus, the overall story.

CAMERA DIRECTIONS

How WE SEE WHAT'S ON THE SCREEN.

The best advice I can give any new screenwriter is to *keep the use of camera directions to a bare minimum if at all.* It's the director's job to decide where the camera will go and what type of shots will best bring a scene to life. Of course, as the screenwriter, you should have a good sense of what the audience sees on the big (and small) screen. But it's best to concentrate on *what's taking place* on the screen not *how it's taking place.* So, the best camera angle technique available to a screenwriter is built right on your computer keyboard. You don't even have to type this camera angle. It's called the *enter* or *return key.* Look at it this way: each new action-description is basically a camera shot. Every time the camera angle changes in the scene, you use a *new paragraph* to describe what we see. It's best to write your action-descriptions as tightly as possible, striving to keep each between one to three sentences in length. This technique is not always practical, and there will be occasions when you need to write longer descriptions. But when used, this simple rule makes the screenplay, overall, much easier to read.

SAMPLE CAMERA TERMINOLOGY

WRITERS WRITE, DIRECTORS DIRECT.

There will be times when you want to use a specific camera angle because it's important to the story or it's important to *emphasize* something to the audience. When you do use them, camera angles are always written in ALL CAPS.

But these terms usually have a technical quality to them that tends to take away from the *tone* of your writing, so use them sparingly *if at all.* Instead, replace most with words that are *reader-friendly.*

Technical Terms	*Reader-Friendly Terms*
Extreme Long Shot	In the Far Distance
Long Shot	In the Near Distance
Wide Shot	Full On
Medium Shot	Feature
Close Up	On or Off
Extreme Close Up	Tight On
Two Shot	Angle On
Three Shot	Angle On
Low Angle	Looking Up
High Angle	Looking Down
Tracking	Moving With

These terms should cover most of the shots you'll ever want to emphasize in a screenplay. You may even want to invent a few *reader-friendly* terms of your own.

ALL THOSE WEIRD ABBREVIATIONS

THE TRICKS OF THE TRADE.

There are a number of shortcuts that are available to the screenwriter, and they're totally acceptable conventions in the industry. See the chart "Screenplay Abbreviations."

Screenplay Abbreviations	*Convention Meaning*	*Sample Usage*
b.g.	background	Joe approaches from the b.g.
f.g.	foreground	Joe runs to the b.g, a car parks in the f.g.
V.O.	voice-over	JOE (V.O.)
O.S.	off-scene	JOE (O.S.)

The difference between **v.o.** and **o.s.** is this: Voice-over is someone *talking over a scene* in which he or she isn't present; o.s. means the character's dialogue is *within the same scene* and he or she is present but not on the screen at that particular moment. For example, the character may be talking from another room and we hear the voice before the arrival.

THE PARENTHETICAL

MAD, SAD, OR GLAD.

This is probably the most overworked and misunderstood convention in screenwriting, especially by new writers who aren't sure whether the dialogue they've written has the proper impact when read.

The simple rule of thumb is to use the **parenthetical** to indicate emotional tone, that is, mad, sad, glad, *only* when it's not clear what the proper tone should be for the dialogue. This is very true when one character is being *sarcastic* . . .

```
                    JOE
               (sarcastic)
          I love you too.
```

Or is teasing another character . . .

```
                    JOE
               (tease)
          I love you too.
```

This tells the actor and the audience how to read this line that has a whole other meaning in another context.

It's always best to try to capture the true emotion in the words, content, and rhythm of the dialogue instead of using the parenthetical as a crutch.

One notable exception is to use the parenthetical as a shortcut for stage directions. In a speech, the character may be talking to several other characters. So you would use the parenthetical like this:

```
                    JOE
          I'm not sure what to do.
               (to Jack)
          What do you think?
               (to Sue)
          Didn't you have this problem last year?
```

TECHNICAL CONVENTIONS

How do you put *that* in a script?

One of the most confusing techniques is writing a telephone conversation. Though there are no specific rules per se, here's a sample scene using a technique that keeps the reader clear on where everyone is during the conversation while avoiding the repeated use of scene headings:

```
INT. BAR & GRILL - NIGHT

Joe holds the telephone tightly to his ear, while shutting out the
rowdy Drunks around him. He looks drunk.

                    JOE
          Honey. It's me.
```

INT. BEDROOM - SUSAN'S HOME - NIGHT

Susan's eyes narrow with anger as she switches the receiver from one ear to the other:

SUSAN
Where are you?

INTERCUT.

JOE
At Mickey's.

SUSAN
Honey...you're not drinking again, are you?

JOE
No, sweetheart. I wouldn't do that.

SUSAN
Good.

JOE
I'm leaving right now.

END INTERCUT.

Susan looks at the LCD clock: "12:20 AM."

SUSAN
Okay, honey. I'll wait up. No, no, I insist. Bye.

Susan hangs up the phone, picks up the remote control and FLICKS ON the TV. Worry washes her pretty face...

Now, if you want to go back to Joe to end this telephone conversation sequence, you use the scene heading for Joe's location after Susan is last seen in the sequence and end the scene in the Bar & Grill.

Another technique that seems to confuse new screenwriters it how to write and use POV, which means point of view. Generally speaking, you use this camera angle when it's important for the reader to literally see something through a character's eyes. Think of it as the camera itself becoming the character's head. It's used like this:

Susan's POV OF THE TV: The late night host takes in the LOUD applause and cheers from his audience.

```
Susan points the remote, TURNS DOWN the sound.
```

Another commonly used camera angle technique is the INSERT. This is used to show shots of *inanimate objects* to the audience. They are called *inserts* to tell the director and producers that this shot can be executed at anytime during the shooting schedule. Here's an example:

```
Susan opens the drawer of the nightstand.

INSERT: An open pack of cigarettes and chrome snub nose .38 pistol.

BACK TO SCENE as:

Susan takes out the pack of cigarettes and fires up one.
```

Notice in the insert, Susan's hand was not used. Her reaching into the drawer was shot on a different angle. This is so the insert can be shot without the actress being present on the set. It also allows for the intricate lighting necessary. However, this is one of those conventions that will not be missed in a spec screenplay, so *avoid* using it.

Here are two more widely accepted technical conventions to follow:

1. All sounds are capitalized in a screenplay, i.e., PHONE RINGS.
2. The first time a major character is introduced, the name is CAPITALIZED.

SCREENWRITING COMPUTER SOFTWARE

IT TAKES THE DRUDGERY OUT.

The easy way to relieve you of struggling with screenplay format is to purchase *computer software*. There are many brands and types on the market. Some are stand-alone programs that are also word-processing programs, some simply convert word-processing program files into screenplay format, while others are sophisticated *macros* that run in concert with popular word-processing programs.

These software programs are usually available in both the PC and Mac platforms. Some are expensive but there's inexpensive software available too. Be sure to ask a lot of questions before purchasing this software and, if available, play with a demo version before investing your hard-earned money. Nearly all of the software manufacturers can be found on the Internet. A few popular stand-alone brands are Final Draft, Scriptware, and Movie Magic Screenwriter.

For those of you still using typewriters, I will pray for you. However, there are several well-known, well-paid screenwriters who still use them. And the last I heard, they began buying up any remaining machines for spare parts when the last typewriter manufacturer went bankrupt. Good luck . . .

NARRATIVE STYLE

SCREENPLAYS ARE VISUAL BY DEFINITION.

Screenplays are not the haven for impressive prose or deep inner thoughts. You're basically restricted to telling your story by what the audience will *see* and by what they will *hear*. So, your style of writing and the words you choose need to create pictures and sounds in the mind of the reader.

You should strive to write your narrative in an active voice and in as much of a shorthand as possible. So instead of writing, "She is SCREAMING at the top of her lungs," it would be more effective to write, "She SCREAMS at the top of her lungs." While both examples are written in the active voice, avoiding the use of words that end with "ing" speeds up the read. Hand in glove with this style is to avoid using words and phrases that give a tentative feeling to the narrative. So, instead of writing, "She seems somewhat doubtful as to what to do next," it would be better to write, "A 'now what?' stare replaces her vacant gaze."

You should also avoid abstract words and phrases while choosing those that produce rich imagery in the mind of the reader. As I mentioned earlier, this is the way to give your work both tone and atmosphere. There are other approaches that you can use to help tell your story as well. Among these are the use of *voice-over, flashbacks, montages*, and *intercutting*.

VOICE-OVER AS A STORYTELLING CONVENTION

VOICE-OVER PERSONALIZES STORYTELLING.

The *voice-over* is a popular device employed in screenplays. Most times, it's the protagonist relating a past story to the audience. Sometimes, the voice-over is not that of the protagonist, but a third party's version of the story. Or even an *"as told to"* version. The latter is generally less effective because it's not telling the tale through the protagonist's point of view. But that doesn't mean it can't work.

The important rule of thumb is simple: use the voice-over technique only if it's *intrinsic* to the story and brings something *new* to the telling. For example, *Forrest Gump* brought his unusual perspective to many famous historical events in which he unwittingly took part. I don't believe anyone can imagine that story being told any other way than through the voice of its simple-minded protagonist.

Though used sparingly in both *Terminator* films, the protagonist's voice-over gives the audience a matriarch's perspective of the relationship between man and machine.

HOW TO FORMAT FLASHBACKS

I believe the best use of flashbacks should include the emphasis on a "visual" style of storytelling . . . such as stark black and white images or distortion. A variation of the flashback might be called *mental flashes*. In the screenplay of *The Fugitive*, they were written as a MEMORY HIT. This may be used to take the audience inside a character's consciousness for a brief time and can contain both visual and auditory information.

MONTAGES

IT'S A TECHNIQUE TO COMPRESS TIME.

Almost all screenplays use this technique. A *montage* is an easy, convenient way to quickly summarize a lot of events in a short period of screen time. It's especially effective in showing a character's transition from one situation in the story to another. Common examples are falling in love or gaining the necessary skills to defeat a villain.

Again, the caution here is to keep these sequences to a bare minimum. Too many montages will slow the pacing of a film or make the film feel *episodic*. The exception to the rule is to use this technique as a *storytelling device* so that it provides a sense of segmentation to the story for the audience. Sagas and epics such as *The Ten Commandments* and *Dances with Wolves* effectively used montage sequences in this way. The use of music also enhances the montage . . . an important factor when you consider many film studios, these days, are also in the music publishing business. The film *Rocky* uses this combination of music and montages most effectively.

INTERCUTTING SCENES

THESE ARE SCENES ON A COLLISION COURSE.

This technique is great to use when you want to grab viewers by the collar and yank them into the story by making them *feel* what the characters are feeling. A great way to create tension and suspense is the **intercutting** together of two or more scenes that ultimately lead to a point of crisis. This technique is especially useful if you are writing a sequence involving a life-and-death situation.

Intercutting Technique Example

```
EXT. SUSAN'S HOME - NIGHT

The Maniac BREAKS THE WINDOW PANE with a vicious blow of his gloved fist.


INT. LIVING ROOM - SUSAN'S HOME - NIGHT

Susan gasps with horror as the GLASS FLIES EVERYWHERE! She turns and
runs for the hallway.

The Maniac leaps through the window with intent to kill.


INT. BEDROOM - SUSAN'S HOME - NIGHT

Susan races to the nightstand in terror.

IN THE LIVING ROOM

The Maniac pulls a big gun from his waistband.

IN THE BEDROOM

Susan snatches open the drawer of the nightstand.

THE HALLWAY
```

The Maniac LOCKS and LOADS the automatic pistol with venom, heads directly for the open bedroom door.

THE DOOR as Susan takes out the gun from the drawer.

The Killer raises his pistol.

Susan turns—raises her gun without a thought.

BOTH GUNS SPIT FIRE!

The Maniac's eyes are calm. A beat, then he drops in a heap.

The gun in Susan's hand trembles. She clenches her jaws in gratified anger, a big hole in the wall behind her.

As you can see by the example, this technique can be an extremely potent way to grab the audience by the collar and pull their emotions into a scene. The first thing to do is to establish the major scenes using scene headings (or sluglines) *before* you start intercutting them. The rule of thumb is to *make sure the reader doesn't get lost in the shuffle of the sequence*. The use of **mini-sluglines** can also enhance the experience for the reader. This technique drops the use of INT. and TIME OF DAY in order to focus on the location of the scene. Also, an effective technique is to vary the lengths of the mini-sluglines as they progress in the sequence so that it takes less time to read each. For example, during intercutting, the sequence's *rhythm* builds like this:

IN THE BEDROOM

THE HALLWAY

THE DOOR

Notice that there are progressively fewer words used in each mini-slugline. This gives the narrative style a *sense of urgency*.

DIALOGUE

NOT JUST CONVERSATION.

My favorite definition of dialogue is this: *What you wanted to say at the time but it didn't occur to you until hours later.* While dialogue is most useful and extremely important to screenwriting, you should be wary of how much you use it to tell your story. *Characters don't talk about the story; they are a part of the story.* So, much more than dialogue, the events of your story should tell it.

If you ever took the time to listen to people talking, you'll quickly find that it's mostly jumbled phrases that depend almost totally on the **context** of the conversation and the situation in which people find themselves. It's not always cogent or elegant. Real discussions tend to be rambling discourses by people who all have personal agendas in the conversation and who rarely listen to what others are saying. Instead, each person is thinking about what they're going to say next.

While this is valuable to observe as a screenwriter, you should avoid this type of authenticity in your dialogue. In drama, each and every word of dialogue has to have purpose.

Dialogue Should Reveal Character

Speech patterns are important. Certain people talk in certain ways. Doctors, lawyers, Indian chiefs all have a special vocabulary from which to express themselves. In addition, these characters have grown up in a certain way in a certain environment with their own special set of experiences. So, the way characters express themselves is most important to unfolding the story.

Here's an example from *Blood Ties* that illustrate how a few simple lines of dialogue can reveal characters' personalities. Dr. Chestnut, Skeeter, and Tish are lost in the rain forest. The roar of a huge jungle cat awakens them. Listen to what each character has to say at the sound of the cat:

```
                    TISH
          What's that?

                    SKEETER
          It ain't "Felix the Cat."

                    CHESTNUT
          Everybody stay calm.
```

These simple lines of dialogue reveal volumes about each character's temperament. Now, here's what they say after an Efe hunter shoots the dangerous cat with a poison arrow and saves their lives:

```
                    SKEETER
          Word! Robin's in the "hood!"

                    TISH
          Thank you, Jesus.

                    CHESTNUT
          Get your stuff; we're getting out of here.
```

In these few words of dialogue, you get the sense that Tish is tentative, Skeeter is brash, and Chestnut is paternal by nature.

To help you understand how to better reveal character through the use of dialogue, it's helpful to use Sigmund Freud's psychological model called *Transactional Analysis*. This theory is based on his concept of *ego*, *id*, and *super ego* and that when people talk to one another, they are "transacting" from a certain viewpoint. There are three viewpoints:

1. Parent
2. Adult
3. Child

From this perspective, you can write stronger dialogue if you—as the writer—understand where each character is coming from in a scene. For example, when a person speaks as a *parent,* he or she is trying to control another character. By contrast, if a character speaks as a *child,* then he or she is being controlled by another character. If both characters are being *adult* about a problem, then they're on even ground in the scene. So you can see, by varying the attitudes of your characters in a single scene you can make the scene more interesting while developing each character. The use of these techniques can also create reversals in a scene—or story—as characters shift from one attitude to another.

In the film *Sling Blade*, Karl is childlike while his new friend—a kid—is adultlike; as the story progresses, Karl and the kid trade attitudes. This growth between the two characters is most obvious in the way they talk—*transact*—with each other over the course of the story.

You can also better control how you develop your characters through dialogue by taking into consideration a simple communication model called *the triad.* It is a variation of *Berlo's Communication Model* that is a way of analyzing the way people talk to one another from three elements: sender, message, and receiver. For example, Joe is on one point of the triad. Sam is on another. And a hamburger is the third point of the triad. Joe likes hamburgers from a certain fast-food restaurant. Sam likes another fast-food restaurant. What is the conversation going to be like if these two are trying to decide on where to go for lunch? It's likely the discussion will be lively. This is a simple example, but the theory of it can help you to write more truthful scenes.

Dialogue Should Reveal Emotion

This is obvious. Dialogue can carry with it anger, sadness, joy, disappointment—any type of feeling. The key is really how each character would express such emotion. For example, if one character shouts all the time, how are we to know when he's *really* angry? Some characters may tell funny jokes when they're really scared to death! Again, it all comes down to specific characters and their mode of operation.

One very clever technique used in this category is to use a clever word or phrase in dialogue as a **mnemonic device** to create an emotional reaction from the audience. This takes you beyond the obvious use of emotions in dialogue. The *mnemonic word* or *phrase* starts out being used with a negative connotation to a positive one. It is used twice, sometimes three times. If used three times, the second use is neutral or transitional in the meaning. For example, in the film *Ghost,* the wife tells the husband that she loves him but the husband replies "ditto." This really ticks off the wife since her husband can't or won't say he loves her. He simply can't help himself emotionally. This is a very negative connotation for the word. The husband dies. As a ghost, he uses "ditto" because he knows it ticks her off. The word takes on a neutral or transitional meaning here to prove her dead husband is there, not to show he loves her. Then by the end of the film, it's the wife who uses "ditto" to tell her dead husband she loves him.

There are other examples:

"My momma always said life was like a box of chocolates. You never know what you're gonna get," from *Forrest Gump*.

"Here's looking at you, kid," from *Casablanca*.

"Be careful among the English," from *Witness*.

"You complete me," from *Jerry Maguire*.

Dialogue Should Advance the Plot

Voice-over narration is the most common dialogue technique used to advance plot. Since dialogue is not real conversation, you should be careful not to put a *news report* in a character's mouth unless he or she is, in fact, a news reporter in the story. There will be times when the characters need to talk about what's going on in their lives (thus the story) and sometimes this is unavoidable. When you find yourself faced with this, try to be clever by using humor or strong emotion.

But here's a not-so-obvious example of plot advancement through dialogue in *Blood Ties*: When Pee Wee's infected cut makes him extremely ill, Chestnut knows he must do something about it:

```
                              CHESTNUT
                  This has gone too far.

Chestnut confronts Zantu. SUBTITLES:

                              CHESTNUT (CONT'D)
                      (native tongue)
                  Zantu, the boy is very sick. You must give
                  me a guide to Stanleyville.

                              ZANTU
                      (sees he means it)
                  Very well...

Chestnut finds Skeeter in the village...

                              CHESTNUT
                  I'm going to Stanleyville. I want you to keep
                  an eye on Tish.

                              SKEETER
                  Nah, man, I'm coming with you.

                              CHESTNUT
                  No, stay here.
```

SKEETER
Come on, "G" let me hang with you. We could do a little male bonding thing...you know, like in the movies...

OFF Chestnut's amusement...

Of course, Chestnut couldn't say no considering Skeeter's convincing way of asking Chestnut to take him on the trek to procure medicine for Pee Wee.

Dialogue Should Create Atmosphere

This short run of dialogue from *Blood Ties* creates a sense that we're in a jungle village:

SUBTITLES:

KENYATTA
(in native tongue)
Zantu, for your generosity, I will pay you very well.

ZANTU
(in native tongue)
I fear you bring bad luck to my village.

Kenyatta is momentarily vexed.

KENYATTA
(in native tongue)
Zantu, we don't bring your village bad luck.

ZANTU
(in native tongue)
I saw it in my sleep. You must take the Children away now.

KENYATTA
(in native tongue)
We have come a long way...

Zantu and Kenyatta stare at each other...

ZANTU
(in native tongue)
When the sun appears again, you'll leave my village.

OFF Zantu's determination...

Also, notice that I've given the dialogue a certain rhythm to give the reader a sense that the characters are using another language.

Dialogue Should Reveal Conflict

Here's a scene from *Blood Ties* between the lawyer hired by Chestnut and Skeeter's mother. This short scene and its dialogue reveal much about the conflicts to come in the story as well as *how* Skeeter grew up:

INT. LIVING ROOM - BANK'S UNIT - DAY

Somber. Worn-out furniture. An old television, new VCR and lots of homemade tapes sit on a room divider that splits the living room from the small dingy kitchen.

MRS. BANKS
What has he done now? He supposed to be in camp. I sent him up there to get him off the street—away from those thugs he calls his "homeboys."
(to the heavens)
God knows I'm trying.

Surprise sweeps Denton's expression.

DENTON
Mrs. Banks, don't you know your son is missing?

MRS. BANKS
What do you mean he's missing?

DENTON
Haven't the police contacted you?

MRS. BANKS
I ain't talked to no police. Phone's been cut off. I work two jobs. Mister, you lucky you caught me home.

OFF Denton's helpless reaction...

Dialogue Should Establish Relationships

Here's another example from *Blood Ties* that helps to establish early on in Act Two how Tish, Skeeter, and Pee Wee are going to relate among themselves as the story unfolds:

Then Skeeter and Pee Wee SEE the BARE-BREASTED EFE WOMEN, all under five feet and dressed in knee-length cloths wrapped tightly around their waists. Skeeter's fear subsides as he elbows Pee Wee:

SKEETER
What time is it?

The hip-hop expression is lost on Pee Wee. He looks at his Boy Scout watch:

PEE WEE
Pacific Daylight Savings Time...it's Eight o'clock.

SKEETER
Nah, man, I mean look at those hotties. Now them some fruit I can deal with.

Tish playfully shoves Skeeter:

TISH
Don't show your ignorance.

Dialogue Should Comment on Action

The following run of dialogue from *Blood Ties* gives the reader a sense of what's going on in the scene and in the story:

INT. YAWL - CONGO RIVER - AFRICA - DAY

Alone, the Lese Tribesman lounges on the front of the boat, stares out at the passing jungle.

Pee Wee, Skeeter and Tish, in the rear of the boat, are soaking in their own sweat.

Tish and Skeeter have shed most of their stylish hip-hop outfits, while Pee Wee has rolled up the pant legs and sleeves of his colorful pajamas—picks at the BLOODY SCAB on his wounded arm:

TISH
Ugh, stop that! That's so nasty.
Cover it up!

Skeeter stares ahead steadily, ignores Tish's girlish behavior...there's something on his mind.

SKEETER
There's only one of him and three
of us. We could bum rush 'em, hook
him up, no problem.

TISH
I'm not "hooking up" anybody.

The Lese Tribesman stares ahead sternly...

TISH
(continuing)
You think he's a real African?

PEE WEE
I think he's a cannibal.

SKEETER
Shut up, fool. Ain't no such thing as
no cannibal. They make that crap up
for the movies.

TISH
Haven't you ever watched National
Geographic?

SKEETER
Nobody asked you nothing.

Skeeter gives Pee Wee a mischievous look, grins.

```
                    SKEETER
              (continuing)
          Man, I been meaning to tell you:
          that is one "phat" outfit you
          sportin'. Nike or Reebok?
```

There are many other things to consider when writing dialogue . . .

THE TRUTH WITH LIES

Try to re-create reality.

Dialogue is a form of expression most people would never use without a lot of thought. Outside of storytelling, we commonly refer to this form of expression as *speechmaking*. Lucky for your characters (and the audience), the screenwriter takes care to avoid writing both haphazard ramblings and preachy speeches. While it's important to try to re-create realistic situations in a screenplay, it's also important to bring something *more* to that reality. Whether it is wit or a quirky viewpoint, good dialogue—in a lot of ways—interprets reality with the infusion of *theme* and *purpose*.

CLICHÉS

"A stitch in time saves nine."

Simply avoid them unless it's the nature of the character to use them. For example, over-the-top villains often take great pride in using clichés . . . such as in every one of the *Batman* films.

You should strive to create original dialogue that's "fresh" and uniquely suits your story's characters. If a line of dialogue sounds like it's been used in other films, then your dialogue will sound stale.

As is with most things, there are times you'll want to put clichés in the mouths of your characters. This technique is called "parody" where you make fun of other movies or characters from other movies in your story. The characters that Arnold Schwarzenegger and Sylvester Stallone have played seem to be the all-time favorites for use in this technique.

VERNACULAR

Time is your worse enemy.

Blood Ties is full of vernacular. For that very reason, I realize that I'm going to have to update some of Skeeter's dialogue continuously until the script is sold. Some of the dialogue will need to be updated by the time it's filmed. Perhaps, by the time the film hits the screen, some looping and dubbing will have to be done to keep the language right on the cutting edge of pop culture.

For that very reason, some of the slang is "invented" and will never be outdated. The easy path is to avoid using a lot of vernacular. But then, you run the risk of missing the opportunity to give your screenplay proper tone. Try to strike a balance but certainly don't be afraid to take risks.

This problem also applies to legal, medical, or any other kind of special jargon. Language changes constantly, and there's not much you can do about it . . . except to rewrite.

Dialects

Amateur trap.

Attempting to write a particular dialect exactly the way it sounds can get you into a bit of a jam with the reader. It's better to write a dialect to fit the rhythm and feel of the particular way characters talk. Here are some examples:

From New York . . .

```
                    SAM
          How's it hanging?
```

From England . . .

```
                    AUSTIN
          Cheerio, mate.
```

From Ireland . . .

```
                    LIAM
          How you be this fine morn.
```

CHARACTER VOICE

Distinctive expression.

How do you prevent characters from sounding alike? There's really a simple rule of thumb: *Know your characters inside and out*. You might even pick people you know and give their personalities to your characters. Imitate the speech patterns and choice of words. But be sure to keep this consistent with the character's background that you've invented. Here's a sample:

```
Sunset. Chestnut sits comfortably, observes activity in the small
village. He WRITES in a SMALL NOTEBOOK as Skeeter watches Efe Hunters
make crude arrows...

                    CHESTNUT (V.O.)
          They say youth is wasted on the young.
          Not in the Ituri Rain Forest. Skeeter's
          street smarts serve him well here. And
          he strongly identifies with the strength
          of the Efe Hunters...

Tish helps Efe Teen Girls patch holes in the huts with large leaves...

                    CHESTNUT (V.O.)
          And Tish's ability to take care of
          herself seems to be serving her well.
          She easily identifies with the Black
          working women of the Efe people...

Chestnut ponders to himself a moment, then writes again:
```

```
                    CHESTNUT (V.O.)
          I don't want to keep these children
          here any longer than necessary. But
          I'm finding it difficult to resist
          the urge to stay...

Pee Wee approaches Chestnut; he's feverish, sweating profusely.

                    PEE WEE
          I don't feel so good, Mr. Chestnut.

Chestnut peels away the dirty bandage on Pee Wee's arm—it's infected,
badly swollen and full of yellow pus.
```

THE NON SEQUITUR

I ASKED FOR YOUR NAME, NOT YOUR ADDRESS!

When characters seem to be talking to the audience instead of one another, we call the run of dialogue a **non sequitur**. This is so easy to unconsciously write it's almost scary. A good way to spot them is to analyze your dialogue by asking yourself, *"Are these people talking to one another?"* or *"Are they repeating information for the benefit of the audience?"* The trick to remedying this problem is to make sure the characters talk directly to one another.

Of course, there will be times when you want to use the non sequitur to your advantage. For example, when a character wants to avoid answering a question or wants to change the subject. So, you might use "avoiding" or "change of subject" in the parenthetical to avoid reader confusion.

A more advanced technique is to run two different conversations simultaneously. The effect is that both characters try to avoid dealing with the problem at hand. Then the non sequitur converges and the two characters come to grips with the discussion at hand.

A visual way to use dialogue non sequitur is to have the characters talk about something that has absolutely nothing to do with what they're doing on screen or that sharply contrasts with what they're doing on screen. There's a wonderful sequence in *Network* where a married near-retirement network executive has his first weekend fling with a pretty ambitious executive. The visuals show a romantic dinner, a stroll along an empty beach at sunset, lovemaking. But the only thing the ambitious woman can talk about is her job.

HUMOR AND FUNNY LINES

CONTEXT, CONTEXT, CONTEXT!

A key issue with humor, especially in drama, is *what's funny to the character and what's funny to the audience*. They are distinctly two different considerations when writing dialogue.

In general, what's funny to the characters has to be carefully related to who the character is and what has happened to the character in the story or relationship.

What's funny to the audience has more to do with timing, context, and irony. Here's a scene from *Blood Ties* that uses humor that's funny (I hope) to both the characters and the audience because the punch line is totally unexpected in the context of this serious situation:

```
They all snuggle up now as Chestnut puts out the small fire. The hut
plunges into SUDDEN DARKNESS. The only sound is the rhythmic PATTER
OF RAIN on the roof of leaves.

                        TISH (V.O.)
            Good night, Mr. Chestnut. Good night,
            Skeeter.

                        CHESTNUT (V.O.)
            Good night, Tish. Good night,
            Skeeter.

A moment, then:

                        SKEETER (V.O.)
            Good night, John Boy.

They all crack up...
```

Writing humor is tricky. It's said that if you have to explain humor, you're in trouble. But there are some rules to consider. The first is the rule of threes. There's a rhythm of *three* to writing humor:

The set-up (or straight line)

The punch line (or big laugh)

The follow-up (or little laugh)

And the icing on the cake is called:

The topper or piling on

In the film *Butch Cassidy and the Sundance Kid*, the two bandits stand at the edge of a cliff while the Mexican army gets closer. They face the choice of being captured or jumping. The set-up is Butch declaring that they must jump. Sundance is hesitant and reveals he can't swim—that's the punch line. The follow-up is Butch saying the fall will kill them both. The topper is how they scream on the way down.

TALKING TO THE SCREEN

AVOID "TALKY" DIALOGUE.

This simply means that unfortunately your characters have become the main purveyors of information about the story to the audience. This is the stuff of daytime drama. In that context, it's a good thing. But in the context of a major motion picture, it's not so good.

It's most important that you attempt to entertain the audience with your dialogue, not bore them to tears. So, keep that in mind when you start giving your characters long, tedious speeches about the history of the universe or something even less interesting except to Carl Sagan and that one brain surgeon in the back row of the theater.

A good technique to avoid "talky" dialogue is to "show" the audience what you feel the characters need to yak on and on about. That might mean creating a new scene or new scenes. That way, the audience is in on what happened already, and you can now have the characters deal with how they feel about what happened without repeating it in dialogue.

Another technique of getting necessary exposition into a story is to *make the information itself the bone of contention* in the scene. That is, the exposition is the reason the characters have a conflicting dialogue.

Still another *sneaky* way to liven up exposition that you absolutely cannot avoid is to *create chaos* in the scene. For example, you could put your characters in a restaurant and someone robs it in the middle of the scene. Or, you could stage the scene at a dog pound during feeding time. There's a wonderful use of this technique in *When Harry Met Sally.* Harry and his best friend go to a football game and end up discussing Harry's divorce. It's all *exposition.* But to make it interesting and funny, the characters get to participate in the "wave" that rolls around the stadium during the entire scene.

Figure 5.1 Sample Act One of *Blood Ties* by Steve Duncan

Written By Steve Duncan

FADE IN:

EXT. CALIFORNIA YOUTH CAMP - TO ESTABLISH - NIGHT

A full moon. Firs nestle around the calm sparkling lake...

EXT. YOUTH CAMP - NIGHT

A CACOPHONY OF CRICKETS and BULL FROGS perform near the plank pier. A well-traveled dirt path leads up to a series of rustic cabins at the foot of a wooded knoll...

INT. BATHROOM CABANA - NIGHT

PAYNE "PEE WEE" FRAZIER, a 13-year-old African-American boy dressed in pajamas illustrated with cartoon characters, takes care of business at a porcelain urinal.

A relieved expression sweeps his youthful, innocent face.

ADULT FEET ENTER...

HANDS IN BLACK GLOVES hold a folded white handkerchief, the other a small bottle that drips CHLOROFORM into the cloth.

All done, Pee Wee moves to a row of wash basins, puts a BOY SCOUT KNIFE–the largest blade open–on the wooden sink, turns on the water faucet.

There's a BOY SCOUT WATCH around his wrist.

With brute strength, the HAND WITH the HANDKERCHIEF COVERS HIS SMALL MOUTH, STIFLES HIS NEAR SCREAM. Desperate, Pee Wee GRABS the BOY SCOUT KNIFE and–

CUTS THROUGH the BLACK GLOVE. The hand jerks away and the KNIFE SINKS INTO PEE WEE'S OWN ARM! BLOOD as Pee Wee goes unconscious.

The blood-stained Scout knife DROPS next to one rubber flip-flop, the only SOUND now is the STEADY FLOW of the WATER FAUCET...

EXT. SUMMER CAMP - NIGHT

SOMEONE'S DISTANT POV: A parked rental car near the cabana as the Kidnaper exits into the murky night, a limp Pee Wee in his arms.

EXT. CABIN PORCH - NIGHT

The "Someone" is a 13-year-old African-American. Stunned, he watches as the Kidnaper PUTS PEE WEE INSIDE the CAR'S TRUNK and drives away.

OFF the Boy's frightened face...

SLOW DISSOLVE TO:

EXT. LOS ANGELES SKYLINE - TO ESTABLISH - DAY

The usual smog hangs over the city...

EXT. UNIVERSITY OF SOUTHERN CALIFORNIA - DAY

The campus full of activity then the rhythm of AFRICAN DRUMS over...

INT. CLASSROOM - USC - DAY

Auditorium style. A TROUPE of AFRICAN DANCERS with DRUMMERS in authentic native kinte cloth costumes put on a show in front of a CLASS of STUDENTS who are WHITE and ASIAN.

DR. KENNETH CHESTNUT, a thirty-something African-American professor, watches the group with great interest. His handsome face is a combination of a rugged athlete and a classic professorial intellectual. As he watches the Dance Troupe, he SEES:

HIMSELF in place of a MALE DANCER in full regalia of the African heritage. Then:

HIMSELF AS THE DRUMMER—pounds the water buffalo skins with vigor, his eyes closed in hypnotic intoxication from the steady beat.

Professor Chestnut, he smiles to himself. The Students come to their feet in STRONG APPLAUSE as the dance ends.

Dr. Chestnut moves to the front of the room as the APPLAUSE finally dies and AD-LIBS "thank-yous" to the members of the Dance Troupe. He turns to his Students:

CHESTNUT

Okay, class, see you Friday. Same time, same place.

Students file out as POLICE DETECTIVE HOROWITZ pushes his way in against the grain. At forty-something, this slightly overweight, scruffy man calmly flips his gold shield at Chestnut:

HOROWITZ

Dr. Chestnut, Detective Horowitz, homicide, L.A.P.D.

CHESTNUT

What can I do for you, Detective?

HOROWITZ

I'm conducting an investigation.

Concern sweeps Chestnut's face as he stuffs papers into his soft-leather briefcase.

CHESTNUT

How can I help you?

HOROWITZ
Does a Mr. Jason Duffy work for you?

CHESTNUT
He's my teaching assistant.

HOROWITZ
Well, sir, I need to ask him a few questions...

INT. CORRIDOR - USC - DAY

Twenty-something JASON DUFFY moves down the corridor. He's African-American, clean-cut, conservative in appearance and has a scholarly, almost "nerdy" quality.

He opens a door and enters:

INT. CHESTNUT'S OFFICE - USC - DAY

Chestnut and Detective Horowitz rise as Jason enters.

CHESTNUT
Jason, this is Detective Horowitz, L.A.P.D.

HOROWITZ
Good to meet you, Mr. Duffy.

Duffy shakes Horowitz's beefy hand gingerly as a confused look sweeps over him. His quality of voice is erudite:

DUFFY
What's this about, Dr. Chestnut?

CHESTNUT
Detective Horowitz wants to ask you a few questions.

DUFFY
Concerning what?

HOROWITZ
Relax, Mr. Duffy, this is routine. Please, sit down.

Duffy throws Chestnut a concerned glare. Chestnut nods with a warm smile and Duffy sits.

CHESTNUT

He's all yours, Detective.

Horowitz refers to a small notebook:

HOROWITZ

Did you organize the South Central Summer Youth Camp?

DUFFY

Yes, sir, I sure did. I'm very proud of that program.

HOROWITZ

Were you at Big Bear Lake this past weekend?

Duffy gives Chestnut an irritated glance, then looks back to the Detective almost indignant:

DUFFY

Yes, I was.

HOROWITZ

Do you remember these youths?

Horowitz produces three photos, gives them to Duffy.

As Duffy shuffles through the photos, Horowitz NOTICES:

A GAUZE BANDAGE WRAPPED AROUND DUFFY'S LEFT HAND.

The FIRST PHOTO is 16-year-old Tisha Toliver, a cute African-American girl in a junior prom dress.

The SECOND PHOTO is 16-year-old Clarence Banks, a roughly handsome African-American boy with a lived-in face who show-boats a gang sign with his hands.

The LAST PHOTO is Pee Wee Frazier posing proudly in a highly decorated Boy Scout uniform.

Duffy stares at the last photo a bit longer, calmly looks up at Horowitz:

DUFFY

(continuing)

They all look familiar. But I don't know them. I surmise they're enrolled in my summer camp.

HOROWITZ
Were enrolled.

CHESTNUT
What's this about, Detective?

HOROWITZ
These youths are missing as of Monday morning.

Duffy and Chestnut are stunned as they exchange glances.

DUFFY
Well, this is very shocking, officer.

HOROWITZ
When did you return to L.A., Mr. Duffy?

DUFFY
Late Sunday night.

Horowitz spies Duffy's bandaged hand with suspicion:

HOROWITZ
What happened to your hand?

DUFFY
I accidentally cut myself while preparing dinner. Surely, you don't think that I had anything to do with this.

HOROWITZ
That'll be all for now.
(to Chestnut)
Thanks for your help, Doc. Listen, Mr. Duffy, don't take any sudden trips, okay?

DUFFY
Okay...

Horowitz nods, LEAVES.

Chestnut gives Duffy a curious stare. But:

DUFFY
(continuing)
I'm late for class.

Duffy exits OFF Chestnut's curious expression...

INT. ABANDONED WAREHOUSE - DAY

Dark room. Pee Wee lies unconscious, blindfolded, hands tied, still in his colorful pajamas, the left sleeve blood-stained.

Next to him:

TISHA "TISH" TOLIVER, the real girl from the prom picture. Normally pretty and prissy, she's blindfolded, unconscious, hands tied. She wears the latest hip-hop clothes, her chemically straightened hair pinned neatly with an array of UNIQUE, SHINY BARRETTES. Next to her is:

CLARENCE "SKEETER" BANKS, the boy in the flesh. He's tough, street-smart in wanna-be gangbanger garb, a gaudy thick ROPE GOLD CHAIN WITH A GOLD MERCEDES BENZ MEDALLION around his neck. His hands are also tied.

He cranks his eyes open. He's groggy, trying to sit up –

A BLACK GLOVED HAND PUSHES HIM DOWN and a HYPODERMIC NEEDLE stabs his arm. Skeeter quickly goes unconscious again.

The Kidnaper goes unseen as familiar FEET MOVE AWAY.

FROM A HIGH ANGLE the three youths lie side-by-side, tied-up, unconscious and thoroughly helpless...

HARD CUT TO:

EXT. USC COLISEUM - DAY

A WOODEN ARROW SLASHES into the BULL'S EYE of a colorful archery target. Chestnut stands in the end zone, the target on the fifty-yard line.

Duffy enters the field from the nearest tunnel as Chestnut reloads his HIGH-TECH ALUMINUM BOW and lets the arrow go.

The ARROW SLASHES into the BULL'S EYE AGAIN!

Chestnut smiles with concern as Duffy arrives.

DUFFY

You wanted to see me, Dr. Chestnut?

CHESTNUT

In all the years I've known you, Jason, the closest you've ever come to cooking is heating a can of Vienna sausages on a dorm heater.

DUFFY

A single man has to learn to cook sometime.

CHESTNUT

Tell me about it...

Loaded with another arrow, Chestnut pulls back the bow, lets the arrow FLY...

IT SPLITS ONE OF THE ARROWS ALREADY IN THE BULL'S EYE!

DUFFY

Robin of Loxley would be very impressed.

OFF Chestnut's confident nod...

EXT. CAMPUS - USC - TO ESTABLISH - DAY

Busy. Students...

CHESTNUT (V.O.)

Then what you're saying Professor Kenyatta is that my research design is flawed...?

INT. CLASSROOM - USC - DAY

Professor SCOTT KENYATTA, a 30ish, oddly handsome African with piercing eyes, sparkling white teeth and tribal scars on each cheek has a look of calm determination.

Each at a podium, he squares-off in debate with Chestnut in front of the same class of white and Asian Students.

Kenyatta speaks with a sharp British accent and his pride competes with his own arrogance:

KENYATTA

One would have to assume that it's impossible to accurately compare today's Black Americans to yesterday's ancient Africans without having actually lived between both cultures.

The Students' eyes swing to Chestnut in unison.

CHESTNUT
Of course. And it's impossible to go back in time, Professor... unless you use one of those Delorian cars and go "Black To The Future."

LAUGHTER from the Students. Duffy smiles to himself but Kenyatta is not amused:

KENYATTA
Perhaps you spend too much time making your students laugh instead of forcing them to think.

Duffy grins broadly, nods in agreement. The Students are serious again as Chestnut reflects momentarily, then:

CHESTNUT
Unfortunately, our time draws to an end. Do you have any final comments, Professor Kenyatta?

KENYATTA
Yes. I'd like to say that I also disagree with your repeated use of the term "African-American" throughout your research.

CHESTNUT
It's not my term, Professor. It's what we wish to call ourselves these days.

KENYATTA
But you are not "Africans." You haven't been for nearly four hundred years. At best, yours is a hybrid culture based on Imperialist Western standards.

CHESTNUT
However, the name does denote a land mass from which black American people have descended. The Italians, the Japanese, the Polish and every other people in America have adopted this type of hyphenate...

KENYATTA
However, Professor Chestnut, they did not abandon their cultures as you have.

The room is tense now.

CHESTNUT
We did not abandon our culture, Professor Kenyatta, we were stripped of it.

KENYATTA
Then why have you failed to fully reclaim it since the so-called Emancipation Proclamation?

The Students are on the edge of their seats. Chestnut thinks a moment, smiles benignly, turns to the anxious Students:

CHESTNUT
And that question is at the heart of your final paper. You are to compare and contrast the cultures of today's African-Americans with those of the first Africans brought to America as Slaves.
(to Duffy)
Jason, pass out the material.

Duffy distributes papers at the end of each row of Students.

CHESTNUT
(continuing)
The pages you now hold in your hot little hands contain excerpts from both mine and Professor Kenyatta's Doctoral theses. We've spent a considerable amount of time on this subject, so it's inadvisable to try to b.s. me.

STUDENT LAUGHTER as Detective Horowitz enters quietly. Chestnut notices but the Detective motions for him to carry on.

CHESTNUT
(continuing)
I don't expect you to choose between my opinions and Professor Kenyatta's.
(kidding)
But if you do agree with me, you could earn a few extra points.

STUDENT LAUGHTER as Chestnut notices Horowitz whisper to Duffy in the back of the classroom.

CHESTNUT
(continuing)
Before adjourning, I'd like to thank our distinguished visiting professor from Oxford University for being a good sport today.

STUDENT APPLAUSE. Kenyatta gives Duffy a look of concern as he exits the classroom trailing Horowitz.

CHESTNUT
(continuing)
Okay, bright young minds, this paper constitutes twenty-five percent of your final grade. Ciao.

The Students stand to leave as Chestnut turns to Kenyatta.

CHESTNUT
(continuing)
Even though we don't see eye-to-eye on this subject, it's certainly an interesting debate for my students to tackle. Thank you.

They shake hands firmly as they move to the door.

KENYATTA
My pleasure. But I have one more question for you, Professor.

CHESTNUT
What's that?

KENYATTA
Where are your "African-American" students..."homeboy"?

INT. CORRIDOR - USC - DAY

Chestnut and Kenyatta step into the hallway to SEE Duffy being led away by Detective Horowitz—in HANDCUFFS.

KENYATTA
It seems your Mr. Duffy has run into a bit of a legal problem.

OFF Chestnut's concern...

EXT. DOWNTOWN POLICE STATION - TO ESTABLISH - DAY

A box-shaped building, no windows...

HOROWITZ (V.O.)
Listen, Doc, I understand your concern. But -

INT. HOROWITZ'S OFFICE - POLICE STATION - DAY

Junky. Lots of files, photos, personal stuff.

CHESTNUT
Don't patronize me, damn it. I know Jason Duffy. He'd have a sleepless night if he stepped on a bug!

Horowitz takes in an impatient breath, lets out a sigh, moves over to PHOTOS of the bathroom cabana tacked to a large cork board. PHOTOS of the youths are there, too.

HOROWITZ
Okay, here are the facts: Mr. Duffy admits to being at the camp that night. We found a blood stained knife next to one of the boy's shower shoes. We also located the rental car that Mr. Duffy drove back to L.A. The trunk contained blood stains that match the blood type found at the scene. The Scout knife could be the murder weapon.

CHESTNUT
Murder weapon?

HOROWITZ
And your man has a fresh wound that could be the result of a struggle.

CHESTNUT
(can't believe this)
Come on, Detective, a grown man struggling with a half-pint 13-year-old? Where's the corpus delicti?

HOROWITZ
We haven't found a body.

CHESTNUT
Then all you have is a little circumstantial evidence and a "hunch."

HOROWITZ
But Mr. Duffy lied.

CHESTNUT
What do you mean he lied?

Horowitz points to the photo of "Pee Wee" Frazier.

HOROWITZ
This boy's parents say Mr. Duffy personally convinced them to let their son go to his camp.

CHESTNUT
I see. Now what?

HOROWITZ
I have 48 hours to file charges. I suggest you find him a good mouthpiece.

OFF Chestnut's concern:

INT. INTERVIEW ROOM - POLICE STATION - DAY

Spartan. A table and four chairs in the middle. Chestnut sits quietly as:

JACK DENTON, a tall African-American man in an expensive dress shirt with matching tie and suspenders, silently reads the police report.

CHESTNUT
Can you get him out of this mess?

Denton gives Chestnut a doubtful stare.

DENTON
From this evidence, the only thing that's going to save Jason is for those three teenagers to walk into the police station—alive.

The door opens as a GUARD escorts Duffy into the room.

CHESTNUT
(continuing)
Jason, are you alright, man?

DUFFY
Yes, sir.

CHESTNUT
Good. This is Jack Denton. He's an attorney.

They shake.

DENTON
Good to meet you, Jason.

DUFFY
While it's very nice to meet you, I must respectfully decline your services.

CHESTNUT
Jason, man, they're going to file murder charges against you.

DUFFY
I didn't kill anyone. Ergo, I don't need a lawyer.

CHESTNUT
Then why did you lie about knowing one of those kids?

Duffy cuts his eyes away.

CHESTNUT
(continuing)
Well...?

Duffy looks Chestnut straight in the eye:

DUFFY
Talk to Professor Kenyatta.

CHESTNUT
What does Kenyatta have to do with this?

Duffy hesitates, cuts Denton a look of doubt.

DENTON
If you lie, Jason, I won't represent you...

Duffy takes in a deep breath, lets it out.

DUFFY
I have nothing more to say.

Duffy looks down at his hands as Chestnut gives Denton a disappointed glance...

INT. LIVING ROOM - APARTMENT - NIGHT

Pitch-black. A key RATTLES in the door, it opens. The overhead light clicks on—it's Chestnut with the BUILDING MANAGER. They enter a COMPLETELY EMPTY ROOM.

MANAGER
Seeing is believing.

CHESTNUT
He just up and moved?

MANAGER
Said he was going home.

Chestnut's mind races a mile a minute.

CHESTNUT
To London?

MANAGER
He didn't say exactly.

Chestnut thinks a moment, then cranks out a stiff smile.

CHESTNUT
Thanks. I appreciate your help.

With a brisk exit, Chestnut leaves the Manager there.

EXT. CHESTNUT'S HOUSE - TO ESTABLISH - NIGHT

It's a large expensive Tudor in an exclusive neighborhood.

CHESTNUT (V.O.)
Jason Duffy has traded my trust for that of Scott Kenyatta's. And for his trouble, he now sits betrayed behind bars accused of murder...

INT. DEN - CHESTNUT'S HOUSE - NIGHT

Pools of light highlight dozens of African artifacts. On the wall are official photos, diplomas, academic certificates, but nothing that even hints at his family life.

CHESTNUT (V.O.)
He has given his allegiance to a man who convincingly challenges my own life's work.

An OLYMPIC SILVER MEDAL in Archery sits in a case on a desk, photos of Chestnut posing with his trusty aluminum bow surround it.

He sits behind the desk, writes in an expensively bound memoir book:

CHESTNUT (V.O.)
Today, a genuine African shook my very soul. And, tonight, now even I sit in doubt...

INT. ABANDONED WAREHOUSE - NIGHT

Face unseen, the gloved hand administers a shot to a blindfolded, already unconscious Tish Toliver.

CHESTNUT (V.O.)
Kenyatta stood proud. He spoke confident. He felt pure. While I have only spent vacations in the Republic of Ivory Coast.

The gloved hand goes to a tray where two other hypodermic needles lie, takes one, gives a shot to a blindfolded and unconscious Skeeter Banks.

CHESTNUT (V.O.)
(continuing)
He grew up on the dark continent. While I slept in the best hotels, he slept among the untamed beasts...

The last needle goes into the arm of an unconscious Pee Wee Frazier...spent boxes of a McDonald's "Happy Meal" nearby.

CHESTNUT (V.O.)
And while I consumed the best gourmet cuisine, he partook of food offered by mother nature.

INT. DEN - CHESTNUT'S HOUSE - NIGHT

Chestnut stares at the page a long moment, then writes:

CHESTNUT (V.O.)
He was born and raised among the descendants of my ancestors. Who am I to call myself an expert of African culture? What gives me the right to teach it...?

Chestnut puts down his pen, serious.

CHESTNUT
(to himself)
Where is Scott Kenyatta and, indeed, where the hell are my African-American students...?

OFF Chestnut's despair:

INT. ABANDONED WAREHOUSE - NIGHT

Three empty large plywood shipping crates with air holes are tied-down side-by-side on the flat bed of a rented truck.

Stenciled on each crate in large black letters is the word "STAN-LEYVILLE." The TRUCK'S ENGINE ROARS TO LIFE and it pulls out of the dusty warehouse...the Driver's face unseen...

EXT. LOS ANGELES AIRPORT - TO ESTABLISH - DAY

Busy...

INT. OFFICE - LOS ANGELES AIRPORT - DAY

Chestnut enters, approaches a young white female CLERK.

CHESTNUT
I'm Dr. Ken Chestnut, I called about a passenger manifest...

CLERK
Do you have the completed form from the front office?

CHESTNUT
Yes, I do.

CLERK
Fine. Just a moment while I query the computer.

The Clerk uses the form at the computer while Chestnut watches impatiently. Finally:

CLERK
Here it is. Mr. Scott Kenyatta, right?

CHESTNUT
That's right.

CLERK
Well, we show he took a flight to the Congo late last night.

CHESTNUT
Africa. Are you sure?

CLERK
Says here he's a representative from the Los Angeles Zoo. He accompanied freight on that flight.

CHESTNUT
What kind of freight?

CLERK
Chimpanzees. Three of them to be exact.

CHESTNUT
Thank you very much.

Chestnut exits OFF the Clerk's polite smile...

EXT. LOS ANGELES ZOO - TO ESTABLISH - DAY

SERIES OF SHOTS: African animals in their cages and habitats, then reveal tourists with cameras...

ZOO MANAGER (V.O.)
Yes, we did send three chimpanzees to Stanleyville, but they were unescorted...

INT. OFFICE - LOS ANGELES ZOO - DAY

Chestnut with the ZOO MANAGER.

CHESTNUT
Are you sure?

ZOO MANAGER
Absolutely. I did the paperwork myself.

CHESTNUT
Do you know a man named Scott Kenyatta?

ZOO MANAGER
No...never heard of him. What's this about anyway?

CHESTNUT
Thanks for your help.

Chestnut leaves OFF the Zoo Manager's curiosity...

EXT. STANLEYVILLE, AFRICA - TO ESTABLISH - DAY

A shantytown. It nestles against the dense Ituri Forest and the banks of the Congo River. It's elbow-to-elbow with White Traders, Africans going to market.

A LESE TRIBESMAN, about 5′ 6″ with a deep complexion, broad shoulders and an expression of interest stands with Scott Kenyatta. We read SUBTITLES:

KENYATTA
(in native tongue)
I have valuable cargo that needs delivery. How much?

LESE TRIBESMAN
(in native tongue)
Depends on its destination.

Kenyatta smiles, he knows he has to negotiate this deal.

KENYATTA
(in native tongue)
I have brought many things from America.

LESE TRIBESMAN
(in native tongue)
That's good for starters...

KENYATTA
(in native tongue)
I want my cargo delivered to Zantu's Village.

LESE TRIBESMAN
(in English)
Then it will cost you considerably...

KENYATTA
You speak English.

LESE TRIBESMAN
(sarcastic)
And you speak my language.

KENYATTA
We have a deal if you don't speak English to my cargo.

The Lese Tribesman frowns with confusion, grins and nods graciously:

LESE TRIBESMAN
(in native tongue)
If you wish.

OFF Kenyatta's own nod and smile...

INT. LINE-UP ROOM - POLICE STATION - DAY

A row of AFRICAN-AMERICAN MEN of similar body type, but different complexions. Among them is a scared and uncomfortable:

Jason Duffy. The others pose unceremoniously against a brightly lit height chart.

INT. OBSERVATION ROOM - POLICE STATION - DAY

Detective Horowitz looks over at Dr. Chestnut and Jack Denton with a solemn expression, then down to the 13-year-old:

Witness from the summer camp.

HOROWITZ

Step up here, son. Remember, they can't see you. Now take your time. Is the man you saw that night in there?

The youthful Witness stares at the line-up through the one-way window...

WITNESS

It was dark. Could you turn down the lights?

DENTON

This is ridiculous, Horowitz.

Horowitz nods to a POLICE OFFICER who turns the rheostat. The lights go down on the line-up and the suspects react.

DENTON (CONT'D)

(warning)

You're crossing the line, Detective.

HOROWITZ

(ignores Denton)

Well, son?

The young Witness squints then points.

WITNESS

That's the one right there.

Chestnut reacts.

WITNESS

(continuing)

Number four. I saw him take Pee Wee and put him in the trunk of a car.

HOROWITZ

Are you sure, son?

WITNESS

Hey, man, I might be a kid but I ain't stupid.

Horowitz shows the boy a photo:

HOROWITZ

Is this the car you saw him put Pee Wee into?

WITNESS
Ymmm...it looks like it.

Horowitz gives Chestnut and Denton a "that's the way it goes" look.

HOROWITZ
Thanks, son. You can go now.

The young Witness is escorted out by the Police Officer.

CHESTNUT
Now what, Detective?

Horowitz gives Denton, then Chestnut a glance.

HOROWITZ
I have to file charges.

DENTON
What kind?

HOROWITZ
Kidnapping. Murder.

Chestnut is displeased...

EXT. THE PORT - STANLEYVILLE - DAY

A crude wooden dock. A 75-foot yawl in need of paint tied there.

ON THE PIER—African Workers carefully open THREE CRATES OF CHIMPANZEES. The Lese Tribesman (we saw with Kenyatta) supervises.

A Land Rover driven by SMITTIE, a rough-looking white man with deep-set gray eyes and deeply tanned skin, stops at the end of the pier. He spies the activity with curiosity, then:

SMITTIE
(Australian accent)
Say, mate! You be needing some transportation for that cargo?

The Lese Tribesman waves Smittie off. He starts to shift the Land Rover into gear but something on the pier catches his eye:

INT. CRATE - DAY

From the dark bottom of the crate—a head...it's Pee Wee. The blindfold is around his neck. He squints at the harsh sunlight, looks at his Boy Scout watch, then around with curious fear. SUBTITLE:

LESE TRIBESMAN
(in native tongue)
Welcome back to your homeland, little man.

Pee Wee climbs out of the crate, GRABS HIS ARM in PAIN.

INT. PIER - STANLEYVILLE PORT - DAY

Pee Wee finds his feet and instantly begins a familiar dance of one who has to go to the bathroom real bad. He looks comical in his colorful p.j.'s, one foot bare, the other in a flip-flop.

From the second crate emerges Tish. She pulls the blindfold from her cute face, squints at the bright sunlight, too.

TISH
(innocently)
Where's the ladies room?

She joins Pee Wee with a slightly more dignified "need to go" twitch as Skeeter emerges from the third crate and the sunlight hits his face in full brightness. He squints defiantly as he climbs out:

SKEETER
Man, I got to pee bad! Where the fuck are we, anyway?

The three teenagers stand together on the pier, give each other curious stares as they all twitch to the rhythm of "I got to go bad."

They are confused at all the AFRICAN CHATTER from the Workers.

Pee Wee looks at one of the Chimpanzees and grins seriously:

PEE WEE
Cheetah, I don't think we're in Kansas anymore.

INT. HOTEL ROOM - STANLEYVILLE - DAY

Kenyatta holds a pair of binoculars at his eyes, his pearly whites glisten with a smile.

HIS POV THROUGH THE BINOCULARS: The Lese Tribesman escorts Pee Wee, Tish and Skeeter onto the rustic yawl. Skeeter refuses help as he climbs aboard unassisted.

Kenyatta drops the binoculars from his eyes, a momentous expression comes over him.

KENYATTA

Now we find out just how tightly bound are the blood ties...

OFF Kenyatta's contemplative smile...

INT. INTERVIEW ROOM - POLICE STATION - DAY

Chestnut and Denton sit on either side of Duffy as he takes in a breath, gives both men an innocent glance, then looks down at his own fidgeting hands.

CHESTNUT

Jesus, Jason, what are you saying?

DUFFY

We just took them into the Angeles National Forest where a friend of Professor Kenyatta posed as an African slave trader...

DENTON

Man, that's called kidnapping.

DUFFY

We didn't hurt them and they never saw our faces.

CHESTNUT

How the hell did you get talked into something like this?

Duffy's eyes light up.

DUFFY

Professor Kenyatta's writings blew my mind, man. He's an African Prince and an intellectual. When he suggested this experiment, I jumped at the chance to help him.

DENTON
And in the process, you've broken the law.

DUFFY
He'll return the kids on Sunday. No harm, no foul. We're all going to be on "Oprah" talking about this.

CHESTNUT
Oprah? Try Court TV.

DUFFY
By Sunday everything will be okay.

CHESTNUT
Jason, man, you've been had.

DENTON
Big time.

Duffy's expression pleads for an explanation.

INT. LOBBY - L.A. COUNTY JAIL - DAY

Chestnut and Denton enter, move to the sign-out table. As Chestnut signs the log:

DENTON
I'll snoop around a little, but I have to tell you, Ken, your man's in deep do-do.

CHESTNUT
(quoting)
"One never goes so far as when one doesn't know where one is going..."

DENTON
What the hell is that supposed to mean?

Chestnut gives the pen to Denton:

CHESTNUT
I'll be in touch.

Denton takes the pen as Chestnut hurries off...

INT. AIRPLANE - IN FLIGHT - DAY

The plane is packed with AFRICANS in suits and native garb.

CHESTNUT (V.O.)
Even though I've been to Africa before, still I feel like a stranger going to a strange land. Questions abound in my mind...

The FLIGHT ATTENDANT serves refreshments.

A pen writes in a small notebook.

CHESTNUT (V.O.)
Why would Scott Kenyatta betray Jason's blind loyalty in such a dastardly manner...?

The Flight Attendant stops at Chestnut's aisle seat. With his serving table down, he stops writing.

There's a book: "People of the Rain Forest" on the table. Chestnut moves the book.

CHESTNUT
Coffee.

The Flight Attendant serves him a cup of hot coffee.

An AFRICAN MAN with leathery black skin sits to Chestnut's right. He smiles, shakes his head "no" and the Flight Attendant moves past.

AFRICAN MAN
Taking a crash course...?

CHESTNUT
You might say that.

AFRICAN MAN
Where are you headed?

CHESTNUT
Stanleyville.

AFRICAN MAN
So am I.

Chestnut nods, smiles, opens the book and reads as he sips coffee.

FADE IN a mellow AFRICAN HARP and the THROATY SINGING VOICE of a Pygmy Tribesman...

DISSOLVE TO:

EXT. ITURI FOREST - TO ESTABLISH - NIGHT

The PYGMY TRIBESMAN PLUCKS the HARP and SINGS native praise to the sun setting on the lush green trees and rich red earth...leaving behind misty gray to black transparent patterns that hover over the distant mountain range...

EXT. STANLEYVILLE TOWNSHIP, AFRICA - NIGHT

The dirt streets of the township are quiet except for an ARGUMENT (in African tongue) between a LESE TRIBESMAN and a pygmy EFE TRIBESMAN.

The Efe Tribesman is much shorter, but enraged nonetheless.

EXT. PORT - STANLEYVILLE TOWNSHIP - NIGHT

A crew ties a small boat to the pier as Dr. Chestnut climbs onto the wooden planks. He carries a medium-sized nylon sports bag, wears a backpack and is now dressed in khaki shirt and shorts.

He looks travel-worn as he makes his way up the pier toward the LOUD QUARREL.

The leather-skinned African Man (from the airplane), walks beside Chestnut as they near the Lese and Efe Tribesmen.

CHESTNUT
What are they arguing about?

AFRICAN
The Efe man is very upset with the Lese Tribesman because he wants to marry his daughter.

CHESTNUT
(somewhat amused)
So what's the problem?

AFRICAN
The Lese people don't feel they must pledge

one of their own daughters for the privilege of marriage as is the custom with the Efe people. America is not the only place where tribal racism is practiced, my friend.

Chestnut throws the African a look as they move past the argument.

EXT. RUSTIC BAR - STANLEYVILLE - NIGHT

An unpainted wooden structure. LOUD VOICES, MUSIC, LAUGHTER inside as Chestnut and the African stop in front:

AFRICAN
You'll find yourself a guide in there, Professor.

CHESTNUT
Thanks for all your help.

The men shake hands firmly, their eyes find one another's with sincerity.

AFRICAN
You're welcome. I hope your safari is a good one.

INT. RUSTIC BAR - STANLEYVILLE - NIGHT

Chestnut enters, moves to the bar. Under the LOUD DIN, he asks the Bartender something, who points to a somber corner of the room.

IN THE CORNER—Drunk, Smittie looks up at Chestnut.

CHESTNUT
Are you Mr. Smith?

SMITTIE
Just call me Smittie. What can I do for you, mate?

Chestnut sits across from Smittie.

CHESTNUT
I need a guide.

SMITTIE
And where might you need to be guided to?

CHESTNUT
I'm looking for three Black children.

SMITTIE
Oh, you'll find lots of them
out there, alright. Them Pygmies multiply
like flies, they do.

CHESTNUT
Three American children...

SMITTIE
Would it be the same three who arrived here
just two days ago?

CHESTNUT
You've seen them?

SMITTIE
I see most things in this neck of the woods,
I do.

CHESTNUT
Will you take me to them?

SMITTIE
Well, you could take the next boat in two or
three days or we could take my Land Rover,
leave tomorrow morning.

CHESTNUT
How much?

SMITTIE
Expensive, it is, mate, with petro, supplies,
inflation running rampant and all.

CHESTNUT
Price is no object.

OFF the glint of resolve in Chestnut's face...

(Structural End of Act One)

AVOID PROMPTING DIALOGUE

THIS CAN RUIN SUSPENSE.

This is a common faux pas of writers at all levels of experience. *Prompting* means you tell the reader what the dialogue is about before he or she reads the dialogue. For example, you might write something like:

```
Jack and Susan sit at the table talking about their problems.
```

Well, that's what the dialogue is about, so why prompt it? Just let it happen for the reader by revising the action-description to read something like this:

```
Jack and Susan sit at the table, both annoyed...
```

Then let the dialogue speak for itself.

NONVERBAL DIALOGUE

Finally, dialogue does not have to be heard. It can be *seen* in the expressions and gestures of characters. There is a scene in *Witness* where the young Amish boy, Sam, discovers a picture of the killer he saw in the Philadelphia train station's bathroom. There is not one word of dialogue as he wanders through the squad room, taking in the strange world, and he comes upon the newspaper clipping in a trophy case. He looks around at various cops then his fearful eyes find the only one he feels he can trust—John Book. Book comes to Sam and the boy points at the murderer—a highly regarded police officer. Book pushes the boy's accusing finger down and gives him a prideful smile for a job well done. It's a very powerful scene and the first plot point of the film.

ADAPTATION

This means taking material from one medium such as a novel, magazine article, a comic book, or short story and transforming it into a screenplay.

Screenwriting and college professor Mark Schwartz, who has worked on many adaptations, comments:

> Why adaptation? Because movies are expensive professional, creative, emotional, and economic gambles. By creating an adaptation from something previously published or produced, the filmmaker knows that on some level the story already works, that it has an audience. Here's a statistic that might surprise you: Over 85% of all movies that have gone on to win the Best Picture Oscar have been adaptations.[1]

There are many examples of successful screenplay adaptations. The *Batman* series of films are all adapted from comic books. Frank Darabont adapted both *The Shawshank Redemption* and *The Green Mile* from Stephen King novellas. The Oscar-winning screenplay for *L.A. Confidential* is adapted from a novel. The same writer adapted the novel *Mystic River* to the screen. *Stand By Me* started out as a Stephen King short story. Even magazine articles can be adapted. Essentially, I wrote the Turner Network Television original film *The Court-Martial of Jackie Robinson* based on a magazine article to which the producers obtained the rights.

Each year, the Writers Guild of America nominates screenplays for its annual awards. Usually half of those screenplays are adaptations. There's no real magic to doing this. The biggest challenge, in my opinion, is converting all the "inner mind" stuff into something that can be "seen" or "heard" while basically staying true to the original story and characters. The process is much simpler when you're adapting a short story since screenplays are essentially short stories anyway. But if it's a novel, then the challenge is much more daunting.

First of all, few novels are written in the present tense. So, you must also change the tense of the novel. If the book is written in the first person, then it gets a bit tricky making the transition. *GoodFellas* is based on a first-person account and was adapted from a novel. The screenwriter had to strike a delicate balance between using voice-over and using scenes that illustrate the first-person telling from the book.

Screenwriter-director-producer Anthony Minghella comments on his process of adapting the novel *Cold Mountain*:

> I don't feel like my job is to copy out the best bits of the book into screenplay areas . . . Having read the book carefully and thought about it, I don't go back to it in the process of adaptation. I don't have it with me when I'm doing the adaptation, and I don't refer to it again. Certain things in the book really spoke to me and moved me, and my job was to advertise them.[2]

You must find the *narrative spine* of the novel. That is, pinpoint the protagonist's journey from beginning to end by cutting away the exploration of the other characters in the novel. Novels have the luxury to get into the heads and background of every major—and sometimes minor—character since there are few limits on length and time. This step gives the screenplay its point of view. Then you must take the events of the novel—the plot—that applies to the protagonist's journey and structure them to fit the limited screen time available for a film. This means changing the pacing of the novel from anywhere between 300 to 1,000 pages to fit the basic two-hour format—120 pages—common to film.

You must somehow convert the inner thoughts of characters into behavior and dialogue. You must figure out how to show character backgrounds in the forward drive. Often, you'll find that the dialogue in a novel needs rewriting for the big screen because of length. Things need to be said quicker in a film than is possible in a book. So, it's not necessarily a word-for-word transfer of dialogue when executing an adaptation.

Sometimes, there are elements in a novel that just won't work in a film. And you have to change those elements into something that does work. For example, in the adaptation of John Grisham's novel *The Firm*, the screenwriters took a few liberties. In the book, the protagonist actually steals the money from the FBI then disappears forever with his brother and wife on a yacht in the Caribbean. In the film, practicing law was the most important thing to the protagonist. This made him more sympathetic to the audience. In the end, the protagonist had to figure out a way to keep practicing law. He did not disappear on a yacht. Instead he goes back to Boston to start his own law firm.

Sometimes what's most challenging is the figuring out a way to keep so much of the richness that comes with a novel while limiting how much will fit into the constricted length of a film. A good rule of thumb is to remember that in film a little goes a long way. You can make your point firmly and move on in a screenplay.

To achieve my adaptation of *Blood Ties* to the novel *Presumed Dead*, I simply reversed the process. I started with the screenplay then expanded it into a novel. The 110-page script became a 400-page manuscript. The manuscript became a 260-page novel in the six-by-nine format. I've included an example that illustrates how I adapted the "hook" (opening sequence) from my screenplay *Blood Ties* into the novel's first chapter.

```
FADE IN:


EXT. CALIFORNIA YOUTH CAMP - TO ESTABLISH - NIGHT

A full moon. Firs nestle around the calm sparkling lake...


EXT. YOUTH CAMP - NIGHT

A cacophony of crickets and bull frogs perform near the plank pier. A
well-traveled dirt path leads up to a series of rustic cabins at the
foot of a wooded knoll...


INT. BATHROOM CABANA - NIGHT

PAYNE "PEE WEE" FRAZIER, a 13-year-old African-American boy dressed
in pajamas illustrated with cartoon characters, takes care of business
at a porcelain urinal.

A relieved expression sweeps his youthful, innocent face.

Adult feet enter...

Hands in black gloves hold a folded white handkerchief, the other a
small bottle that drips CHLOROFORM into the cloth.
```

All done, Pee Wee moves to a row of wash basins, puts a BOY SCOUT KNIFE—the largest blade open—on the wooden sink, turns on the water faucet.

There's a BOY SCOUT WATCH around his wrist.

With brute strength, the HAND WITH the HANDKERCHIEF COVERS HIS SMALL MOUTH, STIFLES his NEAR SCREAM. Desperate, Pee Wee GRABS the BOY SCOUT KNIFE and—

CUTS THROUGH the BLACK GLOVE. The hand jerks away and the KNIFE SINKS INTO PEE WEE'S OWN ARM! BLOOD as Pee Wee goes unconscious.

The blood-stained Scout knife drops next to one rubber flip-flop, the only SOUND now is the STEADY FLOW of the WATER FAUCET...

EXT. SUMMER CAMP - NIGHT

SOMEONE'S DISTANT POV: A parked rental car near the cabana as the Kidnaper exits into the murky night, a limp Pee Wee in his arms.

EXT. CABIN PORCH - NIGHT

The "Someone" is a 13-year-old African-American. Stunned, he watches as the Kidnaper PUTS PEE WEE INSIDE the CAR'S TRUNK and drives away.

OFF the Boy's frightened face...

In the screenplay, the hook is one and one-eighth pages. Now following is the opening sequence adapted into the first chapter of the novel *Presumed Dead*. From screenplay to manuscript, the page count expanded to nine pages. In the printed novel, chapter one is eight pages. Notice how I'm able to delve much deeper into the minds and background of characters and events in the adaptation as compared with the screenplay. This is possible because I'm not limited by the screenwriting rule of only write what you see and hear. Also notice the novel is written in the past tense as opposed to the present tense in the screenplay.

EXCERPT FROM THE NOVEL *PRESUMED DEAD*

CHAPTER ONE

Payne "Pee Wee" Frazier had to take a leak bad and the insisting pressure from his bladder kept him awake. He desperately wanted to jump up and run to the bathroom but he was afraid, not of the dark, but of the horrible things that might be waiting for him in the outdoor cabana every kid at Camp Big Bear lovingly referred to as the Zoo. To Pee Wee and his fellow campers, the toilet was also an ambush zone where vermin and assorted wildlife gathered with the sole purpose of scaring the be-Jesus out of trespassers.

Rising up in his top bunk, Pee Wee glanced around the large rustic bungalow cabin where twenty-three other boys slept in twelve unpainted wood-frame bunks. He stared out of a window covered only with a mesh screen to let in the warm air and keep out the pesky bugs. He could see the Zoo ominously isolated on the top of a nearby grassy knoll. He looked around again at the nearly two dozen sleeping boys—all his own age—and let out a quiet, nervous sigh. He knew most of them but didn't feel like he was one of them.

All of these kids were from the inner city and he lived quite differently than they. At home, his own bed was big, cushy and covered with a comforter containing his favorite Disney characters. Most of these boys slept on stained, sour-smelling, second-hand mattresses with one or more sisters and brothers. A thick, rich blue, double pile carpet hid the hardwood floor of his bedroom. Most of the floors these boys put their bare feet on were, at best, covered with threadworn area rugs. And the walls of his private sanctuary were brightly painted with white puffy clouds floating against a beautiful blue sky, while theirs were caked with several dirty coatings of cheap whitewash. Their homes were located in the loud, over-crowded, dangerous projects of South Central Los Angeles, and his five bedroom Tudor—with den, playroom, pool and Jacuzzi—sat primly in a peaceful Beverly Hills neighborhood.

The campers sleeping around him were poor and Pee Wee knew that was the very reason he was there. His father had consciously enrolled him in a Boy Scout unit located in the African-American community, deciding his son needed to know where he came from. Pee Wee didn't mind it so much. Most of his classmates in the private school he attended were White. And the few African-American kids that attended his school were, like him, financially well-off.

Pee Wee was becoming aware there was something even more dissonant between them that went beyond his and their neighborhoods, something more spiritual, though he wasn't sure what spiritual meant. He had heard his Dad say the word several times, so he looked it up in the dictionary.

He read aloud the definition: " . . . of or pertaining to the spirit or its concerns as distinguished from bodily or worldly existence or its concerns." Pee Wee still wasn't sure what that meant, so he looked up the root word, like he had learned to do in school. On the same page, he found the definition that started him on the path to better understanding: "Spirit: the divine influence as an agency working in the heart of man." So, even though he couldn't put it in his own words yet, he was working on it. He did know he enjoyed being with these boys more than being with his more privileged playmates. These boys had a more aggressive approach to life; they liked to fight it out, not talk about it. He supposed that they had spirit. Getting along with his fellow campers and Scouts was survival of the fittest in the truest sense for Pee Wee. And he liked that.

The pressing urge to pee came back into his consciousness as he tightened his prostrate like a boatswain mate pulling on his best square knot, and then frowned. He knew he shouldn't have drunk so much Kool Aid after the cookout, but, of course, it was too late for regrets. He reached under his foam pillow and pulled out the officially engraved Boy Scout knife his father had given him on his last birthday. He prized the gift dearly. 1992 had already been a special year for Pee Wee. He had just turned thirteen and was now a card-carrying teenager. But he had no idea that this year would be more special than he could ever imagine. Pee Wee opened the largest blade of the razor sharp knife and glanced out of the window again. If he had to go to the Zoo alone, at least he would be armed.

He squinted at the phosphorescent dial of his official Boy Scout watch and suddenly felt like an actor playing a role in a badly written cable TV movie. It was ten minutes before midnight when he eased his legs over the edge of the bunk bed and let them dangle like a rag doll's for a moment, then quietly slipped down to the smooth wood plank floor.

He was six inches shorter than most other kids and, despite the constant ribbing he had to take from some of them, he still wore his favorite pajamas: brightly colored with an assortment of Disney cartoon characters all over them. The floor felt cool despite the warm night, so he reached under the bottom bunk where another boy slept soundlessly and put on his blue and white-trimmed rubber flip-flops. He held his breath as he silently made his way through the maze of double deck beds to the front door. Gripping the Boy Scout knife firmly in his right hand, he opened the door with his left and quietly slipped outside.

He finally took in a deep breath. The full moon put a ghostly glow on the firs that nestled around the calm sparkling lake one hundred yards from the row of rustic cabins. An orchestra of crickets and bull frogs performed a crazy-sounding concerto near the pier where rows of canoes were tied. The insistent music of nature added to his fear. He looked down the well-traveled dirt path leading to the lake past the clay covered parking lot where a dusty old yellow school bus and several late model sedans were parked. He stared at the bathroom in the distant night for a moment more then took the other trail that twisted its way up to the dreaded cabana sitting amidst a clump of skinny pines.

Now standing at the entrance of the toilet, Pee Wee hesitated, bracing his nostrils for the stench of stale urine and feces he knew was there. The only light inside was from a lone 50 watt bulb inside the overhead fixture that was substantially muted by a layer of dead moths inside the plastic cover. He breathed out of his mouth, unglued his feet from the concrete floor and slowly went to the row of porcelain urinals at the back of the cabana.

Standing there in front of one urinal, Pee Wee noticed his own muted shadow matted eerily against the dark wood-stained walls. He tightened his grasp on the Boy Scout knife, found his penis and pointed it toward the basin of the bowl. The pungent smell of the half-used toilet de-odorant bar stung his nostrils as he reflexively took in a whiff of oxygen. He concentrated on the job at hand, relaxed, and a heavy stream of yellow water shot out. A relieved expression swept his youthful, innocent face and he could feel a warm invisible cloud from the rancid fluid drift up. He forgot how he should breathe again and this time inhaled the stale odor of his own urine.

At the door of the cabana, something else quietly entered and listened to the steady flow of Pee Wee's urine. The small boy didn't hear the intruder. He was so relieved that he was finally taking a leak that he forgot about his fear of the wildlife that was known to frequent there. But this invader was not the typical vermin on four legs. This one walked upright and stealthily.

Pee Wee's fears began to re-surface as he cautiously moved toward the row of sinks along the opposite wall. A Hoot Owl startled him as he plopped his weapon on the counter and twisted the knob over the faucet. He stuck his hands under the full stream of lukewarm water, glancing at his face in the dull mirror. His light-brown complexion glowed with perspiration and his face seemed to shine in the dark room. His eyes were round, full of joy despite his smoldering dread, and his lips were pouted just like his father's. A good-looking African-American kid with curly brownish-black hair and midnight black eyes, Pee Wee had learned to enjoy looking at himself in the mirror. It had become a ritual he picked up from his parents; they had taught him to look at his own image in the mirror each morning and each night before going to bed and repeat how great he was. At first, Pee Wee thought it was foolish and felt silly uttering affirmations such as "I, Payne Frazier, am intelligent" or "You deserve the best in life" or "A winner never quits and a quitter never wins." But quickly, the exercise became a way for him to make himself feel good when things seemed to be going bad. Not that things routinely went bad for him. Just the opposite was true. He had always felt lucky to have both his parents together when so many of his schoolmates were not so fortunate. He even got along well with his two older brothers and two sisters.

Pee Wee gave himself a smile, thought how blessed he was, and his fear of being in the Zoo subsided.

As Pee Wee finished washing his hands, the intruder in the cabana—he wore black leather gloves—took out a white handkerchief from his front trouser pocket. He watched his prey for a long second; taking in easy, shallow breaths. He reached back into the same pocket, took out a small bottle of chloroform and carefully dripped some of the liquid into the cloth.

As Pee Wee wiped his wet hands on the front of his pajamas—the paper towels had been long used up—a large leather-covered hand holding the handkerchief suddenly smothered his small mouth, stifling his near scream. Desperation instantly gripped Pee Wee and he instinctively reached for the Boy Scout knife on the counter. His hand fell shy by inches and Pee Wee yanked himself forward to close the short distance. Snatching up the knife he swung his arm around wildly— jabbing it into the attacker's hand. The keen-edged blade sliced right through the thin soft leather. Pee Wee kicked with the fury of an unbroken bronco and the attacker snatched his wounded hand away. The big blade of the small knife slipped and sank into Pee Wee's own tender flesh. Now Pee Wee could feel his consciousness slipping away. His eyes rolled around in their sockets like a possessed evil spirit. His mouth felt parched. He fought with all of his brain's energy to stay aware of what was happening to him. Then he saw the blood. It seemed to be everywhere as he helplessly lapsed into abject oblivion.

The intruder now an abductor held the opiate-soaked handkerchief over Pee Wee's mouth a bit longer for insurance. The fingers on Pee Wee's right hand relaxed and the blood-stained Scout knife dropped to the floor. The abductor swept Pee Wee's small frame up into his arms and one of the rubber flip-flops popped off, landing on the floor next to the knife. Then the abductor stole away from the cabana toilet. He had unwittingly rewritten the fable of the Zoo. Now there was a strange stillness to it, a new aura of horror and the only sound left there was the steady flow of water rushing from the lips of the faucet.

The abductor was in a panic as he hurried toward the clay covered parking lot where he had parked the getaway car. He hadn't planned on anything going wrong. He hadn't planned on a razor sharp knife and he certainly hadn't anticipated such a feisty struggle from the small boy.

From a nearby cabin, a 13-year-old boy named Josh quietly stood on the porch. He had drunk too much Kool Aid too. He gaped with awe as the abductor stuffed Pee Wee's limp body into the trunk of a faded tan vehicle as if he were a bag of dirty laundry. Josh pulled himself back into the deep shadow of the porch away from the light of the full moon, virtually disappearing because of his black-cherry complexion. Fear rushed up into the boy's throat. His heart pounded fiercely like a single bass drum under his rib cage. All of the moisture was sucked from his palette. The boy was confused despite having seen similar scenes of horror in his own neighborhood. He had done nothing then and even though he wanted to do something now, his instincts warned him to stay put, remain quiet and wait for the danger to pass him by. It was his survival instinct that kicked in: see no evil, hear no evil and—above all— speak no evil. He stuffed his finger tips inside each of his ears but he couldn't tear his eyes away as he watched the abductor close the trunk on Pee Wee and get inside the automobile.

The abductor became aware of the pain in his left hand as his right hand groped for the car key lying on the front seat. He could feel the fresh warm blood seeping out of the back of his hand. He also wasn't prepared for fixing a wound. In desperation, he opened the glove compartment and reached in hoping to find a rag or something. Instead, he bled all over the rental agreement folder. Finally, he stripped off his sweat-stained shirt. Underneath was a T-shirt which he simply ripped off of his chest and wrapped around his hand. He fumbled with the car key, his heart pounding in his ears, and he finally jabbed the key inside the ignition, snapping it forward. The car's engine roared to life and spat out a booming backfire.

From his shadow sanctuary on the cabin porch, Josh flinched at the sound. With fingers still plugging both ears, he simply watched as the dusty sedan rumbled out of the parking lot and sped down the tree-lined road, then disappeared like an apparition into the still of the warm summer night.

Josh took in a deep breath and slipped back inside the cabin despite the cramp he was now feeling in his stomach. He climbed back into his bunk and pulled the lightweight blanket up to his chin hoping it would protect him from his fellow camper's fate. He closed his eyes and tried to go back to sleep, but his full bladder wouldn't allow it. So Josh just let his entire body relax and the thin mattress beneath him quickly soaked up the urine like a dry sponge. He held his eyes shut tightly and tried to forget the image of the man stuffing the limp little body into the trunk of a car. A chill surged through Josh's body and he shuddered uncontrollably. Tiny beads of perspiration formed but he pulled the cover up over his face anyway. For insurance.

Producers and studios have a voracious appetite for books and novels that can be optioned to be adapted to the big and small screen. Some screenwriters are doing what I've done—taken a screenplay and transformed it into a novel. Then they shop the film rights of the published book to the studios. The obvious benefit is that the screenplay is already written. But I've personally found that the process of adapting my screenplay to a novel has given me a deeper understanding of the story's premise and its characters. During the adaptation process, I was able to explore other avenues of the plot I could never have in the limited space of a script. So, I'm sure I'll do a major rewrite of the screenplay should I be lucky enough to sell the novel's film rights.

YOUR ASSIGNMENT

START WRITING YOUR SCREENPLAY!

Use the scene outline as your guide. As you write, you may find that some of the material in the outline is not really necessary. If that's the case—get rid of it. You may also find you may need to add material, maybe even some new characters. Do it. Above all, let your *instincts* drive this part of the process. You've allowed your *left brain* to work. That's the more logical side of your thinking. Now it's time to let your *right brain* get a workout. In other words, it's time to write with your *heart*.

The actual writing of the screenplay is more like *magic* than *math*. Now your job is to bring all the elements together cohesively. Your main goal is to *breathe life into the characters*. Give each character dimension. Also, the focus of the *rough draft* process is to simply get the story down on paper in a structure that works. It need not be perfect. In fact, it won't be. You're going to find that some of the dialogue is dreadful. Don't worry about that right now. Think of the dialogue you're writing in this rough draft as *place holders* for the real dialogue to come later. You may find that the structure of the story is not quite right. That's okay for now. You can fix that later. Hey, it's going to take *many* rewrites to get all of this stuff *right*.

NOTES

1. Mark Schwartz has published an adaptation of *Dante's Inferno* in actual screenplay format called *How to Write: A Screenplay* (New York: Continuum International Publishing Group, 2005).
2. Richard Slayton, "Mountain Man," Anthony Minghella's patient climb to the top of Cold Mountain (Los Angeles: Written By, February/March 2004).

PART II

Rewriting the Feature Screenplay

CHAPTER 6

The Rewriting Process

WRITING IS REWRITING . . .

—*Raymond Chandler, author*

Congratulations! You've finally managed to grunt out that rough draft. This is an extremely hard thing to accomplish. So, pat yourself on the back and be very proud. Celebrate and think positive. Resist those nagging thoughts that what you've just finished is a piece of—well . . . instead of going down that road, remember this: you've just passed the first big hurdle of becoming a successful screenwriter: getting to the end. Many who begin the process of writing a screenplay never finish the story let alone 100 to 120 pages of script.

This section of the book is designed as a stand-alone guide that can be followed to rewrite your screenplay. Now, if you really think about it, you'll quickly begin to recognize that everything you've learned up to this point has been about the rewriting process. Along the way of cranking out your rough draft, you've developed a lot of background material and opened many doors to new ideas. Hopefully, your rough draft is not just a perfunctory rehashing of your scene outline. Instead, the material has evolved to another level.

Consider all of this work source material. You've used your creative side quite a bit in the process of bringing your treatment and scene outline to screenplay format. Now it's time to use your analytical side a bit more.

In the real world of the working screenwriter, rewriting is an inescapable fate. Screenwriter Kevin Bisch wrote *Hitch* (starring Will Smith) in about eight months and sent it to an agent who had read, and rejected, another one of his scripts . . . Smith committed to play the lead and the script sold to Columbia . . . when, Bisch concedes, the hard work began—the revisions. "I had no experience being critiqued at this kind of level and getting studio notes," he says. "We had this big attachment and the stakes were high." In the three-year development process, Bisch says a lot of things went right, such as working with great executives. He learned a lot of lessons during the process, especially the importance of collaborating with an open mind. "If you think you're the smartest person in the world, you're in big trouble," he says. "You have to be confident in your idea, yet open to other people's input."[1]

LETTING IT SIMMER

It's an excellent idea to let the rough draft sit on the shelf for a week or more before you even think about starting to rewrite it. Actually, this should be refreshing for you since you've probably been working on this screenplay for months. Simply walk away from it and busy yourself with other things. During this time off, perhaps a few questions about what you've written may pop into your head. Resist all urges to pick it up and read it while the rough draft is "simmering." Simply jot down your thoughts and file them away with the rest of your source material for later reference.

Something magical will happen to you while your screenplay is "simmering." Your mind is a highly sophisticated multitasking computer that'll automatically and subconsciously start seeking out more information about what you've been writing about. You'll start to come across articles, television specials—resources of all kinds—that miraculously relate to your screenplay, because the mind automatically seeks ways to justify decisions and beliefs. For example, you won't focus on a certain kind of car on the road until you buy that model. You'll pull up next to the car and check it out, compare options. You'll start reading the ads in magazines for that car more closely. You'll talk to others who own the same model. What you're doing is making sure that you've made the right decision. Realize that this natural cognitive process will also help you to gather a lot of important tidbits and nuances essential to the rewriting of your screenplay.

One convenient thing about starting the rewrite is that you can do it just about anywhere. You don't need your computer. The only gear you'll need in addition to a copy of your screenplay is a red ink pen and a notepad.

Axiom: There's no such thing as bad writing, just writing that needs to be fixed.

Ideally, you won't start executing the actual rewrite of your screenplay at the computer for weeks. When you do, you're basically going to approach it in sections. First look at your rough draft in the Four Big Chunks:

Act One
Act Two First Half
Act Two Second Half
Act Three

Then look at the rough draft in a more refined way:

Act One
  Pages 1–10
  Pages 11–30

Act Two First Half
  Pages 31–45
  Pages 46–60

Act Two Second Half
  Pages 61–75
  Pages 76–90

Act Three
  Pages 91–95
  Pages 96–Climax–The End.

Remember, these structure milestones are really just guidelines for the shape of your screenplay. Don't get too caught up in making events in the story hit exactly on specific pages. You just need to be in the ballpark to insure good story pacing. Actually, the true value of this approach is to help keep your story structured regardless of the length of the script.

Okay, assuming your screenplay has been simmering for a week or more, it's time to start the rewriting process.

WHAT TO DO FIRST

Novelist-screenwriter Raymond Chandler once wrote "a good story cannot be devised; it has to be distilled." So, after your rough draft has rested, free up enough time to sit alone and read it from cover to cover without interruption to start the distillation process. Don't make notes or evaluate its content as you read. Be a consumer. You'll experience plenty of emotions about your material and, by the end of the read, have a pretty good idea where its weaknesses and strengths lay. Now jot down these feelings and impressions while they're still fresh. Clear your brain of these emotions and observations and save them for later.

ALL BETS ARE OFF

At this point in the creative process of writing a screenplay, I like to think all bets are off. It reminds me that all the work I've done before and while writing the rough draft is not that important anymore. What is important is that my attitude must make a transition, by looking at each new revision as a New Start for the work in progress.

It's your job now to make each new revision become more than the last one. In other words, each rewrite should be considered starting anew. You must do what you have to do to make each new draft better, even if that means altering or changing things set forth in your source material.

Remember, your job now is to let the screenplay be what it *becomes*, not what you thought it was when you were writing the rough draft. I believe it's best to adapt this attitude because it allows you to trust and follow your instincts as a writer. That doesn't mean you can't fix things that you consider being off track—that's an important part of rewriting. It also could mean that where you started probably wasn't the place you wanted to be anyway.

Now, in order to determine the direction of your rewrite, you need to ask yourself a few questions . . .

HONESTLY ANSWER SIX IMPORTANT QUESTIONS

Question One: What's my story really about?

What I'm getting at here is theme. Let's review what that is . . .

When you boil it all down, there are really only five general types of story themes you can write about. They are:

1. Man against Man
2. Man against Nature
3. Man against Himself
4. Man against Society
5. Man against Fate.

Lest I be accused of sexism, one can most certainly substitute Woman for Man in the above basic themes. You need to pinpoint which one of these archetypes you're using, then focus it into a more specific theme. A good way to do that is to convert your theme into a central question that essentially is answered by the end of the screenplay. If necessary, review Theme in Part I of this book.

> Does your screenplay's basic theme fall into one of the above categories?
> If not, you need to fix that.
> Do you know the specific theme of your story?
> If not, you need to find one.

Break out the Bible or *Bartlett's Familiar Quotations*. Both are available on highly searchable CD-ROM. Go to the index and find the one key word that relates to the theme of your story. There's a possibility this may have evolved from your initial idea over the course of writing the rough draft. Then track down a specific passage or quote that fits your story perfectly. This can then become the mantra for the emotional core of your story, and in the rewriting, go beyond the initial clichéd theme you associated with your screenplay.

Question Two: What's the problem in the story?

When we talk about the problem in a story, we're really getting to the reason the protagonist exists in the story. Without a problem or predicament, you have no conflict and probably a flat story. While the main problem for the protagonist is the over-riding difficulty presented, the protagonist should also encounter smaller obstacles that get in the way of dealing with the larger issue at hand. You must be able to clearly define this problem and the obstacles it generates. These should be fairly recognizable to the audience as the story unfolds.

In *Witness*, John Book's problem is dirty cops want to kill a little Amish boy—the only witness to a murder.

In *The Fugitive*, Dr. Kimble's problem is he's been wrongfully convicted of murdering his wife and a U.S. marshal is tracking him down because he's an escaped convict.

In *Jerry Maguire*, Jerry's problem is he has to compete against his former employer—the largest, most unscrupulous sports agency in the world—in order to make an honest living.

In *Erin Brockovich*, her problem is she has to prove a giant corporation is poisoning the water supply of a small California town, which is slowly killing its residents.

So, what is your protagonist's problem and what are the obstacles generated by it?

If you don't know, *you've* got a problem.

If you aren't clear about the answer to this question, then you need to really focus on this during your rewrite. The problem needs to be simple and clearly recognizable by the audience.

Question Three: What's my protagonist's goal?

What the main character wants should be the driving force of every well-written screenplay. The goal can and should be translated into emotions: wants and needs. To be clear: wants relate to *nice-to-have* and needs are *necessary*. Again, at its best, a goal should be simple and easily identifiable by the audience. I often say that you can write a story about a person who wants a glass of water. And it's true. If the character is thirsty enough—say he's floating aimlessly on a raft at sea—he or she will act to get a drink of water. And in this case, it's ironic because the character is surrounded by water albeit undrinkable. If not having water means dying, then the character will be strongly motivated to do whatever it takes to get a drink of water. This is a clear goal with strong *need* behind it. Their want—*nice-to-have*—could be to see the face of their loved ones again. Then it's a simple process of putting logical obstacles, which escalate in difficulty, in the way of getting that drink of water.

In the Oscar-nominated film *Secrets & Lies*, the protagonist has a simple but strong emotional goal in the story: find her birth mother.

The disenchanted Hollywood agent in *Leaving Las Vegas* has a very simple goal: to drink himself to death.

The scientist played by Jeff Goldblum in *Jurassic Park: The Lost World*, simply wants to get his girlfriend off the island where dinosaurs are being cultivated.

In *Gladiator*, the protagonist played by Russell Crowe wants to avenge his family's brutal murder by Roman storm troopers.

The unfolding events in these stories provide obstacles that escalate in difficulty, in turn, complicating each of the protagonist's efforts to accomplish a highly tangible goal.

Can you identify your protagonist's simple goal?

If you cannot, then now is a good time to create one that'll fuel your story's forward movement.

Question Four: What's my protagonist willing to give up while reaching that goal?

What the protagonist is willing to give up in order to reach his or her goal is called the *stakes* in the story. The importance of the protagonist reaching his or her goal is part and parcel to the intensity of the drama and suspense that can be generated for the audience. Is the protagonist willing to give up money to succeed? Or fame? Or even give up life itself? Is he willing to kill another human being to reach his goal in the story? And, the most important question of all: what would happen if the protagonist doesn't achieve his or her goal in the story?

The simple-minded Karl Childers in the film *Sling Blade* is willing to kill in order to protect his new young friend. If he doesn't, his young friend will surely be hurt or murdered.

Jerry Maguire is willing to give up *everything* to be an honest sports agent.

Denzel Washington's troubled Gulf War army officer in *Courage Under Fire* puts his family and army career on the line to find the truth or he will self-destruct, perhaps even commit suicide.

In *Gladiator*, the protagonist had to eventually come to terms with killing a lot of people for sport (as opposed to in war) to get what he wanted in the story. In fact, in the end, he gives up his own life.

What's at stake for your protagonist?

If you don't know—you must find the answer now.

Question Five: How does my protagonist's goal evolve (or change) over the course of the story?

How the protagonist's goal evolves is often referred to as *character arc*. You could even look at it as the "turns in the road" that the protagonist must travel to reach his or her goal in the story. At each new turn, something new is learned or a new skill is gained and, as a result, the character begins to grow as a person. This growth should affect the complexion of the protagonist's goal that started out as being fairly straightforward and now becomes more complex.

In *Courage Under Fire*, the protagonist realizes that his investigation of the death of a female helicopter pilot during the Gulf War has become more about his own search for inner peace and truth than the case itself.

Professor Klump in *The Nutty Professor*, begins to realize that his research to find a way to make himself thin to impress a beautiful co-ed has more to do with his getting in touch with who he is deep down than with the success of the actual experiment.

In the classic film *Casablanca*, Rick—portrayed by Humphrey Bogart—makes the transition from being a cold and calculating American opportunist only interested in making a buck to a caring man who truly wants to help Jews wipe out the evil of Nazism.

In *Finding Forrester*, the young African-American protagonist learns to hang his future on his education rather than on his ability to play basketball.

Does your protagonist's goal change in the course of the story?

If not, then your story may have a feeling of being flat and your protagonist may be coming across as one dimensional or as "one note." This is something that definitely deserves your attention during the rewriting process. Review the part on Character Arc, if necessary.

Question Six: What unexpected gain or result (if any) does my protagonist realize at the end of the story?

The protagonist reaching an unexpected gain is called a story's twist. It's akin to leading the audience down a road in such a way that they have specific expectations, then giving them something quite different in the end.

Red, played brilliantly by Morgan Freeman in *The Shawshank Redemption*, gives up trying to impress the parole board, and this very act is what gets him out of prison and reunites him with his friend, Andy.

In *Pretty Woman*, the prostitute portrayed by Julia Roberts can only win over the man she loves by first giving him up.

In the film *A Family Thing*, written by Billy Bob Thornton (*Sling Blade*), a southern born and bred racist—portrayed by Robert Duvall—warms to embrace his African-American half-brother, played by James Earl Jones.

And in *Lone Star*, two estranged childhood lovers find out they have the same father yet, in the end, decide to remain lovers.

Read the rough draft again.

But this time write notes directly on the pages as you read. Use red ink—it's more dramatic.

CHECK PAGE COUNT AND STRUCTURE

It bears repeating here that when I talk about the number of pages that define each structure milestone, I'm not talking absolutes. The idea is to have some reliable way to keep track of the story's pacing . . . a rhythm, if you will, to the story that the moviegoing audience has come to appreciate and often demand.

Look at the page count as the number of minutes of a finished film. In this way, you have a tried-and-true way to gauge how your story is unfolding totally dictated by the protagonist's desires, the decisions based on those desires, and the actions taken as a result of the decisions.

Again, *this is a guideline.* If it takes fourteen pages to write your structure milestone Pages 1–10, then that's what it takes. However, if it takes twenty pages to write your structure milestone Pages 1–10, then you're probably pushing the envelope of good pacing (unless your film is longer than two hours by necessity). You start to run the risk of making the audience squirm in their seats—creating butt wiggle—if you take too long to tell them what the story is about.

There are, of course, many exceptions to this guideline that work well in films. I will point them out as we explore in more detail the concept of using classic screenplay structure to rewrite.

MAKE SURE PLOTTING IS SOLID

You've probably heard the old writing adage that "character is structure." Well, it's true. Story structure is part and parcel to what the characters do in a story; in other words, the protagonist's behavior. It's very important to keep the protagonist at the center of the story. It's the protagonist who should be constantly facing tough *choices*. It's the protagonist who should make key *decisions* in the story. And it's the protagonist who should experience the *consequences* of those decisions—both good and bad. This is called "telling your story through the protagonist's point of view."

Screen stories can be driven by events or by the protagonist's emotions or both. Either way, the protagonist should be at the center of a decision-making process that causes the story to progress.

Does your story unfold through the protagonist's point of view?

Your protagonist should be in just about every scene of the screenplay. Of course, there will be scenes when this isn't practical to tell the story in a suspenseful way. But if you find you have three, four, or more scenes in a row that don't include the protagonist, this is a red flag. I like to say if you have more than one scene in a row without your protagonist, you could be creating a point-of-view shift in your story. The solution is simple—put him or her right in the middle of the scenes and see what happens. If that's impossible for whatever reasons, put the protagonist in the scene, in absentia—that is, the scene is about the protagonist. It should produce both interesting and challenging "ripples" in the storyline and help to improve the screenplay's overall plotting. You may need to move story elements around a bit.

COMPLY WITH BASIC GENRE CONVENTIONS

Your screenplay *will* fall into one general genre category: drama, romance, Western, comedy, thriller, action, action-adventure, science fiction, horror, or fantasy. Perhaps your screenplay is a hybrid or combination of these general genres such as action-drama, romantic-comedy, sci-fi–thriller, horror-thriller, horror-comedy, and other subgenres. Be aware that the different genres each have their own peculiarities.

Does your screenplay obey the rules of its general genre?

For example, thrillers tend to be plot-driven. In fact, most thrillers—or murder mysteries—actually have two plots.

There are even different brands of thrillers. For example, there's the Hitchcock suspense standard. Then there's the detective story, the horror story, and the one-person-against-the-world thriller or even a combination of any of these.

The point here is that it's a good idea to screen films in the same genre as your screenplay, ideally before you start writing it. But it's never too late to do this and a good time is during the rewriting process.

CONSIDER DIFFERENT STORYTELLING CONVENTIONS

If your screenplay seems flat and overall routine, consider using a nonlinear approach to your storytelling by using a "parallel narrative" storytelling device. Review the part on this subject if you decide to do this.

Can your story be improved by using a nonlinear approach?

If this storytelling convention doesn't help your story, avoid it. This change can sometimes make your story more compelling.

IDENTIFY TYPE OF PLOT

When you get right down to it, a screen story is essentially about one person trying to solve a problem while other people either help or hinder the efforts.

We call this basic spine of the story a *plot*. While it would be wonderful to come up with a plot that no one has ever seen before on-screen, it's simply impossible because it has all been done before. Sorry. So, instead of frustrating yourself trying to reinvent the wheel, why not use these basic structures as a good starting point, then work to make them fresh.

If necessary, go back and review Types of Plots in chapter 3 of this book. Here are the basic types again:

The Hunt
The Journey
The Duel
Unselfish Atonement
Revenge
Coming of Age

Can you identify the type of plot you are using?

To do so means you'll have a clear understanding of your protagonist's plight.

IDENTIFY TYPE OF ENDING

If necessary, review Types of Ending in chapter 3 of this book. Again, they are:

The Hero Wins.
The Hero Loses.
The Hero Wins by Losing.
The Hero Loses by Winning.
The Hero Wins but Loses.

Does the outcome of your screenplay fit into one of these categories?

You might be asking yourself at this point: Why bother to rewrite this screenplay if it's all been done before? Well, the only things that'll set your screenplay apart from all the others will be your unique point of view, dramatic sensibilities, and sense of humor and how freshly you've invented the characters that appear in your story. It comes down to you and the way you interpret life through your own experiences.

SUSPEND DISBELIEF

Whether an audience will buy into your story is a very important consideration, and often writers don't spend enough time dealing with this concept. The audience must be willing to "suspend disbelief" for the two hours or more that your story is on the screen.

For two hours, we believe that dinosaurs walk the earth again in the *Jurassic Park* films. For several hours, we believe a man could be pregnant and deliver a baby in *Junior*. In *Star Trek: First Contact*, we believe that highly superior Borgs exist alongside human beings. We believe the exploits of three Gulf War soldiers in *Three Kings*. And for two hilarious hours, we believe that the aging cast of a past hit science-fiction television series helps an alien race win their independence from a race of lizard aliens in *Galaxy Quest*. In all of these cases, the screenwriter tells a story in such a way that we buy into film reality. The filmmakers present the facts in such a way that we believe them. They cause us to suspend our disbelief.

Is there *film reality* in your screenplay?

Make sure you eliminate or explain any element that causes the reader to pause and wonder if something can really happen or if something is accurate or think, "that would never happen."

YOUR ASSIGNMENT

By this time, you should have generated a lot of questions and found most of the answers—or at least come up with good ideas of how to begin solving the problems in your screenplay. But you're still not quite ready to sit at the computer and start doing the actual rewrite.

You still need to spend more quality time rethinking.

NOTES

1. Rachel Wimberly, "Getting Hitched: An Interview with Writer Kevin Bisch," 12 March 2005, at www.scriptmag.com.

CHAPTER 7

Analyze Scene-by-Scene

THE CHALLENGE OF SCREENWRITING IS TO SAY MUCH IN LITTLE AND THEN TAKE HALF OF THAT LITTLE OUT AND STILL PRESERVE AN EFFECT OF LEISURE AND NATURAL MOVEMENT.

—*Raymond Chandler, author*

As you proceed with planning your rewrite, you may have to move a few scenes around or combine some scenes that seem to have the same effect on the story as another or even delete scenes. This is inevitable. But don't be too quick to discard a scene without making sure it could fit somewhere else in the story.

LOGIC AND REORDERING SCENES

Merely combining two scenes can create a very rich and more meaningful new scene. Even by moving one scene from later in the story to earlier in the story can energize other marginal scenes by giving them fresh and new meaning. *Cause and effect* is an important concept to examine in your screenplay during the rewriting process. We call this *context*.

Write a one-line description of every scene in your screenplay.

Use this *scene-by-scene* collapsed version of your screenplay as the starting point for evaluating its structure and how each scene relates to the others. Here's an example of a scene-by-scene breakdown of the first structure milestone (structure Pages 1–10) from *Blood Ties*:

1. Establish California youth camp, full moon, calm lake.
2. Establish well-traveled dirt path, rustic cabins.
3. Inside bathroom cabana—13-year-old African-American "PEE WEE" FRAZIER is pissing, gets attacked by an UNSEEN KIDNAPPER and stabs him using his Boy Scout knife.
4. Outside—ANOTHER BOY watches as the Unseen Kidnapper drives away with Pee Wee in the trunk of the car.
5. Establish the USC campus.
6. Inside the USC classroom—African dancers/drummers perform for students and DR. KENNETH CHESTNUT, and he imagines himself as one of them, thanks them for the show, then he's approached by LAPD DETECTIVE HOROWITZ.

7. Teaching assistant JASON DUFFY enters Chestnut's office.
8. In Chestnut's office—Detective Horowitz questions Duffy about three missing kids, among them Pee Wee Frazier, with Duffy admitting only to organizing the youth retreat.
9. In an abandoned warehouse—"TISH" TOLIVER and "SKEETER" BANKS with Pee Wee are tied up, unconscious as the Unseen Kidnapper administers drugs from a hypodermic needle.
10. Inside the USC Coliseum—Chestnut practices archery and suspects that Duffy is lying about the kids.
11. Inside USC classroom—Chestnut debates for the class the relationship between American blacks and Africans with KENYATTA—a full-blooded African who casts doubt on Chestnut's expertise and research in this field.
12. In the corridor—Detective Horowitz arrests Duffy for murder.

Note how straight to the point each scene description is written yet still exudes a sense of tone and atmosphere. There's a side benefit to a well-written scene-by-scene—it can later be used as the source of your screenplay treatment for agents, managers, producers, and executives.

At the center of your screenplay are its characters. They should be the reason this story is being told. They should be more important than the backdrop or special effects, even if you're writing a high concept premise.

Let's quickly review the role of characters in storytelling . . .

Verify Dramatic Roles of Characters

The Protagonist. This is who the story is about.

The Fatal Flaw. This is the weakness that makes your larger-than-life protagonist accessible and human to the audience.

The Co-protagonist. This is an antagonist or pivotal character that evolves in his or her relationship with the protagonist, becoming simpatico.

Fish Out of Water. The more your protagonist finds himself or herself in an unfamiliar situation, the more interesting the struggle.

The Antagonist. The character that provides the opposition to the protagonist, thus creating conflict.

The Co-antagonist. Generally a pivotal character that evolves to equal opposition to protagonist.

Unity of Opposites. The common goal that ties the protagonist and antagonist together in the story so neither can simply walk away.

Pivotal Characters. These characters keep the protagonist and antagonist from walking away from the problem and often bring different points of view to the story.

Character Triangles. The emotional relationships between the protagonist, antagonist, and one or more pivotal characters in the story and subplot(s).

The Subplot(s). The relationship that explores the story's theme and puts the protagonist on emotional roller-coaster rides in the screenplay.

Do you know your character triangles?

If characters in both the *main plot* and *subplot* are not clearly triangulated, now is the time to work on this. Diagram them if necessary.

EVALUATE THE PURPOSE OF SCENES

There will be a few scenes that you simply don't need. Often, these scenes are your *darlings*—your favorite for one reason or another. If a jewel of a scene has no real purpose in this story, consider saving it for another. I remember watching a TV interview with actor-director Billy Crystal and he told a story how he had to cut a scene from *Mr. Saturday Night*. He said he really loved the scene but, for some reason, he had to cut it from the picture. He took the very same scene and put it in another one of his films, *When Harry Met Sally*. And it worked.

Evaluate each scene in terms of the following:

> Context: How each scene relates to the one before it, after it, and to other scenes in the screenplay in general.
> Subtext: What's going on beneath the surface of each scene, and does it some how relate to the story's overall theme?
> Intentions: What does each character want to accomplish in each scene?
> Conflict: Is there *opposition* between at least two characters in each scene?

If you don't have these elements in play in each and every scene, it's time to fix that.

Other Concepts

There are a couple of other key concepts you need to apply as you look over the scene-by-scene outline of your screenplay . . .

Are some of your scenes simply back story?

If they are, seriously consider getting rid of them or finding a way to show how this back story affects the story in the present and then put the *back story in the forward drive*. Remember, like us, characters are best judged by their behavior rather than solely by what they say . . .

Does your story have a sense of urgency?

If not, you need to invent *important deadlines* for your protagonist to reach certain objectives in the story and make sure *something is at stake if he fails* to reach those deadlines.

TRACK PROGRESSION OF CHARACTERS

Does your protagonist have a clear "arc" in the story?

If not, you need to fix that as you rewrite. You should be able to clearly identify where your protagonist begins emotionally and where he or she ends up by Fade Out.

YOUR ASSIGNMENT

As you've just experienced, a lot of rewriting is actually *rethinking* and *making notes*. But this time when you sit at the computer, you're going to feel much better than when you started this journey. Why? Because this time you won't be staring at a blank screen.

Axiom: Hindsight is always twenty-twenty.

You now have the advantage of *hindsight* working for you and that'll certainly help you take the material to higher levels.

Consider developing a *Rewrite Plan*. This is a simple document in which you tell yourself (or anyone else who wants to know . . . agents, managers, producers, executives) how you're going to fix each structure milestone in your screenplay. You shouldn't write a long document, just the basic approach and fixes that are needed in clear, precise language. Use the *Story Structure Development Template* as your format.

CHAPTER 8

Rewrite Act One

TAKE THE TALE IN YOUR TEETH . . . AND BITE 'TILL THE BLOOD RUNS, HOPING IT'S NOT POISON; AND WE WILL ALL COME TO THE END TOGETHER, AND EVEN TO THE BEGINNING: LIVING, AS WE DO, IN THE MIDDLE.

—*Ursula K. Le Guin, author*

THE SETUP

Now it's finally time to put butt to chair in front of the computer. If, in fact, you've spent a few weeks being analytical and thoughtful, you should be *chomping at the bit* to get started. If you still have some gray areas in your mind about how to fix some things in your screenplay, don't worry about it too much. In between sessions at the keyboard, spend some of your driving and jogging time rolling the problems around in your mind. Combined with the act of rewriting, this will yield some solutions.

Bottom line, if you can't come up with a good fix, just write something obvious for now. Yes, I'm telling you to write something average or even bad. Just remember it has to be fixed before releasing your first draft for industry consumption.

At this point, you should *avoid getting bogged down.*

Act One is basically the first thirty minutes of a movie. That computes into the first *thirty pages* of the screenplay.

REWRITE PAGES 1–10: THE PROBLEM-PREDICAMENT

The audience needs to have a basic understanding in what they're investing several precious hours of their busy lives and hard-earned money. They want to know the *rules of the game* as it were. That's the overall goal of a film's first ten minutes or so.

The *inciting incident* of a story occurs when something first becomes a problem for the protagonist.

What is the inciting incident in your story?

This is sometimes confused with *point of attack* or *hook* or *opening sequence.* As I've said earlier, the moment that the protagonist's problem begins is not necessarily the *hook.* This need not be a part of the opening sequence in the screenplay. In fact, it can happen well before the story begins—years or perhaps decades before—and we join the story at the point when it begins to directly affect the protagonist. However, it could well be the hook of the story. In fact, the hook and the inciting incident can be two very different events.

What is the hook that pulls the audience into your story?

In most cases, the *hook* is the moment when the inciting incident begins to become a clear problem for the protagonist. So, between pages 1–5, work on opening the story with a scene or sequence that grabs the audience attention and portends of being or becoming a big problem for the protagonist in your story. This *hook* should also orient the audience to the *setting*—where the story takes place and the *world* the story will explore. I like to refer to this as the "closed door" behind which the screenwriter takes the audience. Make sure you are also establishing the *tone* of the story—drama, comedy, action-adventure, horror, sci-fi, and so on—in the *opening sequence*.

What is the central question to be answered by your story?

You should introduce the thematic device or the central question to be answered in the story early on. I've already talked about how this is done in the film *Witness* and *Chinatown*. There are many other examples. Try to come up with the central question for your favorite films. This exercise can help you pinpoint one for your own screenplay if you don't already know what it is.

What visual techniques are you using to relate theme to the audience?

Again, combine both visual and auditory methods to present theme to the audience. In the film *Ordinary People*, the lyrics being sung by a youth choir actually communicate theme in a very subtle way. Be creative with how you present theme to the audience.

Axiom: Characters don't talk about theme, they wallow in it.

What is your Act One metaphor?

A *thematic device*—or visual motif—should be subtle. Often, it is only fully devised by the writer *after* completing the rough draft of the screenplay. So now is the time to fret about this. You may have already instinctively written it in. Now is the time to identify it and use it for dramatic purpose.

Who's the protagonist? and What is the problem?

At a minimum, introduce the protagonist in the opening sequence. You can also introduce the antagonist or the villain. Remember to introduce your protagonist—and all characters for that matter—with *flair* and *style* comparable to their dramatic roles in the story.

Bottom line, somewhere close to page 10, we should know *what the story is about*. And that should center on the protagonist's *problem-predicament* and *initial goal*. I say initial goal because, as the problem escalates, the quest to reach this goal will be interrupted by short bouts to overcome more immediate obstacles in the story. And, in the end, the goal may even change.

Have you introduced the subplot of the screenplay?

If not, do it. You can even put it "inside" a main plot scene. We call this technique the **French scene**. It can be as simple as a trading of glances or one line of dialogue. Ideally, this scene brings the protagonist and his or her *antagonist in the subplot* together and we learn what the problem is or will be in their relationship.

You should rewrite this first structure milestone as many times as it takes to get it right. Go over each element with care and attention. Start to push your scenes, dialogue, and other elements into "fresh" territory. Try to *bend* the rules if you can. Be creative, inventive, and bold. You should do this with each structure milestone during the rewriting process.

REWRITE PAGES 11–30: THE PROBLEM GETS WORSE

At this point, the audience should have a general idea what your story is about. We should be very clear that it's about *the protagonist with a specific problem-predicament.* Now it's time to bring in the other people who will continue or begin to complicate matters. Here are the key questions you must answer while rewriting this structure milestone . . .

Are you introducing all the major characters?

In these twenty or so pages, make sure you're introducing every major character and the conflict each brings to the story. If you didn't introduce the antagonist or villain in the first ten pages, now is the time to do so.

A key to accomplishing this effectively is to concentrate on *character triangles.* The last thing you want to do is to parade a litany of people before your audience without a sense of who they are and what problems they bring to the protagonist and to each other. Remember, clearly present the dramatic roles of each type of character and introduce each in such a way that we quickly understand how each may affect the story. Again, be inventive and clever with the methods you use to introduce these major characters.

Is the problem getting worse?

In fact, your main goal in rewriting this structure milestone is to ensure that *the problem is getting worse for the protagonist.* At this point, you shouldn't be trying to solve anything for the audience. Just show how each major character will create conflict for the protagonist through relationships. Concentrate on how these characters increase the intensity of the problem for the protagonist . . . forcing him or her to spend more "normal" time paying attention to and dealing with the very problem they're trying to ignore. The problem needs to get so bad, so unbearable for the protagonist that he or she finally has to *overtly act* on it.

In *The Fugitive,* Dr. Kimble's problem gets worse when he's placed in shackles and put on a bus heading for death row. In the process, we meet all the key characters that'll provide conflict for the protagonist . . . the prisoners on the bus, Lt. Gerard, and his able cadre of deputy marshals.

In *My Dog Skip,* the protagonist is a lonely boy with no friends. He wants a dog. But his father won't allow it. To make things worse, the bullies at school continue to pick on the boy, tease him, and beat him up. No one appears to love him but his mother.

In *Men of Honor,* the protagonist has joined the Navy to become an elite diver. Things get worse as he's treated very badly simply because he's African-American.

Is your protagonist entering new territory?

Somewhere around page 30, make sure your protagonist *chooses* or is *forced* into an unfamiliar situation—*new territory*—created by the initial problem in the story. The catalyst for this move is best realized through an act committed by the protagonist such as "taking the bull by the horns." This *new territory* or *new life* is the *first plot point* of a total of two that's characteristic of classic screenplay structure. It's the first real *turning point* because no matter what decision the protagonist makes, he or she will still have to solve the present problem. Of course, he or she doesn't really want to do this because it's more comfortable staying in the *old life,* doing things the way they've always been done. Ideally, the protagonist should be faced with a *moral dilemma*—choosing between doing the "right" or "wrong" action— and staring unavoidable change right in the eye. And it's scary.

The Fugitive's Dr. Kimble definitely enters new territory when he decides to hit the road as, what else, a fugitive. John Book in *Witness* enters new territory when he chooses to go to his boss after discovering the murderer is a cop and ends up hiding out on an Amish farm to protect the only witness. *Jerry Maguire's* main character enters new territory when he starts his own sports agency with only one employee and one loyal client. Each of these characters faces a tough choice between *two equally distasteful options.*

Is your protagonist a "fish out of water"?

Is he or she a stranger in a strange land? Of course this is metaphorical unless you're writing a sci-fi piece. It could be a farmer in the big city; an urbanite in a little town; even a playboy truly in love for the first time as Eddie Murphy is in the film *Boomerang*. Your protagonist needs to be dealing with something he or she has never had to deal with before. Your *first plot point* needs to create this feeling for the audience.

Keep rewriting Act One, striving to accomplish every element necessary while staying within a tolerable page-count range for each structure milestone, such as Pages 1–10 and Pages 11–30. Look for ways to combine scenes, replace dialogue with visuals, and make the problem in the story affect your protagonist's current life in an increasingly unbearable way until he or she is *forced to make a tough decision* and, by doing so, enters a *new life*, ideally one that makes him or her a *fish out of water.*

In the finest stories, this new territory indeed foreshadows a new life for the protagonist, having him or her soon realize life will never be the same again.

Does the relationship between the protagonist and the antagonist in the subplot also start to get worse?

If not, fix it. Again, this scene can be "inside" a main story scene or be a transition scene that connects two main scenes. This is the *emotional core* of the screenplay and is the place where you should be *exploring the theme* of the story. To give your screenplay a strong central conflict, the subplot relationship should be the catalyst for discovering how the protagonist solves the problem in the main plot. In fact, in Act One, you should be setting up your overall theme.

YOUR ASSIGNMENT

Act One is very important to your screenplay. You must strive to make *every single element* interesting to the audience and fully engage them in your story.

Axiom: Your first important audience is the professional reader!

Necessarily, there are a lot of things being thrown at the *reader* and you must present these elements with the art and craft of a magician. Act One, more than any other act, needs to be very *tight* if you want the *reader* to stay with you for the rest of the screenplay. Some professional readers will stop if the characters and story don't hook them within the first fifteen pages. Many will stop reading altogether after thirty or so pages, taking the attitude that it's not going to get any better. One professional reader told me that after reading close to one thousand screenplays, he found only a handful that actually got better after Act One.

Rewrite Act One until you're happy with it, and then move on.

CHAPTER 9

Rewrite Act Two First Half

DRAMA IS LIFE WITH THE DULL BITS CUT OUT.

—*Alfred Hitchcock, filmmaker*

THE BIG PICTURE

A SERIES OF CONFRONTATIONS.

Act Two is the middle sixty minutes of a movie. That computes into about *sixty pages* of the screenplay. I call this part of the screenplay the *black hole of storytelling* because this is where most stories get *lost in space.*

One useful way to look at this sixty-page challenge is to think of it in smaller segments. Do this on two levels. The first is as *two thirty-minute halves.* Then slice those halves into quarters. You end up with *four fifteen-minute mini-dramas* that all should build toward the story's climax. This approach makes rewriting your screenplay a much more manageable chore.

It's here in Act Two that the protagonist sets out to solve the problem-predicament in the story using the appropriate logic for the type of situation. For example, if the problem has something to do with the criminal justice process, then there's a legal procedure that American citizens must follow. This includes hiring a lawyer, plea, discovery, jury selection, prosecution, and defense presentations, judge and/or jury deliberation, announcing guilt or innocence, sentencing, and appeals.

If your story involves a football coach who wants to win the coveted world championship, the logical process could include summer camp, pre-season, final roster, regular season, playoffs, and the ultimate championship game. Of course, you can start your story at any point in the logical process and end it at any point. For example, Oliver Stone's *Any Given Sunday* tells the story of a burnt-out coach (played by Al Pacino) trying to win one last championship before retiring. But he is confronted by the changing nature of the game's arrogant self-centered players and its profit-hungry owner. The story begins near the end of the regular season and ends just before the championship game.

If there's no set process for your protagonist's particular situation, then you need to create one. A good starting place is the standard approach to solving a problem used by most *reasonable* people. This, at least, gives you—the writer—a compass to help lead your screenplay out of its troubles during the rewriting process. Whether this approach is used consciously or by pure instinct, we all use it.

The Problem Solving Process

1. Define the problem.
2. Determine personal needs.
3. Determine the nature of the problem.
4. Determine possible solution options.
5. Evaluate each solution options.
6. Determine risks for each solution option.
7. Select the best solution option.
8. Implement the best solution option.
9. Validate if the option solved the problem.
10. If the solution option doesn't solve the problem, select a new one, implement, and reevaluate.

However, in the art of storytelling, this scientific approach should be mitigated by taking into consideration the *nature of your characters* involved in the story. For example, if your protagonist is a man of action, he may move forward against all logic by simply jumping into the middle of the problem to create chaos. But you must remember, the audience needs to have some idea of the protagonist's approach or they will get lost or frustrated with the story because it either doesn't make sense or the hero comes off as stupid or impulsive. So you can use this *theoretical model* to analyze how a problem can be solved, then apply your protagonist's characteristics to the process to come up with his own logic or a variation of it that creates conflict in the story. In fact, now is a good time to go back to your character biographies. This is a very useful way to analyze and approach how to fix the plot of your screenplay that doesn't seem to be working. The reason is simple: *structure is based on your protagonist's behavior (actions) in the story in the attempt to remove each obstacle blocking the path to his or her ultimate goal. In the end, the protagonist's actions are based on what he or she believes and values in life.*

THE FIRST HALF OF ACT TWO—GAINING GROUND

Essentially, the protagonist should be *gaining ground* in his or her quest to solve the problem-predicament at this point in the story. Why? It's important to create a flow to the story that takes the audience on a roller-coaster ride over the entire length of the screenplay. So, if Act One sets up the problem, then the First Half of Act Two should see the protagonist making progress toward solving the problem. Then the Second Half of Act Two should see the protagonist lose (or appear to have lost) all or most of what's been gained. And Act Three should see the protagonist either win or lose in the end. This approach creates an *up-now, down-later rhythm* to the protagonist's efforts in the story.

Having the protagonist *gain ground* in the First Half of Act Two also gets the audience rooting for the protagonist to succeed. This embraces the simple idea that nobody likes a loser. So, if you set your protagonist off losing right out of the gate, then the audience will think of him or her as a loser and quickly lose interest. This doesn't mean that everything the protagonist sets out to accomplish in this First Half of Act Two should succeed. There should be ups and downs, but ultimately, the overall effect on the audience should be that the protagonist has gained more ground toward solving the problem-predicament in the story than he or she has lost. Even if your screenplay is an examination of a loser—the underdog—you need to get the audience behind this character early in Act Two or most people won't care what happens. In this case, small victories—probably very personal ones—can do the trick. The protagonist, Rocky, is an excellent example.

A suitable overall *attitude* to have in your efforts to rewrite the First Half of Act Two is to think of your protagonist as *grappling with change*. Then each of the two mini-dramas has its own specific *attitude* that embraces and contributes to this overall feeling.

REWRITE PAGES 31–45: THE FIRST MINI-DRAMA

BUILD TO THE *FIRST CHARACTER GROWTH*.

Look at this as a separate *small* story that connects to Act One and feeds the next small story. There's a beginning, a middle, and an ending that includes a climax and denouement. You might even call this—and the other three mini-dramas—a fifteen-minute screenplay within a screenplay.

Resisting change

This first little *story-within-a-story* opens with the protagonist facing change in a spiritual and/or physical world that is very different from normal. Think about it: whenever you, in your own life, are confronted with change and find yourself in a new situation, the first thing you do is to rely on the knowledge, skills, and resources you already possess. In other words, you *resist change*. In a general sense, that's exactly what your protagonist should be doing in these next fifteen minutes of the story.

Is your protagonist propelled into this "new territory" or "new life" because of a decision made when faced with a moral dilemma?

The decision that *thrust* your protagonist to this point in the story is very important in creating a sense of jeopardy for him or her. It's important to make the change for your protagonist as dramatic as possible. We sometimes call this making the protagonist a *fish out of water*. In the film *Cast Away*, the character played by Tom Hanks finds himself stranded on a deserted island after a plane crash. In *Almost Famous*, a teenager goes on the road with a rock band. Both have clearly become fish out of water.

Very Important: *If your protagonist doesn't get to this point in the story because he or she is forced to choose between right or wrong, you need to fix that in the rewrite.*

If you find that your protagonist moves into new territory without facing a tough choice, this may be weakening the drama of the story. It also makes the protagonist less active and more passive in the story. Of course, there are times and circumstances in a story when it's not practical or believable for the protagonist to make the decision that moves him or her into a new situation. Sometimes someone else in the story should make that decision. If this is true with your story, then you should try to find another way to present the protagonist with a tough decision. That *other* way should relate to the original decision.

For example, in the film *Saving Private Ryan*, Captain Miller (played by Tom Hanks) is told he must take a squad of men to find Private Ryan and escort him back safely. It's a military order and Miller can't refuse his commanding officer. The screenwriter, Robert Rodat, clearly understands how this circumstance weakens the *first plot point* of the story. So, to make it more dramatic, the writer gives Captain Miller a choice between taking a well-trained soldier who can't speak German and French, thus risking his mission, or take a cowardly administrative clerk who can barely point a rifle—risking the lives of the other soldiers—but speaks both languages fluently. This is a stroke of brilliance by the screenwriter since the decision Captain Miller makes appears to be a minor one but actually decides his fate in the story. In an ironic twist of fate, this decision is ultimately a matter of life and death for the protagonist.

In *Cast Away*, Tom Hanks did not have a choice as to whether he would go down with the plane or not. The plane was going to crash no matter what he did. But once he found himself on the island, he had to decide whether to try to get off or adapt to living there, giving up all hope of rescue.

Over the course of your first mini-drama, the protagonist should also *have trouble adjusting to the new situation*. This is normal for any human being who falls into an unfamiliar situation. So your protagonist shouldn't be any different. This part of the story should serve as an adjustment period, and much of the trouble the protagonist experiences here should be the result of his or her inability to grasp how to function in the new environment. These concepts set the undertow of the mini-drama as the protagonist navigates the sea of his problem-predicament in the story.

The most natural way to create conflict in any story is to set the protagonist on the pursuit of an objective—let's call it a *mini-goal*—that falls into the logical process necessary to solve the problem. It's this pursuit that should activate the antagonist in the story to oppose the protagonist, thus creating conflict. So, the middle of this first mini-drama is generated by the protagonist trying to get back his or her old life by making the problem-predicament go away.

The First Major Obstacle

Make sure the first major obstacle is the result of the antagonist (or villain) opposing the protagonist's efforts. Overcoming this first obstacle should provide a high point—a *mini-climax*—for the first mini-drama. Each structure milestone needs an identifiable obstacle with which the protagonist must deal. And the story's antagonist best creates this complication. Using the example from the criminal justice process, if the protagonist needs a good lawyer, this becomes the mini-goal. If the antagonist somehow makes it difficult for the protagonist to find a good lawyer or one lawyer in particular, this creates a major obstacle. In the film *Philadelphia*, a gay lawyer with AIDS finds it most difficult to find a lawyer who will represent his wrongful termination case. It's the influence of going up against the gay lawyer's former employee (and the fact that nobody really wants to get involved with the deadly disease) that creates the obstacle. This first obstacle in the protagonist's new life need not be a tremendous one, but certainly something important has to be at stake. And it should be sufficiently difficult to make the protagonist realize that he or she is going to have a harder time than anticipated in trying to get life back on track. This is called the protagonist's *first character growth*.

What is the first obstacle your protagonist must overcome?

If there's no obstacle presented to the protagonist, then you may be suffering from *too much exposition* in your story. There's a tendency for writers to want to explain character backgrounds at this point in the story. We think the audience will like or dislike a character because of his or her past. While that may or may not be true, the most important barometer the audience uses to judge how they feel about a character is behavior. What the character *does* right now is a pretty good indication of what the character *did* before we met him or her. What and how a character "chooses" also tells the audience a lot about who he or she is as a person. The audience intuitively cares about your characters' moral compasses. Why? Because that's what drives real people through their own lives—whether their compass is a good one or bad one.

So, the act of the antagonist providing an obstacle or complication to the protagonist generates conflict between these two characters and gives us a sense of this character's mettle. The pivotal characters should naturally take sides and fuel this head-on conflict, creating their own brand of conflict with which the protagonist and antagonist must deal.

In beating the antagonist this first time out, your protagonist should learn that his or her current skills are marginally effective in the new situation. So, after spending six or seven scenes trying, your protagonist should experience *first character growth*. It's a good idea to have a *defining scene* that clearly signals to the protagonist that solving the problem-predicament is not going to be all that easy from this point on in the struggle. The scene should also hint that his or her *old life* is slipping away and that solving the larger problem at hand looms ahead more ominously.

In *The Fugitive*, Dr. Kimble's first obstacle is to get away from Lt. Gerard who, after a harried chase, corners him at the mouth of a dam's drainpipe. When Kimble takes the death-defying leap into the turbulent waters below rather than turn himself over to the U.S. marshal, it's clear to the audience that, if he lives, Kimble is determined to prove his innocence. In fact, he's willing to risk his life to that end. He could simply turn himself in to Lt. Gerard and take his chances with the appeals process of his conviction. Had he done so, this would be a very different story structure. Again, it's what the protagonist does—his behavior—that dictates the structure of the screenplay. That is what you have to consider as you rewrite your screenplay.

The Third Subplot Beat

Does your protagonist realize first character growth in regard to being in emotionally new territory with the antagonist of the subplot?

If not, write a scene. Again, this can be a *French scene* or a transition scene connecting two main-plot scenes. The subplot simply mirrors the structure milestone of the main plot. So, conceptually, the protagonist should experience *first character growth* in the subplot relationship. Often, in the subplot love story, the protagonist will lose his love relationship at this point. A more familiar way of saying this, depending on your story, is *boy loses girl* or *girl loses boy*. This seems to go against the classic structure theory of gaining ground for the main plot. So, in doing so here, you set the stages for an up-and-down emotional roller-coaster ride throughout the rest of the subplot and create a situation that creates the screenplay's *central conflict*. If necessary, review the *Hollywood Love Story Structure Template* to clarify this concept in your mind.

Go through the first mini-drama as many times as needed. Focus on these fifteen (or so) pages only. Make sure all the necessary elements are there and working well. When you're happy, or you feel you've done as much as you can in this first rewrite, move on to the next mini-drama.

REWRITE PAGES 46–60: THE SECOND MINI-DRAMA

Build to the point of no return.

As the protagonist enters the second *mini-drama*, he or she should start to realize that life is going to be different from now on. There should be a strong realization that survival in the new situation is becoming more and more paramount—whether it be physically or emotionally. So, he or she does the same thing you and I would do if pushed into a brand new situation—figure out what it's going to take to persevere.

Gaining New Skills

The byword to the protagonist coping in this fifteen-minute mini-drama is *education*. That is, the protagonist must learn to deal with the existing rules in this new life—which should be quite different from the life in which we met this character. Being a fish out of water can mean being different from everyone else. So, the protagonist now sets out to lessen the chill of that status.

Again, there should be a beginning, a middle, and an ending that includes a **mini-climax** and mini-denouement in this second *story-within-a-story.*

You should set your protagonist on a program of sorts where he or she begins to *gain new skills*. In *The Fugitive*, Dr. Kimble decides to go back to Chicago to find the one-arm man himself. Since he's not a detective but a highly trained physician, he has to figure out how to do this. He calls his attorney (not quite letting go of his past life) and doesn't receive help. He tracks down his best friend (a fellow doctor who turns out to be the villain) and gets a few bucks out of him. He gets new clothes, finds a place to live, reads up on prosthetics, and fabricates himself an ID to more safely gain entrance into Cook County Hospital. So, what Kimble is really doing is learning how to *survive* as a fugitive of the law while still pursuing his main goal in the story: catch the one-arm man to prove his innocence.

Accepting Change

This course of action means Kimble is also *accepting change* in his new life. It's only reasonable that you or I would do the same thing, given these circumstances. The more we know how to survive in a new environment, the more we accept the situation.

How is your protagonist learning new things about coping with his or her new life in this mini-drama?

If your protagonist is not gaining new skills, and, as a result, accepting the new situation, then you need to fix this. In *Cast Away* Tom Hanks's character must learn to catch food, build a shelter, and stay sane by literally befriending a volleyball—giving it the name "Wilson"—that he finds on the beach in the plane crash rubble. In *What Women Want*, starring Mel Gibson, a chauvinist advertising executive must learn how to use to his advantage his new skill of hearing women's thoughts in his head.

The Second Major Obstacle

The first question you should answer here is:

How has the "road not taken" from the first mini-drama going to affect the protagonist in this mini-drama?

This second major obstacle should be greater and harder to overcome for the protagonist. Overcoming it will provide a high point or *mini-climax* for this mini-drama. In dealing with this second hurdle, the protagonist's new skills should be of great assistance. Take care not to let the protagonist lose sight of his goal in the story. Though more difficult than the first, getting around this obstacle should at the very least give the protagonist a modicum of confidence and some self-satisfaction.

What is the second obstacle your protagonist must overcome?

So, this fifteen-minute mini-drama consists of the struggle to learn a new way—*gaining new skills*—to solve the new problem while dealing with a new and greater obstacle to reaching the final goal in the story. But that new way can sometimes be the old way warmed over. Of course, it's at this point that your protagonist should fully realize that the old ways are not going to work. As a result, he or she reaches the *point of no return* in the story.

In this mini-drama's defining scene, it should become very clear to us and to your protagonist that he or she can never go back to the way things were before. Life, as it was known, can no longer exist for the protagonist; it's clearly the time to take the bull by the horns and start over. Your protagonist should reach a *midpoint crisis* in the story. This crisis becomes the *source of motivation* for the protagonist to move forward in the story and try to solve his or her problem-predicament in a more timely fashion. Ideally, this should come in the form of another moral dilemma.

In *Witness* John Book calls his partner from a general store in Amish country to learn that the fish stinks from the head. It turns out that a lot of senior police officers are involved in a widespread illegal drug theft. He can't go back to Philadelphia and be an honest cop without the possibility of losing his life. This is definitely a crisis. In *The Fugitive,* Dr. Kimble turns to deceit to solve his problem by changing his appearance and fabricating a fake ID in order to sneak into the hospital. This crisis is a big step for a man who's painfully honest and a slave to the Hippocratic Oath. Denzel Washington's troubled character had to learn how to get around the strong influence of his commanding officer and win the confidence of key crewmembers in *Crimson Tide* or suffer the consequences of starting a global nuclear war—a big crisis.

Don't forget to use the "choice not taken" and to further complicate the protagonist's efforts later in the story.

The Fourth Subplot Beat

Is your protagonist gaining new skills in the subplot?

If not, create a scene. Again, this can appear "inside" a main-plot scene or can be a separate transition scene that connects two main scenes. Again, the subplot's structure mirrors that of the main plot. So, here, the protagonist should also reach the point of no return in his or her emotional relationship.

YOUR ASSIGNMENT

Now you're halfway through your rewrite. Your screenplay story should have a feel that gives the reader (audience) a clear sense of who all the characters are—especially the protagonist. The general mind-set of the first half of your screenplay should be to *develop the characters by the way they deal with change*. Studio story executives often refer to the process as *mining* the characters.

In the next half, it's time to *let the characters perform*. That is, the audience—clued in to who everyone is—should be able to sit back and watch the protagonist go for it. Studio story executives call this process *forcing the action*.

One more thing: the *element of surprise* is also an important ingredient in your screenplay. So don't be afraid to use "smoke and mirrors" on the audience. Don't be afraid to give the audience misleads. For example, in *The Fugitive,* after we see Dr. Kimble get picked up while hitchhiking,

Lt. Gerard gets a call saying the good doctor has been spotted being picked up by a woman. They go all out to search a house, and we think it's Kimble they've cornered. But it turns out to be the black prisoner who escaped with Kimble after the big train wreck. *The Sixth Sense* is full of misleads. In fact, the entire story is based on the concept of misleading the audience. Most of us believe Malcolm (Bruce Willis) is alive because he's in scenes with his wife, the young boy, and the boy's mother. It's later revealed that only the young boy could actually see Malcolm and the other characters were not aware of Malcolm because he's dead.

In addition, you shouldn't be shy about presenting a character in a different light than they really are. Again, in *The Fugitive*, we had no idea that Dr. Kimble's best friend was the evil villain who hired the one-arm man to kill. However, this was *foreshadowed* (set up) in the early scenes of Act One with the return of Kimble's car keys at the fund-raiser. In *Unbreakable*, we think the character portrayed by Samuel L. Jackson is Bruce Willis's friend (a setup) but it turns out he's an archenemy.

Last, don't forget that the First Half of Act Two is about *winning* or *gaining ground* for the protagonist. *A simple way to see this is that the protagonist is stronger than the antagonist in this part of the story.* This gets the audience behind him or her and cheering for success. That doesn't mean the protagonist can't lose a few battles. It's the overall sense that you want to create for the audience by the midpoint of the story.

Rewrite both first and second mini-dramas as many times as it takes to feel good about them. It doesn't have to be perfect because you're going to repeat the rewriting process many times before you're done with your screenplay. Get it as close as you can for now before moving on to the Second Half of Act Two.

CHAPTER 10

Rewrite Act Two Second Half

EVERY MOMENT OF ONE'S EXISTENCE ONE IS GROWING INTO MORE OR RETREATING INTO LESS. ONE IS ALWAYS LIVING A LITTLE MORE OR DYING A LITTLE BIT.

—*Norman Mailer, author*

You're halfway through the first rewrite of your screenplay. Things should really be jelling for you now. You should have opened up some new doors to new ideas about character, plot, and dialogue.

Despite conflict and frustration up to this point, overall, the protagonist's *gains* should have caused him or her to come to terms with the new situation created by the problem-predicament in the story. He or she should fully understand now is the time to face the music head-on in order to survive and get what he or she wants in the end.

THE SECOND HALF OF ACT TWO—LOSING GROUND

Conceptually, the protagonist now begins *seeking truth*. The protagonist firmly commits to using the newfound knowledge, skills, and resources—even though he or she doesn't necessarily like it—in order to solve the problem and reach the goal that's now much more complicated than he or she ever dreamed it could become.

But to keep the story dramatic and the structure strong—thus entertaining—it's now necessary for the protagonist to start *losing ground* in the story. This helps to keep consistent the roller-coaster ride that you want to take your audience on throughout the screenplay. It's here that you now want to have your protagonist set out to solve the problem-predicament *once and for all*. That is, after having *gained ground*, the protagonist feels he or she is ready to literally end the story in the next fifteen-minute mini-drama. If you think about it, this is a common human trait—to set out thinking that a problem can be solved not knowing whether all the pieces are in place for success. We sometimes call this *faith*, other times we call it ignorance. What it is for your protagonist certainly depends on the kind of character you've created.

In the great majority of films, this is the time in the story when things start to go wrong. The stakes are high and the protagonist starts to lose whatever gains have been accumulated toward success. In essence, there should be a shift in strength in the characters' efforts—the antagonist is now stronger than the protagonist. Psychologically, this makes sense . . . the antagonist has accumulated knowledge and is sufficiently frustrated by losing to the protagonist. Now, he or she works harder and smarter to secure his or her goal in the story.

REWRITE PAGES 61–75: THE THIRD MINI-DRAMA

ALL IS LOST.

You can characterize this mini-story as the protagonist's attempt to solve the problem by attacking it head-on. So far, he or she should have resisted the new situation, adapted to it, and by now *fully embraced it.* So, at this point in the story, there's perhaps a bit of cockiness because the protagonist can see some light at the end of the tunnel.

Does your protagonist feel he or she can now solve the problem at hand?

If not, he or she should be in this mind-set or have few choices but to try. Fix it so the protagonist now sets out to reach the goal in the story once and for all. The audience should be feeling that, by the end of this mini-drama, the hero or heroine will bring an end to the story by defeating the antagonist or villain. Theoretically, the protagonist is looking to get to Fade Out somewhere around page 75. The more convinced he or she (and the audience) is of this outcome, the better. The protagonist decides on a course of action that's based upon previous experience since entering this so-called *new life* at the *first plot point.* But, once again, there's something that looms over the protagonist.

The Third Major Obstacle

The *protagonist should encounter the third major obstacle* in the story and it's a whopper! It's the result, of course, of his attempt to solve the problem once and for all and, perhaps, the pressure built up from all the previous choices not taken in the First Half of Act Two. He should simply fail this third time out. Let me repeat that—*the protagonist should fail!* This creates a major setback in the story, and in the process the protagonist *loses* the obvious solution to the problem. The key pivotal character could be killed or kidnapped or the computer diskette is erased or destroyed.

Ideally, the difficulties presented by this third obstacle should be made more serious by the other two choices the protagonist has passed up in previous mini-dramas.

What is the third obstacle that faces your protagonist?

The defining scene in this *mini-drama* is called the *all is lost* point in the story. It's here that all the wind should be taken out of the protagonist's sail. He or she should want to quit and walk away. But it's just not going to be that easy—too much water under the bridge with other characters. The other characters simply won't let the protagonist walk away from the unsolved problem. They, in effect, are on an unrelenting mission of their own. The antagonist or villain is now the strongest, gaining ground, which is quite the opposite of how it was in the First Half of Act Two. So, to repeat, essentially *the protagonist and antagonist trade places in terms of who is winning and who is losing.*

Dr. Kimble in *The Fugitive* feels all is lost when he takes the risk of going to a tightly secured federal lock-up facility to find the one-arm man on his list of suspects only to learn it's not the man with whom he fought in his bedroom. Lt. Gerard feels the same despair when Kimble escapes from the hospital and disappears in the St. Patrick's Day parade.

In *Clear and Present Danger*, the CIA blows up a home that's supposed to have inside all the drug kingpins in South America who have gathered for a meeting. But the one guy they want the most is late and dodges the wrath of the "smart bomb" that turns the home into a huge hole in the ground. In *Gladiator*, the main character, Maximus, has to take off his mask and is exposed in the coliseum by Commodus, the villain, putting a crimp in his plan to get revenge.

Does your protagonist have a major setback in the story at this point?

If not, fix it. Take away the obvious solution to the problem in the story.

The Fifth Subplot Scene

Does the protagonist feel all is lost?

If not, create it. Again, this can be a *French scene* "inside" a main story scene or take place as you make the transition between main scenes. As I've said before, the subplot structure milestones mirror the main plot but focus on the loss of an emotional relationship. This is where *boy loses girl and it looks like it's forever.*

REWRITE PAGES 75–90: THE FOURTH MINI-DRAMA

BUILD TO *BACK AGAINST THE WALL.*

This part of the story is probably where most screenplays fail the most. You must be aware of the potential of creating a "stage wait" that is simply killing time to getting to Act Three. So, begin this last mini-drama by "kicking the protagonist while he or she is down." Most times, this is accomplished by taking from the protagonist an emotional relationship with a likable pivotal character in the story. In this way, you can create a *dark moment*. More often than not, the subplot scene is the best place in which to do this. This serves to make the audience feel the protagonist has hit bottom. Often, the *tragic character*—as he or she is called—dies. To make this work, along the way, the protagonist should have ideally developed a key relationship with a pivotal character who can help solve the problem, or has the possession of—or knows where to get—something that'll simply cut this problem to its quick. This could be a key witness to the murder or the proverbial computer disk that contains all the damning evidence. Or it could simply be a best friend.

In *Clear and Present Danger*, the dark moment occurs when the children are killed in the blast. This hurts Ryan because of his guilt of neglecting his own children for his job. There's another beat that qualifies more as a dark moment for Jack Ryan when his faithful secretary is murdered by his intelligence counterpoint that has used her for information gathering. In *Top Gun*, Maverick (Tom Cruise) freaks out in combat and his likable "backseat driver," Goose, is accidentally killed in the process but he blames himself.

In *Outbreak*, the highly likable and outspoken doctor played by Kevin Spacey dies soon after structure page 75 to create a dark moment for Dustin Hoffman's character and the audience, who depended on the character to speak for them.

A character need not physically die. In *Mrs. Doubtfire*, the Robin Williams' character's dark moment involves him losing custody of his children. For him, this is the same as death; it's a spiritual and emotional loss. However, there's no dark moment in *The Fugitive* mostly because this film uses *the hunt* plot type. Dr. Kimble has no time to develop an emotional relationship with a likable pivotal character. He is mostly alone during his ordeal in the story. So, every story does not utilize this device.

Is there a dark moment for the protagonist (and audience) in your story?

While it's not an absolute requirement (few things are in artistic endeavor) to have one of these moments in your story, it's a wonderful way to create for the audience a sense that the protagonist has reached the lowest point in the story.

On the Run

At this point, the protagonist is down, been kicked hard and feels the absolute lowest. There's lots of sympathy from everyone except the antagonist or villain. Even though the protagonist should want to cash in his or her chips and walk away leaving the problem unsolved, the antagonist or villain and the important pivotal characters should not allow the protagonist to quit.

Does the protagonist quit and try to walk away from the problem?

If your protagonist is not quitting or strongly considering the option of quitting, then you need to fix this.

The concept of *unity of opposites* should kick into full force here. Whatever it is the *antagonist* wants in the story, now is the best opportunity for him or her to get it. But that can't happen unless the protagonist loses. Perfect unity of opposites exists when the protagonist and antagonist want the same thing in the story, whether is be the diamond, the suitcase full of cash, or the girl (or boy). Still surging with the strength of the victory in the last *mini-drama*, the antagonist or villain should now put the hero or heroine *literally* or *spiritually* or *emotionally "on the run"* in the story.

Is your protagonist running away from the problem in the story?

Along the way, the protagonist should learn something important that is a clue as to how to defeat the enemy. This is an important point in your rewrite. This is where you get to revisit your story's theme. You should do this on two levels: *physical* and *metaphysical*. Answer these two questions in this mini-drama. So, the protagonist should find out the *key thing* he or she needs to solve the problem-predicament of the story. It could be the key witness promises to come forward, the missing computer disk turns up—whatever it is that the protagonist needs to solve the problem should appear or be discovered at this point. This unearthing can be witting or unwitting.

The protagonist should also find out a key thing on a metaphysical level. I'm talking about *universal theme*. Whatever it is your protagonist needs emotionally or spiritually in the story, now is the time for him or her to uncover it. And this should happen on a conscious level since it will serve to jump-start the protagonist's efforts to solve the problem in the story. This is where the *central conflict* pays off for the story. So, if it's important for the protagonist to finally realize that life is not worth living unless it's based on truth and integrity, then now is the time for him or her to realize it, putting the problem-solving effort in the main plot into proper perspective.

But the antagonist or villain should remain *unrelenting*. And if the antagonist or villain finds out that the protagonist now knows how to win, he or she is motivated to re-double efforts to defeat the protagonist or get what he or she wants. The antagonist now pushes the protagonist's back against the wall because he or she can't back down now.

It Comes Down to Only One Choice

Having one's back against the wall really means the protagonist has run out of all options in the story except one. So, somewhere around page 90, the protagonist should realize there's only one choice now: to have a final confrontation with the antagonist or villain. This will constitute the *climax* of the story.

In a moment of clarity, the protagonist gets renewed zest for solving the problem by realizing there's only one option left. This constitutes the second and final *true turning point* in the story (the Second Plot Point) because now, more than ever before, the protagonist realizes exactly what it's going to take to reach the goal, to grab that golden ring.

Is facing the antagonist one-on-one the protagonist's only choice?

Now, the protagonist, in effect, can rely upon the thing that he or she didn't have in order to solve the problem between structure Pages 61–75. In other words, *the protagonist is much smarter as a result of having been defeated by the antagonist and is ready to take him or her on for the final time.*

The Sixth Subplot Beat

Does the protagonist feel his or her back is against the wall in the relationship with the antagonist in the subplot?

If not, add it. I remind you again, the subplot structure milestone should mirror the main plot.

YOUR ASSIGNMENT

You've just navigated through the black hole of your screenplay. The Second Half of Act Two should have been about losing for the protagonist. The protagonist hits bottom and works his or her way back up. Your Act Two should be more exciting and full of confrontations and conflicts for your protagonist. There should be evidence that the central character is growing because of events and experiences in the story. And the audience should feel the protagonist is poised to go for it. This constitutes the protagonist's *arc* in the story.

Now that you've finished rewriting Act One and Act Two, you should be feeling pretty good about your screenplay. By taking this approach, the concept of structure should now be ingrained in the story. However, if you're feeling that it's not quite there yet, that's okay, too. Remember, this is an "additive process." You can always start this entire process over and go through the screenplay as many times as it takes to get it right. And you should repeat this entire process many times to make your screenplay the best it can be.

Axiom: In the end, a lot of little changes add up to big improvements.

So, for now, move forward and deal with whatever feelings you may have of shortcomings in your screenplay during the next revision.

CHAPTER 11

Rewrite Act Three

LIFE IS LIKE A PLAY . . . WITH A BADLY WRITTEN THIRD ACT.

—*Cicero*

This is the place in the story when the pressure cooker should be about to explode. The protagonist should have taken the most reasonable courses of action, and now it's time to fix things once and for all.

REWRITE PAGES 91–95: RECOMMIT TO ORIGINAL GOAL

PAUSE FOR THE CAUSE: *RECOMMIT TO ORIGINAL GOAL.*

The count of five pages is more symbolic than real. This "beat" in the story can be as minor as a glance of determination or one line of dialogue. It can also be a sequence. More than five pages, however, may be pushing the envelope of good pacing. If you plan to push the envelope, it better be very interesting stuff.

The metaphoric question the protagonist asks is *How did I get here in the first place?* But before the protagonist embarks on the ambitious final confrontation—the climax—he or she should first pause to *recommit to the original goal* in the story. I like to call this the *quiet moment* of the story not based on noise, but based on reflection. I also think of this time as the *moment of truth* for the protagonist, the look in the mirror—*Taxi Driver* with Robert DeNiro looking in the mirror—you looking at me?

The protagonist, however, has learned a lot since entering this new life and it's at this point that he or she takes stock in the lessons learned. The screenwriter would do well to go back and revisit the first *mini-drama* that unfolds between structure Pages 31–45 and somehow reflect on what happened there. Focus on the initial *moral dilemma*—the First Plot Point—and whether the right decision was indeed made then. By bringing that reflection to this point of the story—right after the Second Plot Point—and giving it a-lesson-learned sheen, you also give the story a sense of *symmetry*, which means you deliver to the audience a sense that the story has come *full circle*.

In the film *Forrest Gump*, this structure milestone runs onscreen for nearly 15 minutes. This is the sequence when Gump starts running across country to find some answers. The idea of running is actually this film's primary metaphor for *recommitting to his original goal* in the story. Along the way, Forrest is credited with creating many American cultural quips and the popular icon of the smiley face. It is a creatively risky sequence, yet it worked well for the audience.

Yet another good illustration is the sequence when Morgan Freeman's character, Red, gets out of prison in *The Shawshank Redemption*. Red spends about a five-minute sequence trying to adjust to life on the outside. When he finds he can't, he recommits by striking out to find the Tim Robbins character as promised earlier in the film. And he does it by committing a crime—breaking his probation. The original sequence ran nearly twice that length. But director (and screenwriter) Frank Darabont cut it down. In a behind-the-scenes special on HBO, Darabont talked about the cuts and noted that, unfortunately for Freeman, a deleted scene was one the actor personally considered an Oscar performance. (He went on to win the Oscar for his turn in the 2004 film *Million Dollar Baby*.)

This is also a good place in the structure to set up the audience for an *unlikely hero* or *heroine* of the story if you intend to use this dramatic device. Perhaps a pivotal character who has created problems for the protagonist or was not fully committed to helping the protagonist now walks away for the last time only to reappear later at a critical time during the climax to help the protagonist win. However, most unlikely heroes tend to disappear from the story around midpoint so the audience can forget about them. This enhances the surprise at the end.

The Seventh Subplot Scene

Does the protagonist recommit to the original goal in the subplot relationship?

If you don't have this in your screenplay, take a hard look at it.

REWRITE PAGES 96–THE END: THE CLIMAX

Go Head-on into the Final Confrontation.

Essentially, by this time in the story's structure, the protagonist should have a fairly clear plan on how to get what he or she wants in the story. The clear realization, conceptually, is that he or she must find and confront the antagonist or villain in order to reach the goal of the story.

Does your protagonist have a plan of attack to confront the antagonist?

In order to maintain suspense, the plan should not be shared with the audience unless things are to go very wrong. Let the audience see the plan unfold. If the plan is to go off track, then knowing the plan helps to create more excitement and suspense for the audience as they watch the protagonist improvise.

The protagonist should go for it. The plan is set into action for the final confrontation. Lines are drawn in the sand and the two sides—the protagonist and antagonist—begin their quests, each to win in their own way. Finally the confrontation occurs and the protagonist emerges as the victor—perhaps with the help of an unlikely hero or heroine. Or the protagonist loses.

Does your climax involve a face-to-face confrontation between the protagonist and antagonist or villain?

If not, you have a big problem. In 99 percent of films, the face-to-face confrontation is used. Why? Because it satisfies a need for the audience to see the "evil" confronted by "good."

The climax can be characterized as having two levels. The first is the *physical climax*. This generally involves the chase scene, the big fistfight, or the shootout. The second level is the *emotional climax*. This is the most important level on which to base a climax. It's here that every word, phrase, scene, and sequence that you've written should come to a focal point. I like to call it *the moment* in the story. In many films, the emotional climax has little or no dialogue. This is ideal in my opinion since film is primarily a visual medium.

The Mnemonic Word or Phrase

If there's dialogue, it generally comes in the form of a *mnemonic word or phrase*. Remember, this dialogue device starts out in the story carrying a negative connotation for the protagonist and by the end of the story has a positive meaning. It's generally repeated in the story two or three times to show the transition.

If you do decide to have a lot of dialogue in the emotional climax, then it needs to be very dramatic and emotional. In the film *Stepmom*, a dying mother and stepmother confront each other about the future of the children in a restaurant. It's a very quiet but emotional final confrontation. In *Good Will Hunting*, Robin Williams and Matt Damon have a whale of a shouting match that ends on a very tearful note of understanding between the two men. This moment is one of the rare occasions in film when "on the nose" dialogue works well. At this point in the story, the characters should have earned the right to speak their minds. However, you should strive to make the developing dialogue nearly *poetic*.

Do you have a mnemonic word or phrase?

If not, consider it. You may have already written it, and at this point you need only to simply exploit it dramatically.

The Double Climax

Some films use this technique quite effectively to jar an audience who thinks the story is over.

In *Alien*, the lone survivor, Ripley, escapes the apparently invincible alien left behind on the doomed spaceship to get blown up by "mother," the computer—only to discover that the alien is smart enough to get on the shuttle craft, too. Then Ripley faces the alien for the final-final time in a second climax. *E.T.* had two climaxes as well; the first being the government guys catching the cute alien only to let him die. The final one sees E.T. come back to life—that call worked—and the kids are forced into a wild chase to get him to his spaceship before it takes off. In *Air Force One*, Harrison Ford as the President of the United States faces the evil terrorist highjacker, kills him—only to face the fact that his 747 cannot land without total destruction. Take care here. Too many endings will weaken the overall effect of the screenplay.

Do you have or need a double climax?

The Twist

Then there's the *unexpected gain* after the climax.

Does your protagonist get something totally unexpected?

This is usually the result of having done the right thing, a reward of sorts. The *twist* is an excellent way to give a story an uplifting ending when the protagonist has lost in the final confrontation. It's certainly a good way to give a bummer or downer ending an uplifting tone that sends the audience home feeling better about the story.

The Eighth Subplot Scene

Does the subplot relationship have a climax?

If not, you really do need this now. It may even be a part of, or happen in the context of, the main story's climax. Once again, mirror the main plot's structure milestone.

Denouement

Though denouement means untying the knot in French, in storytelling parlance, it means to *wrap up all loose ends* in the story. Therefore, any significant relationships formed with the protagonist during the story should be resolved in a satisfactory way. There can be surprises here. And sometimes the resolution is no resolution. But you should show or at least hint at this to the audience, not leave them without a clue.

Have you tied up all major relationships with the protagonist?

If not, it's a good idea to do so now. Don't get too carried away with this. Your screenplay should end quickly after the climax. Anything longer than three pages is probably too long. Sometimes, the denouement contains the subplot's climax and this can serve to hold the audience's attention as long as it's not anticlimactic to the main plot's climax.

Endings

Here, again, are the types of story endings:

1. The protagonist wins.
2. The protagonist loses.
3. The protagonist wins but loses.
4. The protagonist loses by winning.
5. The protagonist wins by losing.

The bottom line is, of course, that your story has a satisfying ending.

Does your story have a satisfying ending?

If not, you've got to fix this.

YOUR ASSIGNMENT

So, at this point, you've actually done at least one thorough *hands-on* rewrite. The story should be getting better, the characters feeling richer or more human, and the plot line much tighter.

Repeat this entire rewriting process many times.

CHAPTER 12

The Polish

YOU'RE NOT DONE UNTIL YOU ABSOLUTELY LOVE EVERY SINGLE WORD AND PUNCTUATION MARK IN YOUR SCREENPLAY.

—*Steve Duncan, screenwriter*

It's much better to consider this last polish as a series of passes through the screenplay. Each pass should have its own purpose. Here's a list of them:

TRACK EACH CHARACTER'S SCENES FOR CONSISTENCY

Basically, you'll need to do this for each primary character: the protagonist, antagonist, and key pivotal characters. Do one pass per character. You're checking to make sure that each character's sensibilities, attitude, and emotions track from *scene-to-scene* in a believable "arc" through the story.

CHECK EACH MAJOR CHARACTER'S "VOICE"

Check to make sure each character speaks his or her mind in a way that's expected. This includes the use of language and speech pattern.

TIGHTEN EVERY ACTION-DESCRIPTION

If it takes three sentences to write an action-description, try to get it down to one . . . or even down to a phrase. The purpose is to speed up the "read."

Eliminate dialogue where characters give each other information they already know or should know.

This helps to cut down on the "talky" effect of dialogue . . . that is, the characters giving the audience information instead of talking to one another in the context of the scene. Also, check to see that scenes that do require exposition are in the form of an argument or disagreement or set in an unusual location or chaotic situation.

LOOK FOR PLACES TO INJECT HUMOR

By this time, you know your characters very well. It always helps to use a funny line here and there, or a comedic situation to help make your characters become more three-dimensional. Even Hannibal Lecter has a sense of humor.

TIGHTEN EVERY LINE OF DIALOGUE

Get your friends and family—or the local theater group—to read your screenplay aloud. Before working on your dialogue, review its role in a screenplay. So, look over the chapter that covers writing effective dialogue.

Axiom: Characters are a part of a story, they don't talk about it.

MORE THAN JUST POLISHING DIALOGUE

By examining every line of dialogue, you're also focusing on each and every character in the story. You're looking for consistency and logic.

THE "PAGE STARE"

There's one *existential* pass you can make on dialogue. I call it the *page stare*. It means you look over each page without reading it. Just stare at each page for several minutes. For some reason this technique will prompt better lines of dialogue. It's also an effective way to catch typos; they tend to jump out more when you're not reading the words. Just turn the pages one by one and stare. If you can get even one line of dialogue that's better than what's there, it's worth the time.

THE FINAL "SHAPE" OF SCREENPLAY STRUCTURE

Remember that your main goal here is to get a good *read*. You're not trying to impress some director with your knowledge of cinematography. *You want to create a page-turner.* Sound structure is a good way to plan and achieve this goal. Once the plan is firmly embedded into the story and plot, it really doesn't matter how long your structure milestones come out to be. Hell, your structure Pages 1 to 10 might be fifteen or even seven. Structural Pages 60 to 75 might end up being twenty or twenty-five.

For example, in *The Shawshank Redemption*, the structure Pages 31 to 45 all-is-lost milestone, First Character Growth, actually takes twenty-six pages instead of the more classic fifteen. Many films are well over two hours but still closely follow classic structure. The story unfolds in the same way but with a different pace. It's more important that your story progress in this way rather than how long each section of the structure turns out to be. *Braveheart* is a good example of a classically structured story that stretches the limits of each structure milestone. Many of director-producer Steven Spielberg's films fall into this category. However, the *ideal shape* is what will give you the best read. If the pages have dramatic impetus, then don't worry too much about it. If the read slows down in spots, then you should go over the structure milestone and try to reshape it so it gets closer to the ideal page count.

Ideally, you want to write your screenplay so that anyone can pick it up, flip to any page and get pulled right into the story. When you can accomplish that—congratulations! You have a solidly rewritten screenplay.

THE REWRITE IS FINISHED—NOW WHAT?

Put your rewritten screenplay aside for at least two weeks and completely forget about it. A month or even longer would be better. A good distraction is to start working on a new screenplay. Then come back, grab it, and find a nice comfortable spot where you can read the thing cover-to-cover without interruption.

When you're done reading it, you should love every single word and punctuation. You should have not gotten bored for a single moment. You should have been turning those pages anxious to see what happens next, feeling even surprise at your own writing. If this is what happened, then you're truly done! If not, repeat the rewriting process until you do feel this way.

In interviews with *Creative Screenwriting* magazine, M. Night Shyamalan (in 1998) and Robert Rodat (in 1999) discussed rewrites of their screenplays, for *The Sixth Sense* and *Saving Private Ryan*, respectively. Shyamalan rewrote *The Sixth Sense* about ten complete times. It wasn't until around draft five that he realized he was approaching the story in ways the audience had seen before. He literally stripped the story down to its basics and started over for the next five drafts. Rodat rewrote *Saving Private Ryan* in eleven complete drafts. Rodat explained that he likes to use the first four or five drafts to get the story and structure right. Then he uses the remaining drafts to concentrate on character and dialogue.

Axiom: Learn to love rewriting. In the end it's this process that makes your script excellent.

Now, before you send it to your agent (or out to prospective agents), I suggest you take a few days to feel good about your creation. Put it on your nightstand for several nights so you see it when you go to bed and when you wake up. It'll make you smile inside. Your screenplay is a child that you've created in the womb of your imagination. But now it's all grown up. It's time to let your baby go out into the big bad world. You're going to receive all kinds of suggestions from people in and out of the entertainment industry. Everyone has an opinion. There are only two rules I believe screenwriters should follow religiously after sending one of their babies out into the world . . .

Rule #1: *Never forget you're looking for the one person who will love your screenplay and also have the power to purchase and/or get it produced.*
If there is more than one interested person, that's icing on the cake.

Rule #2: *Rewrite your already thoroughly rewritten screenplay (which you already love) only if the feedback from several different sources is consistent about the same element(s).*

Otherwise, you'll drive yourself insane trying to please everyone who reads your screenplay. When you get that agent or option or sale, the real work begins. *Rewriting* for those who have a personal and financial stake in your screenplay is going to be your biggest challenge. Good luck and happy rewriting. It never stops until the film from your screenplay is released to the public.

CHAPTER 13

The First Draft Spec Feature

FENG SHUI OF SCREENWRITING—THE YIN AND THE YANG

WRITING AND SELLING ARE TWO VERY DISTINCT ARENAS.

Try hard to keep these two processes separate. Persistence and timing are the most important elements. Most new screenwriters begin by writing a **spec** script (one that is written without a contract or payment). A lot of new screenwriters want to know *"Now that I've finished my first spec screenplay, what should I do?"* My answer is always *"start writing another one."* Of course, there are other things you need to be concerned with now that you've pushed your first child out into the world. Like a parent, you're still responsible for the care and feeding of your "baby." But now, you must work with others. A representative is one of them.

FEATURE AGENTS AND MANAGERS

IT'S A LOVE-HATE RELATIONSHIP.

Having an **agent** is like being married without sex—unless you're married to your agent. In my opinion, that's like performing your own heart surgery. It seems everyone gets an agent in one's own unique way. Sometimes it doesn't happen until the screenwriter has virtually sold the script himself or herself and then the agents start to come out of the woodwork.

Let me first explain the difference between an agent and a manager. The essential difference is that an agent can legally negotiate a contract for the screenwriter. Managers can't. The role of the **manager** for writers has grown considerably in the past ten years. It used to be that actors had managers, not writers. But as the competition increases in the industry for talent, agents have not paid as much attention to developing writing talent as they have in the past. Managers simply picked up the slack. In your career as a screenwriter, you'll definitely need an agent. But you don't necessarily need a manager. You can have both, and at some point, you'll need an **entertainment attorney** too.

The important thing to remember about agents, managers, and attorneys is that they work for you. On the flip side, they're working to make a living, too. Agents, by law, get 10 percent of the selling price of the screenplay. Managers generally get 15 percent but can negotiate a larger percentage.

Attorneys generally require a retainer fee and bill on an hourly basis. Some lawyers will work on a project-by-project basis for 5 percent of the selling price of the screenplay. This is why agents and managers are most interested in screenwriters who are in it for the long haul—writers who have a stack of promising scripts that show multifaceted talent. Ironically, it's the first sale that'll *pigeonhole* you as a certain type of screenwriter. For most, that's not a big problem unless one can't get work in the particular area in which one has been pigeonholed.

In my opinion, it's important for you to work at finding your own agent or manager. It's a very personal decision. A good start is to obtain a list of "signatory" agents from the Writers Guild of America. There's a branch in Los Angeles and one in New York City. This list will indicate what agencies are willing to consider new screenwriters and they are contractually obligated to abide by the guild's **Members Basic Agreement**, which sets forth the union working rules. There's no list of managers, although you can find plenty of them listed in the *The Hollywood Creative Directory of Agents and Managers*. This directory costs money and is available in book form or electronically on the Internet (which is updated more often).

Once you choose agents and/or managers to approach, write solid query letters to them. Include a description of your screenplay and your background. If agents are interested in reading your screenplay, they will write you back or call. It's not a bad idea for you to call these agents as a follow-up to your query letters. Or even call them before you send query letters to make sure they are still open to new clients.

What makes a good query letter? First, it should be no longer than one page. Realize this letter gives the reader a pretty good clue as to what kind of writer that you are. It represents you. So, it should be well written. That also means no typos, misspelled words, or grammar errors. Here's a good format to follow:

First paragraph: *Hook* the reader with an engaging first line. Then tell the premise of your screenplay in one or two sentences (sound familiar?).

Second paragraph: Suggest the actor or actors who might be perfect to star in your screenplay and/or how your screenplay fits into the current marketplace (this is a business). Be realistic.

Third paragraph: Tell the agent a little about yourself—but only the facts germane to you being a writer or your experiences in life as it relates to your screen story. You should always call yourself a *screenwriter* . . . not an aspiring one . . . regardless of that day job.

Last paragraph: Give your phone and fax numbers and your e-mail address if you have one. Ask the agent to read your screenplay and advise him or her that you'll make a follow-up call in several weeks.

Be sure to make that follow-up call. And be prepared to pitch your screenplay over the phone.

Some people say these days that it's a waste of time to send a query letter because agents and managers don't read them. Well, maybe many of them don't. But some do. And you must take every opportunity possible if you want to attain representation.

The process of finding an agent or manager can be a tedious but rewarding experience. When you connect with someone who warms to your work as well as your creative talent—it's like winning the lottery. What you gain is someone who will praise you, push you, and criticize you, occasionally tick you off, and—in the process—help build your career as a professional screenwriter.

The Internet

With the widespread use of the World Wide Web, many agents, managers, studio executives, and producers subscribe to or offer websites that post screenplays. How this process works varies widely.

Some websites are free. Most require a monthly payment in order to post your properties. There is also a ton of screenwriting contests listed on the Internet. The only words of wisdom I can give you in this area are *approach with caution*. Investigate before turning over your material to the *world* to read.

THE PITCH

IT'S A SURPRISINGLY VERBAL BUSINESS.

Pitches are meetings where the screenwriter describes the story. These *pitch meetings* can also take place over the telephone. The opening sequence of screenwriters pitching film ideas in the Robert Altman opus *The Player* is eerily authentic.

Learning the art of the pitch is important. Basically, you have about ten minutes to grab a producer or executive's attention and get them interested in a story while they continue to conduct their daily office routine. It's a daunting experience that's more and more reserved for experienced screenwriters who already have screen credits.

You still need to learn how to pitch because even your agent will ask you to pitch ideas to him or her. So will producers when you least expect it. Always be prepared to pitch your latest idea and certainly all of your finished screenplays. Practice on your significant other, friends, and family. If you see eyes glaze over, then you have a problem with your pitch. But if they get involved in your storytelling, you're on to something.

Salesmanship is an important skill for screenwriters to develop. So, take a few pages from people who sell for a living. Here are several very important guidelines to follow:

What Does the Buyer Need? It helps tremendously to know what a producer or studio executive is looking to purchase before you go into a pitch meeting. Otherwise, you're taking a shot in the dark. The ironic thing is that you still have a chance to sell a good idea or screenplay premise regardless of what they're looking for.

Emphasize Benefits. Always tell the target of your sales pitch how your screenplay is going to benefit him or her. If you're talking to studio executives, their interest is in making a hit film or attracting a hot actor or director to a project. If it's agents, their interest is in finding the right studio or producer to push your screenplay or seeing his or her name in *Daily Variety* and earning a 10 percent commission on the sale's total price. Bottom line: potential buyers are most interested in the answer to the question, *What is this going to do for me?*

Ask for the Order. Never fail to put a gentle pressure on potential buyers by asking for what you want. That's why you're going through the process, right? What if they say no? They will more often than not. That's the reality of this business. But use the "no" as an opportunity to get another pitch meeting or to send another one of your screenplays for reading. People feel bad or at least a little guilt when they have to turn down writers. So, take advantage of one of their rare moments of weakness.

There are also lots of colorful stories of how screenplays have been delivered to potential buyers, locked in briefcases with a phone number to call for the combination, or the one where actors showed up dressed like characters in the story to deliver the screenplay to a studio executive. This is salesmanship but it is also high risk. In my opinion, nothing replaces good old-fashioned storytelling or an excellent idea presented precisely.

Be prepared for your agent search by writing a very strong logline of your finished screenplay. That's a two- or three-sentence pitch of your screenplay. It has to present the essence of the story but with a bit of sizzle to it. It's like an advertisement.

You want to create interest. Also, you should write a one- or two-page synopsis of your screenplay. This should present the story's beginning, middle, and ending in an exciting way. *If you plan to enter your screenplay into contests, you will need a one-page synopsis.* However, don't forget, you want to entice the reader to want to read your screenplay. *Don't give this to anyone unless they insist on it.* You don't want to discourage anyone from reading the entire screenplay.

THE SYNOPSIS

There's an art to writing a synopsis to your screenplay. Here are some basic guidelines:

Start with a solid logline of no more than three sentences that really give the essence of the screenplay. This is sort of a cross between your one-sentence premise and an advertising hook.

Tell the story in broad strokes. If your screenplay is plot driven, then you will have to summarize events. The goal is to capture the major plot points that tell the story.

Keep the synopsis length between one and two pages, single-spaced, no longer. The point of the synopsis is to encourage someone to read your screenplay because most people in the industry do not like to read (unless they're paid to do it).

Use visual language, glittering generalities, and create *sizzle* for your story.

Here is a general outline for a synopsis:

> The *hook*.
>
> Explain the protagonist's problem-predicament.
>
> Tell how the problem gets worse for the protagonist.
>
> Describe the protagonist's moral dilemma (first plot point).
>
> Describe how the protagonist *gains ground* in the story by overcoming one or two major obstacles presented by the antagonist.
>
> Describe the protagonist's major setback and how the antagonist *loses ground*.
>
> Describe how the protagonist bounces back from the setback and back against the wall (second plot point).
>
> Describe the climax and ending.

If you follow this general flow, you'll end up with a pretty solid synopsis of your screenplay. By the way, this is also a good outline for developing a pitch of the screenplay. Finally, avoid using writer's vocabulary or jargon. Be a storyteller!

SAMPLE SYNOPSIS

ONE DEAD SLOB, TWO VILLAGE IDIOTS, THREE SOUL BROTHERS

A Dark Comedy-Thriller Screenplay Written By Steve Duncan

A 22-year-old prodigy professor finds herself being stalked by a killer after the murder of the chancellor and unwittingly uncovers a dark family secret as her divorced ambitious mother and father compete to get the dead chancellor's job.

The story opens with *Angela Brown* hiding in the closet of her old Gothic house, wearing a negligee while listening to her stalking killer approaching. She turns and looks us right in the eye and begins to tell the story . . . It all started with the murder of *Chancellor Burkhardt. Chief Meyers,* the only cop in town, decides on his prime suspects: Angela, her mother, *Rose,* and her father, *Gene.* Rose is promoted to interim chancellor at Bartlett College and quickly promotes her daughter Angela to fill her now vacant position. This does not make Gene happy. Then someone tries to kill Rose. Angela falls for her own replacement—*Brad,* a handsome fellow from California. The town's journalist—school-dropout-turned-editor of the local paper also investigates. Angela and her father are attacked by a geek swinging a baseball bat. She discovers her father is taking a mysterious drug.

Put off by Gene's strange behavior, Angela turns private detective and discovers the murder weapon in her father's closet. She also finds out that the mysterious prescription is used for schizophrenia. Meanwhile, a stranger visits the dropout newspaper editor and reveals Chief Meyers's shady background. When Rose is attacked again at her own home, she lies to Angela and Brad about not knowing who it is. She knows. Angela feels that her mother is lying to her and goes to the doctor who wrote her father's prescription. He turns out to be a psychiatrist. Now Angela is sure her father killed the chancellor. The dropout newspaper editor uncovers that Chief Meyers shot down a young black boy while serving in the Boston Police Department and the young boy was the son of this mysterious visitor.

Angela finally confronts her mother about the schizophrenia. Her mother takes Angela to confront Gene together. Rose shocks Angela by shooting him, right before her very eyes. While Rose is arrested and pleads self-defense, Angela goes to the childhood address listed in her dead father's medical file. She discovers that her grandfather is none other than Mr. Kensington, the richest man in the state and primary contributor to Bartlett College's endowment. Kensington tells Angela to back off. While Boston Police interrogate the baseball bat-swinging geek, Angela discovers the murdered corpse of the psychiatrist. Rose finally confesses to Angela that she knew the truth all along. Rose's case gets dismissed as self-defense while Angela finds a lockbox containing proof that Gene's not her real father! Angela feels betrayed by Rose.

Meanwhile, Chief Meyers is arrested for murder since the only eyewitness has recanted her testimony. After learning that Kensington has died in his sleep of a drug overdose, Angela brings Rose into a meeting with Kensington's attorney. It's revealed that Angela will inherit all of the old man's money as long as she works at Bartlett College. Rose is to get nothing and goes berserk! We learn that Kensington had had Gene sterilized when he was just a young teenager and that Gene *is* her biological father but not through Rose! Angela is the product of Gene's impregnation of his adopted mother—Kensington's late wife.

Outside the attorney's office, Angela is accosted by the released baseball bat-swinging geek who promises to get even. The stalking assassin now finds Angela hiding in her closet—it's Rose with a gun. Before killing Angela, she reveals that Kensington had had her sterilized as well to prevent her from getting pregnant when the old man sexually abused her! And that she's the one who killed the old man with the overdose. But Brad shows up and wounds Rose in a shootout. And in the attic of the Gothic house, Rose leaps through a window to her death, committing suicide. All ends well as Angela resigns from Bartlett College, giving up millions of dollars in order to become a professor at Harvard and earn her own way in life . . .

(*Note:* The screenplay placed seventh in the Writers Digest 1999 Writing Competition.)

THE BUSINESS OF SCREENWRITING

IT'S A BUSINESS.

Let me repeat that louder—it's a business! *Spec scripts* drive the film development market. These are screenplays written outside the influence of a studio or producer or pay, with the hope they'll be produced. Some big producers even work with screenwriters while they're writing a spec script, before taking it to a studio.

Studio deals—whether "Exclusive" or "First Look"—tend to be reserved for the "hot" writers and/or writer-directors or experienced producers. Actors who emerge as stars also may sign major studio development deals.

Agents and managers often try to marry your spec script with a writer, producer, director, star, or combinations thereof, who have these studio deals. This is referred to as *packaging*.

Development hell is an accepted phrase for being hired to write a screenplay or to rewrite your First Draft screenplay with an eye toward making it into a film. This is lovingly referred to as *hell* because it seems that most days in this process is in the hands of Satan. Everyone has an opinion, everyone wants his or her way, and often, the screenwriter is left out of the decision-making process altogether—except when facing the computer screen. That's always all alone. But the good news is you're getting paid to write when your screenplay is in "development."

Bidding wars are much talked about but in the large scheme of the entertainment industry, it's a rare occurrence. There's not that many multimillion dollar spec scripts being bought over the run of a year compared with all the others being written and marketed. Thousands of screenplays are registered at the Writers Guild of America every year. Thousands are read by various studio executives, their staffs, agents, actors, directors, and producers and hyphenates of every type. Few become the center of a bidding war. Most screenplays go through a rigorous process that may take years before it falls into the right hands under the right business conditions to get purchased at average market value. It's good to know this because it should give you the perspective you need to keep writing. Many hit movies take years to get mounted. Time does not betray the quality of good writing. If anything, time *verifies* quality.

THE WRITERS GUILD OF AMERICA

THIS IS "BIG BROTHER" IN THE TRUEST SENSE.

You can become a member of this guild when you sell a screenplay. There's a fee to join, and you pay quarterly dues based on the income you receive from screenwriting or a modest flat rate if there is no writing income. The WGA also provides its members with valuable services such as credits arbitration, collective bargaining, professional development, health and pension plans, the management of residual income, and even a social life. You can find out more about the Writers Guild of America by visiting its website at www.wga.org.

It's a big club where relatively few members work on a regular basis, let alone make a living at writing screenplays. How to financially survive as a screenwriter is, of course, an eternal question all of us face.

THE FINAL SHOT

The biggest mistake writers make across the board is to put work out on the market before it is ready. So . . .

Rewrite! Rewrite!! Rewrite!!! And then rewrite some more . . . until you love every single comma, period, word, phrase, and line of dialogue.

Then prepare for more rewrites if you're lucky enough to sell your screenplay.

PART III

Writing for Television

To write for television, you should be familiar with the basic concepts of story premise, plot, character, dialogue, the rules of story structure, and screenplay format. However, there's one big difference in television versus feature film writing that you must grasp immediately.

Rule breaking by freelance TV writers is a no-no!

The most important thing to remember about writing an **episode** of a current television series is this: It's not your job to change or fix what you think is wrong with an established program or to invent new characters for it. Your job is to *mimic* the series perfectly and write its characters accurately within the bounds of an original story that befits the series' week-to-week blueprint.

In fact, a successful "spec" episode has to read like it was written by one of the show's producers. To be noticed, it should be better than what the program has written and aired to date while staying within the boundaries of the series concept. Your story premise should fit into the series. If the series utilizes more than one storyline in each episode—which is the case in most drama and comedy series—then you must develop more than one storyline for your spec teleplay.

The examples presented in this text are designed to illustrate basic format and approach. Each series has its own rules, conventions, and little quirks. Read teleplays for the series for which you are writing; check the Internet for available downloads of teleplays. Many downloads that are available online are *transcripts* of episodes. That means there's only dialogue and the script is not in proper teleplay format. If you're in Los Angeles, there are bookstores at which you can purchase teleplays. Some are via the mail or you can visit the Writers Guild of America to use their library. You can read teleplays there; however, you will not be allowed to copy or check them out.

Much of this part of the book embraces what I call the *classic television series structure.* This approach—in a word—works. And it's surprisingly universal from series to series. If you want to be arty and push the boundaries of a particular television series, I can confidently say you're barking up the wrong tree. That's the domain of writers who create new series. Most of this section applies both to drama and comedy. However, I've included a chapter on the *situation comedy* to cover significant differences.This part of the book is designed to be used as a stand alone. So, I review some key screenwriting basics but with an eye toward how they apply to television writing. Let's get started.

CHAPTER 14

Which Series to Write

WRITING FOR A NEW SERIES

It's very tough for any writer who's not on staff of a new series to **pitch** and/or sell a "spec" teleplay to that series. The first year of a series is highly volatile. Often, the program's producers themselves spend the first half of the first season searching for the heart of the series. There's no way for anyone to know which character or, more important, which actor playing a particular character will strike a chord with viewers and critics. And sometimes characters leave the series in the first season.

For you to write a spec script for a brand new series is akin to going to Vegas and playing craps. You have no way of knowing what the creators will do with the characters—especially in the first twelve or thirteen episodes. But most important, nobody knows how long a new series will stay on the air. So, you would be better off to write a spec script for the most respected television series on the air.

WRITING FOR AN ESTABLISHED SERIES

It's much easier to write or even get the opportunity to pitch a story idea to an established series. Well, it's not exactly easy. But, if a program has been on the air for two years or more, it's established and more open to stories from freelance writers. If a show is marginal in the ratings, then it's always at risk of being canceled. It's hard to second-guess the network executives who, themselves, don't always know which series they will keep year-to-year.

One important fact to remember is, if you're going to write for an established series, the obvious stories are generally a waste of your time. You should strive to come up with unique storylines that have not been used on the series. Admittedly, this is a difficult thing to do and it presupposes that you've watched every single episode that's been produced. Internet websites have become a partial solution to this problem by offering a place to download information that often includes loglines or story summaries of every episode that's been produced. Of course, this doesn't include the stories that were rejected. That's an unknown with which we all have to live.

Once you have your idea, start developing it into a story with a beginning, a middle, and an end. If you haven't done so, do your homework on the particular series you're writing and assemble a **series bible**. A bible is a document that contains pertinent information on the series' premise, franchise, characters, and produced episodes.

Remember, you need to get the stars of the series involved in your storylines. This is sometimes called to **service the money**. So, use each and every main character in the series in some dramatic role—protagonist, antagonist, or pivotal character.

After a series gets its second year order—announced usually around May of each year—and the program is earning respectable ratings and/or critical acclaim, that's a clear nod that it's safe to write a spec teleplay for that series. The key word here is *respectable*. It's sometimes hard to make a list of these shows, but it's the kind of thing you (and agents) simply know by watching TV, reading *TV Guide* and other entertainment publications. If a series is winning awards and praise then that's a good sign even if it isn't in the Top Twenty Ratings Winners.

Booming Times for the Drama

The one-hour drama thrived in prime time during the 2004 to 2005 season (September through May). In no particular order, the following series appear to have legs to stay on the air for years to come. These are among the series for which you should consider writing a spec:

Desperate Housewives
Boston Legal
Lost
Law & Order franchise
CSI franchise
Without a Trace
The Shield
Nip/Tuck
Monk
Smallville
Everwood
The O.C.
Grey's Anatomy
Cold Case

Since television is a dynamic medium—a politically correct way of saying viewers are fickle and unpredictable—some of these series could and will be canceled at any time. And other series will become hits. So, check your local listings before proceeding.

Tough Year for Comedy

Situation comedies (sitcoms) had a tough time finding audiences in 2004–2005. Here are the few that remain good candidates for which to write a respectable spec:

Scrubs
Two and a Half Men
Will & Grace

Again, this fortune could turn at any time. Before *The Cosby Show* appeared in 1984, critics announced that the sitcom was dead. Then after that series became a big hit, many critics revised their proclamation to announce drama was dead on television. So, it's all come full circle in just over one decade. Again, check your Nielsen ratings before deciding which comedy you will write for your spec.

THE BASIC STORYLINE PREMISE

Once you've decided on what series to write, whether drama or comedy, you need to come up with a solid story premise. In today's ensemble oriented series, you'll need to come up with more than one story premise per episode. These are called **multiple storylines**. As a general rule, situation comedy has always used multiple storylines in each episode.

Let's now look at the basic elements needed to develop a solid premise for a television storyline.

THE AREA

WHAT IS THE *THEME*?

Most writers of teleplays begin here because this is the place where a television series can truly explore specific subjects through its regular characters. A good example of an **area** is *date rape*, or *international art thief*, or *serial killing*, or *doctor-assisted suicide*, or *police corruption*. Of course, the type of series for which you are writing heavily influences this choice because it should somehow fit into the general context of the program's genre. If you're writing for a sitcom, the area would most likely be something like *faithfulness* or *parents lying to a child* or the ever popular theme of *sex*. Sitcoms tend to stay away from "heavy" themes such as murder and rape. Occasionally, you will catch an episode of a comedy that's very serious, but it is rare even then there will be laughs.

The basic idea here is to insert the characters' beliefs and values that regularly appear in a television series—who are called the **series regulars**—into a specific subject area so that we—the loyal viewers—can get to know more about each of these characters each week. Some writers and producers also call this the *arena*. Putting one or more series regulars into a specific subject area or arena should always lead to the next important element of the premise—*a problem*.

THE PROBLEM

WHAT IS THE SOURCE OF *CONFLICT*?

The most dramatic type of problem for a television character to face comes in the form of a *moral dilemma*. This type of predicament always offers the protagonist of the story a choice between doing what is *right* or what is *wrong*. And the most powerful dilemmas in drama and comedy always offer equally distasteful choices to the protagonist.

THE PROTAGONIST

WHO IS THE STORY *ABOUT*?

At the heart of every story is a character who's grappling with a specific problem. The story is told from this character's point of view, and the solution to the problem should ideally come as a result of the actions of this character.

THE PROTAGONIST'S GOAL

WHAT DOES THE PROTAGONIST WANT?

The act of solving the problem involves the protagonist developing a clear and precise goal. Whether it is to "stop a criminal from killing again" or to "help some poor soul die in peace" or—in the case of a comedy—to "trick a child into telling the truth," this goal is best complicated when the very solution puts the protagonist at the doorstep of yet another problem. When you can do this as a storyteller, you're creating a suspenseful and compelling drama or comedy that always portrays hard choices and, perhaps, offers a few responses to the problem at hand.

Generally speaking, the protagonist in a storyline of an episode is a character who appears each week on that series. There are some exceptions to this but, for the most part, series producers and network executives prefer to feature the stars—the **money**—as the producers sometimes affectionately call the actors.

THE ANTAGONIST

WHO GETS IN THE WAY?

Someone must complicate the protagonist's efforts of solving the problem in a storyline and that's the job of the antagonist. Of course, giving this "dramatic role" to a series regular is the ideal—especially in ensemble programs. Series that feature only one, two, or three regular characters usually leave this dramatic role for guest stars to take on. In fact, some series include this as a part of the program formula.

Also falling into this category is the villain. Because villains tend to be despicable and unlikable, this dramatic role tends to fall more to guest stars than a regular character in a series. However, when this is the approach, an astute viewer easily guesses whodunit. The cable series *Monk* is especially guilty of this weakness. So, my guess is the audience savors how Monk will figure out the case more than who actually is guilty. There are, of course, exceptions such as the character J.R. Ewing from the classic prime-time soap series *Dallas* (1978–1991). Audiences loved to hate this character. It's an unusual phenomenon for this type of character to be embraced by the audience in prime time. It tends to be the stuff of daytime soap opera.

Now combine all of these elements to come up with a sound story premise:

1. An area or arena
2. A problem
3. A protagonist
4. A strong goal for the protagonist
5. An antagonist who opposes the goal.

One other element is also necessary—*a setting*. This is provided to you as part of the television **series franchise**. Carefully look over the Sample Storyline Premises and use them as a guide to developing your own.

SAMPLE STORYLINE PREMISES

TOUCHED BY AN ANGEL—"SEPARATE LIES"

A Spec Written by Steve Duncan & Jean V. Duncan

A-Story: Tess assigns Monica to help a wife find and reconcile with her bigamist husband who faked his death in order to focus on a secret marriage.

B-Story: Tess assigns Andrew to bring to light fraud in a chain of funeral homes that fakes deaths and funerals for financial gain.

C-Story: The son from the abandoned marriage finds the brother he always wanted in his "dead" father's second marriage.

Runner 1: The father who abandoned his son must reconcile with him.

You should have noticed how precisely the premise for each storyline is written. They're short and hard-hitting. You must work hard to make each of your premises read in the same straightforward manner. Rewrite each as many times as it takes to accomplish this. It's from clearly conceived premises that you will be able to successfully generate solid stories.

STORY

We'll examine *television story structure* later, but the most important thing to do at this point is to expand your basic premise for each storyline into these three components:

Beginning: How a story starts—the inciting incident, the hook, how the protagonist gets involved, what's his or her goal to finding a solution, and who's complicating the effort. Include the protagonist's moral dilemma.

Middle: How the story unrelentingly gets more complicated by the protagonist confronting the efforts of the antagonist who is trying to create a different solution or even the same solution with a different approach.

Ending: How ultimately the protagonist succeeds or fails in reaching his or her goal of solving the problem at hand and the lessons learned by all.

Character "Arc" in Story

This is a simple concept already discussed in Part I of this book. It means that characters—primarily the protagonist—goes from one emotional place in the story to another and this transition or growth or even change happens gradually over the course of the entire story.

Each character should experience an *arc* in an episode. However, it's not so uncommon for a particular character not to change in one episode. So, in this case, a character may grow or change over several episodes, an **episode arc**; a full season, a **season arc**; or even over several seasons, a **series arc**.

STORY VERSUS PLOT

At this early stage of your teleplay's development, it's very important to distinguish between story and plot. So, let's review these concepts:

Story is "what happens." We sometimes call this the **narrative or spine**. Bottom line, "story" deals with the emotions of characters—especially focusing on those of the protagonist. These emotions are always sensitive to the problem at hand and what the protagonist *wants, needs, and feels* about particular solutions.

Plot is "how it happens." On the other hand, plot deals with specific events that are caused by the actions of the characters. How they behave is what generates the basic plot of a storyline.

You can clearly see that story *generates* plot—not vice versa. So, while developing your basic story, stay away from the "how it happens" stuff and concentrate on what the protagonist wants, needs, and feels in each of your storylines. This is sometimes called *writing from the inside out*.

THE PURPOSE OF A SPEC TELEPLAY

The Writers Guild of America recommends that series producers give out at least two freelance scripts each season. This is not a requirement or a part of the Members Basic Agreement (the MBA). The irony is that the series for which you write your spec is probably the last place you'd want to send it to be read, because it's tough to impress the people who write the program every week. Besides, the reality is that most of the "freelance" assignments go to friends of the staff producers. These friends tend to be writers with experience and good credits. Also, studios often invoke the *right of assignment* clause to compel writers who are under contracts called *overall deals* to write for their series. The writing fee is then charged against the writer's contract, essentially giving them free episodes. Your spec, then, is better off being read by the producers of a series with a similar franchise. If you write a spec for one cop show, then all the other producers of cop shows should be the primary targets for your spec.

On a fairly new series—the first two years—the staff writes stories that best fit the concept of the series but generally strive very hard to avoid using the most obvious ideas for storylines. So should you. You really have to come out of left field with your premises and stories. Write something the series producers might never think of writing. Those are the teleplays that most get noticed.

You're writing a *spec* for one reason and one reason only: *Prove you understand how to write for television.* The spec teleplay should open doors for you as a writer. These doors include gaining representation such as an agent and/or manager. This, in turn, gets you the opportunity to pitch ideas to series producers. It's an incredible long shot that someone will actually purchase your spec script. However, it is possible. I address a career as a television writer in a later chapter.

YOUR ASSIGNMENT

Develop story premise(s) for one episode of the series for which you intend to write. Remember that it's important for you to choose a series that is respected and that you also enjoy watching regularly.

Also, develop a practical analysis—a bible—of that show. Include a clear description of the series premise, its format, and character sketches of each regular character to make sure these characters are clear in your mind. Most TV programs have a website containing a lot of background information and assembling a bible is as simple as downloading web pages. Read interviews with the series creator and producers to gain valuable insight into their thinking. Also, the website *www.tv.com* (formerly, www.tvtome.com) lists every series ever produced and provides in-depth information on each such as a cast list and a description of every episode produced. This is an excellent resource for television writers.

The better you understand the series, and the more you personally like it, the better your spec episode will turn out.

CHAPTER 15

Television Characters

TV SERIES CHARACTER DEVELOPMENT

The reason audiences come back to a series week after week is its characters. Therefore, it merits another discussion as it relates to your efforts to turn your premises into full-blown storylines.

One very important idea to understand about character development in a series is to know that it's not your place as a freelance writer—an outsider—to fix or change any of the characters. That does not mean you can't take the existing characters right to the edge of a personality quality that already exists. Human beings are unpredictable and capable of any action given a set of circumstances. However, if you choose to do so, by the end of your "spec" episode you must put things back to where they were in the ongoing series. Suppose you decide that a series regular gets pregnant in the episode you're writing. Then by the end of that storyline, she better be without child. You might kill off a character but it better be that he was just missing and presumed dead by the end of the episode.

It's perfectly fair game to play around with the characters but take care to have these characters behave and think in the established framework. It's shaky ground because you do want to be as original as possible without violating the basic principles of the series creator.

CHARACTER TRIANGLES

The principle of character triangles apply to television writing just as it does to feature writing. The heart of *dramatic action* centers on how your characters' emotional decisions ignite physical behavior toward other characters in the story. Therefore, the ideal scheme for focusing each storyline is to clearly triangulate the basic dramatic roles. This means each storyline has a strong *protagonist, antagonist,* and at least one *pivotal character* that bring a different point of view to the central problem-predicament. Of course, there can be more than one pivotal character involved in each problem and, in television, this is more the rule. Essentially, you want to create opposition and a method of refereeing the issue or theme of each storyline.

THE ROLE OF THEME

Television has become the best medium with which to explore social themes of all kinds. Whether it's drama or comedy, many series utilize ideas or incidents that are virtually *ripped from the headlines*. The long running series *Law & Order* is based on real legal cases and has spawned a spin-off of two series: one that deals with sex crimes and the other that shows the law and criminal points of view in the story. These two new *Law & Order* franchises also use the "ripped from the headlines" approach. So, themes are all around you: in newspapers, magazines, and in television news reporting. Also look to your friends, neighbors, family, and personal relationships to help you develop and write your television stories. Much of television explores the stories of regular or average people who face universal problems, but are given dramatic leaps for entertainment purposes.

THE AUDIENCE IS VERY IMPORTANT

I suppose audiences who faithfully watch particular series feel they know the characters personally. After all, the characters do come into their households at least once a week. In the case of daytime drama, it's five days a week. The characters share with viewers deep, moving, poignant moments as well as emotional highs. And it's always fascinating to observe your friends going through problems that you particularly don't relish having in your own life.

When it comes right down to it, most television series explore the essential thematic rudiments associated with *family*. Whether it's a group of cops in the same squad room or the nightshift in a crime investigation unit or a henpecked husband-sportswriter whose intrusive parents live across the street, television series are essentially about a group of people who share a close, common environment. And that is, fundamentally, the definition of the television audience itself.

Having said that, it's important to understand that television does not exist expressly for the programs. The medium exists for the *advertising* to reach varied audiences. The characters are simply vehicles to bring a larger audience to the same place on a regular basis so that corporations can expose their products to potential buyers. Certain characters attract a certain type of viewer, and it's this concept that drives the business of television writing. It's called **demographics**. If the audience is offended by certain characters and stops watching a program, that program will not survive. And it doesn't matter if it's extremely creative or well written. The number of viewers a program attracts on a weekly basis—*the ratings*—drives the success or failure of a television series.

Premium cable audiences don't have this particular power, since they pay to watch. The cable TV business is not driven by sponsorship, per se, although *product placement* is a growing trend on premium cable television series. Product placement involves characters using particular brands in scenes or even mentioning specific products in dialogue. But even on cable, the number of viewers a series garners is what keeps it thriving. And, on paid television, the creativity becomes paramount because it separates their programs from those of network or commercial programs.

Many networks and premium cable stations have turned to the concept of *branding* to attract a particular type of audience. I'll talk more about this in a later chapter. But, for example, the Lifetime network advertises itself as Television for Women. TNT adopted the slogan "We Know Drama." Certain premium cable channels program series to attract adults by showcasing mature subjects in more realistic ways. HBO, for example, brands itself with this slogan: "It's not television, it's HBO."

YOUR ASSIGNMENT

Take each of your storylines and create character triangles. Focus on the series regulars and *service* each character, which means to get them involved in a storyline.

CHAPTER 16

Television Writing Basics

Let's take some time to focus on how some basic screenwriting concepts apply to writing for television.

SERIES BASIC STORIES

While classically structured stories have a beginning, a middle, and an ending, television stories more often than not can go on for very long stretches of time. Some storylines in TV last for several episodes, some for several seasons, and others go on for the entire run of the series. So, what you're doing with your stories is taking a *micro*-view that somehow fits into the *macro*-view of the series. This may sound obvious on its face but think about it—you're creating one tiny odd-shaped piece of a larger puzzle that has perhaps a hundred pieces (there are, on average, one hundred episodes in a five-year run). So, when it comes to the type of stories you want to invent, you most certainly must take into account how many years the series has been on the air. Series creators and producers look at ideas as primarily first-year, second-year, or third-year stories. The thinking beyond the third year is that a five-year run is very possible. This leaves more room for creative freedom. However, the first three years of a series is a very fragile time since it's a known phenomenon that if an audience likes the characters involved, it will stick with a program even if it has a string of not-so-good episodes or an overall terrible season. So, the stories must appeal to the audience in such a way as to engender loyalty to the characters and their journey.

Unlike feature films, series television is a unique art form because the underlying principle of its design is to take a long time to develop and explore a group of characters. Rather than being limited by two hours, you can write about characters for one hundred or more hours. So, television stories take a *slice of life* and structure them into four (or five) acts if it's drama or two (or three) acts if it's comedy. This "slice" then fits into the bigger long-term picture. It's not all that difficult for a series to create too many slices that lead it in the wrong direction, ultimately causing cancellation. Research has shown that once an audience goes away, it rarely comes back.

So, think of your stories in a way that will give your "spec" teleplay the longest shelf life possible. Looking at how television series formats are evolving in the first decade of the twenty-first century, it's unrealistic to think that a spec will have a shelf life longer than one season without having to be rewritten.

DRAMATIC ACTION

Dramatic action writing involves providing the characters, especially the protagonist, of a story with tough choices. The most dramatic way to do this is in the form of deciding between *right* and *wrong*, which depends on the social morals of not just the viewing audience but the characters themselves and, less we too quickly forget, the corporations who run advertising during the series.

As you develop your episode, know that your storylines will be most appealing and entertaining in the television format if they explore *moral dilemmas* through the characters. Constantly force the characters of your storylines to choose between two equally distasteful options. In television, you must also flavor these moral dilemmas with the franchise of the series. So, if you're writing for a law show, explore *legal* moral dilemmas. If you're writing for medical series, explore *medical* moral dilemmas. If you're writing a comedy about family life, explore *parental* moral dilemmas. From 1984–1992, one TV program—*The Cosby Show*—literally helped parents raise their children over two hundred episodes. The producers hired Dr. Alvin F. Poussaint, a Harvard professor of child psychology, to consult on the series. The parenting techniques were honestly presented but in a very humorous manner. After its first season (finished third in the ratings), this series reigned number one. Each week, Cliff and Clair Huxtable faced parental moral dilemmas and the audience learned from them.

SERIES PLOTS

Series plots is another one of those basic concepts that seems to be self-explanatory. But when it comes to a television series, the logic of how an episode or season unfolds is volatile. In television, audiences have learned that anything can happen. Even characters can be replaced with another actor. A character's background can be tweaked or embellished over the course of a series run. In 1986, it was revealed that an entire season of a series, *Dallas*, was just a dream in order to bring back to life a popular character that had been killed. In the 1994 pilot of the medical series *ER* a nurse died at the end, and then miraculously came back to life the next week. This also happened in the 1981 pilot of the ground-breaking police drama *Hill Street Blues*.

As a freelance writer, you have less flexibility in this regard. You must figure out the logic of a character in a story based on the episodes that have been aired. You have no way of knowing what will happen down the road or what's in the grand plan. So, temper your story and character development to avoid painting yourself into a corner. It's very easy to write a plot that makes a lot of sense to all the episodes that you've seen only to have that basic logic go completely out of the window in one airing.

So, tread lightly when it comes to writing stories that relate too closely to the continuing logic of current storylines in a series. Focus on each character's journey instead and try to come out of left field with your plot.

WRITING EFFECTIVE DIALOGUE FOR TELEVISION

Television is a dialogue-driven art form. So, let's quickly review the purpose of dialogue as it applies to teleplays:

Reveal Character

You must know the series regular characters very well. Much of who a character is will be revealed in the way he or she talks, the choice of words (vocabulary and slang), his or her speech pattern, and his or her basic values and beliefs. So, as you study the series for which you're writing, you should make a vocabulary list for each character. Listen to the rhythm of the character's delivery and make a list of each character's moral concerns. All of this will help you to mimic the characters without creating a caricature.

Advance Story

The key thing here is to be clever with the way you write your dialogue when it's necessary to give the audience important information about the story. One well-used technique is to let the important information and facts become the source of conflict among the characters. If they must tell the audience parts of the story, have them disagree over it.

Reveal Emotions

This is pretty obvious. But the key in studying the characters of a series is to understand what makes a character emotional—whether it's anger or laughter—and how that character exudes these emotions. Some characters will be quiet when they're angry while others will shout when they're happy.

Establish Relationships

How a character speaks to other characters is important when writing dialogue. For example, a father might use very different words and tone when speaking to his daughter than when speaking to his son, or to his mother, or to a foe. Let the dialogue help you in this area.

Comment on Action

This involves using dialogue to have the characters tell the audience important exposition that has happened off-camera. It also allows the characters to talk about how the present relates to past events in the story or in his or her life.

VISUAL WRITING TECHNIQUES AND PAGE FORMAT FOR TV

Unlike feature films, narrative style is not that important in the teleplay. Even though it is important to write with style and flair, teleplays do not heavily use action-descriptions. As I mentioned earlier, TV is a dialogue-driven art form. So, don't get too crazy with long visual descriptions. The series *Buffy the Vampire Slayer* (1997–2003) aired a two-hour episode in season six where there was no dialogue in the first hour. It was considered ground-breaking, and it even was submitted to the Television Academy for Emmy consideration.

So, keep the action-descriptions lean and mean and to the point when writing a teleplay.

BASIC TELEPLAY FORMAT

The format of a teleplay varies depending on the type of series for which you're writing. The one-hour drama uses the same format as a feature film except that there are four (or five) acts and these acts are indicated in the teleplay. Television movies use the same format, too, but there are seven acts that are indicated. Comedy uses a very different and specific format that employs double-spacing and other conventions that have to do with the nature of multi-camera production. I'll address more specifics in the chapter on the situation comedy. Included in this book are sample drama and comedy teleplays to illustrate format.

BASIC SCREENWRITING CONVENTIONS

Storytelling conventions such as voice-over, flashbacks, flash-forwards, and magic realism should only be used in series television if, in fact, the series uses these conventions as a part of its weekly execution. Otherwise, only the producers can get away with using them.

The series *Ally McBeal* (1997–2002) uses *magic realism* to get inside Ally's—and other characters'—imagination. Some programs have characters "break the fourth wall" by talking directly to the audience, as is the case in the critically acclaimed series *Once and Again* (1999-2002). The series *Any Day Now* (1998–2002) takes two women—one white, the other African-American—and flashes them back to their childhood relationship as part of the storytelling in each episode. Each of the three *CSI* series franchises uses a visual technique to take the audience inside the body of corpses as well as to illustrate different scenarios of how a murder was committed from various points of view.

If you want to be creative and impose special storytelling conventions on a series that does not use them, you're taking a huge risk that whoever reads your spec teleplay will feel that you don't understand the show for which you're writing or don't understand how to write for television in general.

CENSORSHIP

What you can show and say on a particular series merits a quick discussion. Study the series carefully and take care not to violate what's acceptable or unacceptable. On *The Sopranos* (1999–2006), language has no boundaries because it airs on a premium cable channel. On the other hand, most series on commercial networks have to monitor language very carefully. There aren't many specific words that haven't been used on commercial television. But there is a limit to how many times a word can be used and in what context.

Also, one must consider how far one can go visually. Graphic violence or nudity is carefully monitored by commercial networks. I remember when the series I created for CBS, *Tour of Duty* (1987–2000), was in development, the network "standards and practices" executive insisted that because this series is about war, it was okay to show a soldier being blown up if he stepped on a mine. But I couldn't show the body coming down and hitting the ground without legs. When I was writing and producing an episode of the ABC series *A Man Called Hawk* (1989), the network censor insisted I couldn't use the word "abortion" in dialogue. It had to be cut. Commercial cable networks such as FX are pushing the limits of censorship with each new season with edgy fare such as *The Shield* (first on the air in 2002) and *Nip/Tuck* (first on the air in 2003).

Carefully study the series for which you're writing and learn where the line is on that particular program when it comes to language and what's typically acceptable. If you cross the line, again, you run the risk of a producer or agents believing you don't understand how to write for television.

CHAPTER 17

Overview of Television Structure

THE THREE-ACT STRUCTURE AND TELEVISION

A significant difference between writing a feature film and writing an episode of television is *commercials*. You've got to fit them into the flow of the story or you risk losing viewers. The way we do that is to build in **act breaks**. While series on premium cable use the same dramatic flow of building to act breaks, they aren't interrupted with commercials. The reason is simple, the audience is very accustomed to "feeling" the act breaks. And, to some degree, the concept of act breaks fit the natural *rise and fall* of good drama.

In classic film structure, there is also this feeling of act breaks, but there are no commercials. When a feature film is shown on commercial television, commercials are added. So, for TV, the film is essentially edited to the classic *structure milestones*—Pages 1–10, 11–30, 31–45, 46–60, 61–75, 76–90, 91–The End.

Comparing classic film structure to the structure for a television one-hour drama yields the following:

Feature Film	*One-Hour Drama*
Act One	Teaser or Prologue
Act Two	Acts One, Two, and Three
Act Three	Act Four

The *Teaser* or *Prologue* theoretically uses the *first plot point* of the feature's act one. Then the concept of "series of confrontations" used in a feature's act two are also used in the one-hour drama's first three acts. And finally, the feature film's third-act climax is used in the TV drama's act four.

Now, let's take a closer look at television structure.

THE ONE-HOUR TV FOUR-ACT STRUCTURE

The four-act structure is generally used for prime-time dramas. Depending on the network, one episode—not including the commercials—can be as short as forty-five minutes or as long as forty-eight minutes. The other twelve to fifteen minutes are used for advertising and network promotions.

Depending on the network and series itself, a teleplay will run fifty to sixty pages long. Ideally, each act is of equal length, but a good average is fifteen pages per act.

The Teaser or Prologue

The **Teaser** or **Prologue** is a short opening sequence that "hooks" the audience and reels them into an episode. It's as short as one minute and can be as long as five minutes, depending on the series. Series with continuing storylines will include a montage labeled "previously on . . . " before the Teaser to bring viewers up-to-date on storylines that affect the current episode. How Teasers are written varies from show to show and network to network. Some series do not use the Teaser. But it's rarely absent since this is a device that effectively lures viewers and serves to discourage channel flipping.

THE FIRST-RUN TV FIVE-ACT STRUCTURE

A "first-run" series is one that produces never-seen-before episodes but is not on the major networks. This is most commonly called *syndication*. The very first series to ever create new episodes "off-net" was *Fame* (1982–1987) based on the 1980 feature film of the same name. A familiar example of this type of series in recent times is the *Star Trek* series franchise that include *Star Trek: The Next Generation* (1987–1994), *Star Trek: Deep Space Nine* (1993–1999), *Star Trek: Voyager* (1995–2001), and *Enterprise* (2001–2005).

These one-hour programs tend to have less time for story and more time for commercials because of the financial model associated with syndication. So, in order to get more commercials in, the five-act structure is used.

The running time for the actual story is as short as forty-two minutes and as long as forty-five minutes. From a practical standpoint, each act is approximately ten to eleven pages with the overall length of the teleplay around fifty to fifty-five pages. However, first-run syndication has all but disappeared from television as original programming and has been replaced with a programming concept called **repurposing**. This means episodes from prime-time networks now rerun them on other cable networks owned by the mother corporation. This is possible because all of the major networks (NBC, ABC, CBS, FOX, UPN, and The WB) are owned by or themselves own giant multinational media companies.

Exceptions to the Rule

Because of the fast-pace formula of *ER*, the producers write seventy-page scripts, and then edit the filmed episode to proper length. More often than not, it is dialogue that gets cut. A series called *Quincy* (1976–1983) also had to have scripts that ran longer than the average fifty-five to sixty pages. But it wasn't because the show was fast-paced; it was because the star, Jack Klugman, delivered his dialogue at a rapid-fire pace.

The best way to learn the acceptable length of a series scripts is to get your hands on several episodes. But you're always safe to keep your "spec" script between fifty-five and sixty pages because your script is not being written for the series producers but as a demonstration of your understanding how to write for television.

DEVELOPING THE EPISODE STORY

When you start developing your teleplay's story, it's better to think of *beats*—the major *moves*—of a story rather than specific scenes. Here's a simple guideline:

- One beat per three pages of written script.
- Prime time: five major beats per act
- Off-net: four major beats per act

This does not include minor or transition scenes such as establishing shots of cars driving up and away. In television, the budget is important; however, you shouldn't worry about that at this early stage of your teleplay's development. That's a function of rewriting, and I'll talk more about that later.

USE OF MULTIPLE STORYLINES

Think of your storylines as "A, B, C, and so on." These different stories can have related or unrelated themes. This is dictated by the series formula. On series that use **continuing storylines**, many of the minor stories are fodder for future stories. So, generally, one can assume that an A-story is the centerpiece of an episode. The B-story is right behind that in dramatic importance, the C-story behind the B, and so on.

Relationships are often explored or established between series regular characters by using *runners,* which are "arcs" to an emotional relationship instead of full-blown storylines. These runners are also used as fodder for future stories in future episodes.

There are some series that only use an A-story. Generally, these series will include what's akin to a subplot relationship to *emotionally* augment the single story. This subplot can also be viewed as a runner. The series *The X-Files* (1993–2002) often uses this technique since its formula includes only an A-story. But one of the elements that made this program a big hit was the sexual tension between the two lead characters, Mulder and Scully. After the Mulder character was written out of the series, the producers focused on Scully's relationship with her new partner.

Another technique that's used to create a feeling of personal emotions is called **running dialogue**. These are side remarks—sometimes called *throwaway lines*—that characters express while in the throes of solving the problem in the story. But they are not throwaways; these remarks are based on a character's strongly held values and beliefs. Nearly all series use this technique. A good example is evident on the long-running cop drama, *NYPD Blue* (1993–2005). One detective, Andy Sipowicz, has a hatred for cops who betray other cops on the job and believes brother shouldn't turn on brother. On another cop series, *Homicide: Life on the Streets* (1993–1999), Richard Belzer plays a detective who had a conspiracy theory for everything. This character has gone on to appear as a regular on the series *Law & Order: Special Victims Unit* (first on the air in 1999) by moving from Baltimore to New York City.

THE BOTTLE SPEC STORY

The "bottle spec" story is a technique that's usually used by series producers to stay on budget when costs have gotten out of hand. So, the writers "bottle" up the characters in a small number of locations or sets to tell the story. For example, the entire cast of a show could get trapped in the basement of a building when the power goes out and personal dramas unfold.

This technique can also be used by freelancers to write spec scripts for those series whose formula utilizes strong **continuing storylines**. This way, you can create stories that exist outside the continuing character arcs. A **bottle story** should be unique and smack of a one-shot occurrence. But be careful. If you write the most obvious ideas for a bottle story, the chances of the series producers using that same idea are very, very good and this will render your spec teleplay obsolete.

The key to writing a bottle spec is creativity and originality used within the boundary of the series modus operandi.

YOUR ASSIGNMENT

Write a *short story* for each of your storylines. Write no more than one page each. Give each story a beginning, a middle, and an ending. This is much like developing and writing the Basic Story Synopsis in feature film screenwriting. Concentrate on what happens not on how it happens. That means you should focus on each protagonist's "wants, needs, and feelings" toward solving the main problem-predicament.

The next chapter will give you some practical tools that you can use to turn the short story into *beats*.

CHAPTER 18

Developing the One-Hour Episode

SCENE OUTLINE DEVELOPMENT TECHNIQUES

In this chapter, it's time to get more practical. Here are some techniques you should use as you move forward, developing your episode . . .

Beats versus Scenes

In episodic television, writers find it to be more productive to develop each storyline separately using the technique of "**beats**" versus scenes. Specific scenes are then formulated later in the process.

So, what's a beat? Well, it's an event that significantly creates forward movement in the story. For example, let's say a detective in a cop show has to interrogate three suspects over the course of a day of investigation. In the end, he comes up empty. It takes three separate scenes to write this. But the one beat is "Cop interrogates three key suspects and comes up empty each time."

Label your beats using an alphanumeric system. This helps you to keep track of each storyline when you inevitably start moving stuff around. It also gives you a sense of the rhythm at which your episode is unfolding.

Use the *Beat Sheet Development Template* (see below) as a tool to help you develop the pacing for each separate storyline.

Beat Sheet Development Template

Note: There can be more than three storylines, and runners are optional. The number of beats per storyline can vary. The following is an all-inclusive sample of the format.

A-Story Premise: (Describe your premise in one line.)

A1. (Describe the beat.)
A2. (Describe the beat.)
A3. (Describe the beat.)
A4. (Describe the beat.)
A5. (Describe the beat.)
A6. (Describe the beat.)

A7. (Describe the beat.)
A8. (Describe the beat—the climax.)

B-Story Premise: (Describe the premise in one line.)

B1. (Describe the beat.)
B2. (Describe the beat.)
B3. (Describe the beat.)
B4. (Describe the beat.)
B5. (Describe the beat—the climax.)

C-Story Premise: (Describe the premise in one line.)

C1. (Describe the beat.)
C2. (Describe the beat.)
C3. (Describe the beat—the climax.)

Runner 1 Premise: (Describe the premise in one line.)

R1-1. (Describe the beat.)
R1-2. (Describe the beat.)

Runner 2 Premise: (Describe the premise in one line.)

R2-1. (Describe the beat.)
R2-2. (Describe the beat.)

The number of beats is based on an average of twenty beats per episode. Of course, there can be more but not too many more. If you've got more than twenty-five beats in one episode, you're probably trying to put too much stuff into your episode.
You're severely limited by time when writing for television.

Looking at the sample beat sheet, you see that the A-Story has more beats, thus setting the overall tone of the episode and providing a *primary point of view* for the episode. The B-Story has less beats, so does the C-Story. Runners are a good source for exploring character relationships at an emotional level—whether dramatic or humorous—and tend to be oriented on a situation rather than the plot.
From series to series, the number of beats per storyline or the presence of runners in an episode will be different from the sample provided. Use the basic format of the template to help you develop your material.

For programs that only feature an A-story, you need only develop a subplot instead of a B-story. This series design resembles the storytelling of a feature film even though the structure of the episode is four or five acts.

After developing the beats one story at a time, the next step is to integrate them into the *act structure* of an episode. Now the prime directive shifts to paying attention to *how* the story dramatically unfolds. Use the *Beat Sheet Template—Act Structure Format* (see below) to help structure your story beats.

Beat Sheet Template—Act Structure Format

Note: The following is only an example of a sample format. Your beats will be different for your episode.

The Series Name
Your Episode Title

Act One

A1. Teaser
B1. (Describe the beat.)
C1. (Describe the beat.)
R1-1. (Describe the beat.)
A2. (Describe the beat.)

Act Two

B2. (Describe the beat.)
C2. (Describe the beat.)
A3. (Describe the beat.)
B3. (Describe the beat.)
A4. (Describe the beat.)

Act Three

A5. (Describe the beat.)
R1-2. (Describe the beat.)
B4. (Describe the beat.)
A6. (Describe the beat.)
R2-1. (Describe the beat.)

Act Four

C3. (Describe the beat.)
R2-2. (Describe the beat.)
B5. (Describe the beat.)
A7. (Describe the beat.)
A8. (Describe the beat.)

The arrangement or order of beats is somewhat arbitrary. However, look closely at the example and you'll see that each storyline is introduced in act one. If you feel like you've just entered a math class, in a way you have. Even though it's arbitrary, your instincts will also help you to arrange the order of the beats by feel. Expect to rearrange things anyway once you start writing.

There's one other very important theory to consider: these beats need to fit into the *dramatic milestones of structure*.

GENERAL EPISODIC STORY STRUCTURE

Here's a quick summary of all the elements you need to develop your episode. I'm including the *Four-Act Teleplay Structure Milestones*.

Teaser or Prologue

One to three pages (minutes).

Usually one major beat, the number of scenes varies. This can tease other storylines as well, but it's highly unusual to do so except maybe in a series with a large ensemble cast.

Structure Milestone: *Hook the audience to the story's situation.* This is usually, but not always, the A-story. Motivate the audience to stay and watch and not flip to another channel.

This is analogous to the *first plot point* of a feature film, which ideally involves a *moral dilemma.* The bottom line here: the problem is presented to the audience, often by presenting it to the protagonist in the A-story.

Act One

On average five major beats, the number of scenes varies. Can be more or less beats, it depends on the pacing of the series.

Structure Milestone: *The protagonist becomes aware of problem and realizes it's not going to be easy to solve.* In this act, the protagonist in each storyline generally has other concerns and problems to attend to and doesn't have the time or inclination to get involved in anything else. But a new problem is now added to the list. As the act evolves, this new problem quickly gets to the top of each protagonist's list of priorities. And by the *act break*, each protagonist realizes he or she can no longer ignore this new problem or put it on the back burner.

This is analogous to the first mini-drama in act two of a feature film where the protagonist *resists change* and *has trouble adjusting* to a new situation.

Act Two

On average five major beats, the number of scenes varies. Can be more or less beats, it depends on the pacing of the series.

Structure Milestone: *The protagonist gets involved with the problem, which causes it to get worse.* Generally, the new problem is something of which each protagonist is not totally equipped to handle at the time. It's something new or mysterious and each protagonist needs to figure out what it'll take to make this new problem go away. So, each strike out to discover how to do this and, as a result, affects the new problem in such a way that it gets worse rather than better. By the *act break*, each protagonist realizes he or she must do something quickly to solve this problem or it will spin out of control.

This is analogous to the second mini-drama in act two of a feature film where the protagonist *gains new skills* and *accepts change.*

Act Three

On average five major beats, the number of scenes varies. Can be more or less beats, it depends on the pacing of the series.

Structure Milestone: *The protagonist tries to solve the problem once and for all but in the wrong way, fails, discovering the right way in the process.* Generally, in order for each protagonist to prevent the new problem from getting totally out of control, he or she decides to try to solve it despite not having all the information or skills necessary to do so. Of course, each protagonist fails for a major setback in the storyline. This is the lowest point in the story for each protagonist.

This is analogous to the fourth mini-drama in act two of a feature film where the protagonist *tries to solve the problem once and for all, fails, and all is lost.*

Act Four

On average five major beats, the number of scenes varies. Can be more or less beats, it depends on the pacing of the series.

Structure Milestone: *The protagonist finally solves the problem with flair. This is the climax.* It's only after failure that each protagonist gets a clue as to how to really solve the new problem. Now armed with the *key thing needed all along* to solve his or her problem, each protagonist sets out to solve the new problem and either succeeds this time or fails again.

Wrap up loose ends.

This is analogous to both the fourth mini-drama of act two where the protagonist is *on the run* and *scrambling* until his or her *back is against the wall* combined with the act three climax of a feature film. This includes each protagonist discovering the *key thing* that leads to the ultimate resolution.

All of this is theory, of course. It's intended to guide you as you develop and write your teleplay.

Pay attention to this but do not become a slave to it.

I can't emphasize enough how important it is to watch the series and learn how the producers of the series make the most of this general theory to meet their own creative needs. But I guarantee you'll find that nearly all one-hour dramas follow this basic format and structure theory.

THE IMPORTANCE OF ACT BREAKS

Since a television program exists *absolutely* to give advertisers a platform to sell products, how you end each act is very important. The idea here is to make the audience stay tuned to the particular network, watch the commercials, and continue to watch the program after the commercials are done. The act break is akin to a *mini-climax*.

You have a couple of ways to conceptually approach the act break:

1. *Character Hook.* This involves an emotional moment for a character in the storyline, usually a protagonist in one of the storylines.
2. *Action/Situation Hook.* This involves the protagonist of one of the storylines caught in danger, an impossible situation, a big surprise, or something physical such as a fistfight or car chase.

THE SCENE OUTLINE

The scene outline is the result of fleshing out the beat sheet developed from the template. Included here is a Sample Scene Outline for the series *Touched by an Angel* (1994–2003) as a guideline. This is the actual working document that was used to write the "spec" teleplay. When a writer gets an assignment, this is the format generally accepted by producers. The scene outline is often submitted to the Current Programs Department (they manage the series on the air) at the studio and network for notes and approval before the go-head to write the teleplay is given to the writer.

SAMPLE SCENE OUTLINE

TOUCHED BY AN ANGEL
"Separate Lies"
Written By Steve Duncan & Jean V. Duncan
TEASER

FADE IN:

EXT. SMITH HOME—DAY

An establishing shot of a well-cared for suburban home. The White Dove flies over the shot . . .

INT. KITCHEN—SMITH HOME—DAY

Inside, invisible to humans, TESS introduces MONICA to her next assignment, FRANK SMITH (45, Caucasian, balding, ordinary wouldn't-hurt-a-fly kind of guy), who appears to be a happy, loving father to his 10-year-old son, ALBERT (the kid next door), and husband to his wife, SARAH (also 45, Caucasian, mousy, a touch overweight). Their household is a 1990s version of the Cleavers.

INT. LIVING ROOM—SMITH HOME—DAY

Frank kisses Sarah good-bye; he's going on a business trip. Tess tells Monica that Frank is a sales representative for a large computer chip manufacturer and he's on the road every other week. Monica remarks that his family must really miss him, only seeing him half the time. Tess remains unusually reserved, hinting Frank is not telling all to his wife.

EXT. FRONT YARD—SMITH HOME—DAY

Sarah and Albert wave goodbye to Frank. They watch the car turn the corner and disappear from sight. As they head back into the house they hear an awful CRASH! Sarah panics. She tells Albert to stay put as she runs in the direction of the awful sound.

EXT. STREET—DAY

Just as Sarah turns the corner, she sees Frank's car EXPLODE! A large truck speeds away as people in the neighborhood pour out of their homes to witness the aftermath of the accident. Sarah is speechless, frozen. Then she realizes Albert has followed her. Tears well up in both of their eyes as they helplessly watch the car burn. Albert sobs the word "daddy . . . " Also watching (still unseen by humans) are Monica and Tess. Tess nods with a laconic stare, utters "The heart is deceitful above all things, Monica, and desperately wicked . . . " Monica looks for Andrew but he's nowhere to be found. As Monica stares at Tess in confusion, Tess says: "Monica, Andrew's not here because nobody has died here today . . . " OFF Monica's surprise, we . . .

FADE OUT.

END OF TEASER

MAIN TITLES
ACT ONE

FADE IN:

EXT. SMITH HOME—MAPLEVILLE—DAY

To establish . . .

INT. LIVING ROOM—SMITH MAPLEVILLE HOME—DAY

Monica and Tess pose as the Funeral Directors. They are with Sarah in her home, planning the services. Monica is still confused over the entire assignment. It's obvious Sarah is very broken up by the passing of her husband as she falls into uncontrollable tears and grief . . . runs into the den . . . So, Monica guesses her job is to give solace to the widow and help her get past this tragedy. But Tess informs her that that isn't the nature of her assignment.

INT. DEN—SMITH MAPLEVILLE HOME—DAY

As she and Tess talk to Sarah, Monica quickly realizes the woman is a well-adjusted, god-fearing woman who is taking the situation in stride as best she can—she really loved Frank. We learn that she and Frank were happily married for their 10 years except for one thing—his job put a wedge between them. The company had put Frank on the road during the first year of marriage, and he even missed Albert's birth. On the wall are lots of photos of Frank with Albert and Sarah during happier times . . .

EXT. BACK YARD—SMITH MAPLEVILLE HOME—DAY

Invisible as angels, Tess shows Monica Albert in the backyard playing alone. Albert's behavior is odd. We learn he has no friends and he wants a brother more than anything else in the world . . . "Even more than a Tickle Me Elmo doll," adds Tess with a devilish grin. Monica laments now he may never get his wish . . . unless Sarah remarries soon . . . but her biological clock is running down fast—she's pretty much past the age of childbearing without medical assistance . . . They observe the sadness in Sarah's eyes and face as she watches Albert play alone in the yard . . .

Monica, bordering on insubordination, demands that Tess reveal her assignment and stop playing games. Tess uses Monica's emotions to make her point: "Imagine trying to function in life with just half of what you need . . . with just a half-full heart . . . " Monica agrees that that would be awful but that a whole lot of families are doing it these days . . . with the divorce rate over 50 percent and all. Tess says that Monica's assignment is to help Sarah and Albert fill the empty half of their lives and hearts . . . " adding, "But there's going to be a lot of pain in the process." And time is running out for Albert . . . ANDREW appears at that moment and Monica asks him how Albert will die. "A car accident," responds Andrew. "Unless you do your job well," adds Tess.

EXT. FUNERAL HOME—DAY

To establish . . .

INT. CHAPEL—FUNERAL HOME—DAY

At Frank's funeral services, we meet JACK TENNISON, the owner of the funeral home, which is just one of many in a national chain. We learn that this man goes through funeral directors like changing his expensive suits. He's rude, abrupt and rather doubts that Tess and Monica will last very long in his employ (this is the subplot). Andrew shows up to observe the closed casket funeral.

INT. OFFICE—FUNERAL HOME—DAY

We learn that Andrew's posing as a State Consumer Affairs Official when he confronts Tennison with the fact he's investigating claims of fraud against the funeral home. They clash.

INT. HALLWAY—CHAPEL—FUNERAL HOME—DAY

As the grieving family and friends go through the services . . . Andrew reveals to Monica that the body in the casket is not that of Frank Smith's, but of a John Doe homeless man whose death he oversaw the day before. "Then where's Frank Smith?" asks Monica. Tess responds: "Alive, well, and happy—he thinks. And, angel girl, it's time for you to start earning your wings." Monica wants to know why she had to go through all of this. Tess responds: "To know the hurt he's left behind . . . remember the glass is not half-empty but half-full . . . " OFF Monica's understanding of that we . . .

FADE OUT.

END ACT ONE
ACT TWO

FADE IN:

EXT. SMITH HOME—ELMSTOWN, OREGON—DAY

Tess and Monica show up at another home in a neighboring city, Elmstown. (Explain both cities are close to the state line, less than fifty miles apart.) They see Frank Smith as he happily arrives "home" to his bigger, nicer house. He enters to . . .

INT. LIVING ROOM—SMITH HOME—ELMSTOWN, OREGON—DAY

. . . greet another "ideal" family, but with a different wife and son. Frank greets his wife, JANICE (younger and prettier than Sarah but also mousy and shy with low self-esteem issues.) His 9-year-old son, FRANK JR. is bright, energetic, and confident. He happily greets his dad as Monica and Tess "pop in." Monica gets the full import of her assignment. Frank Smith is a bigamist with two families in neighboring small towns. He's led this double life for 9 years.

INT. HALLWAY—CHAPEL—TENNISON FUNERAL HOME—DAY

Frank Smith's funeral services are over. Sarah, young Albert, and the family proceed out with Tess and Monica in tow. The family leaves. Other friends exit as Tess and Monica wait and watch. Tess explains that Frank Smith finally chose to be with his second family full time. So, he faked his death in the car crash. He thinks that the insurance money he left for Sarah and Albert will help them get over losing him, as well as ease his own guilt. It was all a very elaborate scheme staged in concert with Jack Tennison, the owner of the funeral home chain. This is not Tennison's first time staging a fake death. He is paid thousands of dollars to make such arrangements. Tess lets Monica know that she and Andrew will take care of Tennison. Monica's assignment is to guide Frank Smith and both his families to the truth. OFF Monica's curious face . . .

EXT. SMITH HOME—ELMSTOWN, OREGON—DAY

To establish . . .

INT. LIVING ROOM—SMITH HOME—ELMSTOWN, OREGON—DAY

Frank enters with Monica. He introduces her as a special gift to Janice. Monica is a paralegal. She is there because Frank has drawn up a new will and wants Monica to explain it to Janice. Frank praises Janice for her brains and beauty—inside and out. He wants her to go on a shopping spree. Anything she wants. He has a new lease on life and wants himself, Janice, and Frank Jr. to start life anew. He's gotten a promotion and doesn't have to travel anymore. As Monica and Janice sit down together, Frank Jr. enters. Frank tells him that he's finally got the time to build that tree house Frank Jr. has always wanted. They exit to go buy the wood and supplies. Janice doesn't know what's gotten into Frank. But she likes it. He's really happy about the new promotion and that he won't be on the road anymore. Monica knows differently.

EXT. TENNISON FUNERAL HOME—MAPLEVILLE, WASHINGTON—DAY

To establish . . .

INT. OFFICE—TENNISON FUNERAL HOME—MAPLEVILLE, WASHINGTON—DAY

Andrew and Tess uncover incriminating evidence against Tennison. Tennison enters to find them. They confront him. Andrew informs Tennison that he is being shut down. Now they must break the news to the dozens of families destroyed by the schemes.

INT. LIVING ROOM—SMITH HOME—MAPLEVILLE, WASHINGTON—DAY

Tess and Andrew are with Sarah. Young Albert listens from a nearby hallway. Sarah can't believe it. She won't believe it. There's only one way Sarah will know the truth.

EXT.—SMITH HOME—ELMSTOWN, OREGON—DAY

Sarah stands at the door with Tess and reluctantly rings the bell. Janice opens the door. Curious, Frank soon comes to the door. In the b.g., Albert watches from the car. OFF Frank's utter shock . . .

FADE OUT.

END ACT TWO

ACT THREE

FADE IN:

INT. LIVING ROOM—SMITH HOME—ELMSTOWN, OREGON—DAY

Frank has big problems. Sarah is devastated. Janice is horrified.

EXT.—SMITH HOME—ELMSTOWN, OREGON—DAY

Albert waits in the car for his mother. Frank Jr. comes home from next door. He sees Albert and approaches the car. He convinces Albert that the parents will be inside for a long time. They could get in a quick game of hoops. The basket is set up in the driveway. Albert gets out of the car. The two boys play and get along instantly.

INT. LIVING ROOM—SMITH HOME—ELMSTOWN, OREGON—DAY

Tess informs Frank that he may also face criminal charges for faking his death. Monica adds that neither will is valid. Sarah, Janice, and Frank all go at it. Sarah threatens to divorce him. He'll never see Albert again. Shocked, Janice wants to know who Albert is. Janice nearly faints to hear that Albert is Frank's son, born the first year he married Sarah 10 years ago. Frank Jr. was also born the first year she and Frank were married. He's 9. That means their marriage isn't legal. Frank Jr. is illegitimate! Janice will never forgive Frank. Frank wants a chance to explain. But there is no explanation for what he did. It was immoral and illegal. They all yell and scream at each other—just as—Frank Jr. and Albert enter. They heard everything. Frank Jr. starts to cry. Albert takes his hand and they run out together.

EXT.—SMITH HOME—ELMSTOWN, OREGON—DAY

Albert and Frank Jr. exit the house and take off up the street. Frank, Sarah, and Janice are right behind them. The boys cut through a neighbor's yard and disappear.

INT. LIVING ROOM—SMITH HOME—ELMSTOWN, OREGON—LATER THAT DAY

Sarah and Janice pace the floor worried sick for their children. They eventually share stories and compare events from their lives with Frank. Tess and Monica remain for moral support and possibly legal counsel. They are happy to see the women bond. After a moment, Frank enters. Sarah and Janice pray he's found them. He has not.

EXT. STREETS—DOWNTOWN ELMSTOWN, OREGON—DAY

Albert and Frank Jr. board a bus.

EXT.—SMITH HOME—ELMSTOWN, OREGON—NIGHT

The police are with Sarah, Janice, and Frank. They are near panic. Sarah informs them that she has called home. No answer. They aren't there. The police assure them they will do everything they can to find the boys. The entire department is looking for them. Sarah and Janice cry into each others' arms. They pray their boys are safe.

EXT. BACK YARD—SMITH HOME—MAPLEVILLE, WASHINGTON—DAY

To establish . . .

INT. ALBERT'S TREE HOUSE—DAY

Albert and Frank Jr. finish their fast food sandwiches and fries by flashlight. It's a real life camp-out. Albert talks about how he felt when he saw his father's car explode. The boys talk about the good times they've had with their dad. They know he's in trouble. And eventually he might have to choose which one of them he will live with. The prospect makes them sad. Why can't they all live together? They just want to be brothers. They vow to never leave each other—no matter what. Night approaches. Albert turns on his flashlight. It doesn't work. They decide to light a camping lantern. Darkness falls as Albert and Frank Jr. fall asleep in the tree house side by side.

EXT. BACK YARD—ALBERT'S TREE HOUSE—NIGHT

Darkness . . . as the faint lantern glows from within the tree house.

INT. LIVING ROOM—SMITH HOME—MAPLEVILLE, WASHINGTON—DAY

Exhausted, Sarah enters her dark, empty home.

INT. KITCHEN—SMITH HOME—MAPLEVILLE, WASHINGTON—DAY

Weary and tearful, Sarah enters the dark room and goes to the refrigerator for a glass of water. She stands in the dark and drinks it. Just then, the front door opens and closes. Startled, Sarah is frightened. After a moment, the kitchen light goes on. It's Frank. Sarah is furious. How dare he use his key! This is no longer his home. Frank argues that he's there to try to figure out where Albert and Frank Jr. could have gone. As they argue, Sarah turns and notices—out the window—the faint light in the tree house. Frank sees it as well. Sarah is out the door calling Albert and Frank Jr. Frank telephones Janice then tears out.

EXT. BACK YARD—ALBERT'S TREE HOUSE—NIGHT

Sarah and Frank call for Albert and Frank Jr. No answer.

INTERCUT:

INT.—ALBERT'S TREE HOUSE—NIGHT

Albert and Frank Jr. are sound asleep around the lantern.
Below, Frank and Sarah continue to yell for the boys. They know Albert and Frank Jr. are sound sleepers. They could sleep through anything. Frank decides to go up after them. He climbs the thin, fragile ladder. The first two steps he takes break. He looks for something to hit against the bottom of the floor of the tree house. He finds a tree limb. He jumps and jumps to reach it, but to no avail. He finally finds a short ladder. He is barely within arms reach of the tree house. He reaches and reaches. Inside the tree house, the boys are still sound asleep. But, the lantern is moving from Frank shaking and knocking against the tree house. The lantern tilts dangerously, until—it falls over, spills kerosene, and the flame ignites A FIRE.

EXT. BACKYARD—ALBERT'S TREE HOUSE—NIGHT

Sarah screams as she sees SMOKE simmer from inside the tree house. She runs to call the fire department. As Frank calls out to his boys . . .

FADE OUT.

END ACT THREE

ACT FOUR

FADE IN:

EXT. BACKYARD—ALBERT'S TREE HOUSE—NIGHT

Small, growing flames emerge from the tree house now. Frank runs back with a water hose. He manages to get the fire under control. We hear Albert and Frank Jr. calling for help.

INT. ALBERT'S TREE HOUSE—NIGHT

Through the smoke, Albert and Frank Jr. call out for help. Frank and Sarah call back for them to stay calm. Help is on the way. Albert notices that the floor of the tree house is giving away where the fire had been.

EXT. BACKYARD—ALBERT'S TREE HOUSE—NIGHT

Frank and Sarah notice the floor of the tree house crackling apart. Before they know it—the fragile tree house begins to crumble. Frank throws himself under it. The tree house, Albert, and Frank Jr., all come crashing down on Frank—as Janice, Tess, Monica, and Andrew arrive . . .

EXT. HOSPITAL—MAPLEVILLE, WASHINGTON—NIGHT

To establish . . .

INT. HOSPITAL—EMERGENCY UNIT—NIGHT

Sarah, Janice, Tess, and Monica pace and wait. After a moment, an ER Doctor approaches. He tells them that the boys are in stable condition, though weak. They are trying to clear their lungs. They inhaled quite a lot of smoke. Mr. Smith is in critical condition. He suffered severe head injuries when the boys and the debris from the tree house came down on him. It's touch and go. Sarah and Janice want to see their boys. The ER Doctor says, "Okay, but only for a short time." Sarah and Janice exit with the Doctor. Tess confides to Monica and Andrew, "Frank Smith wanted his first family to think he was dead. Be careful what you ask for . . . " Andrew nods in agreement, then exits after the ER Doctor into . . .

INT. HOSPITAL ROOM—EMERGENCY—NIGHT

The ER Doctor, Sarah, and Janice enter. Saddened, Sarah and Janice pause to look at Frank, unconscious, bandaged, and bruised badly. They proceed to Albert and Frank Jr.'s bedsides. The boys are weak, but stable. They are worried about their dad. They repeatedly ask if Dad will be okay. Andrew enters and goes to Frank's bedside. The boys want their dad to be okay. The Doctor quiets the boys. Albert and Frank Jr. ask if they will stay brothers. Janice confides that they will move to Mapleville so that he and Albert can go to the same school. The Doctor directs two ORDERLIES to wheel the boys' gurneys out. Their room is ready. Yes, they're in the same room. He wants to keep them overnight for observation. As the boys are moved past Frank's bed, they tell him, "We love you, Daddy." Sarah and Janice share a look then gently take hands as they follow the boys' gurneys out. The ER Doctor goes to Frank's bedside. Frank's eyes open. He struggles to talk. ER Doctor tells him to take it easy. Frank must know if his sons are okay. Andrew and the Doctor confirm they are stable. He relaxes momentarily. Frank then insists on seeing Monica. The ER Doctor says for only a minute. He exits to get her. Frank asks Andrew if he's there to arrest him. No. The State is still investigating the charges. But expect them to come. He has to pay for what he did. Frank knows. Monica enters. Frank confesses he's ready to die—for real this time. For nearly 10 years he wasn't man enough to choose one family. He truly loved each of them. He wants to make sure his children and wives are taken care of. He doesn't deserve them. He deserves to die. He only hopes one day they will forgive him. Monica and Andrew reveal that they are angels sent by God. God loves him and will forgive him if he'll only look to God. Frank's intentions as a good father and provider may have been sincere. But he was wrong in how he went about it. God is the ultimate good Father, the ultimate Provider. Frank sobs. All he wanted was to be a good father to both his children, and good provider. Will God give him another chance? Can God, his sons, and his wives ever forgive him. Monica nods, "Yes." Frank admits he does want to do right. He will face the consequences and struggle to regain his boys' love. Monica adds, "You never lost it."

FADE OUT.

END ACT FOUR
THE END

Story and teleplay © Steve Duncan Productions

BASIC TELEPLAY ACT FORMAT

Each show has a different look and uses different storytelling conventions. But they all fundamentally use standard teleplay format. You should get a script of the particular series for which you're writing and look for its nuances, then follow them religiously.

Some software manufacturers are selling computer file templates of popular television programs for their screenwriting software. These files come prepackaged with the series character names, standing sets descriptions, margins and format settings. If you're using a particular brand of screenwriting software, check with the manufacturer to see if these templates are available. A good place to check is the software company's website on the Internet. However, because of the dynamic nature of episodic television, these templates tend to become outdated very quickly.

SERIES FORMULA

The pacing of storylines varies with each series. You must watch the show to get a feel for the following:

1. How the scenes unfold. This includes the use of the French-scene technique, fast-paced editing, dialogue overlaps, voice-over, and the balance between the use of exterior and interior sets and locations.
2. The average running time of scenes. Some programs use scenes as long as five minutes on a regular basis. While others use very short scenes.
3. The types of visual transitions or "motifs" used, such as magic realism, "shaky cam," or fast-cutting music video style establishing shots.

The French-scene technique applies to stage plays but has been made popular by the classic police drama *Hill Street Blues*. Today, most series with ensemble casts will use French scenes to weave their stories together.

A French scene is essentially a *scene within a scene*. For example, a character may enter a scene that's in progress. This starts a new scene—the French scene—and ends that new scene by leaving the room. The old scene can continue the same beat or a new scene can begin a different beat. This gives the effect of storylines crossing paths, or literally bumping into each other. Again, study the style of the program for which you're writing and imitate it religiously.

HOW TO ANALYZE A SERIES APPROACH

The *Beat Sheet Template—Act Structure Format* is an excellent way to "chart" storylines for a particular series episode. If you do this several times, you'll quickly get a graphic sense of the show's style, pacing, rhythm of storytelling, and inventory of transitional devices. You could even track the length of each scene, which gives you a sense of how many pages are typically used for scenes in the series. The general guideline is still "one page equals one minute." As I've advised before, you should also get your hands on, or take a look at, a typical teleplay from the series for which you're writing.

YOUR ASSIGNMENT

Using the *Beat Sheet Template—Act Structure Format* as a guide, analyze several episodes of the program for which you're writing.

Next, develop a beat sheet for each of your own story premises based on the same approach learned from analyzing series episodes.

Finally, flesh out the details of the beat sheet into a scene outline. Take care to apply the basic structure theory to your acts in the beat sheet and scene outline.

CHAPTER 19

Writing the One-Hour Teleplay

Before you start writing the teleplay for your episode, let's review some basics.

ANATOMY OF A SCENE—NECESSARY ELEMENTS

Each scene of a storyline should contain the storyline's protagonist interacting either with the antagonist, pivotal character(s), or both. When writing each scene, remember to ask yourself the right questions.

Character Motivation

Why does a character do what he or she does in a story?

There needs to be reliability to a character's behavior in order for the audience to believe the character. You must also be aware of the emotions that a character has experienced in the last scene and how that affects the current scene. There must be consistency and you must keep the audience aware of a character's emotional transitions.

Intentions

What does each character in a scene want?

When a character goes after his or her desires, this interaction with others is what creates conflict. Every character should want something, even if it isn't wanting anything.

Subtext

What are the emotions simmering beneath the surface of the scene?

That is, what's not being said in the scene but is still present in the sense of the scene. Ideally, subtext is felt not discussed. However, in television, discussion tends to be a way of life. It's ideal to use some perspective of the story's theme as the subtext of each scene. This provides a scene with its depth, richness, and texture.

Context

How does the current scene relate to previous and future scenes?

The true power of a single scene often comes from what has happened before and what it portends for the future. Scenes should build upon each other in order to create certain audience expectations. It's what you do with these expectations that create suspense and drama in a story.

Dialogue

What is being revealed from how the characters talk to one another?

Dialogue has many purposes. But its most important function is to *reveal character*. In television, dialogue is also important for providing to the audience character and plot information that budget and time restraints don't allow to be presented visually. But don't forget, nonverbal dialogue can also be very valuable in storytelling.

Now that you have your scene outline written, let's take a more in-depth look at each part of the teleplay's structure.

THE TEASER OR PROLOGUE

The Teaser usually runs from one page to as long as five pages or minutes. Sometimes referred to as a *cold opening*, the Teaser usually presents only one major beat of the main story or, in the case of a series that uses multiple storylines, the A-story. Occasionally, multiple storylines series will open with a different beat than one from the A-story in an attempt to vary itself. Often, series producers will even break the rules of the series because they—not necessarily the audience—are getting bored with the series formula. Don't let this distract you from the fact that you must follow the basic formula religiously. That's your job as a freelance writer. Those who read and judge the quality of your "spec" teleplay will do so against the series formula, not on how you improve it.

The number of scenes in a Teaser varies. Series that use "continuing storylines" often begin with a short segment containing the voice-over that begins with "previously on . . . " This segment shows clips from previous episodes that serve to bring the audience up-to-date so that the current episode's subtleties make sense. This is not part of the Teaser.

The main purpose of the Teaser or Prologue is to *hook* the audience into a storyline's problem or predicament for that storyline's protagonist. Generally, the Teaser is dramatic and ends with a cliff-hanger so the audience will come back after the *main title sequence* or first commercial. More and more, the series that utilize the *continuing storylines* approach have been introducing setups for several storylines in longer Teasers.

You should avoid getting overly creative with your Teaser and departing from the series formula. Remember—your job is to mimic the way the series for which you're writing uses the Teaser from week to week or during those occasional bursts of creativity presented by the series producers.

ACT ONE

The number of scenes varies and the pacing of each act depends on how each series functions from week to week. While writing your teleplay's act one, bear in mind that the main purpose of

Act One is *to make the protagonist aware of the problem-predicament in each storyline*. So, here, you must introduce the problem to be faced by each of the protagonists.

Generally, each storyline's first beat is presented in the first act unless the first beat is used in the Teaser for series that use multiple storylines. Runners don't strictly follow this rule because there are generally only a few scenes to a runner in an entire episode. Or a runner is introduced strictly as fodder for a future episode. You should have carefully studied the series for which you're writing and analyzed more than one episode by now. Mimic that.

As you begin to write the first episode, be aware of each character's speech pattern, vocabulary, and relationships already established in the series. For example, if two cops are partners, you're treading in deep water if you break up the partnership in your episode. If you do materially alter the series established concept or character relationships, then you must put it all back the way you found it by the end of your episode.

Also be aware that you can easily fall into the trap of creating a caricature of a series regular character. This often happens when writing quirky characters in a series. Examples of popular quirky characters—past and present—are: Sipowicz of *NYPD Blue*, Belker of *Hill Street Blues*, Quark of *Star Trek: Deep Space Nine*, Munch of *Homicide: Life on the Street* and *Law & Order: Special Victims Unit*, Grissom of *CSI: Crime Scene Investigation*, and Denny Crane of *Boston Legal*.

The "act break" is a very important aspect of this and every act you write. You must provide the audience with a reason to continue viewing. Think of the last scene in each act as a *mini-climax* that motivates each protagonist to do something more in the next act.

Also, remember, each act runs about fifteen pages for a prime-time series—NBC, ABC, CBS, FOX, The WB and UPN—and about ten pages for *off-net* or syndicated series (which tend to be five acts).

ACT TWO

In the second act, your goal is to *get the protagonist involved with the problem which, in turn, makes it more complicated*.

The problem *gets worse*.

The act break for the second act is most important. This happens on the half-hour mark when new shows begin on other networks. Viewers are very susceptible to "surfing" in pursuit of something better on another channel. It's your job to keep them where they are. So, you must hook the audience with a cliff-hanger that brings them back after the commercial break or their surfing voyage. Generally, this *mini-climax* shows that the protagonist is in some type of jeopardy as a result of getting involved in the problem.

ACT THREE

In the third act, *the problem-predicament intensifies*. The protagonist tries to solve it but fails. Or, at the very least, makes the problem worse than it was before. This is commonly referred to as the *reversal*. Bottom line, it's a major setback for the protagonist.

The act break, again, is very important. Generally, this third mini-climax shows the *protagonist defeated or at the lowest point in the story as a result of trying to prematurely solve* the problem.

Figure 19.1 Classic Teleplay Structure

Structure	*Pacing*	*Dramatic Goal*
Act One	15 pages	Protagonist becomes aware of the problem
Act Two	15 pages	Protagonist gets involved, complicating the problem
Act Three	15 pages	Protagonist tries to solve the problem, fails, and intensifies it
Act Four	15 pages	Protagonist solves the problem

ACT FOUR

In the last act—after a bit of scrambling and being on the run, the *protagonist resolves the problem in the story*. The protagonist's discovery of a *key thing* to solving the problem or removing the predicament from the story sparks him or her to *go for broke*.

Ideally, *each storyline has its climax in the last act*.

It's very important in this last act break to *deal with all loose ends* after the climax of each storyline. Series often leave some loose ends in order to continue them into future episodes. I suppose you can do that with your spec episode, but make sure the loose end is not one that contradicts the series established modus operandi and character relationships. Or, at least, make sure there's a sense that the loose end can be left alone without attention in the near future. My advice is to avoid leaving loose ends in a spec teleplay because it could easily be construed as poor writing. Series producers can get away with more than you.

Be sensitive to the way a series likes to end its episodes. For example, the long-running *X-Files* almost never solved the problem in the story. Usually, an *X-Files* audience was left with the feeling that the problem will move on to someone else or that the protagonist—or anyone—was not strong or smart enough to solve the problem. But they gave it one hell of a run for its money.

In this first decade of the twenty-first century, executives at the commercial networks (free television) are concerned with what they call the *audience satisfaction factor* and put a lot of pressure on series producers to have the storyline protagonist(s) reach his or her goal by the end of the hour or half hour. A classic example of how this affected how a series is written is *Alias*. Entering its third season in 2005, the series was not on the air in the fall of 2004. Instead, the series producers retooled from its original concept, which was very daring and certainly unusual, to a classic structure approach. The first two seasons essentially had each episode begin with act four from the previous episode and the viewers saw that climax, and then proceeded to see acts two through three. Then the episode had a cliff-hanger at the end of act three and the audience had to wait until the next episode to see the climax. In the later seasons, the series takes more of a *Mission Impossible* (original aired 1966–1973, remake 1988–1990) approach each week.

TELEPLAY STRUCTURE AND FIVE ACTS

Though the five-act structure has all but disappeared with the death of the first-run syndication market, it bears a discussion since television is so unpredictable. The five-act structure does not neatly fit the classic TV structure theory. Or so it may seem. The best way to address this "extra act" issue is to simply develop and write the episode using the four-act structure approach. In theory, the five-act structure uses less time in each act. So, the extra act is a combination of acts two and three in a four-act structure but broken into three equal parts.

In other words, you're stretching out the structure theory of *the protagonist getting involved in the story* and *the protagonist tries to solve the problem but fails, making it even worse.*

While these two acts would be fifteen pages each in the classic four-act format, they become three ten-page acts in the five-act format. So, take the second and third acts you've developed using the four-act structure theory and break it up into three ten-page sections. Then take care to end each ten-page act with a strong dramatic scene to create the act break. You still cover the thirty pages necessary, and with acts one and five running at ten pages each, you cover your one-hour time limit.

YOUR ASSIGNMENT

START WRITING YOUR TELEPLAY.

An ideal goal is to set aside four or five days to write the rough draft. Your goal could be to write one act per day. It's no easy task to write ten to fifteen good pages per day. This is mentally exhausting. But if you've done your homework—analyzed several episodes of the series, written a precise premise for each storyline, developed a story for each premise with a beginning, a middle, and an ending, structured your story and turned the story into a Beat Sheet, and developed specific scenes for each act—you should be having fun writing this rough draft.

So, go ahead and crank out your rough draft.

CHAPTER 20

Rewriting the One-Hour Teleplay

Rewriting is the rebirth of the original process of developing your teleplay. By simply re-following the development process, you'll get the most out of your rewrite.

LET THE ROUGH DRAFT SIMMER

First, put your rough draft "spec" teleplay aside for at least one week, longer if possible. This will help to give you a fresh eye to the material. If you feel the need to start rewriting right away, resist it. Instead, start a folder labeled "teleplay rewrite" and jot down all the thoughts that come to mind while the thing simmers. Also, *view episodes* of the series while your teleplay is in "simmer" mode. Pay attention to every detail in each episode. Your brain will automatically alert you to any glaring errors that are in your teleplay. It's very eerie when that happens.

READ THE ROUGH DRAFT AGAIN

After the teleplay has simmered for a week or more, it's time to re-read it. But this time, bring a red pen, and mark up the teleplay with your thoughts and impressions. Identify typos and dialogue that needs revising. Write in the margins of the script or on a separate piece of paper every idea that pops into your skull. Try to do this in one sitting. If you don't have the time for one fell swoop, complete the procedure one act at a time.

ANSWER THE KEY QUESTIONS

Now honestly answer the following key questions about your impressions of the teleplay:

What is each storyline really about?

Get to *theme* here: the lesson learned, the message to the viewer. This should be felt by the viewer and is realized through the protagonist's, or protagonists', experience(s) in solving the problem(s) in the episode. This is what gives an episode "texture," richness, and depth.

What is the problem or predicament faced by the protagonist in each storyline?

Simply identify the challenge facing each protagonist. It needs to be clear and simple for the audience.

What is the goal of the protagonist in each storyline?
Identify how each protagonist intends to overcome the challenge in the episode, not necessarily the result. It's only through the audience's understanding of each protagonist's intent that success and failure can be measured.

What does the protagonist in each storyline have to give up to attain his or her goal?
Identify the sacrifices made and what's at stake for each protagonist. Also pinpoint what undesirable results will occur if each protagonist fails.

Does the protagonist's goal in each storyline change during the course of the episode?
This is character growth or "arc" through the episode. Remember, you're pretty much limited to keeping the series regulars in the same spot they started because it's not your place to change the series characters or format. So, stick to taking series regulars through territory that's well within the boundaries set by the series creators, even if the series appears to be "broken" in certain areas. Concentrate on the goal for solving the problem in front of each protagonist in your episode. Avoid attempting to deal with a "season arc."

What unexpected gain or result does the protagonist in each storyline realize at the end of the episode?

This is what's popularly called the *twist* in a story, the *surprise*. Audiences appreciate surprises in storytelling.

USE STRUCTURE TO REWRITE

AS YOU REWRITE EACH ACT, KEEP IN MIND THE STRUCTURAL GOAL OF EACH.

Rewrite Act One

This includes rewriting the Teaser. The structural goal is: Protagonist(s) becomes aware of the problem or predicament. Here, you *introduce the problem* and cliff-hang the act break to portend the protagonist(s) will get involved in the problem. This is equivalent to Enter New Territory in a feature film screenplay.

Rewrite Act Two

The structural goal is: Protagonist(s) gets involved with the problem or predicament. Here you *complicate the problem* and cliff-hang the act break to portend the protagonist(s) will next try to solve the problem.

Rewrite Act Three

The structural goal is: Protagonist(s) tries to solve the problem or predicament but fails—for *a major setback*. Here you must *intensify* and cliff-hang the act break to portend the protagonist(s) will quit.

Rewrite Act Four

The structural goal: Protagonist(s) discovers the key to the solution and *resolves the problem or predicament*. Each storyline has its climax. Wrap up any loose ends that generally focus on relationships developed during the episode while attempting to solve the problem.

PASSES AND POLISHES

Do the following rewrites concentrating on one thing per pass for a total of six thorough passes through the script:

1. *Track each character's scenes for consistency.* Do this for every series regular character in each storyline but especially for each protagonist. You are checking to make sure that each character's sensibility, attitude, and emotions track from scene-to-scene in a believable arc through the story.
2. *Check each character's "voice."* This is paramount for each series regular. What I'm talking about here is speech pattern, vocabulary, and, more important, what a character will or will not say or do in the context of the series blueprint.
3. *Tighten every action-description.* Teleplays generally don't have a lot of fancy descriptions, although creating tone and atmosphere is important to any piece of material. Get rid of *overwritten* descriptions.
4. *Eliminate dialogue where characters blatantly give one another information they already know or should know.* This is a biggie in television because this medium characteristically uses dialogue to feed information to the viewer. You need to be clever in the way you do this in a teleplay because dialogue is a staple of the art form. The key is make information the *reason* for a fight between characters.
5. *If appropriate for the series—look for places to inject humor.* However, you must stay within the boundaries set by the series creators for each character and the tone of the series itself. But almost every drama on television today incorporates some brand of humor. If it's a comedy teleplay, the whole thing must be funny.
6. *Tighten every line of dialogue.* Read your lines out loud. Go back and review the purposes of dialogue if necessary. It's a good idea to assemble a group of actors (or friends) and read the teleplay out loud. In comedy, this is very important. This is where you execute what's called a *punch-up*. That is, make the laughs funnier or add more humor.

THE FINAL SHAPE OF YOUR TELEPLAY

Depending on the series, each act must come in at the required page length. Commercial television is driven by, you guessed it—commercials. You simply cannot write a twenty-minute act when the ads must be played after twelve minutes. So, pay attention to this—it's very important!

WHEN TO STOP REWRITING

When you're done doing all of the above, go back to square one and let the thing simmer some more; longer than a week—a month if possible. Continue to view the series each week or watch your recorded episodes. Let that highly sophisticated multitasking computer called your brain help you to find errors in your teleplay or opportunities to improve your story and characters. Look for the characters' catch phrases or nervous habits, anything that'll make your teleplay more authentic.

Now start all over again. Yes, that's what I said—start the process all over again!

You should do this entire process at least three times from beginning to end before you even start to think you're done rewriting. In this way, time becomes your ally instead of your enemy.

A common mistake for writers at all experience levels who are new to television is to show the industry their material too soon. If you're on some kind of deadline to deliver your teleplay, then cut out the long simmering time. Take a one-day breather and just go through the process as many times as you can within the time you have before it's due. You're completely done when one of two things happens:

You run out of time. It's a common practice in television for producers and staff writers to never stop rewriting an episode until it absolutely has to be shot—and then they still loop new dialogue and record wild lines during the editing process!

You love every single word and punctuation mark in your teleplay.

Then you're done. Well, for now anyway.

Figure 20.1 Sample Teleplay for *Touched by an Angel, "Separate Lies"* by Steve Duncan and Jean V. Duncan

TOUCHED BY AN ANGEL

"Separate Lies"

Written By

Steve Duncan
&
Jean V. Duncan

FIRST DRAFT

TOUCHED BY AN ANGEL: "*Separate Lies*"

TEASER

FADE IN:

EXT. SMITH HOME - MAPLEVILLE, WASHINGTON - DAY

A very nice suburban home. The White Dove flutters past...

INT. KITCHEN - SMITH HOME - MAPLEVILLE - DAY

FRANK SMITH, 45, is your average balding, wouldn't-hurt-a-fly kind of guy in a business suit. He drinks coffee as –

SARAH SMITH, 45, frumpy, overweight, docile and reeking of timidity, puts a plate of pancakes in front of –

ALBERT, 10, an average kid-next-door, bright, energetic.

ALBERT
Dad, will you be back home in time
for my game tomorrow?

Frank sadly shakes his head. Before he can respond –

SARAH
Albie, you know Dad has to travel for
his job.

Albert pouts, he doesn't want his dad to leave.

FRANK
(playful)
Come on, straighten out that face.
It might get stuck and you'll have to
go around looking like this all the
time.

Frank makes a goofy face that gets a laugh from Albert.

Sarah joins in with a smile, as

BING! The angels Tess and Monica APPEAR...

(CONTINUED)

CONTINUED:

MONICA
Such a happy, loving family.

TESS
Don't rush to judgment, Angel Girl.
Observe and learn...

Frank stands and gives Albert a kiss,

FRANK
Hit one out of the park for your old
man, okay, champ?

ALBERT
Okay.

Frank grins. Sarah is relieved, they've soothed their son.

INT. LIVING ROOM - SMITH HOME - MAPLEVILLE - DAY

The Smith family stops at the door where Frank's well-worn brown suit bag and briefcase wait. Frank and Sarah embrace:

SARAH
Honey, I could get a nursing job.
I've never really used my degree.
With the extra income you won't have
to travel so much.

Frank sighs, then hugs Sarah tightly for dear life.

FRANK
No, Sarah. We've been through this.
I want you here at home for Albert.

Sarah grins and bears it. She understands.

Tess and Monica observe:

MONICA
It's so sweet to see they're still
very much in love.

(CONTINUED)

CONTINUED:

TESS
(skeptical)
Chocolate is sweet, too. But you have too much of it, it'll make you sick.

MONICA
Tess, you're unusually critical. What's going on?

TESS
You'll see soon enough.

Frank pick ups and hugs his son Albert for dear life.

ALBERT
I love you, Dad.

FRANK
I love you more, champ. So, what do you want me to bring you back this time?

ALBERT
You know... a little brother.

Sarah sighs. Starts to protest, but –

FRANK
Tell you what, son, when I get back, Mom and I might start doing something about that. I promise.

ALBERT
(face aglow)
All right-t-t!

Sarah beams and blushes with surprise.

EXT. FRONT YARD - SMITH HOME - MAPLEVILLE - DAY

Sarah and Albert, Tess and Monica watch Frank get into his car and drive down the street and turns the corner.

(CONTINUED)

CONTINUED:

MONICA
So, my assignment is to help them prepare for a new little one...?

TESS
Actually, you're going to prepare them for a new "big" one. A really big one.

Monica's brow folds in confusion.

Then – CRASH – THE LOUD CRUNCH OF METAL.

Sarah grabs Albert's hand.

Monica gives Tess a worried look. Tess remains stoic.

SARAH
Stay here, Albie.

Near panic, Sarah runs toward the awful noise...leaving young Albert behind on the front yard.

EXT. STREET - MAPLEVILLE - DAY

Sarah turns the corner to see – Frank's CAR EXPLODE! A large truck speeds away. People pour from their homes.

Sarah is frozen. Speechless.

ALBERT (O.S.)
Was that Daddy's...?

Sarah looks down to see Albert beside her – crying. Tess and Monica are behind him.

Sarah hugs Albert tightly, turning his face away from the ball of fire. SIRENS SCREAM IN THE DISTANCE.

TESS
The heart is deceitful above all things, and desperately wicked...

Monica looks around the chaotic scene:

(CONTINUED)

CONTINUED:

MONICA
Is Andrew working this case?

TESS
Don't bother looking for him, honey, nobody has died here today... at least not physically.

Off Monica's surprise and bewilderment, we:

FADE OUT.

END OF TEASER
MAIN CREDITS

ACT ONE

FADE IN:

EXT. SMITH HOME - MAPLEVILLE - DAY

To establish...

INT. LIVING ROOM - SMITH HOME - MAPLEVILLE - DAY

An emotional wreck, Sarah opens the front door to:

Tess and Monica both in basic black attire.

TESS
Hello, Mrs. Smith.

SARAH
Do I know you? You look familiar.

TESS
We spoke on the phone yesterday. I'm Tess, from the funeral home. This is my assistant, Monica.

MONICA
We're very sorry about your loss. There are only a few documents we need you to look over and sign...

Gravely distracted, Sarah just stares at them.

TESS
May we come in?

After a beat, Sarah snaps, remembers her manners:

SARAH
Oh, of course. I'm sorry. It's, well...it's been very difficult.

Tess and Monica enter, follow Sarah to sit on the sofa. Sarah unconsciously remains standing with a painful smile.

Monica glances around the room – FAMILY PHOTOGRAPHS EVERYWHERE. She tries to ease the sadness in the air –

(CONTINUED)

CONTINUED:

MONICA
You have a warm and beautiful home, Mrs. Smith.

Sarah tries to loosen her stiff smile. It's not easy.

Tess notices a certain FAMILY PORTRAIT of Sarah, Frank and Albert.

TESS
They say you can tell a lot about a family by sitting in their living room. Yes...there's a lot of love here.

Sarah fixes on the family portrait, moves toward it in silence. Her hands brush the portrait. Her thoughts drift. After a beat, she struggles to speak...

SARAH
(softly)
Frank is... was...a good man. A good father. A good husband.
(beat)
We had so much...but so little time together. His job kept him on the road two or three weeks of the month.

MONICA
That's a lot of time away from home.

SARAH
(reflective)
It doesn't feel like he's dead... Seems like he's just away... on another business trip.

An awkward moment of silence lingers...then:

TESS
It's hard to adjust to everything life brings our way.

(CONTINUED)

CONTINUED:

SARAH

We had a full life. High school sweethearts, married young. I'm glad I was finally able to give him a child. We were happy.

MONICA

Some people never find that kind of happiness.

SARAH

Albie and I didn't want for anything.

(beat)

Well, Albie has always wanted a little brother.

Sarah's voice trails off. Monica and Tess respect the moment. Then –

MONICA

It's a difficult time... especially when a young child is involved.

Sarah's eyes drop to the floor:

SARAH

Yes...very difficult.

Again, her words hang pensive in the air... until:

TESS

We should get this paperwork started, Mrs. Smith.

Monica opens her briefcase and spreads documents out.

MONICA

Fortunately, your husband had already seen to most of the details in advance. We just need a few signatures from you.

Sarah's glare stays focused on the floor. She is not there.

Monica and Tess exchange glances of concern.

(CONTINUED)

CONTINUED:

TESS
Mr. Smith had his affairs very much in order. You and your son will be well provided for.

Monica lays out the papers and holds a pen up for Sarah.

After a beat, Sarah's eyes lift, go up to –

FOCUS ON - THE PEN in Monica's hand. Then,

THE PAPERS spread out on the coffee table.

Sarah reaches out – HER HAND TREMBLES. She draws it to her mouth in an attempt to contain herself. But, can't...

SARAH
(voice cracking)
Forgive me...

Sarah runs from the room. Leaves Monica and Tess in silence, near tears, feeling her pain.

They hear Sarah's SOBS O.S.

MONICA
It breaks my heart to see such an unselfish woman suffer so much.

TESS
(nodding)
And it's so unnecessary.

MONICA
Tess, there's something you're not telling me about this case.

TESS
The time will come, Angel Girl. Now, we see through a glass darkly, but soon face to face.

As Tess and Monica gather their things to leave...Sarah's SOBS O.S. grow LOUDER...

(CONTINUED)

CONTINUED:

ON Tess and Monica's troubled expressions...

EXT. BACKYARD - SMITH HOME - MAPLEVILLE - DAY

A tree house is perched in a large oak.

BING. Monica and Tess appear under the massive tree. They look up into the tree house –

TESS
A young boy's hideout is sometimes his only friend.

MONICA
Albert is hiding from so much pain.

INT. TREE HOUSE - SMITH BACKYARD - DAY

Albert looks out of the little window down into the yard below. (He can't see Tess and Monica looking up at him.) He's a very unhappy boy...

EXT. BACKYARD - SMITH HOME - MAPLEVILLE - DAY

Tess and Monica looking up at the tree house and Albert's sad, lonely face in the little window.

TESS
This child lived for the days his Daddy would come home. Unfortunately, the only thing that might pull Albert out of this is....

MONICA
(knowingly)
A little brother.

TESS
He wants one more than any child wants a Tickle Me Elmo doll.

MONICA
Do you think Sarah will remarry?

(CONTINUED)

CONTINUED:

TESS
Only Sarah and God know that.

Sarah's face appears at the rear window of the house. She looks out into the backyard...up at the tree house that holds the sad swollen eyes of her son. She starts to cry again.

MONICA
Tess, I'm ready to do something. I want to help Albert and Sarah.

TESS
And you will, Monica. You will.

MONICA
But when? When do I start to help heal their broken hearts?

TESS
Your assignment is to lead Sarah to the truth. And very often, the truth hurts.

MONICA
They couldn't possibly hurt more than they do now.

Tess lays a firm eye on Monica. She means business.

TESS
It's hard to imagine, but what Sarah and Albert are about to know could be very devastating.

OFF Monica's caring looks at Albert...then Sarah...

EXT. TENNISON FUNERAL HOME - MAPLEVILLE - DAY

To establish...

INT. CHAPEL - TENNISON FUNERAL HOME - MAPLEVILLE - DAY

Tess and Monica make arrangements for a funeral service.

(CONTINUED)

CONTINUED:

JACK TENNISON, 60, in an expensive Italian suit. A man who looks as rude as he is enters like he owns the place. And quite frankly, he does. Tennison is looking for someone.

Tess leaves Monica to meet Tennison:

TESS
May I help you, sir?

TENNISON
I'm looking for the new director...

TESS
That would be me.

TENNISON
(disbelief)
You're the new director – of my funeral home?

TESS
If your name is on my check, it must be yours. Is there something I can do for you?

TENNISON
(sarcastic)
Yeah, sell more and start increasing my profit margin.
(nasty)
You're the last hire those pinheads in H.R. will shove off on me. What is your name?

TESS
Tess.

TENNISON
Tess what?

TESS
Tess will be fine.

TENNISON
Now do you know who I am, Tess?

(CONTINUED)

CONTINUED:

TESS
Yes. And from your disposition, I also know "what" you are, but I don't use that kind of language.

Before Tess can unload her true righteous indignation —

MONICA (O.S.)
Tess, I could use your assistance with this...

Tess puts wrath on hold and gives Tennison a testy smile as Monica arrives with a notebook in her hand.

MONICA
(continuing/to Tennison)
Hello, sir. Please excuse me.
(then)
Tess, we need to finalize the Smith service. It begins in an hour and several people have come early and are inquiring about viewing the body....

TENNISON
(rudely interrupting)
That is a closed casket service!

Tess turns to Tennison.

TESS
We are aware of that, Mr. Tennison.
(beat)
This is Monica, my assistant.
(then)
Monica, this is Jack Tennison, the owner of this establishment.

MONICA
A pleasure to meet you, Mr. Tennison. Did you know Frank Smith personally?

TENNISON
(protective)
No. But I handle all of my patrons and their families with personal service.

(CONTINUED)

CONTINUED:

Tennison gives Tess a short-tempered glare. Then, he spots:

ANDREW — at the door, dressed in a cheap, ill-fitting government-type suit.

As Tennison heads toward Andrew, Monica gives Tess a curious glance:

MONICA
What is Andrew doing here?

TESS
(playfully)
Andrew in a funeral home... A match made in Heaven. Which is more than I can say for that suit.

Monica smiles.

MONICA
(playful scolding)
Tess...

They turn to see Andrew and Tennison shaking hands:

TESS
Andrew had better count his fingers after shaking with that guy. He's as crooked as the day is long.

OFF Tess and Monica's curiosity as Tennison and Andrew walk away together:

INT. OFFICE - TENNISON FUNERAL HOME - DAY

Tennison enters with a phony smile, feigning hospitality. He motions for Andrew to have a seat.

TENNISON
So, what brings Consumer Affairs all the way down from the state capital to one of my humble little funeral homes?

Tess and Monica stop at the door.

(CONTINUED)

CONTINUED:

TESS
We'll be in the sanctuary if you need us....

TENNISON
(short/to Tess and Monica)
No, go ahead. This is a private meeting.

ANDREW
If they're employed here, I'd prefer them to stay.
(to Tess and Monica)
Ladies... please come in. Have a seat.

Tess and Monica enter hesitantly off Tennison's glare.

TESS
We're preparing for a service. I hope this won't take long.

ANDREW
Not at all.

TENNISON
(to Andrew)
What in hell is this all about?

Tess leans to Monica's ear:

TESS
He got the destination right. His evil self is working on an express, one-way ticket to the fiery furnace.

Monica smiles discreetly.

ANDREW
Since you put it so bluntly, Mr. Tennison... I'm investigating a number of complaints of fraud filed against your chain of mortuaries.

(CONTINUED)

CONTINUED:

TENNISON
Fraud? You have to be kidding.

ANDREW
No, the State is very serious.

TENNISON
Exactly what kinds of complaints were filed?

ANDREW
Well, to name a few – exhuming remains to make room for new ones. Selling the same plots three and four times. Removing headstones...

TENNISON
(interjects/annoyed)
I get the point. For the record, I categorically deny all charges.
(fiery)
Now, if you'll excuse me. I have an honest business to run.

Tennison is on his feet and out the door. OFF Tess, Monica and Andrew as they exchange looks:

CUT TO:

INT. CHAPEL - TENNISON FUNERAL HOME - MAPLEVILLE - DAY

Filled with grieving family and friends. On the front row, FEATURE Sarah draped in black with Albert closely by her side in a new and very uncomfortable suit.

The closed casket there. A Minister stands at a podium.

MINISTER
There are three occasions that bring family and friends together the most. Births...weddings... and funerals. These are life's most important transitions. And they bring out strong emotions...

INT. HALLWAY - CHAPEL - TENNISON FUNERAL HOME - DAY

Andrew, Monica and Tess observe the services inside.

In the b.g., Tennison watches them. After a long beat, Tennison turns abruptly and exits.

MONICA
Is Mr. Tennison involved in this assignment?

Tess and Andrew exchange knowing looks.

TESS
Yes, Monica, he is very involved.

ANDREW
You see, Frank Smith isn't in that casket...

Monica gives Tess a look, then back to Andrew:

MONICA
Is it empty?

ANDREW
No. I guided the passing of a homeless man yesterday. No family, no friends. Very few people know that he's in that casket, and not Frank Smith.

MONICA
Then where is Frank Smith?

CUT TO:

EXT. STATE HIGHWAY - DAY

The regal red Cadillac convertible – top down – speeds down the black-top. Tess behind the wheel. Monica at shotgun, her red locks blow in the wind...

EXT. STATE HIGHWAY - DAY

Tess's red chariot blows past a highway sign: "Welcome to the State of Oregon..."

EXT./INT. RED CADILLAC - PARKED - DAY

Tess and Monica watch A SEDAN turn into a driveway.

MONICA
Tess, when are you going to tell me why we drove up here?

TESS
Let those who have ears... hear. And those who have eyes... see.

Tess casts her eyes over Monica's shoulder. Monica turns to see:

EXT. FRONT YARD - SMITH HOME - ELMSTOWN, OREGON - DAY

A modest home. THE SEDAN STOPS IN THE DRIVE.
FRANK SMITH gets out, grabs his well-worn brown suit bag and briefcase.

He looks toward Tess' parked car:
Frank's POV – No Cadillac or Angels. BACK TO SCENE as:

Frank Smith looks around with great satisfaction. He is pleased as he takes in a deep cleansing breath of fresh air.

INT./EXT. RED CADILLAC - PARKED - DAY

Shocked, Monica looks at Tess. They continue to watch as:

Frank heads for the house – A woman and A boy exit the house to meet him on the porch. They all hug lovingly.

TESS
Are the clouds beginning to part for you now, Angel Girl?

OFF Monica's baffled amazement...

FADE OUT.

END OF ACT ONE

ACT TWO

FADE IN:

EXT. SMITH HOME - ELMSTOWN, OREGON - DAY

Tess and Monica watch from the Cadillac as Frank and the woman and the boy enter the house in a loving group hug...

TESS (O.S.)
Yes, Frank Smith is a smooth operator. Two separate families only fifty miles apart.

INT./EXT. RED CADILLAC - PARKED - DAY

Tess and Monica:

TESS
Divided by a state line — and his selfishness, Frank Smith has two houses. Two wives. Two sons. Two lives.

MONICA
In God's name, how long has he been doing this?

TESS
God didn't come up with this system. This was a Frank Smith production. He's been living separate lies for over 9 years.

OFF Monica, she still cannot comprehend the situation...

INT. LIVING ROOM - SMITH HOME - ELMSTOWN, OREGON - DAY

JANICE SMITH - docile and plain, mildly overweight and frumpy, she is Sarah Smith ten years younger.

JANICE
How was your trip, sweetheart?

(CONTINUED)

CONTINUED:

FRANK
Good. Very, very productive.

FRANKIE (Frank Jr.), 9, is bright, energetic, and confident. He wears a Seattle Mariners baseball cap.

FRANKIE
What did you bring me, Dad?

Frank slowly opens his suit bag and pulls out a new baseball mitt. As he presents it to his son:

FRANK
There you are, champ. A catcher's mitt.

FRANKIE
Wow! Gee, thanks, Dad! You're the best.

Frankie hugs his father, then takes off running.

FRANKIE.
(continuing)
I'm going to try it out right now!

JANICE
No running in the house –

Too late. Frankie is gone.

Frank and Janice are face-to-face now. Alone...except for:

Unseen angels Tess and Monica who observe:

FRANK
I've got great news.

JANICE
What is it?

FRANK
(big smile)
The company took me off the road. No more traveling!

(CONTINUED)

CONTINUED:

JANICE
Oh, Frank, thank God!

TESS
Nope, this was all Frank Smith's doing.

FRANK
There's more. I'm getting a big raise. Now you don't have to work those temp jobs.

Janice is beaming. She and Frank hug:

FRANK
(continuing)
I'll be coming home to you and Frankie each and every day for the rest of our lives.

JANICE
I've prayed for this day.

TESS
Be careful what you pray for, girl. It's prayers like those that keep us angels working overtime.

OFF Tess and Monica as they shake their heads and sigh...

CUT TO:

INT. CHAPEL - TENNISON FUNERAL HOME - NIGHT

Empty. Frank Smith's funeral services are over. The CAMERA FINDS – Tess and Monica now sitting in the last pew.

MONICA
How could a man do this to people he says he loves?

TESS
Frank Smith doesn't know the meaning of the word.

(CONTINUED)

CONTINUED:

MONICA
Why did he choose one family over the other? And why now?

TESS
He was stretched thin. He couldn't go on living like that.

MONICA
I don't understand how he could do that to Sarah and Albert.

TESS
I don't either, but it's your job to sort it out and reveal the truth...to Frank Smith – and to both of his families.

MONICA
It's not going to be easy.

TESS
No, it's not. But that's why you get the big feathers, Miss Wings.
(beat)
Meanwhile, I've got bigger fish to fry.

ANDREW (O.S.)
Tess...<u>we've</u> got bigger fish to fry. You know how I like to cook.

Andrew appears – sitting at the other end of the pew.

TESS
Then we better shake some angel feathers. This train is pulling out of the station.

ANDREW
Have I told you lately, how much I like working with you?

(CONTINUED)

CONTINUED:

MONICA
(playful)
Yes, working with Tess isn't just a job, it's an adventure.

OFF Monica, Tess, and Andrew's grins...

EXT. SMITH HOME - ELMSTOWN, OREGON - DAY

To establish...

INT. LIVING ROOM - SMITH HOME - ELMSTOWN - DAY

Frank enters with Monica by his side, calls out:

FRANK
Honey. I'm home.

JANICE (O.S.)
Be right down.

Frank turns to Monica:

FRANK
Now I don't want my wife to think she's not okay. I –

MONICA
(interjecting)
Trust me, Mr. Smith, any woman would appreciate a gift like this. Your wife will be overjoyed.

FRANK
Great.

JANICE (O.S.)
Hi, honey.

Janice enters...surprised to see a woman in her living room.

FRANK
Sweetheart, I want you to meet Monica.

(CONTINUED)

CONTINUED:

MONICA
Hello, Mrs. Smith.

FRANK
Monica is a consultant.

JANICE
Really? What kind of consultant?

MONICA
A beauty and fashion consultant. Your wonderful husband has hired me to give you a complete makeover.

Janice takes a moment to comprehend,

FRANK
It's your birthday gift, honey.

Janice smiles and kisses Frank.

JANICE
Sweetheart, that's so thoughtful.
(to Monica)
What do I have to do?

MONICA
Prepare yourself to be pampered, and shop 'til you drop.

That brings an even bigger smile to Janice's face.

FRANKIE (O.S.)
Hey, Dad.

They turn to see Frankie enter with blueprints.

FRANKIE
Dad, you promised we were gonna start building the tree house.

That hits Monica as betrayal but she maintains a smile.

JANICE
Frankie, don't be rude. Say hello to Miss...?

(CONTINUED)

CONTINUED:

MONICA
Monica will be fine.

FRANK
Sorry, ladies, duty calls. You two go on and have a good time.
(to Frankie)
Son, give me five minutes to change clothes, then we head for the lumberyard.

FRANKIE
All right!

Frank kisses Janice on the cheek, then he and Frankie exit...leaving the two women alone.

JANICE
My husband is a new man. It's like a miracle. Do you believe in miracles, Monica?

MONICA
Oh yes, I believe in miracles.

JANICE
Our lives are perfect now. And it's going to stay that way...

Monica knows differently. Still, she smiles...

INT. MASTER BEDROOM - SMITH HOME - ELMSTOWN - NIGHT

A large room. Janice leads Monica inside.

JANICE
My closet is over here.

Janice leads Monica into the:

INT. WALK-IN CLOSET - MASTER BEDROOM - SMITH HOME - ELMSTOWN - NIGHT

Several rows of drab clothes – navy, black, and gray.

(CONTINUED)

CONTINUED:

MONICA
I see you like subtle colors.

JANICE
I'm not a flashy kind of person. I don't like being noticed.

MONICA
Well, a little color in your wardrobe goes a long way.

INT. MASTER BEDROOM - SMITH HOME - ELMSTOWN - NIGHT

Janice now sits in front of the mirror on her dressing table. Monica leans in behind her.

JANICE
It's going to take more than a little color. Look at me...

Janice drops her eyes, avoids looking at her image.

MONICA
I see you, Mrs. Smith. You're a beautiful woman.

JANICE
(blushing)
It's your job to say that.

MONICA
Yes, it is. But I don't say it unless it's true. Beauty comes from within. It's my job to help you bring out <u>your</u> beauty.

A pregnant beat passes. Monica and Janice search each other's eyes...their souls connect:

(CONTINUED)

CONTINUED:

MONICA
(continuing)
Tell me...how you feel about yourself...on the inside?

Janice glances at herself in the mirror, then:

JANICE
I've never thought about it.

MONICA
Perhaps it's time you did...

OFF Monica's sincere and inviting smile:

CUT TO:

INT. HALLWAY - CHAPEL - TENNISON FUNERAL HOME - DAY

Tess and Andrew watch as TWO FBI AGENTS and REPORTERS march into the hallway and head their way.

The Agents flash their badges.

TESS
He's in there, Mr. FBI, destroying evidence.

Tess is pleased as the Group heads toward the office.

ANDREW
Tess, 'Vengeance is mine, says The Lord.' He will repay.

TESS
(smiling)
There's nothing wrong with me admiring his payment plan.

INT. OFFICE - TENNISON FUNERAL HOME - DAY

The FBI Agents enter. The REPORTERS in their wake to find Tennison and a LAWYER, anxious, rifling through files.

(CONTINUED)

CONTINUED:

FBI AGENT

John Charles Tennison?

TENNISON

Who the hell are you?

The Agents' badges come up:

FBI AGENT

FBI. You are under arrest.

The other FBI Agent then notices a small fire in the trash can. He douses it and lifts out several charred documents.

FBI AGENT

Are you guys destroying evidence?

The Lawyer gives Tennison a look, then, he goes for it:

LAWYER

(fast-talking)

No. In fact, Mr. Tennison asked me to, and I flatly refused. I'm no longer his counsel. I quit. I'll even turn State's evidence.

Tennison is furious.

LAWYER

(to Tennison)

John, you never paid me enough to go down with you.

The PRESS GOES WILD WITH QUESTIONS as Tennison is handcuffed and led away...CAMERA LIGHTS FLASH.

Invisible to the Crowd, Tess and Andrew observe:

ANDREW

Now what?

TESS

Now for worm number two.

OFF Andrew's knowing glance...

CUT TO:

INT. LIVING ROOM - SMITH HOME - MAPLEVILLE - DAY

Sarah is crying her eyes out. Andrew and Tess sit with her.

INT. top of the staircase - SMITH HOME - MAPLEVILLE - DAY

Teary-eyed, Albert lies on the floor. His head pressed against the rails of the staircase. He watches and listens to his mom, Tess and Andrew downstairs in the living room.

INT. LIVING ROOM - SMITH HOME - MAPLEVILLE - DAY

Sarah wipes the tears from her face.

SARAH
Are you certain it's my husband?

TESS
Yes, Mrs. Smith. He is alive.

SARAH
But the crash...the explosion?

ANDREW
He wasn't in the car, Mrs. Smith.
His body wasn't in the casket.

SARAH
(reeling)
Why did you people put me through this...why in God's name would Frank do this to me and our son?

TESS
We had no choice, Mrs. Smith.

ANDREW
It was the only way the funeral home owner could show his hand.

SARAH
I'm going to your superior.

Andrew and Tess trade subtle smiles.

(CONTINUED)

CONTINUED:

ANDREW
He's always available.

SARAH
I'd like you to leave now.

Sarah leads Tess and Andrew to the door...

EXT. PORCH - SMITH HOME - MAPLEVILLE - DAY

Tess and Andrew exit. Tess turns back –

TESS
Mrs. Smith, they who have eyes shall see.

Sarah looks Tess right in the eye.

SARAH
What does Bible scripture have to do with any of this?

TESS
It has everything to do with all of this.

Sarah does a double take on Tess. They share a moment.

ANDREW
It's an hour's drive.

TESS
Fifty-one minutes at my pace.

Tess and Andrew offer their most sincere expressions.

OFF Sarah's indecision...

CUT TO:

INT. MASTER BEDROOM - SMITH HOME - ELMSTOWN - DAY

Monica exits the closet with an armful of drab clothes.

(CONTINUED)

CONTINUED:

MONICA
The thrift shop will be glad to see these.

Janice takes colorful new clothes from shopping bags. She crosses Monica heading into the closet.

JANICE
And I'm glad to see these here.

They share a smile. The DOORBELL RINGS O.S. from downstairs.

INT. LIVING ROOM - SMITH HOME - ELMSTOWN - DAY

The DOORBELL RINGS again. Frank and Frankie watch TV.

FRANKIE.
I'll get it.

Frankie runs to the door and opens it to:

Sarah. Tess and Andrew stand behind her. Sarah's face folds into curiosity as she looks at Frankie. Tears brim.

Frankie stares speechless at the strange teary-eyed woman.

FRANK (O.S.)
Who is it, Frankie?

FRANKIE.
Two ladies and a man. One of the ladies is crying.

Frank appears, looks up and locks eyes with Sarah...

SARAH
(mortified)
Oh, my God...

JANICE (O.S.)
Honey, what's going on here?

Then Sarah SEES:

(CONTINUED)

CONTINUED:

Curious, Janice approach and hugs Frank around the waist.

SARAH
Oh, my God...!

JANICE
Frank, do you know these people?

Frank can't bear Sarah's pain. He reaches out to her, but Sarah coils at the possibly of his touch.

SARAH
Don't touch me.

FRANK
I'm sorry, Sarah. I'm so sorry.

SARAH
Don't touch me!

JANICE
(utterly confused)
Frank, who is this woman?

Unspeakable tension fills the air.

FRANK
(barely gets it out)
She's...she's... my...wife.

Janice goes weak in the knees. OFF everyone's tension...

FADE OUT.

END OF ACT TWO

ACT THREE

FADE IN:

EXT. FRONT YARD - SMITH HOME - ELMSTOWN - NIGHT

Albert's curiosity peaks. His face pressed to the window of his mom's car. He gets out, tries to see what's happening on the porch. Albert thinks he sees his father. His face lights up in expectation. He bolts for the porch.

Frank sees Albert running toward him. His face lights up.

ALBERT
Dad...!

FRANK
(emotional)
Son....

INT. LIVING ROOM - SMITH HOME - ELMSTOWN - NIGHT

FRANK'S POV - ON Albert as he reaches the porch, face aglow, arms outstretched.

Frank bends down, opens his arm to hug Albert, but:

Sarah steps between them in unrelenting defiance.
Albert peeps around his mother's skirt.

Frankie peeps around to get a look at Albert.

The two boys exchange curious, friendly looks.

Awkward silence. What can anyone say? They wait.

Frank is mortified.

Janice is horrified.

TESS
Frank, you've got a truckload full of explaining to do. So you might as well invite us all in.

(CONTINUED)

CONTINUED:

Frank hesitates a moment, then steps aside.

TESS
(to Albert and Frankie)
You boys go to Frankie's room and play while us grown folks get down to business.

INT. LIVING ROOM - SMITH HOME - ELMSTOWN - NIGHT

Albert follows Frankie. They exit to –

INT. HALLWAY - SMITH HOME - ELMSTOWN - NIGHT

Albert and Frankie stop to face each other.

ALBERT
What's your name?

FRANKIE
Frankie. Grown-ups call me Frank Jr. – same as my dad.

ALBERT
He's my dad, too. They told us he was dead, but I didn't want to believe he was.

Frankie frowns...doesn't understand any of that.

FRANKIE
So, we're brothers, huh?

ALBERT
I think so.

OFF the boys' nods of agreement...

INT. LIVING ROOM - SMITH HOME - ELMSTOWN - NIGHT

Sarah and Janice sit across from each other with Tess, Monica, and Andrew seated in the middle.

(CONTINUED)

CONTINUED:

Frank paces nervously.

MONICA (O.S.)
Mrs. Smith, I think your closet...

All eyes turn to Monica as she bounds down the stairs, looks up and stops in her tracks. She fixes on Tess and Andrew.

MONICA
Oh, you're here.

JANICE
(shocked)
Monica, you know these people?

Culpable, Monica nods as she sits next to Andrew and Tess.

JANICE
Frank, what the hell is going on?

ANDREW
Mr. Smith, let me say, as a State Official, anything you say might be held against you. Criminal charges will likely be filed against you.

That sets a new tone in the room.

FRANK
I didn't plan to hurt anybody.

TESS
But you did, Frank. And you broke the law in the process.

Guilty, Frank sighs in resignation as he searches for words.

INT. HALLWAY - SMITH HOME - ELMSTOWN - NIGHT

Albert and Frankie tiptoe closer to the living room and listen to the adults' conversation with great interest:

FRANK (O.S.)
I never meant for it to go this far.

(CONTINUED)

CONTINUED:

SARAH (O.S.)
You took it this far, Frank.

JANICE (O.S.)
How could you marry me when you already had a wife...and a son?

SARAH (O.S.)
For God's sake they look like they're the same age.

Albert and Frankie's young faces fold in pain and confusion.

INT. LIVING ROOM - SMITH HOME - ELMSTOWN - NIGHT

Frank has now found a solitary seat, his head in his hands.

FRANK
(surrendered)
Albert is four months older.

The full import of that hits Janice and Sarah equally. Tears well up in their eyes.

FRANK
I love them both, more than I love life.

SARAH
How ironic! You faked your own death and left Albie and me to come live here — with them!

Janice can't believe what she's hearing.

JANICE
(shocked/to Frank)
You did what?!

Frank struggles to make eye contact, but he can't. His silence speaks volumes.

(CONTINUED)

CONTINUED:

SARAH
(voice cracking)
I'm getting out of here. Where's my son?

Sarah stands, looks around for Albert.

SARAH
(calling out)
Albie...? Albert, let's go home.

No response. After a moment –

A DOOR OPENING AND SLAMMING SHUT!

The adults react. Sarah and Frank run to the door.

EXT. FRONT PORCH - SMITH HOME - ELMSTOWN - NIGHT

Albert and Frankie tear down the porch and run into the well-lit street as:

Frank and Sarah rush out, with Janice in their wake:

FRANK
Albert!? Frankie!? Come back!

Frank runs after them.

EXT. STREET - SMITH HOME - ELMSTOWN - NIGHT

Running for dear life, Albert and Frankie reach the corner and turn down the street...

Moments later, Frank reaches the corner. He turns, stops:

FRANK'S POV - the street is empty, quiet. No one in sight.

Desperate, Frank spins, looks in every direction. Nothing.

FRANK
(calling out)
Albert! Frankie! Where are you?!

(CONTINUED)

CONTINUED:

No response...only a melody of crickets fills the still night air...As Frank's eyes search helplessly:

EXT. FRONT YARD - SMITH HOME - ELMSTOWN - NIGHT

Sarah, Janice, Tess, Andrew and Monica stand in front of the house as –

Frank trots toward them, gasping for breath.

SARAH
Where are they?

JANICE
Did you see where they went?

Frank breathes deeply and shakes his head. As he heads to his car –

FRANK
I'll go look for them. Call the police.

Sarah and Janice turn inside. OFF Frank's guilty pause...

EXT. TAXI STAND - DOWNTOWN ELMSTOWN - NIGHT

A CABBIE behind the wheel, making notes. Albert and Frank Jr. open the back door, crawl inside the parked cab.

INT. TAXI CAB - PARKED - NIGHT

FEATURE - A plastic Jesus on the dashboard.
The nonchalant Cabbie doesn't bother to look up:

CABBIE
Where to?

A beat, then:

ALBERT
We want to go to Mapleville, please...sir.

(CONTINUED)

CONTINUED:

The Cabbie looks in the rearview mirror, then over his shoulder. At the sight of the boys –

CABBIE

(surprised)

Washington? You fellas realize we're in Oregon now, don't ya? I'd be crossing state lines.

ALBERT

Yes, sir.

CABBIE

How old are you kids?

FRANKIE

Old enough to take a cab.

CABBIE

Where are your parents? You boys wouldn't happen to be running away from home, would you?

ALBERT

No, sir. Here's the address.

Albert takes out a wallet made in shop class and boldly shows his school I.D.

ALBERT

(continuing)

And this is the door key. See...

Albert pulls out a chain from around his neck with a door key attached.

ALBERT

(continuing)

Please, sir. My mom'll pay you.

FRANKIE

Yeah. And she's worried sick about us.

(CONTINUED)

CONTINUED:

The Cabbie eyes the school I.D. and gives it back to Albert as he looks at the boys with suspicion...

ON Albert and Frankie's confidence and solidarity:

SLOW DISSOLVE TO:

EXT. SMITH HOME - ELMSTOWN, OREGON - NIGHT

To establish...

INT. LIVING ROOM - SMITH HOME - ELMSTOWN - NIGHT

Sarah, Janice, Tess, Andrew, and Monica together. Emotional exhaustion.

The PHONE RINGS. Janice snatches it up,

JANICE
(into phone)
Yes.
(listens, disappointment)
Nothing. Did you try that camping spot I told you...
(listens)
You did. Okay.
(heavy sigh)
I suppose we'll just have to wait...
Thank you.

Janice hangs up the phone.

SARAH
Was that Frank?

JANICE
No. The police. Nobody's seen them yet.

SARAH
Maybe Frank has already found them...

(CONTINUED)

CONTINUED:

Sarah and Janice share the agony, hoping against hope.

Andrew gives Tess a look:

ANDREW
Tess, I've really got to go... now.

Tess and Monica know he's right.

Andrew rises,

ANDREW
(to Sarah and Janice)
I'm sure your children will be found...safely...and very soon...

Sarah and Janice barely acknowledge with nervous sighs.

Off a nod to Monica and Tess, Andrew exits.

MONICA
(quiet whisper)
Tess, I'm really beginning to worry about the boys. It's been a couple of hours.

TESS
Angels are watching over them, Monica. God takes care of children...

On that, Frank enters. Tess eyes him:

TESS
(continuing)
...and fools.

Monica can't help but smile a tiny bit, as:

Janice and Sarah turn and look to Frank in anticipation.

Guilty and disappointed, Frank drops his head.

(CONTINUED)

CONTINUED:

FRANK

Not a sign of them...anywhere. I looked every place I could imagine...except...

(then hesitant)

...our...

SARAH

(cuts him off)

Say it, Frank...our house...in Mapleville. I've been calling there every five minutes. There's no answer.

JANICE

You have a house in Mapleville?

Frank avoids eye contact. Sarah nods.

JANICE

(continuing/to Sarah)

Those houses are very expensive. Do you work?

SARAH

(slightly ashamed)

No. I have a degree in nursing, but...I've never worked.

Janice gasps in disbelief. Then lets Frank have it:

JANICE

You bastard! She's never worked and you can afford a house in Mapleville?! And here I'm working two jobs just to help make ends meet!

Twisting in the trap, Frank has no response.

MONICA

Ladies, please, harsh words aren't going to help us find your little boys...

(CONTINUED)

CONTINUED:

JANICE
You stay out of this, Miss...Miss beauty consultant. This is none of your business.

SARAH
Beauty consultant?
(to Monica)
You told me you work with her at the funeral home in Mapleville.

Tess returns a confident look.

MONICA
(stuck)
Well, actually, I do....

JANICE
What? You're a beauty consultant for a funeral home?

SARAH
Who are you really?

JANICE
Yeah. For all we know you could be wife number three!

Monica looks to Tess. Tess can't help but grin. Frank springs to his feet:

FRANK
Stop it! Stop it right now!

He gets everyone's attention. The ladies relent.

FRANK
(continuing)
Dear God, I just want my boys back – safe and sound. I just want my boys!

Frank breaks down. His head sinks into his hands as he flops on the sofa and cries.

(CONTINUED)

CONTINUED:

Janice and Sarah both want to console him, yet they won't allow themselves. They each withdraw in silence.

OFF Monica and Tess as they witness the painful moment...

EXT. BACKYARD - SMITH HOME - MAPLEVILLE - NIGHT

Establish Albert's tree house in its perch...

INT. ALBERT'S TREE HOUSE - NIGHT

Dark. Albert tries his flashlight. It flickers off and on, off and on. It then goes out for good. Albert takes out a kerosene camping lantern. He strikes a match and lights it.

Albert and Frankie are both exhausted, drained. They break open a bag filled from their refrigerator raid. They eat like two hungry, growing boys.

FRANKIE
(off the surroundings)
This is way cool.

ALBERT
I helped Dad build it last year. It took almost all summer.

FRANKIE
We were gonna build one. We had the plans and wood and stuff.
(beat)
Did a good job.

ALBERT
Yeah. I been thinking...

FRANKIE
'Bout what?

ALBERT
How cool it is to have a brother to do stuff like this with.

(CONTINUED)

CONTINUED:

SIRENS interrupt – draw their attention. The boys hold their breath as the sound gets further away and finally fades into the night... All is back to normal –

FRANKIE
You think Dad really faked like he was dead?

ALBERT
I don't know. I saw his car blow up and they said he was dead. But I never believed them.

FRANKIE
Did you see his body all burned up and stuff?

ALBERT
Nope. They wouldn't show it to us. And Mom didn't wanna see it.

FRANKIE
Sounds like he's in big trouble.

ALBERT
Yeah.

That hangs in the air for a moment then the boys chomp on their sandwiches in silence. Then:

ALBERT
(continuing)
Hey, if you and Dad don't get to build your own tree house, we can share this one.

FRANKIE
Really?

ALBERT
Yeah. That's what brothers are for.

FRANKIE
Yeah. That's what brothers are for.

(CONTINUED)

CONTINUED:

The boys grin and slap palms.

ALBERT
You think they'll make us live in different places?

The prospect gives them pause, makes them sad. Frankie glances out the small window.

FRANKIE
I hope not. I like it here.

ALBERT
Hey, let's make a pact. Brothers stay together forever.

FRANKIE
Okay. Brothers forever. We need a secret handshake or something.

Albert nods in agreement. As they work out a handshake...

EXT. BACKYARD - ALBERT'S TREE HOUSE - NIGHT

Still. Dark — save the faint glow of the lantern inside the tree house...giving it a magical glow...

INT. LIVING ROOM - SMITH HOME - MAPLEVILLE - NIGHT

Sarah, Janice and Frank enter with fiery determination. Tess and Monica follow in their wake.

FRANK
I'll look upstairs.

SARAH
I'll check Albert's room. Janice, the kitchen's that way. The light is on the right.

Sarah points, Janice heads that way as the trio split up — leaving Tess and Monica in the middle of the living room.

(CONTINUED)

CONTINUED:

MONICA
It's a good thing that cab driver notified the police.

TESS
It's a good thing that cabbie had a heavenly co-pilot.

Tess and Monica look upward with thankful smiles.

INT. KITCHEN - SMITH HOME - MAPLEVILLE - NIGHT

Janice enters in the dark. Her hand searches the wall for the light switch, when – she catches sight of the glow from tree house outside.

JANICE
(screams)
I think they're here!

EXT. BACKYARD - ALBERT'S TREE HOUSE - NIGHT

Janice exits running from the house toward the tree house.

JANICE
Frankie! Are you up there!?

Sarah and Frank exit the house with Tess and Monica on their heels...

FRANK
Albert!

SARAH
Albert! Answer me. Are you up there?

INT. ALBERT'S TREE HOUSE - NIGHT

Albert and Frankie are sound asleep.

(CONTINUED)

CONTINUED:

EXT. BACKYARD - ALBERT'S TREE HOUSE - NIGHT

Frank, Sarah and Janice at the foot of the big oak tree:

JANICE/FRANK

Frankie!

SARAH/FRANK

Albert!

Tess looks over and:

BING! Andrew appears.

His presence concerns Monica.

AT THE FOOT OF THE BIG OAK TREE

Frank climbs onto fragile dangling rope ladder. SNAP – it breaks. The rope and Frank crumble to the ground.

Frank recovers and runs to the toolshed.

SARAH

They must've gone to sleep.

JANICE

Frankie can sleep through anything.

SARAH

Albert can too.

As they exchange a common motherly moment –

Frank returns with a short aluminum ladder. He climbs on, grabs for a tree limb. Almost...it's just out of reach.

SARAH

Albert!

JANICE

Frankie!

(CONTINUED)

CONTINUED:

They continue to call out as Frank tries again. This time he lunges for a limb...but, misses. BOOM! He and the ladder hit the ground hard.

INT. ALBERT'S TREE HOUSE - NIGHT

Albert and Frankie stretch and turn. THE LANTERN at their feet – it TIPS OVER. Kerosene spills – AN INSTANT FLAME!

EXT. BACKYARD - ALBERT'S TREE HOUSE - NIGHT

FIRE AND SMOKE stream from the wood structure.

Sarah and Janice SCREAM.

FRANK
Call the fire department!

Sarah runs for the house.

JANICE
Frankie! Albert!

The tiny door of the tree house opens. The boys peer out.

ALBERT/FRANKIE
We're here. Help!

FRANK
Can you jump!?

THE BOYS' POV - Looking down. The rope ladder is gone. It looks like a very long way.

ALBERT
Dad, I'm scared!

FRANKIE
Me, too.

Inside – growing FLAMES LICK at the boys' feet. Then –

(CONTINUED)

CONTINUED:

A THICK STREAM OF WATER.

Frank aims a water hose, DOUSES THE BOYS AND THE TREE HOUSE.

Underneath, Janice SEES – the smoky, splintered, water-logged floor of the tree house – as it COMES APART.

JANICE
Oh, God – no!

The FLAMES ARE OUT. SMOLDERING SMOKE. Frank stands at the base of the big oak tree. He drops the water hose and opens his arms.

FRANK
Boys, you have to jump! Now!

As Albert and Frankie muster their courage – the WEAKENED STRUCTURE CRUMBLES!

AT THE BACK DOOR

Sarah exits –

SARAH
Albert! Frank, no!

IN SLOW MOTION – THE SMOLDERING WOOD FRAME CRASHES DOWN ON TOP OF Frank – Albert and Frankie among the debris!

Invisible to all but Tess and Monica, Andrew approaches the tangled pile of wet, smoldering wood and bodies.

As DISTANT SIRENS GET STRONGER...

OFF Andrew's unsure glance to Tess and Monica...

FADE OUT.

<u>END OF ACT THREE</u>

ACT FOUR

FADE IN:

EXT. OPEN ROAD - MAPLEVILLE - NIGHT

Two ambulances blow by – SIRENS BLARING.

INT. AMBULANCE #1 - SPEEDING - NIGHT

Frank on a gurney. He is badly hurt. In a frenzy, the Paramedics work on him.

Andrew, invisible to them, observes solemnly...

INT. AMBULANCE #2 - SPEEDING - NIGHT

Albert and Frankie side-by-side, each on a gurney. Paramedics clean minor cuts and bruises on the boys...

Albert looks over at Frankie. He tries to talk but can't muster the strength. Neither can Frankie.

Both still frightened and shaken, they exchange weak smiles.

FEATURE their hands touching. They manage a feeble execution of their secret brotherly handshake...

INT. CAR - SPEEDING - NIGHT

Janice drives. She's a mess. Monica in the passenger seat.

MONICA
I'm sure they're going to be fine.

JANICE
It's all Frank's fault. I'll never forgive him for this.

OFF Monica's concern...

(CONTINUED)

CONTINUED:

INT. TESS'S LONG RED CADILLAC - SPEEDING - NIGHT

Tess at the wheel. Sarah next to her. She's a mess.

TESS
No need to fret. They're in God's hands now and that's the safest place for them.

Sarah's expression is stark and blank. She stares out of the window, oblivious to the passing scenery...

CUT TO:

EXT. HOSPITAL - MAPLEVILLE - NIGHT

To establish...

INT. WAITING ROOM - TRAUMA UNIT - HOSPITAL - NIGHT

Sarah, Janice, Tess, and Monica pace the floor...

An E.R. physician, DR. MEYERS, approaches the ladies from the b.g. Hopeful eyes fall on Dr. Meyers:

DR. MEYERS
Hello, ladies, I'm Dr. Meyers.

Janice and Sarah stand, anxious...

JANICE/SARAH
(in unison)
How's my son?

Sarah and Janice exchange quick glances, then back to:

DR. MEYERS
The boys are stable and in good shape. They inhaled a lot of smoke so we're clearing their lungs. It's a miracle they weren't seriously injured.

(CONTINUED)

CONTINUED:

Tess and Monica share thankful smiles.

SARAH
Thank you, Dr. Meyers.

JANICE
Yes. Thank you.

TESS
How is Mr. Smith, the father?

Dr. Meyers is not so enthusiastic now.

DR. MEYERS
Which one of you is Mrs. Smith?

JANICE/SARAH
(perfect unison)
I am.

Dr. Meyers blanches with confusion.

TESS
A common name...and a long story.

DR. MEYERS
Well, I'm afraid Mr. Smith is in critical condition. He's unconscious, in a coma. He suffered severe head trauma and his spine was also injured...
(dramatic beat)
There may be some paralysis. We'll know better when the swelling around the spine subsides.

The news hits Sarah a bit harder than Janice.

JANICE
Can I see my little boy?

Sarah's eyes ask the same question.

(CONTINUED)

CONTINUED:

DR. MEYERS
Of course. But only for a few minutes. And, please, don't encourage them to talk. Their lungs need time to rest.

Sarah and Janice nod as Dr. Meyers motions for a Nurse to take the women in...

Dr. Meyers gives Monica and Tess a final remorseful glance then he turns and exits.

MONICA
What a shame. Frank Smith pretended to be dead, and here he is – at death's door.

TESS
He set all of this in motion.

They turn and – their feelings are confirmed:

Andrew is there. He trails Dr. Meyers down the hall.

OFF Tess and Monica's serious expressions...

INT. TREATMENT ROOM - TRAUMA UNIT - HOSPITAL - NIGHT

Dr. Meyers enters with Andrew in tow. They see –

Sarah and Janice paused near Frank's bed. Sarah is concerned and saddened. Janice's contempt masks her pain.

An Attending Nurse draws the curtain around Frank's bed to include Dr. Meyers and Andrew.

Sarah and Janice continue to the other side of the room: FEATURE Albert and Frankie on separate gurneys side-by-side:

JANICE
Honey, mommy's here.

FRANKIE
How's Dad...?

(CONTINUED)

CONTINUED:

JANICE
Sweetie, don't talk. The doctors want you to rest.

ALBERT
But Dad....

SARAH
(intervening)
That goes for you too, Albie. Your father's going to be fine.

Sarah and Janice trade uncomfortable glances...a pall so thick you can cut it. The women hug their sons.

JANICE
Frankie, I was worried sick when you ran away.

SARAH
Please don't do anything like that again, sweetheart.

The boys cast their eyes down. They're truly sorry.

Dr. Meyers steps over with Two Orderlies:

DR. MEYERS
We'd like to keep them overnight to be on the safe side.

Sarah and Janice manage a smile. Sarah kisses Albert. Janice kisses Frankie.

ALBERT
Are we in the same room?

DR. MEYERS
Yes.

Albert grins from ear to ear. So does Frankie.

Sarah and Janice witness the bond, stepping back as The Orderlies push the boys' gurneys toward the door.

(CONTINUED)

CONTINUED:

DR. MEYERS
(to Sarah and Janice)
And we have a parents' room right next door...

Sarah and Janice exchange a brief, non-committal glance.

SARAH
Thank you for everything.

OFF Sarah as she offers Janice a smile of reconciliation...

INT. HALLWAY - TRAUMA UNIT - HOSPITAL - NIGHT

The Orderlies push Frankie and Albert's gurneys past Frank's bed.

The curtain is peeled back just enough to reveal Frank – his eyes closed...his body motionless.

ALBERT/FRANKIE
We love you, Daddy.

The gurneys continue into the hall and up the corridor.

FEATURE - Frank's bed. Andrew steps into frame at Frank's beside. He places his hand on Frank's forehead. Frank has a peaceful expression...almost like he's dead...

Sarah and Janice move to the entrance to block the view. In unconscious unity they slowly turn their backs on Frank.

Janice hurries up the corridor. Sarah proceeds in the opposite direction past:

Tess and Monica who have witnessed it all.

TESS
Looks like it's going to be a long, busy night.

MONICA
I hope it's a healing night.

OFF their serious expressions as Monica stands...

(CONTINUED)

CONTINUED:

INT. CORRIDOR - HOSPITAL - NIGHT

Janice stops her hurried pace to sit on a bench. A mix of anger and anxiety, she tries to gain composure.

MONICA (O.S.)
It's very hard watching those we love being hurt, isn't it?

Janice turns to Monica, now instantly seated beside her.

JANICE
He's my baby. He's all I have left now.

MONICA
I think Frank truly loves you.

JANICE
Frank is a liar. What we had was a lie.

MONICA
He's the father of your child.

JANICE
Why don't you just go away? I'm not going to talk about my life with a total stranger.

Janice turns away. Monica stays still, gives Janice an angelic smile.

MONICA
Janice, be not forgetful to entertain strangers. For thereby some have entertained angels unaware.

Janice is very irritated now. She turns to let Monica have it... But her venom is greeted by –

Monica in A WARM, ANGELIC GLOW. She offers Janice her heavenly smile.

(CONTINUED)

CONTINUED:

MONICA
(continuing)
Janice, I am an angel sent by God.

Janice takes a moment to absorb this.

JANICE
What does God want from me? Haven't I suffered enough?

MONICA
God wants you and Frankie to be happy. It hurts him to see you suffer. You'll find peace when you forgive.

JANICE
Frank doesn't deserve to be forgiven – by me, or God, or anybody. If God really loves me, he'd punish Frank for what he's done.

MONICA
God isn't that kind of Father, Janice. I believe if you search your heart, you'll admit that Frankie needs his father. Frank has been and is a wonderful dad to your son.

Janice looks at Monica's soft face aglow. She softens.

JANICE
It just hurts so much.

Janice fights back the tears... Her eyes well up.

MONICA
God understands. He cares. He loves you. Open your heart to Him. He'll take away the pain.

ON Janice as she sinks her head into her hands and sobs:

(CONTINUED)

CONTINUED:

JANICE
(crying)
Oh, God, help me...What am I going to do?

After a long beat, Janice struggles to contain herself. She raises her head. Monica is gone...

ON Janice, as she sits alone, teary-eyed and pensive...

INT. HOLDING ROOM - TRAUMA UNIT - HOSPITAL - NIGHT

Dr. Meyers and a Nurse examine Frank, still comatose.

DR. MEYERS
His vitals are still steady. And there's brain activity.

After a long beat, Frank's eyes slowly crank open.

FRANK'S POV - fuzzy, blurred images of the doctor and Nurse. Frank struggles to form words:

FRANK
What... what happened...?

DR. MEYERS
You had an accident, Mr. Smith.

FRANK
(now desperate)
My boys... Where are my boys?

DR. MEYERS
They're here. They're just fine. Please try to relax.

Frank breathes easier.

Dr. Meyers lifts the sheet from Frank's feet, takes an instrument and rubs it along the bottom of his feet.

(CONTINUED)

CONTINUED:

DR. MEYERS
(continuing)
Do you feel this, Mr. Smith?

Nothing from Frank. Dr. Meyers shoots the Nurse a look of concern.

DR. MEYERS
(continuing)
How about this?

FRANK
(getting worried)
I don't feel anything.

DR. MEYERS
It's okay, Mr. Smith. You're coming along. Just try to rest. I'll look in on you later.

Dr. Meyers offers Frank a comforting nod, then he and the Nurse exit.

Frank's eyes follow Dr. Meyers and the Nurse as they leave.

Andrew now appears beside Frank.

ANDREW
Hello, Frank.

FRANK
(startled)
You're here to arrest me, aren't you?

ANDREW
No. But there will be consequences for what you've done.

FRANK
(remorseful)
Jail is too good for me. I deserve to die – for real.

ANDREW
You're not going to die...

(CONTINUED)

CONTINUED:

Frank gives Andrew an odd look. Then:

Andrew's ANGELIC GLOW illuminates the room and Frank's face.

ANDREW
(continuing)
Frank, I'm an angel sent by God.

Frank is perplexed.

FRANK
Why would God send me an angel?

ANDREW
Because God loves you.

FRANK
I don't deserve to be loved.
I lied to Sarah, Janice, and my sons.
What kind of man does that?

ANDREW
A man who has made mistakes. Now it's up to you to rectify those mistakes. God wants to help you.

Frank's eyes well up.

FRANK
They'll never forgive me.

ANDREW
But God will, and he'll help set things right. Just ask Him.

FRANK
(voice cracking)
I...don't think I know...how...

Tears stream down his face now.

ANDREW
Just seek Him, Frank. Seek Him with a pure heart.

(CONTINUED)

CONTINUED:

ON Frank as he closes his eyes.

FRANK
Oh, God, please forgive me. I want to do what's right...

After a long beat, Frank opens his eyes. Looks toward Andrew, but – Andrew is gone. OFF Frank's teary and mystified expression...

INT. HOSPITAL - CHAPEL - NIGHT

The chapel is empty. Sarah gingerly steps inside and stands at the entrance. Somber, she takes a deep breath then approaches the altar. She sits on the first pew, clasps her hands, then bows her head.

TESS (O.S.)
(whispering)
I knew there was something I liked about you, Sarah Smith.

Sarah turns – beside her sits Tess...a grin on her face.

SARAH
I didn't hear you come in.

TESS
Don't mind me. We're here to talk to the same person. I'm sure He can hear both of us at the same time.

Sarah gives Tess a curious look.

SARAH
You're not really from the funeral home, are you?

THE WARM GLOW now surrounding Tess answers that question.

Sarah's eyes soften, she's not surprised.

SARAH
You're an angel.

(CONTINUED)

CONTINUED:

TESS

Yes.

SARAH

When you came to the house, I felt like I'd seen you before.

(reflective)

But so much was going on.

TESS

Is any of it coming back to you now, Sarah Marie?

SARAH

(quiet revelation)

You were there the night my mother told me she was sick.

TESS

Yes. You were only about six or seven years old.

SARAH

(tearing up)

A few weeks later you came to my room and woke me up so I could be with her to say good-bye.

Tess nods affirmative.

TESS

Such a brave little girl. What happened to that faith-filled child, Sarah Marie?

SARAH

Life. One tragedy after another. I just got numb. Stopped seeing angels.

TESS

You stopped believing, Sarah Marie. We've always been here.

They each take in the fullness of that truth.

(CONTINUED)

CONTINUED:

SARAH
I looked for you when Frank died...well, left. Didn't know where else to turn. I counted on Frank for everything.

TESS
The way you used to count on God?

Sarah nods woefully.

TESS
(continuing)
You can still count on Him. God loves you. He never stopped loving you, Sarah Marie.

Sarah feels the import of Tess' words. She drops her head.

SARAH
I believe that.

TESS
You know what you have to do. It starts and ends with you.

The tears start to come now. Sarah's emotions spew:

SARAH
You want me to forgive Frank? How can I? He's given me nothing but heartache and....

TESS
(interjecting)
And a beautiful son...

Sarah knows Tess is right.

TESS
(continuing)
And something your son has always wanted...a little brother.

Right again. The tears flow.

(CONTINUED)

CONTINUED:

SARAH
(crying)
From another woman...that he married.

TESS
Baby, God knows you're hurting. But earth has no sorrow that Heaven cannot heal.

CLOSE ON Tess - warm, sincere and intent...

TESS
(continuing)
Let the healing begin... with you, Sarah.

CLOSE ON Sarah - she tries to control her tears, wipes her tear-stained face. In surrender, Sarah glances up. Tess is gone. Not surprised, Sarah clasps her hands...and prays...

INT. TRAUMA HOLDING ROOM - HOSPITAL - NIGHT

Frank's eyes are closed.

SARAH (O.S.)
Frank...

Frank looks up to see Sarah at the door. She enters. They share a moment in silence. As Frank motions to speak, Janice enters. She and Sarah trade looks. Tess, Monica and Andrew POP IN... and observe:

FRANK
(voice cracking)
All I can say is, I'm sorry. I'm very sorry.

Janice and Sarah can't hold back. Their eyes fill up.

SARAH
You did a lot of horrible things, Frank. But you also did some good. You gave my...our son something he's always wanted. Something I couldn't give him...
(OFF Janice)
...a brother.

(CONTINUED)

CONTINUED:

Janice gathers her anger, gives Sarah a surrendering nod.

OFF Tess, Monica, and Andrew's – joyful and tender smiles, REVEAL they are now in the:

EXT. BACKYARD - SMITH HOME - MAPLEVILLE - DAY

Tess, Monica, and Andrew look on with delight as:

Albert and Frankie work together to rebuild the tree house.

FRANKIE
Our new tree house is gonna be awesome!

ALBERT
Yeah. Think we'll finish it before school starts?

FRANK (O.S.)
We can if we stick to it...

Frank – in a wheelchair – rolls to the boys with blueprints in his lap. Elated, the boys run to meet their father as they gather to point out things on the blueprints.

FRANK
(continuing)
Now that Frankie and his mom live up the street, we can work on the tree house every day.

ALBERT/FRANKIE
All right!

Beaming, Albert puts his arm around his brother Frankie... then they execute their secret handshake.

Pleased, Frank smiles proudly at the boys, knowing how blessed he truly has become.

ON Monica, Tess, and Andrew as they grin.

(CONTINUED)

CONTINUED:

MONICA
I think Frank and his family have finally found true happiness.

TESS
Yeah. And with therapy and hard work, Frank should be on his feet again before long.

ANDREW
He's got a lot of community service work ahead.

MONICA
It was nice of Sarah to give him time to recover.

SARAH (O.S.)
Guys, lunch is ready.

Tess, Monica and Andrew turn to see Sarah exit the back door with a tray of sandwiches. Peaceful and fulfilled, she sports a nurse's uniform and a certain air of confidence. Sarah puts the tray on the nearby patio table.

SARAH
(high-spirited)
Move it or lose it. I have to be back at the hospital in an hour. I'll get the lemonade.

As Frank and the boys make their way to the back door, Sarah reaches the back door, then promptly turns back and fixes her eyes on Tess --

SARAH
(for Tess only)
See ya around, Tess.

With a wink, Sarah goes back inside. Monica and Andrew as they exchange curious grins at Tess - she chuckles and gives them a wink. At the Angels' delight as they look up toward the tree house in process -

The White Dove flutters from the trees...FREEZE FRAME, and:

FADE OUT.

<u>END OF ACT FOUR</u>
<u>THE END</u>

CHAPTER 21

Writing the Situation Comedy

THE SAME BUT DIFFERENT

In this chapter, I address the essential differences in writing the one-hour drama and writing the situation comedy. However, bear in mind that all the same general rules and the basic process of writing a one-hour drama also applies to writing a half-hour comedy.

When developing and writing a sitcom "spec" teleplay, you should do the following:

- Analyze episodes currently airing.
- Develop a bible for the series.
- Develop multiple premises for an episode.
- Develop each premise into a storyline with a beginning, a middle, and an ending.
- Convert each storyline into "beats."
- Expand the beats into a scene outline.
- Write the teleplay.
- Rewrite the teleplay.

However, there are significant differences between drama and comedy:

- Running time: a half-hour versus one-hour length
- Story structure: two acts versus four acts
- Teleplay format
- A focus on humor versus drama

For comedy series producers, the process of turning out an episode each week is also significantly different from the process used to develop and write a one-hour teleplay. And it's necessary for you to understand this process if you have ambitions to join a comedy writing staff or become a producer of television comedy.

WHICH SERIES TO WRITE

As in choosing the right one-hour drama for which to write a spec, you must choose the right comedy series as well. Again, this means selecting a series that is respected by critics, thus agents, producers, and executives. As in drama, check the Top Twenty Program Ratings and look up what critics have to say about certain comedy series.

THE DRAMEDY

In the series development area, networks are taking a very hesitant look at using the one-hour format for comedy series. A significant trend in this direction began with the David Kelly's one-hour comedy *Ally McBeal* (1997–2002). The initial huge success of this series even prompted the **Academy of Television Arts and Sciences** to pass a special rule that the comedy category for the coveted Emmy didn't have to be produced in the half-hour format. (The Academy of Television Arts and Sciences is not a guild or union and does not engage in contract negotiations or oversee employment. This organization created the Emmy, produces the award's broadcast, and is very influential for most professions who work in the television industry.) The ruling came as the result of complaints from studios and producers of the half-hour format. Because of the cost of producing a one hour versus a half hour, no one knows if this will become a trend on network television. But you can bet your last dollar it will stop cold if there's a run of unsuccessful one-hour comedies. However, as of the 2004–2005 development season, the premium cable companies such as HBO and Showtime are demonstrating a strong interest in the dramedy TV genre. Their development in this area has been mounting over the past several years because commercial networks (free TV) have shied away from this genre and, despite the success of *Ally McBeal,* continue to have a difficult time programming series of this type. The HBO series *Sex and the City* (1998–2004) is arguably the most successful dramedy in recent television programming.

As far as agents, producers, and managers are concerned, one hour is not half hour. So, if you choose to write a comedy that's produced in the one-hour format, producers of half-hour comedies will not, in most cases, consider that spec as a reliable barometer of your ability to write a sitcom.

THE SITCOM PROCESS

Because series producers work differently in comedy than in drama, it affects you, the freelance writer, more after you've pitched and been assigned to write an episode. Writing your comedy spec is the same lonely experience as writing a one-hour drama or a feature film. You sit in a room all alone (or in a coffee shop with your laptop—still all alone) and do it. But that's not the case if you find yourself working on the staff of a situation comedy. Being on the staff of a television series is the equivalent of a daytime job in the real world and is an important goal for all TV writers to strive toward.

The Writers Room

The "Writers Room" is the affectionate moniker for where all the staff writers meet to hash over ideas for episodes and get notes from the producers on scripts in progress. Some might equate it to competing in the Roman Coliseum or a boxing ring; it can be both an exhilarating experience and a horrible nightmare. Generally, each **staff writer** is contractually assigned a certain number of episodes to write. A certain number of episodes may go to freelance writers. At any given time, the writing staff and producers are working on five or six episodes in various stages of completion. Essentially, everyone sits around a big table and pitches ideas and jokes. Once an idea is approved and assigned to a writer by the **executive producers**, the room is used to *break the story*. Every staff writer participates as the assigned writer pitches the beginning, middle, and ending of his or her episode's A-story and B-story. Rarely will half-hour comedy use more than two storylines. However, in order to *service* a large ensemble cast, there might be several *runners* used. These are often "gags," thus the phrase *running gag*.

Once the story is agreed upon, the assigned writer goes off and writes the rough draft. Then the rough draft is distributed to all the staff writers. Supervised by the **story editors**, and/or **producers**, staff writers assemble in The Room to hash over the rough draft. It's here that things get competitive. All the writers are vying to be funny. Writers want to get their ideas and jokes into the teleplay.

If you're a freelance writer who has written a teleplay on assignment, it's unlikely you'll be in this meeting. You'll work primarily with a story editor and/or producer until you finish the rough draft. Then you will come in for "notes." These notes are generally given by a producer. You go home and incorporate the notes into your draft. Officially, you should get to do a second draft and polish. But often, it is the producer, story editor, or staff writer who will do this. The primary reason is time. However, you still get paid for all the steps whether you get to do them or not. If you're funny and a very good writer, then there's a superb chance you'll see the episode through the second draft and polish.

Ultimately, the fate of your screen credit lies in the hands of the writing staff and producers. Because they must then take the teleplay to the next important step, which will yield more rewrites. However, your screen credit has some protections built in by order of the Writers Guild of America's Basic Members Agreement (the MBA). I'll address this more later.

The Table Read

The "table read" begins the week that the episode will be taped. A series' week doesn't necessarily mirror the real work world. The start of a week in television can be Wednesday. But, for our purpose, let's say it's Monday. The Table Read involves the actors of the series sitting around and reading the script aloud for the first time. They may have received a copy of the script by messenger on Sunday. The writers and producers are there. But more important, the studio and network executives are present. The main goal is to see what's funny and what's not funny. Notes will fly like fur in a cat fight during and after the table read. Then the writers retire to The Room and work on the teleplay until the time comes to *put the episode on its feet*.

The Walk Through

Now it's Wednesday. Actors assemble on the series' sets with a revised script in hand. The director *blocks* each scene with camera shots in mind. *Blocking* simply means decisions are made on how the actors will move through the sets, make entrances and exits, and use props. Physical humor is generally added beyond what's already in the script. Writers are there to tweak dialogue and make the episode funnier. After the run through, the writers retire to The Room and make changes and adjustments to the script. Always, the essential focus is to make the episode funnier.

The Dress Rehearsal and "Tech" Run Through

Now it's Thursday. The actors dress their parts for the episode so wardrobe can make sure all the costumes fit and look proper on camera. The actors should be "off book," which means they have memorized their lines. The cameras are "hot" at this session for the technical crew to make sure everything's working properly. The lighting is tweaked for the final blocking. The sets are *dressed* with props. And, yes, the writers are present to listen and to rewrite.

Tape Day

It's Friday. A live audience comes in for the taping. Scenes are generally shot in chronological order so the audience can follow the story. This necessitates several costume changes. While this is going on, a stand-up comedian entertains the live audience so boredom doesn't set in. Everyone is there, including someone from the network. If a joke falls flat during the taping, then the writers are busy behind the scenes coming up with new lines of dialogue to try on the next take or, more likely, to incorporate after the audience leaves the studio.

Pick Ups

Once the audience is gone, the actors and crew—and writers—stay to do "pick ups." This means they fix the unfunny lines in the episode and do necessary reshoots. Rarely does this involve shooting an entire scene. It's usually just single lines of dialogue to improve punch lines. This often goes into the wee hours of the morning since the actors get the weekend off.

On many sitcoms, the writers come in on Saturday to start the process all over again for the already written next episode that's due for the Table Read on Monday.

Hiatus

Because of the fast-pace pressure of producing a live-on-tape episode each week, comedy series usually take a one-week vacation each month, called a *hiatus*. So, theoretically, every three weeks, everyone gets a one-week vacation . . . except the writers. They're usually writing at home or in the office and sitting around The Table. This allows the writers to stay ahead of the production process so the pressure is not so severe from week to week. Whether this tactic works or not depends on how well the series is being managed by the executive producers and studio executives. On well-managed comedy series, the work week is much like a nine-to-five gig in the real world. This is generally true for hit shows that have been on the air for many years. It is rarely true for a new series.

SITCOM STORIES

A most significant difference between a dramatic story and a comedy story is, in a word, *simplicity*. Dramatic stories tend to plot more by depending heavily on events. Comedic stories have little plot and are more reliant on *predicaments*. That's where the label "situation" comedy is derived.

For example, in a 2004–2005 season episode of *The King of Queens*, the A-story is about the wife who reads an article about couples who replace communication with sex. She thinks this is bad. The husband can't see why (because most husbands on sitcoms are not too bright). So, she declares a moratorium on sex for two weeks. The story revolves around that fact that a perfectly wonderful relationship starts to fall apart while the couple goes about trying to fix it. This is the *predicament* or *situation* from which the story and humor are developed. The protagonist is the wife. The antagonist is the husband in the A-story.

The B-story revolves around the husband's coworker who has been kicked out of the house in an earlier episode by his wife. He's now bunking with a male friend (a series regular character) who starts to act as if the two are married. The coworker is the protagonist and the male friend is the antagonist in the B-story. This predicament *mirrors* the A-story's situation. The husband from the A-story is a pivotal character in the B-story.

The Runner involves the wife's father, who lives with the newly sexless couple, dating an annoying woman with whom he wants to have sex only because she's slept with Frank Sinatra. The father is the protagonist and the annoying woman is the antagonist. The father is also a pivotal character in the A-story. This runner is the *antithesis* of the primary predicament.

As you can see, these are all very simple premises for stories that are generated by sharing the same theme in some way. This is very often the case on most well-written comedies. You should analyze the series for which you're writing to see if this is an approach that's often used.

Instead of focusing on a big plot, the comedy focuses on different minor situations that are created by the major predicament. The humor is generated from the characters' efforts to remove themselves from the minor situations.

For example, in the *King of Queens* episode, the A-story put the husband and wife into different minor situations to test how well they now communicate since sex has become off limits. The list of minor situations that are created from the major predicament includes the following:

1. The wife comes home late from work and wants to go right to bed.
2. The husband and wife go out for a romantic dinner.
3. The wife gets a list of how to make love without sex.

You can see how simple this approach can be.

In nearly every sitcom series, the same basic underlining themes are used over and over. Actually, there are essentially only two of them:

#1—We're all in this together.

#2—It's okay to be yourself.

So, when developing your stories for a sitcom, keep it simple. Remember, most situation comedies are about some form of family. To create a story, exploit a predicament by putting the series regulars in situations that generate conflict in the family. Remember, the more ridiculous or serious the situation, the more comedy potential.

WRITING "FUNNY"

Being funny is very important when writing a sitcom spec. And the humor has to be the same type of humor that's the hallmark of the series for which you're writing. If it's a series that depends heavily on physical humor, then you have to write physical humor. If it's a series that depends on smart humor that's generated from the characters themselves, then that's what you have to write. Here are two basic rules of thumb for writing comedy:

1. Drama is at the heart of comedy.
2. Humor emanates from conflict.

It certainly helps to be funny if you want to write comedy teleplays. But being funny is often not enough. You must also master the *structure* of writing humorous dialogue.

The Area

The "area" simply means you have to start with something on which to extract humor. Most times, it's a *situation*. Let's say your characters have to attend a funeral. The area is a funeral. On its face, going to a funeral is not funny. But there are ways to extract humor from the characters who attend the funeral. So, start by looking at the different facets of a funeral. For example:

1. People cry at funerals. A mourner's crying can be exaggerated and become funny by escalating from quiet sobbing to loud wailing.
2. People view the body at funerals. How different personalities perceive the actual corpse in repose can be exaggerated in lines of dialogue: "He looks better dead than when he was alive."
3. There are flowers at funerals. The wrong flowers are delivered at the last moment, perhaps the banner reads: "Bon Voyage" and a card reads "Have a Great Holiday."

Look at your story, its scenes and find the areas from which you can extract humor.

Comedy Dialogue Construction

It's said that if you have to explain how to be funny, then you're in big trouble. But that's not necessarily true for writers. The first thing you need to understand is *why people laugh?* People generally laugh when

1. *they're uncomfortable with something; and*
2. *when something unexpected happens.*

Put the two together and you have the beginning of humor. One of the key techniques for creating comedic dialogue is to take the audience down a familiar path, make them think they know what's coming next in the dialogue, then give them something completely unexpected.

Two people viewing a corpse in repose at funeral: "He looks so good . . . " says one onlooker, the other says, "Yeah, he looks better dead than when he was alive." That second line is not expected. A classic nonverbal example of this is the circus clown who points a gun at another clown, pulls the trigger and a flag comes out that reads "bang." The gun makes us feel uncomfortable even though we know it's not a real one. This creates a sense of *tension*. The flag coming out with the word "bang" instead of a bullet relieves the tension. And because the flag is unexpected, it generates laughter.

A more sophisticated use of this physical humor technique is used by the Harlem Globetrotters basketball team. There is a gag where one of the players takes a bucket from the sideline, chases a referee around the court with it, then splashes him with the bucket of water. Later in the game, the same player gets mad at the referee again and this time the referee runs into the bleachers with the spectators. The crowd is tense with nervous laughter as they expect to get doused with water along with the referee. But the bucket contains confetti. This relieves the tension and it gets a huge laugh. To use this technique in a sitcom teleplay, set up a situation that's very serious (in the context of the story and situation) early in the story and that creates certain expectations. Then later in the story, pay it off with the unexpected.

In general, comedy dialogue is a combination of this technique of *threes* and *timing*. In other words, there's a *three-beat rhythm* to joke construction in dialogue. They are:

1. The *straight line*. The setup of the joke is not necessarily funny. In fact, this first line is most effective when it's most serious.
2. The *punch line*. This is the pay-off of the serious line and should generate a big laugh.
3. The *follow-up*. This is sometimes called *piling on* or *the topper* because it creates smaller laughs based on the punch line. There can be more than one follow-up to a punch line and writers call it *a run*.

As an example, I've taken a bit of creative license with a classic Mae West joke:

1. Straight line—"*You told me to come up and see you sometime . . .* "
2. Punch line—"*Well, big boy, is that a gun in your pocket or are you just glad to see me?*"
3. Follow-up or Topper—"*You'd better come in before that thing goes off.*"
4. Physical comedy fits into the same construction.

A look or reaction can be a setup, punch line, or follow-up. Or you can use a combination of dialogue and physical emotions.

Timing and rhythm is important.

Let's say you have a character whose line is, "You're not going to make a nickel on this crazy scheme." This can be a funnier line when delivered by an actor if instead of the two syllable word "nickel" you use the three beat phrase "twenty-five cents," putting equal emphasis on each of the three words.

Character counts.

The other part of this equation is to incorporate a character's background and sensibilities. On the long-running sitcom *Frasier*, much of the funny dialogue comes from the erudite, snobby world-views of Frasier and his brother, Niles. So, to make this line even funnier using character, Frasier might say, "You're not going to make one Euro, Shekel, or Botswana Pula on this ill-conceived ruse." Notice, I've used three different kinds of money and purposely chosen the last type to have three syllables. The use of money from around the world takes advantage of the characters' background as highly educated men of the world.

Some words are just funnier than others.

I've never heard an explanation why. For example, it's funnier for a waiter with a tray of finger snacks to break the tension of a serious scene in a comedy by asking "Ramacki?" rather than "Hors d'oeuvres?"

SITCOM PAGE FORMAT

How your teleplay looks compared with the one-hour format is very different. It's nothing like standard feature screenplay format. The way a page is written for a sitcom has a lot do with production. Here are the basic differences:

Only about two-thirds of the page is used for dialogue and action. This is done so that the director can plan out camera shots and mark them on the script.

Dialogue is double-spaced. This gives the actors and directors room to make notes on the script page. It also makes it easier to use at the Table Read.

Action-descriptions are single-spaced and written in all caps. This more clearly separates the action from the dialogue when reading the script.

Scene headings are underlined and include names of the characters that appear in the scene in parentheses. This makes it easier to breakdown the script for sets, props, and wardrobe.

Half-hour teleplays usually run between forty-five to fifty-five pages long. This is true mostly because so much of the script is double-spaced for production convenience. Because of this, in sitcom teleplays, two pages equal one minute in terms of running time.

Take a look at the sample sitcom *Frasier* spec teleplay in this chapter. Rather than trying to duplicate the format using a regular word-processing program, I think you'll find it's much easier to use screenplay software.

SITCOM STORY STRUCTURE

The half-hour comedy uses a two-act structure. Like its story, sitcom structure is very simplistic. Here are the components:

Teaser or Prologue

Like the one-hour teleplay, the Teaser serves the same function: *to grab and draw in the viewer*. Unlike the drama, the Teaser can have absolutely nothing to do with the A- or B-story. Sometimes, the Teaser sets a runner into motion. How to use the Teaser depends on the series for which you're writing. The length of a Teaser is very short, no longer than two minutes, which computes to about four script pages.

Act One

The first act generally *sets into motion the problem-predicament* for each of the storylines' protagonists. Each protagonist becomes aware of the problem and intensifies it by getting involved. The act break is often dramatic with a humorous spin. The length is somewhere around twenty-five pages, which is about twelve minutes.

Act Two

The second act generally sees *each protagonist try to solve the problem-predicament only to make it worse*. This effort backfires and creates a reversal in the story. This is commonly called *the act two bump*. This bump is usually a big surprise to each protagonist as well as to the audience. This event is what leads each protagonist to the *climax or resolution of the problem-predicament*. The length is somewhere around twenty-five pages, which is about twelve minutes.

Tag or Epilogue

Tag or epilogue is a short scene and is designed to *button up* the story's loose ends. In comedy, all the characters come back to where they started in the story. Often, the tag punctuates the "we're all in this together" theme and is topped with a laugh or a warm poignant moment. This style of tag can be as short as thirty seconds (one page) and as long as two minutes (four pages).

The tag can also run on the screen as part of the credit roll. If it does, it's usually about thirty seconds long. Some series actually use this style of tag to show funny outtakes from the episode or to demonstrate to the audience that a conflict between characters is now mended and they are back on good terms.

The basic structure of the half-hour sitcom is very simple. Analyze the series for which you're writing and you'll see how that particular program uses these elements.

Figure 21.1 Sitcom Structure

Structure	*Pacing*	*Dramatic Goal*
Teaser	2–4 pages	Funny runner or introduction to the A-story
Act One	25 pages	Introduce problem-predicament, protagonist(s) gets involved, complicating it
Act Two	25 pages	Protagonist tries to solve problem, intensifies it, creates a setback (reversal)
Tag	1 page	Wrap up loose ends, or funny outtakes, reinforce theme "we're all in this together"

PURPOSE OF A SITCOM SPEC

The same rule applies in comedy as in drama—the spec teleplay's main purpose is to demonstrate your ability to write for a television comedy series. It also demonstrates that you're funny. Sending a spec to the same series for which you've written it most likely will end in rejection.

Figure 21.2 Sample Teleplay for *Frasier,* Act One, "Shrinkz 'N' the Hood," by Jean V. Duncan

FRASIER

"*Shrinkz 'N' the Hood*"

Written By

Jean V. Duncan

(Act One)

FIRST DRAFT

FRASIER

"SHRINKZ 'N' THE HOOD"

TEASER

A

FADE IN:

INT. RADIO STUDIO - DAY

(FRASIER, ROZ, BARNEY (V.O.), BARNEY)

FRASIER IS AT THE CONSOLE IN THE MIDDLE OF HIS BROADCAST.

ROZ IS AT HER POST IN THE BOOTH.

FRASIER

Roz, our next caller please.

ROZ

Dr. Crane, it's the same young man who called yesterday and wouldn't give us his name.

FRASIER

Perhaps he'll honor us today, Roz.

FRASIER PRESSES THE PHONE BUTTON ON HIS CONSOLE.

FRASIER (CONT'D)

Hello, young man, and how are we today?

BARNEY (V.O.)

Ain't no 'we', dog. I'm me, and you you.

FRASIER

(FISHING) And whom might you be, son...?

BARNEY (V.O.)

Why you hatin'?

FRASIER

I don't know what that means, but I'm sure I'm not doing it unintentionally. Now why don't you tell me your name? It's clearly a problem for you.

BARNEY (V.O.)

Yeah. So? Deal with it, G. You down with O.P.P. (LAUGHS)

FRASIER

What is O.P.P.?

BARNEY (V.O.)

On this tip, it means Other People's Problems.

FRASIER

And what is the problem with your name?

BARNEY (V.O.)

It's whack.

FRASIER

Whack? Is that your first name or your last name? (SOTTO) That is dreadful.

BARNEY (V.O.)

Ah, man!

FRASIER

I'm sorry, Whack, I didn't mean to....

BARNEY (V.O.)

(INTERRUPTING) Man, my name ain't no whack. I mean, it's whack, but... just forget it.

FRASIER

I'm sure it isn't that bad. (COVERS THE MIC) It couldn't be as bad as your manners, or your grammar. (OPENS MIC) Please tell me your name, son.

BARNEY (V.O.)

(RELUCTANT) All right. It's... (BEAT) ...Barney.

FRASIER

(SMILING) Barney is a fine name. There are lots of well-loved and heroic individuals with whom you share your name.

BARNEY (V.O.)

Yeah, I know, Barney Rubble, Barney Fife, and Barney that toe-down purple dinosaur. Nobody cracks on them 'cause they be famous, and think they all that.

FRASIER

Perhaps you're experiencing Barney-envy.

BARNEY (V.O.)

What?

FRASIER

Perhaps you feel ashamed of your name because you're not as popular or celebrated as those other Barney characters.

BARNEY (V.O.)

Man, you buggin'!

FRASIER

Just remember, (SINGS) I love you. You love me. We're a happy family... (THEN SERIOUS) Barney, my point is that in time you will come to like your name. You're young. Lighten up. Use a little humor.

BARNEY (V.O.)

Oh, yeah, well humor this, G!

SFX: DIAL TONE.

FRASIER REACTS A BEAT THEN DISCONNECTS THE CALL.

FRASIER

We'll be right back after this commercial break. (OFF AIR) Damn, he hung up again.

ROZ

Can't win 'em all... (TONGUE IN CHEEK) ... homeboy.

ON FRASIER'S DISAPPOINTMENT, WE,

CUT TO:

END OF TEASER

ACT ONE

B

FADE IN:

A BLACK SCREEN. IN WHITE LETTERS: "YOUR BLEEDING HEART"

CROSS FADE TO:

INT. RADIO STUDIO - CONTINUOUS - DAY

(FRASIER, ROZ, OLDER CALLER (V.O.), BARNEY (V.O.)

FRASIER AND ROZ STILL IN THE COMMERCIAL BREAK.

FRASIER

Roz, you're being snide and insensitive toward a young man who appears quite insightful...

ROZ

(INTERJECTING) And quite hooked on Ebonics.

FRASIER

That's so elitist.

ROZ

Now there's an example of the elite calling the kettle upper echelon.

FRASIER GIVES ROZ A TERSE LOOK THAT SILENCES HER.

FRASIER

Well, Roz, if the shoe mixes metaphors. I just wish I could help the kid.

ROZ

Barney sounds like he can take care of himself.

FRASIER

He's obviously masking a lot of pain. He's crying out for help.

ROZ

Yeah, slamming the phone in your face screams "Help." (THEN) We're back.

FRASIER SIGHS THEN PRESSES THE BUTTON ON HIS CONSOLE.

FRASIER

This is Dr. Frasier Crane.

ROZ

Mrs. McNamara on line two.

BEFORE FRASIER CAN SPEAK,

OLDER CALLER (V.O.)

Dr. Crane, you should be ashamed of the way you toyed with that nice young man's emotions. Ashamed I say!

FRASIER

But, ma'am, I....

DIAL TONE.

FRASIER

Hello? (COVERS THE MIC) I tire of the theme.

ROZ

Well, he's back-k-k. Barney is on line three.

FRASIER

(EAGER) Barney, I'm so glad you called again.

BARNEY (V.O.)

(PROPER) I must thank the very nice lady who spoke so highly on my behalf.

FRASIER

Barney, is it you?

BARNEY (V.O.)

Yeah, dog. Whatzup?

FRASIER

Indeed, I should ask you that question. Why did you hang up?

BARNEY (V.O.)

Don't playa-hate, G.

FRASIER

Gee, that doesn't sound good. I didn't know I was doing that. By the way, what is 'play or hay'?

BARNEY (V.O.)

Playa-hate. I guess old folks say 'don't diss me' – don't disrespect me. Don't envy me. Get it?

FRASIER

Barney, I meant no disrespect. I apologize. I want to help.

BARNEY (V.O.)

Nothin' you can do for me, G.

FRASIER

Well, 'gee', I beg to differ. I'm a trained professional.

BARNEY (V.O.)

Then hook me up. Get me a job.

FRASIER

Well, I...uh....don't know.

BARNEY (V.O.)

Yeah, I get it, the ole liberal bleedin' heart shuffle. At least a brotha knows where he stands with the Conservative Right. (PAUSE) We stand in the welfare line. We stand in the unemployment line. And always at the back of the line.

FRASIER

Barney, how old are you?

BARNEY (V.O.)

Old enough. I'm seventeen and a half.

FRASIER

Are you still in school?

BARNEY (V.O.)

Yeah.

FRASIER

Well, have your secretary call my secretary. I think we....

BARNEY (V.O.)

Get off that, man. I ain't got no secretary.

FRASIER

(CORRECTING) You don't have a secretary. I mean — have the secretary of your school call....

BARNEY (V.O.)

Man, you tryin' to play me like Tiger plays The P.G.A. My school ain't got time to do nothin' for nobody. If you don't wanna help, just say so.

FRASIER

Barney, listen. Today's audience is my witness. I will secure employment for you. At the very least for the summer.

BARNEY (V.O.)

I flipped burgers last summer, G. I'm lookin' to move up.

FRASIER

Okay. No fast food... no food service. A real job.

BARNEY (V.O.)

(EXCITED) That's phatt, man.

FRASIER

Excuse me?

ROZ

(INTERJECTING) He's thanking you, Dr. Crane. And thank you, Barney. We'll be right back.

SHE HITS A BUTTON ON HER CONSOLE, AND THEY GO TO BREAK. ROZ CROSSES TO FRASIER AT HIS CONSOLE.

ROZ

Frasier, are you crazy? How are you going to find a job for this kid? You don't know anything about him.

FRASIER

How difficult can it be to find employment for a bright and interesting young man who is clearly willing to work?

CUT TO:

C

FADE IN:

A BLACK SCREEN. IN WHITE LETTERS: "IT'S A TOUGH JOB, BUT FRASIER'S GOTTA DO IT"

FRASIER (V.O.)

Why is it so difficult to find employment for a bright and interesting young man who is clearly willing to work?

CROSS FADE TO:

INT. FRASIER'S LIVING ROOM - DAY

(FRASIER, NILES, DAPHNE, MARTIN)

FRUSTRATED, FRASIER PACES THE FLOOR AS NILES, MARTIN, EDDIE, AND DAPHNE SIT AND WATCH.

FRASIER

I've called three head hunters and nothing!

NILES

Frasier, have you seen this young man's C.V.?

DAPHNE

Oh, my goodness. That sounds contagious.

FRASIER

C.V. is Curriculum Vitae...

MARTIN

Fancy words for resume.

DAPHNE

Back home a call from your mother or father was enough for any suitable employment. Of course, the only jobs available were in the local factories. And I'd rather work me tail off for the likes of you than sort the innards of farm animals all day. Though sometimes I think I've made a dreadful mistake.

DAPHNE EXITS TO HER ROOM.

MARTIN

From what you say, Frasier, this kid sounds like he's from pretty tough stock.

FRASIER

So?

MARTIN

Remember the first time you and Niles wandered to the wrong side of the tracks during our vacation on Martha's Vineyard?

FRASIER

It was a terrifying experience.

MARTIN

Yeah. Your mother made me put on my uniform, stop the train, and escort you back safely.

NILES

(TREMBLES) Yes. It was absolutely horrible. That miniature town looked so real as we ran our little trains through it on the tracks.

FRASIER

I wonder, what ever happened to that train set?

MARTIN

Frasier, are you sure you want to take your little train set to the other side of the tracks? The last thing these kids need is drive-by therapy from you two.

FRASIER

Dad, I gave my word. I think a meaningful job could set Barney ...using your tireless train metaphor...on the right track.

NILES

(PROUDLY) Yes, look what intelligence and higher education have spawn in Frasier and me.

MARTIN

For what it's worth, when I was on the force, our Community Relations Department set up all kinds of programs for kids. Talk to somebody at the station.

FRASIER

Dad, that's it. I'll talk with Cheryl Raymond in Community Affairs. Maybe she can arrange a paid internship.

MARTIN

The station gets an employee, the kid gets a few bucks, and you and Niles X get to satisfy your guilt.

FRASIER

Come on, Niles, we've got to go see Cheryl Raymond.

NILES

What's this 'we' stuff, home-brother.

MARTIN

It's homeboy, Niles. Homeboy.

NILES

Well, if I must.

FRASIER

You must.

FRASIER LAYS A CHASTENING EYE ON NILES. THEN, ALA DENZEL WASHINGTON IN "MALCOLM X" – FRASIER PUTS HIS HAND UP AND DRAMATICALLY POINTS HIS FINGER TOWARD THE DOOR.

NILES TAKES HIS MARCHING ORDERS, AND EXITS. FRASIER EXITS BEHIND HIM.

CUT TO:

D

FADE IN:

A BLACK SCREEN. IN WHITE LETTERS: "HEY, BROTHER, CAN YOU SPARE SOME TIME?"

CROSS FADE TO:

INT. KACL RADIO - CORRIDOR - DAY

(CHERYL RAYMOND, FRASIER)

FRASIER ENTERS THE CORRIDOR FROM THE STUDIO WITH HIS JACKET AND BRIEFCASE IN HAND. CHERYL RAYMOND APPROACHES. SHE IS AN ATTRACTIVE, SPIRITED AFRICAN-AMERICAN WOMAN IN A CONSERVERATIVE BUSINESS SUIT.

CHERYL RAYMOND

Terrific show, Dr. Crane.

FRASIER

Well thank you, Ms. Raymond. It's a pleasure to see you again.

CHERYL RAYMOND

I have good news. We've set up a tour of the station for Barney Jeffries and a few other young people from his high school.

FRASIER

Wow, that was fast.

CHERYL RAYMOND

Well, I was excited by our conversation the other day. When a man like you offers to give something back to the community I have to move fast.

FRASIER

So, when does this take place?

CHERYL RAYMOND

Tomorrow. Meet them fifteen minutes before your show then spend an hour or so afterward... if that's alright with you.

FRASIER

(SURPRISED) Tomorrow? I think tomorrow is fine.

CHERYL RAYMOND

Great. Thank you, Dr. Crane.

SHE STRUTS AWAY, LEAVING FRASIER TO PONDER. AND WE,

FLIP TO:

E

FADE IN:

A BLACK SCREEN. IN WHITE LETTERS: "WHATZUP, DOC?"

CROSS FADE TO:

INT. RADIO STUDIO - DAY

(NILES, FRASIER, CHERYL RAYMOND, BARNEY, LILITHA, TEEN)

FRASIER AND NILES ENTER ARGUING.

NILES

Why am I here? I thought the object was to get your young man a job...not take me away from mine.

FRASIER

I need you as a filter. I don't know what goes on in the minds of young people these days. You're my younger brother, you're as close to adolescence as anyone I know.

NILES

Am not.

FRASIER

Are to.

NILES

Am not!

JUST THEN, CHERYL RAYMOND ENTERS WITH SEVERAL HIGH SCHOOLERS.

TWO AFRICAN-AMERICAN BOYS, ONE AFRICAN-AMERICAN GIRL, HISPANIC-AMERICAN BOY, AND ASIAN-AMERICAN GIRL. ALL HIP-HOP EXCEPT THE AFRICAN-AMERICAN GIRL.

CHERYL RAYMOND

Hello, Dr. Crane. Young people, I am pleased to introduce KACL Radio's foremost broadcaster, Doctor Frasier Crane.

FRASIER AND NILES SMILE, WAVE AND NOD.

FRASIER

Hello, everyone. This is my brother Dr. Niles Crane. He's also a psychologist.

FRASIER IS THEN CAPTIVATED BY THE AFRICAN-AMERICAN GIRL'S HAIR. SHE IS LILITHA, 18, ATTRACTIVE AND POISED, SHE IS PROPER AND HIGH-COLLAR CONSERVATIVE. HER INTRICATE BRAIDS ARE PULLED UP INTO A TIDY BUN.

FRASIER

(TO LILITHA) What a beautiful intriguing design. How do you do that with your hair?

LILITHA BLUSHES. BUT BEFORE SHE CAN RESPOND, A TALL, HANDSOME, BRAWNY AFRICAN-AMERICAN KID INTERVENES,

BARNEY

Yo, dog, get up off her.

NILES

(TRANSLATING) I think that means relent, Frasier.

FRASIER RELENTS AS THE TWO AFRICAN-AMERICAN GUYS EYE HIM AS THEY FORM A WALL SIDE BY SIDE.

FRASIER

Barney? You're Barney. I'd know that voice anywhere.

FRASIER EXTENDS HIS HAND, BUT BARNEY, A TALL, WELL-BUILT HANDSOME YOUNG MAN TAKES A TOUGH STAND. HE LOOKS FRASIER UP AND DOWN. THEN THROWS HIS ARMS OPEN AND HUGS FRASIER.

BARNEY

(THRILLED) Whatzup, dog?!

FRASIER

Fine, Barney, I'm fine.

BARNEY

Check it out, this is my girl, Lilitha. Ain't she all that, G?

FRASIER LOOKS CURIOUSLY AT NILES,

NILES

(TRANSLATING) I think that means she's special, beautiful...and all of that sorta thing.

FRASIER

Yes, lovely. Nice to meet you... (UNSURE) Your name again...?

LILITHA

Lilitha...like your ex-wife's name...just add an "A." You don't talk about her on the air as much. That's a sign of growth.

FRASIER LOOKS CLOSELY AT LILITHA, HER STERN POSTURE AND MANNERISM. HE FINDS THE RESEMBLANCE IS UNCANNY.

FRASIER

I see.

LILITHA EXTENDS HER HAND TO FRASIER. SHE HOLDS IT A LITTLE LONGER THAN USUAL, LOOKS HIM STRAIGHT IN THE EYE.

LILITHA

It's a pleasure to meet you. I already feel like I know you.

BARNEY

She's been into your show since day one. She's the reason I started checking out your show. See where you comin' from. 'Cause, me myself, I ain't up on the brainiac tip, ya know.

MACHO, BARNEY GIVES THE OTHER TWO GUYS A POUND.

CHERYL RAYMOND

Well, you've met Barney and Lilitha. This is Marcus, Ramon and Joy. They're all seniors interested in broadcasting.

LILITHA

I've been accepted into Princeton, in psychology.

FRASIER

Very impressive, Lilitha.

BARNEY

First we all gonna be hooked up as interns, making bank, right?

CHERYL RAYMOND

Yes. The station has approved five positions for paid interns.

TEENS

All right! Yo, yo, yo!

CHERYL RAYMOND

Okay, young people. Dr. Crane is busy now. We'll talk with him later, after his show.

LILITHA

(TO FRASIER) May we watch?

CHERYL RAYMOND

(INTERJECTS) No, we have other things to see here at the station. Come along now.

THE KIDS SIGH IN DISAPPOINTMENT AS THEY START TO EXIT.

BARNEY

Hey, maybe you brothas...get it? Brothas?

FRASIER IS STUMPED.

NILES

Got it. Brothers... double entendre. We are blood related brothers, and we're like soul brothas. That's very clever.

BARNEY

I like you.

BARNEY PUTS HIS ARM AROUND NILES' SHOULDER. NILES PUTS HIS ARM AROUND BARNEY.

NILES

I like you, as well... brotha.

BARNEY

So, you'll be judges in our Weekly Rap.

NILES

Is it some sort of recital?

LILITHA

People rap, sing, dance, read poetry. It's a contest we have every Friday.

NILES

Oh, yes. Frasier and I are there. We be down!

NILES, BARNEY, LILITHA, AND THE OTHERS EXIT. OFF FRASIER'S STUPEFIED EXPRESSION, WE:

FADE OUT:

END ACT ONE

CHAPTER 22

The Economics of Television Writing

In this chapter I cover business basics. Paying attention to the production costs of your "spec" episode is important in its initial development, but it's more imperative during the rewriting process. If you offer up a teleplay that would cost more than the average production budget for a particular series, you're basically telling producers that you can't work in the television environment because you don't understand its financial side. The producers who read your spec teleplay have the power of putting you on staff, so you want to make the best impression you can with your teleplay.

Although knowing about the basic economics of television won't necessarily help you to write a better episode, it certainly gives you better insight as to how and why some deals get made while others don't. The only *real* logic used to make creative decisions is taking into consideration the business deal.

LICENSING FEES AND DEFICITS

A typical one-hour dramatic episode for the 2004–2005 season had a cost between $1.5 million and $3 million. Series that become successful because of a popular large ensemble cast generally get more expensive when the initial contract expires, which is usually after the first three years. It's estimated that the series *ER* costs in the neighborhood of $10 to $13 million per episode.[1] In fact, nearly all of the original cast members have been replaced to reduce the cost of the series. As this series nears its run, the big factor of whether it stays on the air is the cost-profit ratio.

While most sitcom per-episode budgets generally hover around $1 million when they first hit the airways, these costs always escalate with the success of the series. It's reported that in the final season of *Friends* (1994–2004), the costs were somewhere between $5 million and $10 million per episode.[2] The cost of on-screen talent is the single largest reason behind rising costs in television production since writers generally write for scale and producers try to keep their fees reasonable when they negotiate. For the 2005–2006 television season of *The King of Queens*, its star, Kevin James, reportedly earned $500,000 per episode. This trend has given rise to new series development outside of the Big Three Networks—NBC, CBS, and ABC—and aided UPN and the WB in establishing themselves beyond fledging status. Alternatively, with the five largest networks competing fiercely for rating points, the rapid rise of "reality television" on these nets have also opened the door for a new generation of basic cable networks such as TNT, TBS, and notably USA and FOX's FX to get into the one-hour drama, halfhour comedy, television movie, and mini-series business.

Talk and game programs—called *strip shows*—are much cheaper to produce than scripted series. For example, venerable syndicated game shows such as *Jeopardy, Wheel of Fortune*, and *The Price Is Right* videotape five weekly shows over a single weekend. While "reality" series such as CBS's *Survivor* and MTV's *Real World* fall under this category, these series' costs have escalated with their success. Ironically, in a survey, audiences do not consider the *Survivor* series as reality but as a drama.

The budget of television films can range anywhere from $2 million to $20 million (or more) for a mini-series. This art form is becoming more the domain of premium pay cable networks such as HBO and Showtime who can attract feature film actors to essentially uncensored material.

Studios get some production money from the network. It's called a **licensing fee**. It's generally only a portion of the complete cost to produce an episode. The studio must then provide financing for the **deficit** of each produced episode. Generally, the networks license the use of an episode for 80 to 90 percent of the total budget and the studio must invest the rest themselves. Networks make back their money through advertising sales revenue, while studios make back theirs in what's called the *after* or *ancillary markets*. Most times this is domestic and foreign syndication, video rentals and sales, and other unique forms of distribution. The possibilities continue to expand as technology develops more means of program distribution. The practice of **repurposing** programs is a growing trend as networks make deals with one another to rebroadcast certain series or air reruns on networks they already own. In this way, financers can reduce their negative cost and earn higher profit margins on each advertising dollar received.

Networks can own their series by financing them in-house. This has changed the way networks develop programs in a big way. But still making a profit is the primary motive.

The emergence of technology such as the DVD (digital video disc) is changing the way networks make money. Many of their series both on and off the air are being sold in collector's editions. This trend has been fueled by the merging of networks with large media corporations that have strong distribution capabilities in the retail marketplace. Examples of networks and corporations that are financially linked in 2005 are: Universal Studios *and* NBC; ABC, A&E *and* Disney; CBS, UPN, MTV, BET, Showtime *and* Viacom; The WB, TBS, TNT, HBO *and* Time-Warner.

CO-PRODUCTIONS

In order to make back investments sooner, often a studio or network will enter what's called a **co-production** deal. This means that several investors put up money to spread out the liability and divide the expenses in such a way that the entire production budget is covered. Each investor splits profits in exclusive designated markets. For example, an American studio might enter a co-production agreement with Germany. The two share the entire production costs and split profits according to domestic and German distribution rights. This way, every party begins making money on the *first dollar* as opposed to waiting for *back-end profits*. This form of investing is used extensively with television movies, especially expensive mini-series.

So, why should you care about all of this business mumbo jumbo? The overall effect is that all of these tactics induce studios and networks to invest money into new programming development. The more programming, the more work for writers.

HOW MANY SPEAKING ROLES

When writing your spec teleplay, be conscious that every time a character speaks, it costs money. So, keep speaking roles outside of the cast of regulars to a minimum. For example, instead of giving three cops one line each, give all the lines to one cop and use the others for atmosphere only.

Also, control the number of characters outside the series regulars. Concentrate on telling the story by *servicing* the regulars. Series producers like to write in juicy guest star roles but that's generally frowned upon in spec teleplays.

The bottom line is controlling the number of actors needed in your script outside the regular characters makes your teleplay more *producible*.

HOW MANY SETS AND LOCATIONS

Be conscious of how many sets and locations you use in your teleplay. One rule of thumb is if you must use a set outside of the *standing sets* (the sets used on a weekly basis), then put more than one scene in that "swing" set.

If the series has scenes *on the streets* that are locations outside the studio sets, be aware of how much the series for which you're writing uses locations. When you analyze typical episodes, count the number of location scenes and that'll give you a pretty good idea of how many are acceptable for the show.

If at all possible, design your story to take place in as few locations or sets as possible. Concentrate on using the standing sets, especially when writing a sitcom script.

Again, this makes your script more producible and illustrates that you have a clear understanding of how to write episodic television.

ACTION SEQUENCES AND BUDGET

Car chases and shoot-outs cost more money than dialogue-driven scenes. Study the series for which you're writing and count the number of action sequences used in a typical episode. You might find a particular show will have one action sequence per act, or two per show—usually one in the first half (act two break) and one in the second half (usually the climactic scene).

Otherwise, your spec episode will be too expensive and cast a dark shadow on you as a potential TV writer.

PRODUCTION SCHEDULES

Few one-hour series are totally studio-located productions. Most split the production between *in-studio* shooting on sets and shooting *on the street* in real locations. Some series primarily shoot in Los Angeles but go back to actual locations to shoot street locations in the city in which the series takes place. This was done with *NYPD Blue* and *ER*. Episodes for the hit series franchise *CSI*—Las Vegas, New York, and Miami—are also shot primarily in Los Angeles. Generally, when this happens, exterior locations for several episodes are shot during one visit, usually over a period of a week or two. Then these scenes in the actual location are edited into the rest of the episodes that are shot in L.A.

Once a teleplay is put into pre-production, it must be *boarded* for production. During this process, casting, wardrobe, and other details are also underway.

The Board

The board is a foldout panel that carries color-coded strips for each scene in an episode. It lists all pertinent information gleaned from the teleplay to generate *call sheets.* A call sheet indicates the locations to be used that day, work time for each actor and crew member, and provides each department with important information such as wardrobe, props, effects, and stunts.

The board is organized by priority based on specific factors such as actor availability, studio or location, day or night. It's a big juggling act because things frequently go wrong during production and schedules have to be rearranged.

The typical one-hour drama for prime time is shot in eight days, not including weekends. There are a lot of union rules that affect how this can or cannot be executed—too numerous to get into here. But schedules are most dramatically affected by a concept called *turnaround*, which provides for a certain amount of time between work days and how long certain people can work based on a lot of factors. For example, there are strict work rules for minors.

There are usually two crews designated A and B. Directors are assigned to a crew and, at any given time, one episode is in *prep* while another is in *production*, while still another is in *post.* Certain key production members serve on both crews. These positions almost always include the *director of photography.*

The Process

Prep means a script is being broken down for the reality of production. It usually last five to seven days; every detail is paid attention to: what characters will wear, hand and set props, production design, special effects, and stunts. If necessary, locations are scouted by the **director** and locked-down for shooting by the **location manager**. The script is constantly being revised to accommodate these factors. Casting of characters written outside the series regulars takes place as well.

Production means the teleplay gets photographed. Once a teleplay leaves prep and goes into production, another script goes into prep. If the A crew is shooting one script, the B crew preps the new one, which will go into production when the current episode finishes being shot. Producers and executives view "dailies" as footage is processed and might rewrite some scenes or reshoot them as necessary, using the director and crew in production. The growing use of high-definition video is changing the process significantly as it eliminates film processing. This speeds up the **post-production** process.

Post means editing begins on the episode coming out of production. There are a lot of details that need attention. Generally speaking, the following steps must be accomplished:

- Rough cut
- Editor's cut
- Director's cut
- Producers' cut
- Studio's cut
- Network's cut

The advent of nonlinear editing using digital software on a personal computer has helped make this process less intimidating and less time-consuming. Digital editing allows the producers to create different "cuts" quickly for comparison as well as to make changes mandated by the studio or network.

During post, the edited episode has to be *spotted* for sound effects and music. *Sweetening* then begins, which could include the looping of wild lines called *automatic dialogue replacement* (ADR), sound effects, and the music score. If there are digital effects or *computer generated images* (CGI), they are usually worked on separately then edited into the episode along the way.

Once all of these major procedures—and many others—are completed, the episode is *mixed down* and *dubbed* for broadcast.

These steps apply to sitcoms and television movies.

NOTES

1. Josef Adalian, "NBC Staying with 'Friends'—Peacock Pays $150 Mil for Final Year," 11 Feb. 2002, at www.variety.com/articles.
2. Josef Adalian, "King's Ransom for Queen Leah Sitcom Thesp Gets Royal Treatment from CBS," 20 July 2005, at www.variety.com/articles.

CHAPTER 23

Writing Original Teleplays

THE DEVELOPMENT PROCESS

Many people wonder why certain television series get made. Well, that's one of those things that can only be explained by the executives who make those decisions. But generally, networks try to put on series that appeal to every segment of the audience. That includes viewers who like "silly" entertainment. The most valued segment to the network consists of viewers who are eighteen to twenty-five years olds. This slice of the audience is most prized because advertisers want to reach this market more than any other because they tend to be more innovative, take more chances, and, because they have less responsibility, have more disposable income to buy stuff. Advertisers' research has proven that a consumer becomes loyal to a certain brand of product at an early age.

So, series are developed with an eye toward a certain **demographic** because advertisers want to reach certain kinds of consumers. The largest television audience demographic is women eighteen to forty-five years of age. So, many series programs are designed to appeal to females in general. This is especially true in the television movie department. Women make many of the purchasing decisions in a family household, so advertisers are very interested in appealing to this group.

If you're interested in writing original material for television, it's important to understand which *demographic* will be attracted to your project.

THE FINE ART OF HOMOGENIZING

Simply stated, television tries to appeal to the broadest audience as possible. Although this is becoming more and more true just for certain networks, cable television is taking a different approach by offering a certain brand of entertainment. Examples abound: The Sci-Fi Network appeals to science fiction junkies; Comedy Central to viewers looking for a laugh; and Lifetime to women viewers. There are others such as Showtime, offering "sexy" series appealing to adults, and HBO who puts on series that appeal to a more "sophisticated," predominantly male, audience. The bottom line is that they are all trying to reach the same pool of people out there in the vast wasteland by using different program appeals.

In recent years, the major networks have been losing a piece of the viewing audience to other networks, many of which are classified as pay TV. This trend is predicted to continue as more and more cable networks come on-line with highly specialized series program appeals. This is called *niche* programming and is the future trend of television programming predicted by most industry mavens.

How television programs get developed varies from studio to studio and network to network. But the general process goes something like this:

1. Series idea pitched to a studio.
2. A studio options or buys series idea.
3. A studio pitches series idea to a network.
4. A network buys series idea.
5. A studio and a network collaborate on developing a pilot teleplay.
6. A pilot teleplay is ordered into production.
7. The produced pilot is picked up for series production.
8. The new series goes on the air.

Of course, somebody can always say "no" along the way and stop this entire process. In that case, it's back to square one and start over. There are other ways series get made as well. Some studios have the financial power to order a full season of episodes, generally twenty-two. Others will order forty-four episodes, especially for pay cable series, looking to make a long-term investment so the series can be syndicated later on free TV. Examples are HBO's *The Larry Sanders Show* (1992–1998) and *Dream On* (1990–1996) and Showtime's remake of the *The Outer Limits* (1995–2002) and *Stargate SG-1* (1997–present). HBO's edgy series *The Sopranos* (2000–2006) is being edited for general audiences for syndication. But these premium cables consider thirteen episodes a full season, not twenty-two like their commercial counterparts.

Certain stars command large episode orders for the deal to be made in the first place. For example, Roseanne Barr and Bill Cosby had the power of mass appeal and several years of episodes were ordered up front. This, of course, is rare. But as networks and studios merge in terms of ownership, and network in-house studios produce more and more of their own product, this trend will certainly grow. This approach to the business is also being fueled by the competition to retain the exclusive services of writers who have a strong track record of creating hit series.

CREATING A NEW SERIES

Creating a new series is probably one of the hardest deeds to accomplish in television for a new writer. Even veteran series creators have a tough time getting one to stick with an audience. It's important to remember that studios and television networks are in the business of making profits. The jobs of executives are at stake if they fail to deliver hit shows. There's a lot of money spent up front to hire star talent, develop, produce, and promote a new television series. Still, it's a very expensive gamble.

This is why studios and networks turn to writers and producers who have a track record in developing new television programs. Some writers and producers have become as famous as the actors who star in their series. And this makes them more marketable to the networks and serves to open more doors for the studios who hire them. These famous writer-producers sign major *development deals* and exclusively work for one studio and network. Because of this, many buyers are not looking to bring in outside writing talent but, instead, to "get their money's worth" from the folks they're already paying big bucks.

Spec Pilots and Development

Yes, it's true that today, there's less opportunity for the newcomer to create a new series than five or ten years ago. But that doesn't mean it can't be done. It's just harder to do. I'd like to think that a good idea for a new series will somehow find its way to the little screen despite the fact it's a new writer who invented it. Sometimes they do. Because there are ever-expanding forms of distribution, more studios are developing pilot teleplays outside of the normal process of firm network commitments to star talent and studios. It's simply not as risky today as it was when the only game in town was the three big networks.

There's also more of a trend these days for new writers (and experienced ones) to write a pilot episode on "spec." That means writing it for free before ever officially contacting anyone in the business. The *spec pilot* is proof that the new or experienced writer has a unique vision and can execute it in "prototype" teleplay form. If you write a spec pilot teleplay for a new series, chances are you'll be able to get studios and networks to read it because it's free! They can always say no without spending one red cent. However, if they like what they read, then you're on your way to fame and fortune. However, actually getting an executive to read your spec pilot is yet another big hurdle you'll have to jump. The best starting place to this achievement is an agent or manager.

So, if you think you have a great idea for a new television series—whether drama or comedy—this chapter briefly offers some basic information to help you get started.

SERIES PREMISE AND FRANCHISE

The **series premise** is the fundamental reason the characters of a series are tied together, that is, to solve crimes or save lives, or in the case of a comedy, it could be to stay married or raise children properly.

The **franchise** is the general *setting* in which these characters share their relationships. A franchise is *more* than a setting. It's the "well" from which stories can be retrieved. The deeper the well, the longer the series will run. In drama, *Cops, Docs, and Lawyers* seem to be the favorite franchises because each involves life and death situations as an "organic" part of the setting. *Family* is another favorite. Many dramas present their ensemble casts as a type of family. This franchise is the staple of soap operas and sitcoms in prime time. Most series have regular characters who are metaphors for (or really are) father, mother, son, daughter, uncle, aunt, cousin, and so on.

The Series Concept or Format

The **series concept** or format is generally a document that's five to ten pages long. Its purpose is to explain the entire series. It's a sells pitch, clear and simple, and should be well written. Here's a typical outline of a series concept:

A Hook. Grab the reader quickly with a clever sentence or two.

The Premise. Explain the underlying premise of the series and its overall *week-to-week* aim.

The Franchise. Explain the backdrop or setting for the series.
Broad Explanation of Series Approach. Explain how the characters' interaction with one another and within the franchise will generate stories on a weekly basis.
Series Regular Character Thumbnail Sketches. A half-page or so on each regular character in the series. Include major **recurring characters**, if any.
Loglines for Episodes. Using the *TV Guide* format, write a short description of twelve to twenty-two episodes. The loglines should focus on the series regulars multiple storylines and have a bit more detail than a real *TV Guide* description.
Long-Term Arc of Series Regular Characters. You can also include a short explanation of how the series regulars' relationships will evolve and change over time, especially during the first season.

Still, buyers generally want to hear a pitch of the format before reading it. And that means getting a meeting with important personages at studios and networks. Before that, agents will want to hear it. Then a long list of "underlings" will want to hear it—their job is to screen material for their bosses. The catch-22 is that nobody really wants to meet with newcomers. They say they're looking for new talent, but feel it's too risky and they're afraid you might sue them if they already have something similar to your idea in development (which happens more often than you may think).

It's important to have a personal set of contacts that include one or more of the following: *an agent and/or manager, a producer with a track record, a studio executive, and a TV network manager.* The more of these ingredients you have, the better your chances are for success. If you're new, try contacting writer-producers with track records and get one interested in your material. If a "showrunner" likes it, he or she may then purchase it, or execute an "if come" deal with you and "attach" themselves to the project. Then they take it to the buyers.

Some quick definitions: An *if come* deal is a simple contract that's usually a page or two that states the basic terms of payment and participation in a project for all parties concerned. These terms do not go into effect until someone actually purchases the project. *Attaching* a writer-producer to a project simply means the producer will work on the project, thus guaranteeing to the buyer a chance of success based on the producer's track record. A **showrunner** is a writer-producer who has successfully created or worked on a series for television.

Make sure you understand where you stand in the process, and be aware it's very easy to become overwhelmed (seduced) by show business double-talk. That's why it's a good idea to have access to an entertainment attorney to help sort out confusion that surely will crop up.

The Two-Hour Back-Door Pilot

Because it's so risky to purchase and produce a one-hour pilot for a program that might not get "picked up," studios and networks sometimes turn to the television movie format to hedge their investment. Despite a recent decline in the television movie on network schedules, they figure if the two-hour doesn't work as a pilot, at least they have a product they can still exploit for profit.

Bear in mind, the two-hour **back-door pilot** is not like a regular television movie. It has to be *more.* Even though its format is still seven acts, how you use this structure is quite different from a normal television movie.

The primary difference is this: the back-door movie has to achieve two major goals:

1. satisfy the audience's need for a story with a beginning, a middle, and an ending; and
2. leave a feeling that the characters can continue indefinitely in future weekly stories.

The really well-written back-door pilot spends the first hour—acts one, two, and three—introducing characters into the series premise and franchise primarily using a central storyline, an A-story that leads into the second hour. The second hour—acts four, five, six, and seven—"plays" more like a typical weekly four-act episode despite the fact that there's a single central story. The B- and C-storylines carry the four-act structure in this last hour so it's important to nurture the secondary storylines in the first hour. You could also say that the two-hour back-door pilot is like writing two episodes that are "To be continued . . ." The long-form pilot does utilize multiple storylines but they are most effectively dramatically contributing to the central A-story.

The special nature of the back-door pilot is this: *You must develop your characters extremely well in the first hour and let the audience sit back and watch them do their "weekly" thing in the last.*

For more on the seven-act structure, see the section Writing Television Movies.

The Series Bible

The *series bible* is the basic background information on a series. It starts with the *concept* or *format* and is generally expanded to more detail after the series is sold and produced. This becomes the "common" document from which writers, producers, directors, and executives work. It establishes the rules of character and story. This often evolves as the series goes on, taking into consideration the fact that certain actors "break out" or the audience prefers one direction to another in the series. The series bible also grows to include every storyline produced as well as the ones that have been rejected. All of this information is placed in a series of three-ring binders for easy reference by the story editors and producers.

The Series Regular Cast of Characters

As I've already mentioned, we often call the series regular characters the **money**. They're the reason a series becomes popular. Therefore, you have to *service the money* each week in each episode. Here's a general overall view of how that's done.

Character Arc

You service them on three levels:

Per Episode—Characters experience growth over the course of one hour.

Per Season—Characters experience growth over the course of twenty-two hours (or thirteen for premium cable).

The Run of the Series—Characters experience growth over the course of 110 hours, which is the ideal goal of a five-year run (or fifty-five for premium cable).

Character Counterpoint

What makes this work is the following:

Opposites Attract—Each character should be a different person.

Conflict—Characters should form relationships based on disagreements because agreeing is boring. This is called *counterpointing* characters.

Rotating Counterpoint with Character Arc—Characters often change their minds and form new relationships based on new disagreements.

Using Guest Stars

Guest star characters often help to put a certain spin on a series and help to attract audiences. But most series prefer to let their regular characters drive the storylines. Some programs actually base the series on *guest stars*. The most famous one is *The Love Boat* (1997–1986) and, recently, *Diagnosis Murder* (1992–2001). These are generally one-shot appearances.

Some series sign a guest star for two to three episodes and bring them back over the course of a season. For example, *The Practice* (1997–2004) used this approach several times a season by picking up storylines that appeared to have ended but the character does something else that requires the legal services of one of the series regulars. Continuing in this tradition is the series spin-off *Boston Legal* (2004–present).

Another growing trend is to bring in actors as *guest regulars* who appear over a six to thirteen episode arc. This affords the producers a grand opportunity to kill a character familiar to the audience for "sweeps," which is the ratings periods. It also gives the show a breath of fresh air and occasionally yields new regular cast members if the audience grows to like a particular character played by a guest star actor. The Academy of Television Arts and Sciences even has an Emmy Award category for guest stars on a series. This frequently encourages feature film stars who normally do not act on television to take a role.

Developing Weekly Episodes

When you start to think of all the possible stories you can explore on your new series, keep the following in mind:

- *Fill In Long-Term Gaps*
  In putting together a concept for a new series, you should consider the long-term potential of the character relationships and story possibilities. It doesn't have to be set in concrete, but the long-term potential needs to be fairly clear. A series concept that looks like it can only get a season or two before running out of gas most likely won't get developed. Well, some actually are developed, and most don't succeed as a result.
- *Challenge the Premise*
  Demonstrate how the series can be taken to its edge on a regular basis and how the premise feeds conflict from week to week. This is called *testing the premise*. Generally, pilots try to take the series premise to the edge. And, generally speaking, a series will test its premise three to four times a season. Lately it has become fashionable to test a series premise during the ratings periods called *sweep*—November, February, and May—as well as at the end of the season by using a tantalizing *cliff-hanger*.

  How do you test the premise? Kill a main character! Take the franchise away! Try to remove the core reason for the series to go on. Or at least give that impression only to have the day saved at the end of the hour or the start of the next season. Sometimes, series are tested unintentionally when an actor decides to move on with his or her career or can't agree on a new contract. So, the writers will send that character off the series in an extraordinary style.

- *Challenge the Characters*
  Demonstrate the potential for bringing in new characters and getting rid of present characters. Feature different series regular characters in your sample weekly episodes.
- *Explore the Bounds of the Franchise*
  Try to take the series beyond itself. It's sometimes referred to as **spin-off** potential. Show as many different facets of the franchise in the type of episodes you want to see in the series.

Creating Series without Franchises

Series without franchises are generally referred to as *anthologies*. This type of series depends entirely on stories rather than characters that appear week to week. They also depend on using a wide variety of recognizable actors on a weekly basis.

The series *The Outer Limits* is an excellent example. An old favorite is *The Twilight Zone* (1959–1965). You can catch this classic series during holiday marathons. Premium cable TV is leading the way in bringing back this art form with such series as Showtime's *The Hunger* (1997–2000) and Showtime's *Red Shoe Diaries* (1992–1999).

On the networks, a few series managed to merge the two concepts. Shows such as *Early Edition* (1996–2000), *Touched by an Angel* (1994–2003), and *Promised Land* (1996–1999) had small core casts and relied heavily on using guest stars with an anthology-type storytelling approach.

Nirvana—The Five-Year Run

Ideally, for the producers and networks, a series will run for at least five years. So, characters often get reinvented several times over—sometimes ending up where they started in the pilot. That means you must develop a series that has potential for at least five years worth of episodes. The magic number seems to be one hundred. It's celebrated by studios and networks because it means money in syndication sales for the studio that owns the series.

And *series creators* generally have a piece of that action.

WRITING THE TELEVISION MOVIE

The networks call them *MOWs* (**Movie of the Week**). They tend to appeal to the women in the audience. A nickname for the type of movies being produced these days is *woman in jep*. "Jep" means jeopardy. This has expanded to include *family in jep*. Many of these premises are ripped directly from the headlines and usually involve a furious battle to get television rights up front from the real life people.

The networks have been trying to wean the audience off of this fare by developing more "original" movies. But the audience has stubbornly continued to view the jep movies in large numbers. The crown jewels of every network's movie schedule are the **mini-series** that broadcast during the rating sweep periods. They are almost always based on material from another medium, mostly novels, sometimes famous fables. Selling an original mini-series is almost impossible because the cost is so great. The networks cannot afford to develop and produce one without it having a "built-in" audience.

Cable calls their television movies **made fors**. These days, cable is where nearly all of the original television movies are being produced. In fact, each year, it's cable who wins the most Emmys in this area. Even cable is getting into the mini-series business. In 1998, HBO broadcast *From Earth to the Moon* in twelve parts and it was a huge hit. In 2001, this cable-caster aired a ten-part mini-series based on a novel of the same name, *Band of Brothers*. Other mini-series that have seen success are *Battlestar Galactica* (2003), *Spartacus* (2004), *Traffic* (2004), and *Angels in America* (2004).

Cable can produce movies that have strong adult appeal since premium channels have no advertisers to appease. This is not the case for such networks as USA and Lifetime, who, despite being pay cable, still depend on advertiser support for income. But this segment of cable movies is growing tremendously. Turner Network Television (TNT) and Turner Broadcasting Station (TBS) are making an impressive number of original films each year while non-cable networks are cutting back. Both of these cable stations are owned by Warner Brothers.

Television movies made for *syndication* are rare. This is because of the financial models that apply to the loose net of independent stations that depend on low cost fare for profit. Most of these movies get syndicated through co-productions where the producers are playing by a different set of profit-making rules.

The driving force for television movies is advertising sales and sponsorship. Some TV movies get made because one company buys the lion's share of the national advertising time, leaving only space for local ads.

Writing an original teleplay for a television movie is a tough row to hoe. In my opinion, the best way for newcomers to approach this opportunity is to obtain the *real life rights* to a story. If you want to get into writing television movies, there are some things you should know.

Spec MOWs

Television generally acquires an idea and/or the rights to a story. Rarely is a spec television script purchased. You should first write a "treatment." This is a synopsis of your story *under* ten double-spaced pages and broken down into seven acts. If you're a new writer, don't get your hopes up for writing the teleplay. Chances are you won't be allowed. With a good writing sample, maybe you'll get a shot on the next sale.

Types of Stories

Most television movies are *character driven,* ideally about women. They're about the girl next door who gets raped. Or the abused housewife who sets her husband on fire. Or a true story ripped from the headlines. Audiences watch TV for the characters. For this reason, producers and networks like strong themes with universal appeal. Like series television, stories about families appeal to buyers. Stories about the average woman fighting the system are also very popular. And these stories must be very emotional. There's a short list of actors who draw big ratings for TV movies. You have a better chance of selling a TV movie treatment if one of these actors is perfect for the lead role.

Budgets

Television movies have much smaller budgets than feature films, more or less. So, as with series television, you must watch the number of characters, sets, and action-sequences that are included in your treatment. This is true even for original cable films.

Structure

Commercial television (free) movies use the seven-act structure. As with series TV, you must make room for commercials. Therefore, you must include the act breaks in the script just as you would in a weekly series teleplay. Here's a breakdown of the seven-act structure:

Act One
- Twenty-two to twenty-four pages long
- Equivalent to the feature's act one
- Ends on the first half hour, needs a strong dramatic act break

Act Two
- Thirteen to fifteen pages long
- Equivalent to the feature's first mini-drama of act two

Act Three
- Thirteen to fifteen pages long
- Equivalent to the feature's second mini-drama
- Ends at the top of the first hour, needs a strong dramatic act break

Act Four
- Thirteen to fifteen pages long
- Equivalent to the feature's third mini-drama

Act Five
- Thirteen to fifteen pages long
- Equivalent to the feature's fourth mini-drama
- Ends on the half-hour, needs a strong dramatic act break

Act Six
- Thirteen to fifteen pages long
- Equivalent to the feature's act three

Act Seven
- Thirteen to fifteen pages long
- Equivalent to the feature's act three

However, premium cable movies do not use the seven-act structure because there are no commercials. They are written exactly like feature films.

Selling a TV Movie

Contact producers and/or production companies who are in the business of making TV movies. Watch the credits of television movies to see who the producers are and what production company made the film. You can also find out who produces television movies by reading the trades, such as the *Daily Variety* and the *Hollywood Reporter*, on a regular basis. Finally, you can also consult the *Hollywood Creative Directory*. Ideally, you'll want your *representation* to make the contacts on your behalf.

WRITING DAYTIME DRAMA

The first thing a writer does to develop an original **daytime drama**, popularly called *soap opera,* is to write a *bible*. The bible runs three to four hundred pages. It contains a treatment of the basic premise, character biographies for every series regular, the first six months of storylines, and an explanation of how each storyline will weave in and out of the series.

Daytime dramas are written by a variety of writers:

The **headwriter** is on staff and supervises all writing.

Breakdown writers are usually freelance. Some are on staff. A breakdown is a scene outline for an episode.

Staff writers generally write most of the installments. Some of them specialize in writing certain character's storylines and dialogue.

Freelance writers are usually part of a pool that producers can turn to for help to handle the sheer volume of writing that has to be done. Some of these writers rarely see the producers and work through e-mail and fax.

If you're interested in writing for daytime television, you definitely need an agent with good contacts on the series. Generally, one needs to have a strong track record but new writers break in every year. Some networks have new talent programs that actively seek writers in this and other areas of programming.

WRITING REALITY TELEVISION

Many of the programs that fall into the category of **reality television** are considered to be *writer proof* by the industry. That means they do not use writers. Some *game shows* use what is called *researchers* to come up with questions and answers.

Reality drama series such as MTV's *Real World* and *Survivor* do not use writers. The producers of *Real World* say the episodes do not come out of someone's imagination, instead, the producers find the story in documentary-style videotaped material. However, these types of reality series do use the *series episodic technique of multiple storylines*. And in unfolding these storylines, they also use the *two- or four-acts structure*. This is achieved not by writers writing a script but by producers in the editing room using the principles behind writing an episode. To aid in this process, producers cast the "real" people using character types that will engender conflict. The reality, no pun intended, is that game shows will always be a staple of television programming. Game shows have certainly evolved to become more edgy, such as *Fear Factor* (on the air in 2001) and *The Amazing Race* (on the air in 2001). This new type of fantasy game show has also spawned hits such as *The Bachelor* and *The Bachelorette*. Talk shows will continue to flourish as well. But, in my opinion, only a few reality drama series will survive the test of time. *Real World* hit MTV in 1992 and has firmly earned its place in television history; so has *Survivor*, which hit the airways in fall 2000; both are still going strong. These types of reality series use producers who understand story and structure and represent a clear opportunity for writers to use their skills in the editing process.

Improvised series are becoming an important part of television since the success of Larry David's HBO series *Curb Your Enthusiasm* (he created the hit series *Seinfeld*). This program has firmly set the pace for this new form of reality/drama/comedy television. In this situation, the writer comes up with a story and scene outline and the actors improvise the scenes during actual production. This is a growing genre on television.

Television news is another form of reality programming. This goes beyond the nightly news and extends to such series as *20/20, 48 Hours, Dateline,* and the venerable *60 Minutes.* But these programs are written by members of the Writers Guild of America called "news writers." These writers are primarily trained in broadcast journalism. An interesting trend is that some of these network news programs are also using the four-act dramatic structure and are increasingly highlighting only one story per episode.

CHAPTER 24

A Career Writing for Television

WRITING ON STAFF

There's so much television being produced that it requires consistent work weeks like any other profession. Writers are provided offices, computers, staffs of secretaries, and assistants in order to get the job done.

Your journey to becoming a TV staff writer begins with that "spec" teleplay. The spec attracts representation—an agent or manager. The representatives schedule pitch meetings for you. You win several episodic assignments and write teleplays that get produced. These screen credits become your track record, and producers will hire you to write on staff on the basis of your track record. Once a *staff writer*, you can move up to *story editor*, then to *executive story editor*, then to **co-producer** to *producer* to **supervising producer** to **co-executive producer** and finally to the exalted position of *executive producer*.

Writers have enormous power in television and that's why they become producers. Once you reach the ranks of producer, you're known as a *showrunner.* Many of these producers who work on hit series are enticed into signing exclusive deals with studios and networks to develop and create new series whether their specialty is drama or comedy. For that reason, many feature film screenwriters are also joining the ranks of television writers. However, there are many staff writers who simply like working on staff and do not wish to take on management responsibilities by becoming producers.

There are few non-writing producers working on staff in series television. Those who do are mostly **line producers** whose job is to manage physical production and budgets, not the writing process. Some producers get their titles through directing. Yet others are just figureheads who manage the talent responsible for creating and/or starring in the series.

Few television writers work year after year for an entire career. For most, this climb to the mountain top takes years. There are times when experienced writers have "dry spells" and fail to get on staffs. They then must turn to freelancing or live off their savings or go hungry.

WRITING FREELANCE FOR TELEVISION

Freelance writing for television can be summed up in one word: *tough*. The reality is that television series *staffs* write most of the episodes. But those freelancers who do get assignments do so because they are good writers with a proven record of delivering quality material on time. As a freelancer, even experienced TV writers have to write a new spec script. In comedy, because of the group effort created through "the table" process, producers want to make sure that even an experienced writer can indeed write a teleplay on his or her own. Some sitcom writers have a reputation for being very funny and often land consulting jobs to punch-up scripts with jokes.

It's possible to sell a teleplay to a long-running series because these producers are always looking for fresh stories, but it's highly unlikely. Series like the *Star Trek* programs are always open to reading new and experienced writers' spec teleplays, though this is becoming less so. However, you must first sign a release if you do not have an agent. Some series that are produced outside the United States are written almost exclusively by Canadian or dual-citizenship writers.

The good news is that the marketplace for television writers is constantly expanding. Freelancing is hard but if you want to be a television writer, you will have to do it.

GETTING A TELEVISION AGENT OR MANAGER

Agents want to read spec teleplays. That's the bottom line. Agents also want to be confident that you can pitch your ideas. It's extremely difficult to work in television without an agent or manager. So, work hard on your spec teleplay, they're the key to your future in television writing. Write more than one TV spec. Some agents and producers will read a feature screenplay but ultimately you'll need that teleplay sample.

Television is very competitive for everyone. Even though new writers are their future lifeblood, agents are busy and don't have a lot of time to spend with newcomers. The best first step to getting an agent is to write a query letter. You can get a list of agents interested in television writers from the Writers Guild of America. *Do not send a script with your query letter.* However, have copies at the ready should an agent ask to read your teleplay. Also, be prepared to pitch episode ideas to agents when you meet with them. That means you need to work on story ideas for the series for which you would like to write. Despite the fact that the agent is satisfied with your material and ability to pitch and agrees to set up meetings with producers, you may *not* be asked to sign a contract. In television, this is sometimes called a *sweetheart deal* or *hip pocket deal*. Most likely you won't be offered a representation contract until you receive an offer of employment.

You can also meet agents at writers' forums and seminars. Agents often attend special luncheons designed to connect writers to representatives. If you attend this sort of function, your goal should be to connect as a human being to a potential agent. Then the process should evolve naturally in its own unique way.

An agent earns 10 percent of what the writer earns. If the writer does not earn a cent, neither does the agent. Remember, the agent works for you and should always work in your best interest. In fact, agents are legally bound to do so because they are *signatories* to the Writers Guild of America's Members Basic Agreement or MBA. That means they must follow the rules therein. If you find you don't like your agent, you can always fire him or her. The WGA rule is that if, after ninety days, the writer—that's you—is not offered employment, the writer can terminate the agreement. All it takes is a registered letter informing the agent you no longer wish to be represented by him or her. But be careful not to burn any bridges with agents. Try to leave on friendly terms because that very same agent you weren't happy with may come across an opportunity and throw you a fish someday.

A *manager* can also be a valuable member of your career team. More so than agents, managers see themselves as *cultivators of talent*. Since managers can't legally negotiate contracts or search for employment for his or her clients, they can help the writer make important connections in the vast industry network. Managers also help the writer to focus on writing the most saleable material for the marketplace. Some managers have those figurehead executive producer titles on television series and thus have enormous power and access to those who hire writers. And managers often own or work for production companies that develop and produce television series.

The *entertainment lawyer* is another valuable member of the television writer's team. The lawyer's job is primarily to look over contracts, make sure all the proper clauses are included, and ensure no loopholes exist that work against the writer. However, if you are assigned to write episodes for series television, these are standard WGA contracts that are air-tight. The attorney comes into play when you start to write above and beyond episodic TV minimums. If you negotiate to become a producer, you need a legal eye to check over the contract before you sign it.

THE ART AND SCIENCE OF TV PITCHING

Once you get an agent, he or she will use your spec teleplay to set up pitch meetings with producers of television series. Pitching is a must for television writers. You can't get around it. So, if you're a quiet person who hates talking to people, you'd better get over that if you want to work in television.

Pitching is nothing more than salesmanship. For example, when you go to buy a car, the moment you enter the showroom, you've demonstrated to the sales staff that you are fair game to be pitched. And if someone doesn't come over to help, you'll be upset about the quality of the dealership's customer service. The ground rules are the same when you enter a producer or executive's office. Both parties understand their respective roles are *seller* and *buyer*.

The process of pitching is similar to presenting a commercial of your ideas to a producer. Here's the structure of a TV commercial:

Attention
Interest
Demand
Action

This model is called AIDA. You must somehow grab the listener's *attention*, create *interest* in your story, build a *demand* for your story, and get the buyer to *act*. It's that simple. First pitch the "area" with an interesting "hook." Then tell the producer the beginning, middle, and ending of each storyline of your episode, always focusing on how the series regular characters are involved in the dramatic roles of protagonist, antagonist, and pivotal character. You've got about five minutes to pitch each episode idea. So you have to be concise and interesting. Hit the highlights and stay away from details of the plot. And be enthusiastic. If you're not excited about your story, don't expect the listener to become excited.

You should be prepared to *pitch three to five episode ideas*. You don't want to put your eggs in one basket with only one highly developed episode. It's best to have more than one loosely developed idea. If the producer is interested, he or she may even offer suggestions on how to develop an idea. If this happens, you're on your way to getting an assignment.

There is a two-meeting rule in television pitching. If the producer meets with you for a second time on the same story idea, the producer must purchase the story. Your agent should be aware of this rule. But you should be aware of your rights as well. That's when the WGA comes into play.

TV AND THE WRITERS GUILD OF AMERICA

The WGA protects television writers like no other type of screenwriting writer. TV is big business. There are strict rules for nearly everything associated with writing for television. The guild not only negotiates compensation and benefits for TV writers but also collects and manages residual payments from reruns from all over the world. The guild also settles writing credit disputes if you're rewritten by another writer. If you work as a TV writer, you can be sure just as with death and taxes that you *will* be rewritten. This *credit arbitration* takes place in complete anonymity by three peers who determine who gets what credit after reading every single draft.

The WGA contract also covers all areas of TV writing, including daytime and movies for television. Recently, minimum standard contracts for animation writers have been established and significant progress for minimum compensation and rights for material that appears on the Internet has been achieved. The guild is also aggressively pursuing the establishment of basic working rules for the writing of reality series, however, what "writing" means is still being defined. You can obtain copies of the Members Basic Agreement from the guild. Once you become a member, copies are automatically sent to you. To become a member, you must sell your writing to a signatory company. It takes the sale of a teleplay or screenplay that you've written yourself or with a writing partner to get full membership. If you only sell a story, you get credit toward full membership. Check with the WGA on current membership requirements.

CHAPTER 25

Becoming a Professional Screenwriter

NETWORKING

Someone once said, "there's only one way to break into the entertainment business as a writer and it's different for everyone . . . " This is a rather glib piece of wisdom, but unfortunately, it's true. However, there are some activities that new screenwriters can pursue that appear to get most on track toward productive careers.

First of all, getting the big script sale for one million dollars is abnormal. It's a nice dream, but don't put that kind of pressure on yourself as you start out pursuing your writing career. A great majority of careers begin on a modest level and grow with small but steady gains. Most "first breaks" have two things in common:

- at least one well-written screenplay or teleplay; and
- at least one important contact in the industry.

Fortunately or unfortunately, it is true that who you know is an important factor. But an important person has a job to do. His or her career is on the line with every creative decision. So, it's in his or her best interest to work with the best talent than can be found. Those who ignore this important concept, do not last very long in the industry. So, while it's very important to make contacts, it's equally important to have well-written material. Without excellent material, an important person in the industry will not give you the time of day.

So, how do you develop important contacts in the industry? Go to where they are and network. Attend writers' conferences, seminars, and industry lunches. Join industry associations, volunteer for industry community service groups or work as an intern for production companies. Once you land an agent and/or manager, they will help you make connections. But it's pretty much your responsibility to network.

DEVELOP YOUR CRAFT

Develop an arsenal of scripts. The more variety of types and genres, the more likely you'll attract interest to your material. Learn as much about writing as you can. Read magazines on writing, go to seminars, and take classes. But you'll do yourself the most good by practicing your craft. That does not mean you need to write a full-blown feature screenplay or teleplay every time. You can also write scenes and short film scripts for practice. Yes, that's what I said. Like any other profession, writers need to practice too. You can write story treatments. You can write short stories, even a novel. The more you write, the better you learn to use the tools of the trade.

Write every day. You hear this all the time. But for some reason, new writers tend to scoff at this advice. But professional writers of all types do write every single day. It's what we do. The pages won't happen until you put your butt in the chair and your fingers on the keyboard. Technically, writing doesn't always happen when you're sitting at the computer. It happens twenty-four hours a day, seven days a week. It happens when you're awake and while you're sleeping. You can't get away from writing if you want to be good at it. So, you must love writing above all things. It must be the one thing you want to do most with your life. When and if you feel that way, then writing every day is a no-brainer. On a practical level, look at your weekly calendar and *block out time for writing*. If you have to get up two hours earlier before going to work, then that's what you have to do. If you have to stay up a few hours later at night, do it. Instead of watching a rerun on television, go somewhere quiet, close the door, and write. Use your commute time to think about story and character. Carry a micro-recorder in the car, your briefcase or purse so those great ideas don't slip away. Keep a pad and pencil inside your nightstand to jot down those bolts of lightning that hit you at three in the morning. Writing is creative, but it's also a discipline.

Don't be afraid to write badly. My philosophy is *there's no such thing as bad writing, there's writing that needs to be fixed*. Get your ideas down on paper. Once you learn them, don't be afraid to break or bend the rules. It's okay to push the creative envelope. If you learn the process, it will help you be a good screenwriter.

LEARN THE BUSINESS

Screenwriting is a business. It's not like writing a poem. Screenplays are written for one reason and one reason alone—to sell to become films. Teleplays are written to be produced for airing. You've got to understand the industry in which you wish to work. It's not that hard to do. Start with a subscription to the *Daily Variety* or the *Hollywood Reporter*. There are weekly editions of both and you can buy these trade newspapers off the rack at newsstands. Read at least one of them from cover to cover Monday through Friday. Read even the boring little articles on distribution financing. Read about writers' deals, executive assignments, and especially the daily industry-watch columns. Read magazines on screenwriting. Go to websites on the Internet. Pour over what has been sold and what is in production. Your mind will collect these facts and put them into some kind of sensible order all on its own. So, when you have the instinct to write a certain kind of screenplay, it's not necessarily coming from your gut as much as from your intelligence. Facts are adding up in your head and making you more savvy about how to succeed in the business of writing. Attend classes or seminars on the general areas of the entertainment business. Read books about the industry. Ask questions of those who do different jobs. Find out how your agent or manager works. Ask an executive about how he or she does the job. Be curious about how the industry makes its money and profits. Network with working screenwriters and learn from their experiences. But above all, understand that as a writer, you must strike a healthy balance between *art* and *commerce* if you are to succeed and build a career.

Follow the Three Ps. The best way to stay motivated as a screenwriter is to avoid desperation. Agents, managers, executives, producers, and so on can smell it. The three Ps are the following:

Persistence—Quite often, it's not the most talented writer who builds a successful career, but the writer who's the most unrelenting. You simply have to keep trying no matter how many times you're rejected.

Patience—Rejection is 99 percent of the entertainment business. Compared with the number of screenplays being written and the number of them that can be produced, only a very small fraction of them will ever see the light of day. So, while you're waiting for that next big step in your career, keep writing and honing your craft.

Pay Check—Obviously, it's very difficult to be creative if you can't provide the essentials of living for yourself and/or your family. So you must find a way to make some money while you pursue your writing career. Ideally, you should get a job inside the entertainment industry. That way, you increase your chances of making important connections and building key relationships with individuals who can help you down the line. But don't feel bad if you have to be a waiter or salesman or grocery store clerk. Everyone has to do something to make money because making money in the entertainment business as a writer is extremely difficult and volatile.

The Role of Luck. Yes, luck is an important factor in an entertainment career. However, someone once said, "*The more you write, the luckier you get.*"

Appendix

Exhibit 1

CHARACTER DEVELOPMENT TEMPLATE

Full Name:
Dramatic Role (protagonist, antagonist, pivotal character):

Physiology Profile
Sex
Age
General Appearance
General Health
Abnormalities (defects if any)

Sociology Profile
Race and Religion
Class Status Home life—past and present and the influence of it
Education
Occupation and Abilities
Key Relationships
Politics—where stand on current important issues
Hobbies

Psychology Profile
Sex life
Ethics, Values, Moral Standards
Drive and Ambition
Frustrations, Disappointments
Temperament

IQ
General Attitude toward Life
Complexes (if any)

Qualities Important to the Story
How will the audience feel about this character?

Exhibit 2

BASIC STORY DEVELOPMENT TEMPLATE

(Use the answers to the following questions to begin developing the foundation for your Basic Story Synopsis)

Beginning (Act One)

1. What clever or interesting "hook" will introduce the story to the audience?
2. What does the protagonist want and why can't he or she have it?
3. What things happen to make the protagonist's problem or predicament "get worse?"
4. What forces the protagonist into a "new situation?"

Middle (Act Two)

1. What keeps the protagonist from adjusting to the new situation in which he or she finds himself or herself involved?
2. What does the protagonist need to know, learn, and/or do to be more successful in his or her new situation?
3. What does the protagonist finally try to do in order to solve his or her problem?
4. How does he or she fail this time for the first "major setback?"
5. How does the antagonist continue to hurt the protagonist after the major setback?
6. What finally makes the protagonist realize the only way to solve his or her problem is to confront the antagonist once and for all?

Ending (Act Three)

1. What is the protagonist's original goal and how does he or she "recommit" to it?
2. What must the protagonist do to create a "final confrontation" with the antagonist and try to get what he or she wants in the story once and for all?
3. What happens in the final confrontation between the protagonist and antagonist and how does the protagonist *get* or *not get* what he or she wants in the story?
4. What "unexpected gain" (if any) does the protagonist realize?
5. With whom (major characters) does the protagonist need to take care of unfinished business?

The End

Exhibit 3

STORY STRUCTURE DEVELOPMENT TEMPLATE

Pages 1–10: Introduce tone, place, time, and what the story is about. Cleverly introduce the central question that gives a clue as to the theme to be explored throughout the story.

Pages 11–30: Set up all conflicts for the main characters in the Main Story and Subplot. Solutions will come as the story progresses. The Protagonist's problem gets worse.

Pages 31–45: Protagonist moves into new territory by committing to pursuing a new goal. Build to Protagonist first character growth that's the first true realization that his or her life is changing. Protagonist encounters and overcomes first major obstacle while resisting change.

Pages 46–60: Protagonist starts to get into big trouble. The Protagonist now leaves behind the old situation, starts to gain new skills, and becomes committed to the new situation. Protagonist encounters second major obstacle bigger, more serious than the first and overcomes it. By page 60, reaches the point of no return in pursuit of goal.

Pages 61–75: The Protagonist sets out to solve the problem and it looks as if all is lost when the Protagonist fails to overcome this third obstacle. A new, larger obstacle looms. The Protagonist wants to give up but the antagonist, now stronger than ever, won't allow it.

Pages 76–90: The Protagonist is literally and spiritually "on the run" and "scrambling" in the story. By page 90, back is against the wall. Along the way, discovers the missing element needed to defeat the antagonist or villain. Protagonist has no choice but to go for broke.

Pages 91–95: Start the Protagonist's journey to getting the golden ring. Restate the central question of the story, and Protagonist's recommits to the new life. Revisit what happened between pages 31 and 45 to give story symmetry.

Pages 96–110: Build to the climax of the Main Story: The Protagonist gets the golden ring, but it's not exactly what was expected, it's something else entirely . . . and more than expected (the "twist").

Pages 111–115: Wrap up Main Story illustrating the growth of the Protagonist. Hint: People don't change, they grow. Tie up loose ends.

Note: Classic screenplays are 120 pages. However, today, most screenplays average about 115 pages.

Exhibit 4

CLASSIC HOLLYWOOD MALE* PROTAGONIST LOVE STORY STRUCTURE

Between Pages 1 and 10

1. Boy meets Girl.

Between Pages 11 and *30*

2. Boy is confronted by a "problem" with Girl, ends up falling in love with her.

Between Pages 31 and 45

3. Boy loses Girl—his own fault.

Between Pages 46 and 60

4. Boy gets Girl back.

Between Pages 61 and 75

5. Boy loses Girl again—her doing, looks like forever.

Between Pages 76 and 90

6. Boy gets Girl back.
7. Boy loses Girl once again—this time by no fault of his own (an outside force).

Between Pages 91 and 95

8. Boy gets Girl back.

Climax

9. Boy, having learned his lesson, confronts and eliminates the influence of the outside force forever.

Denouement

10. Boy and Girl live happily ever after.

* *Of course, this works for a Female Protagonist, too!*

Exhibit 5

TELEVISION BEAT SHEET DEVELOPMENT TEMPLATE

A-Story Premise: (Describe the premise in one line.)

A1. (Describe the beat.)
A2. (Describe the beat.)
A3. (Describe the beat.)
A4. (Describe the beat.)
A5. (Describe the beat.)
A6. (Describe the beat.)
A7. (Describe the beat.)
A8. (Describe the beat—the climax.)

B-Story Premise: (Describe the premise in one line.)

B1. (Describe the beat.)
B2. (Describe the beat.)
B3. (Describe the beat.)
B4. (Describe the beat.)
B5. (Describe the beat—the climax.)

C-Story Premise: (Describe the premise in one line.)

C1. (Describe the beat.)
C2. (Describe the beat.)
C3. (Describe the beat—the climax.)

Runner 1 Premise: (Describe the premise in one line.)

R1-1. (Describe the beat.)
R1-2. (Describe the beat.)
Runner 2 Premise: (Describe the premise in one line.)

R2-1. (Describe the beat.)
R2-2. (Describe the beat.)

Note: There can be more than three storylines, and runners are optional. This is only a starting point for format.

Exhibit 6

BEAT SHEET TEMPLATE: SAMPLE ACT STRUCTURE FORMAT

The Series Name
Your Episode Title

Act One
A1. Teaser
B1. (Describe the beat.)
C1. (Describe the beat.)
R1-1. (Describe the beat.)
A2. (Describe the beat.)

Act Two
B2. (Describe the beat.)
C2. (Describe the beat.)
A3. (Describe the beat.)
B3. (Describe the beat.)
A4. (Describe the beat.)

Act Three
A5. (Describe the beat.)
R1-2. (Describe the beat.)
B4. (Describe the beat.)
A6. (Describe the beat.)
R2-1. (Describe the beat.)

Act Four
C3. (Describe the beat.)
R2-2. (Describe the beat.)
B5. (Describe the beat.)
A7. (Describe the beat.)
A8. (Describe the beat.)

Note: This is only an example. It will be different for your episode.

EXHIBIT 7

A STRUCTURE ANALYSIS OF THE FILM *WITNESS* BY STEVE DUNCAN

THE FILM WAS DIRECTED BY PETER WEIR FROM A SCREENPLAY WRITTEN BY EARL W. WALLACE & WILLIAM KELLEY, STORY BY WILLIAM KELLEY & PAMELA & EARL W. WALLACE.

This is the author's interpretation of the images and dialogue in the film produced by Paramount Pictures. An analysis follows each summary section and attempts to explore the techniques used by the screenwriters and filmmakers. The film analysis is based on comparing the finished film with the screenplay's Revised Draft dated April 8, 1984. No direct excerpts from the screenplay are used in this analysis.

Pages 1–10: introduce tone, place, time, and what the story is about. Cleverly introduce the central question that gives a clue as to the theme to be explored throughout the story.

The film opens with sumptuous shots of a verdant countryside. A procession of horse-drawn buggies carrying Amish families through wind-blown fields of grain toward a distant, quaint farmhouse provides the backdrop for the opening credits. The music is haunting, even foreboding, a stark contrast to the graceful images on-screen that seem to be from another era.

Inside the old-fashioned farmhouse, the Amish men, women, and children—dressed in the same plain black and white Quaker clothes—gather around a wooden coffin. We meet Rachel Lapp, a fetching Amish woman (*Kelly McGillis*), and her eight-year-old son, Samuel (*Lucas Haas*). Also, there's the family and clan patriarch Eli Lapp. As the bishop says final words in an antique German dialect, we realize the person in the coffin is Rachel's husband. Afterwards, the traditional repast: lots of food and conversation. We meet Daniel Hochleitner as he delivers his condolences to Rachel. He's young, witty, strong, and very interested in impressing the grieving widow.

Later, one ancient buggy carrying the Lapp family slows the progress on the highway of huge eighteen-wheeler trucks. We suddenly realize that we are in the present, not the past, as the immense vehicles are forced to wait for a chance to overtake it. At their destination, the local train station, all—including Hochleitner—sees off Rachel and young Samuel for a visit to relatives who live in the City. Eli's last line of dialogue to Rachel has a watchful tone as he tells her to be careful among the English. As the train chugs out of the rural station, Samuel animatedly points out the window for Rachel to see Hochleitner riding his buggy like a Roman gladiator trying to keep pace with the departing train. It's obvious to us that this man really likes Rachel.

As the train cuts through the emerald Pennsylvania countryside, Samuel sees a kaleidoscope of hot air balloons staging in a vast field . . . and soon, the distant urban cityscape looms. Inside the Philadelphia train station, mother purchases tickets for Baltimore and learns that their train is delayed. As they find their way to the waiting room, Samuel is in utter awe of the pay phones, the escalators, and other technology everyone else takes for granted. He's especially intrigued by a majestic statue of an angel holding a dead soldier in her arms . . .

Samuel has to go to the bathroom. Inside, his height forces him to use a toilet in a stall instead of the urinal. While inside the stall, a Black Man (*Danny Glover*) and a Caucasian Man enter. Without warning, they attack a Young Man who's washing his hands. It's a savage and brutal murder at the blade of the Black Man's knife. Afterwards, the Black Man retrieves a notebook hidden in the restroom and we realize young Samuel has witnessed the entire transgression through the crack of the restroom stall door.

The Black Man whips out a huge gun and—for good measure—double checks the room before departing. A frantic Samuel can't lock the stall's broken latch as the Black Man starts a systematic search. Just as he gets to the one containing Samuel, the boy gets it locked in the nick of time. The Black Man tries to open the stall but can't. He kicks it. The door holds. Samuel slips under the partition into the next stall just as the Black Man's second vicious kick rattles the door's hinges—his gun coming in with intent to kill. But Samuel stands on the toilet seat in the next stall and holds his breath as the Caucasian Man returns to beckon the Black Man before he can discover Samuel. With heart-stopping fear—Samuel listens as the Killer and the Caucasian Man leave him alone with the murdered Young Man laying face down in his own pool of blood . . .

Pages 1–10 Analysis: The tone of the story: Drama; the place (or setting): Amish country; the time: present day. In these pages, we get an excellent sense of what this story is about: A sheltered young boy witnesses a brutal murder and, no doubt, will have to identify the killers for the police. In the process, we also get a sense that two worlds with very different lifestyles are on a collision course. We get a clear picture of the backward, peaceful lifestyle of the Amish attempting to co-exist within the modern society of the time. It's not until the image of a huge eighteen-wheeler having to wait for a chance to past a horse-driven buggy that we fully realize we are not in another era. This juxtaposition of images provides us with an ultimate contrast and cleverly introduces the "central question" of, "Can these two very different worlds continue to co-exist?"

Also, within the first few minutes of the story, we meet the protagonist, Rachel Lapp, and Samuel Lapp who—for the time being—serves as Rachel's antagonist. This relationship in the main story will be moved into the subplot as the story progresses. Eli and Hochleitner are introduced as Rachel's pivotal characters. In the Philadelphia train station, we meet a henchman in the Black Man. He will prove to represent the true antagonist in the story and a representative of the villain (whom we haven't met yet).

This is what's called an *open story*. While there are some unknown facts, we—the audience—have seen the Killer's face, though we really don't know much about him. So, for the time being, much of the suspense comes from wondering "what's going to happen next" and the "why" of the murder. So far, we only know that the Black Man was killed for an innocuous notebook hidden in the restroom of a train station. We really don't know what's at stake for the characters. This just seems like a temporary delay to the trip. Much of this time has been spent introducing characters and the setting of the story. The emotional core of the story presently exists with young Samuel's utter fear of having witnessed a barbaric, violent act of murder and the fear of the unknown yet to come as he enters the world of the criminal justice system. This, in effect, introduces the underlying theme of the story: the delicate fact of a nonviolent society co-existing with one that turns on violence. When you distill this down to the five general story themes, you basically have "man against man." Though this film was written and produced two decades ago (1984), it still holds up to what exists in our society today.

The pages 1–10 structure actually takes twelve and one-eighth pages in the screenplay and about seventeen minutes to unfold in the film. So you can see the concept of structure is not an exact science (nor should it be). Up to this point, only one short sequence in the screenplay was omitted in the final cut of the film. That sequence portrayed the train passing through the dirty slums of Philadelphia and Rachel forcing Samuel to turn his eyes away from it. The sequence was probably photographed and left on the editing room floor for reasons of "running time."

The stage is now set and it is time to meet other characters who will bring conflict into the story . . .

Pages 11–30: set up all conflicts for the main characters in the main story and subplot; solutions to come as the story progresses.

In the train station, young Samuel finds himself surrounded by the constant crackle of police radios and the barking of commands by the investigation squad. Rachel frets over the activity and her son's exposure to this seamy part of modern society as they become innocent bystanders in the flurry of all the official activity.

We meet John Book (*Harrison Ford*), a tough-as-nails Philadelphia homicide detective with a wry sense of humor, as he exits the men's room. With him is his black partner, Carter. Book interrogates a Black Custodian who reveals that it wasn't he who reported the murder, but "the kid in the funny threads." As Book questions Samuel, Rachel gets more irritated with the situation. She becomes outraged when Book discovers the boy has actually witnessed the murder "by a black man" and insists that Samuel go to the police station to look at mug shots.

Book's unmarked sedan carrying Rachel and Samuel takes a side trip to a local nightclub in the Philadelphia ghetto. Book extracts a Black Thug from the bar with the violent panache that's typical of his character—jams the hoodlum's face to the car window for Samuel to identify. It's frightening for the boy and his mother. But Samuel says the man's not the killer. Rachel voices her distaste for this barbaric process to Book and she fully realizes this is going to be more than an inconvenient detour.

Book takes Rachel and Samuel to his sister's home for the night. Elaine and Book immediately fight when he learns she has a man in the house despite the fact that she has two young children there. Elaine is not happy to see these Amish people and Samuel doesn't want to stay there either.

The next day, Samuel is subjected to a police lineup of suspects. Rachel and Book continue to clash as Rachel tries to save her son from police procedures. Though they don't get along, we sense there's a certain mutual intrigue brewing between them. At lunch in a restaurant, Rachel, Book, and Samuel eat hot dogs. Rachel reveals that Elaine has said some revealing things about her brother, John Book, during their layover. The most telling being that Book thinks he's right about everything and he's the only one who can do anything about crime. Samuel lets out a whooping belch, which shocks Book as being rude and amusing. But Rachel announces that her son has a good appetite.

Back at the precinct, Samuel wades through more mug shots. Book has to take an important call, leaves Samuel to wander through the busy police station. The curious young Amish boy draws clear affection from the other police officers and a sneer from a perpetrator out to have a little fun while handcuffed to a chair. Then Samuel approaches a large glass case full of trophies, plaques, and framed newspaper accounts of outstanding police duty. Samuel stops with curious eyes and then suddenly freezes. The music is haunting as the ambient sound fades away. It's as if Samuel is suddenly alone in the world. Inside the glass case—prominently displayed—a headline reads "Division Chief McPhee Honored for Youth Project." Accompanying the story is a picture of McPhee . . . clearly the Black Man who slaughtered the young cop in the train station men's room.

Samuel is riveted to the picture as John Book joins him. Taken by the boy's fearful expression and, without dialogue, Book realizes he's found their man. As Samuel points at the picture of McPhee, Book quickly takes his hand to conceal the forbidden act of implicating a police officer to murder. He gives the boy a gentle smile instead . . .

Pages 11–30 Analysis: The first new important character we meet is John Book. It's here that a significant shift in character relationships takes place: Book becomes the protagonist of the main story; Rachel becomes Book's antagonist; and Samuel remains Rachel's antagonist as his relationship with his mother becomes part of the subplot that will feed the main story. Two character triangles have now been clearly established: (1) Rachel (Protagonist), Samuel (Antagonist), and Eli (Pivot Character) and (2) Book (Protagonist), Rachel (Antagonist), and Samuel (Pivot Character). As you can see, these characters possess what's sometimes referred to as *unity of opposites*. Book—tough, violent, and male—is the antithesis of Rachel who is soft, spiritual, and female. Rachel—a doting mother—is the antithesis of Samuel who is a mercurial little boy. At this point, nobody can solve their own problem without the others failing.

It quickly becomes clear that Book and Rachel will clash as he forces her son to participate in a criminal justice system in which the Amish do not believe nor participate. We briefly encounter the conflict that exists between Book and his sister, Elaine, which establishes her as an important pivotal character in the story. In the shooting script, one other character was introduced, Deputy Chief Schaeffer, but the filmmakers saw fit to postpone this introduction in the final cut.

Here are all the deletions that took place from the screenplay in the Pages 11–30 Structure:

1. A scene where Book clashes with the Chief of Detectives over who's going to handle the murdered cop case.
2. A meeting between the Deputy Chief of Police Schaeffer and John Book who reveals there's an eyewitness to the murder and that the dead cop was undercover chasing the theft of police evidence (drugs); Schaeffer gives Book just twenty-four hours to solve the case (a ticking clock).
3. A sequence of Book trying to find a hotel room for the Lapps and Rachel refusing on religious grounds.
4. A scene depicting the fact that Carter and Book have worked through the night after dropping off the Lapps at his sister's house.
5. An entire domestic sequence that features Samuel mistakenly walking in on Elaine and her boyfriend, Fred, making love; Elaine and her boyfriend having a screaming match; a conversation between Rachel and Elaine after Rachel has marshaled the efforts of the three boys to clean up the house; Rachel and Elaine bonding in a quirky sort of way over the different points of view concerning women and men's relationships.
6. Some dialogue between Rachel and Book is cut during the police lineup scene.
7. The restaurant scene originally took place in a park.

At this point of the story, the director decides that he had sufficiently developed the clash of societies and moved to concentrate on the crime-solving effort by the protagonist. The focus of the clash now shifts from the monolithic concept of social differences to a more personal one between Book and Rachel with the boy clearly caught in the middle. Why? Because Samuel seems to be intrigued by John Book while Rachel refuses to admit that she shares the emotion. And screen stories are about PEOPLE not concepts. The moment that John Book moves into a "new life" occurs when Samuel reveals that the killer is a respected police officer. The protagonist's situation is "new territory" because the idea that a cop would kill another cop and abuse the public trust is simply earth shattering to Book. This is very new and shocking to a man who has dedicated his adult life to truth, justice, and catching the bad guys. Now, one of the bad guys is supposed to be a good guy. The telling moment of Book's dilemma is revealed when he stops Samuel from pointing at the cop's picture for fear that someone might see it. John Book realizes the rules have suddenly changed and he's not sure what to do next.

The Pages 11–30 Structure in the screenplay actually runs from pages 13 to 36—twenty-two and a half pages. Not bad in "structure theory." But the page 30 "new life" defining scene takes place at exactly twenty-nine minutes and thirty-six seconds into the movie's screen running time. To maintain this "pacing," the filmmakers cut out stuff from the script. I'm sure they shot all those scenes but decided—after viewing the "editor's cut"—the story's pacing was too far off to effectively keep the audience engaged. This is fairly typical for many films during the translation from the written word to celluloid. Sometimes the screen time of a scene takes longer (sometimes shorter) than the number of pages it takes to write it. Also, actors bring a certain amount of unexpected information to the screen through their glances, their chemistry, and off-the-cuff ad-libs. In this case, the director thought it would be more suspenseful to reveal what's at stake a bit later in the story than indicated in the screenplay—a scene where Book meets with Deputy Chief Schaeffer. In viewing the film, I—and many others—think he was right to do so. This delay keeps the story moving ahead.

Now, our protagonist, John Book, has entered new territory and he's faced with a complicated "moral dilemma"—the choice between right and wrong.

Pages 31–45: protagonist moves into new territory by committing to pursuing a new goal. Build to protagonist first character growth that is the first true realization that his or her life is changing. Protagonist encounters and overcomes first major obstacle.

Book goes to the home of his boss, Deputy Chief of Police Schaeffer. His wife and daughter are there and it appears to be your typical East Coast middle-class family. In the home's study, Book reveals the identity of the murdering cop as being McPhee. Book is excited, this can be important to his career. Schaeffer plays it straight down the middle as Book describes what he believes is the motive—$22 million of stolen drugs from their evidence locker. Schaeffer wants to know what Book is going to do. Book wants to add manpower from outside the department . . . he doesn't know the extent of the corruption yet. Schaeffer agrees, shows genuine concern, and wants to know where the only eyewitness to the murder—Samuel—is being kept. Schaeffer tells Book to move the boy and to keep it just between them.

Later, Book pulls into the underground parking garage of his apartment building. He gets out of his car with his dry cleaning and heads toward the elevator. As he passes rows of parked cars, he hears the faint sound of a car door. He turns—nothing. At the elevator, he presses the button and waits impatiently, but another sound behind him pulls his attention. The music is foreboding as Book turns to see McPhee stroll toward him; the Black Man smiles, almost friendly. The moment seems endless as everything slows down to a dreamlike state. Book hears Schaeffer's voice inside his mind asking who else knows and he remembers his own response to the question of as being just us. McPhee's big pistol fills his hand and rises in super slow motion as the elevator doors ding. The double doors slide open to reveal a middle-aged couple on their way out for the evening. McPhee opens fire! The couple scrambles, lucky to escape sudden death as Book rolls to the slick pavement and returns fire. Book shouts at the couple as McPhee runs for his car. The elevator door closes at the exact moment that McPhee's car screeches away. Book gives a brief chase as the garage falls silent as McPhee's car disappears. He leans heavily against a parked car and opens his jacket. He's been hit, blood soaking his white shirt.

Still hurting from the gunshot wound, Book goes to his sister's house. He tells Elaine to hide his car in the garage and refuses to tell her anything except to pretend she's never heard of Rachel and

Samuel. Carter gets a call from Book. He's concerned as Book tells his partner to locate Rachel's address written on his desk calendar and destroy it. He won't tell Carter why, just that Schaeffer is dirty. Carter rips the page from Book's desk calendar and is startled by two plainclothes detectives on his way out of the precinct.

Schaeffer shows up at Elaine's. She won't let him in. He wants to know where Book is. She's adamant that she doesn't know and he loses his temper. McPhee watches as Schaeffer gives up the interrogation. He tells his henchman he doesn't believe she knows anything. Schaeffer asks about Book's partner, Carter, and tells McPhee to lean on him.

An old Volkswagen breaks the sloping horizon of Lancaster County just at first light. Book's the driver and in excruciating pain. Next to him, Rachel holds a sleeping Samuel. From a distance, Eli watches the strange car approach, cross the barnyard, and stop. Samuel leaps out and runs into the old man's arms. Rachel gets out but Book can't—he's in too much pain. She asks if Book will come back to take Samuel to trial. Book tells her there won't be a trial.

Eli and Rachel watch as Book's car pulls away. He wants to know who the man is. In the near distance, the car swerves off the road and crashes into a tall birdhouse, comes to rest against a bank of earth. They run to find Book passed out behind the steering wheel.

Rachel gives medical aid to Book and he comes to momentarily. He won't let her take him to a hospital because he knows the gunshot wound will be reported. Book reminds Rachel that if they find him, they'll find her boy. Then he slips into unconsciousness again.

Rachel gently touches Book's handsome face . . .

Pages 31–45 Analysis: The only scene cut from the original screenplay took place in Book's car: he and Rachel argue—she doesn't feel safe and fears her son will be hurt. It was only one page. In the final cut of the film, the story picks up with Book's dilemma of whom to turn to for help. He goes to his boss, Schaeffer. This is the first time in the film we meet him. He plays it straight (we think) with Book. We learn what's at stake—big money and a police conspiracy. Schaeffer confides in Book to keep the entire matter between them. And we get a clear sense of the mentor-mentee relationship between them. This was a clever mislead for the audience that was only revealed when Book was shot by McPhee in the garage parking lot. At this moment, the protagonist (and the audience) realizes who the "true antagonist" in the story is—Deputy Chief of Police Schaeffer! And he's sent his Henchman, McPhee—the cop murderer—to do more of his bidding.

In classic screenplay structure theory, between pages 31–45, the protagonist tries to survive in new territory using skills acquired in his or her "old life." It's at this juncture in the character's development that he or she tries to rely on the skills he or she already has at his or her fingertips. In this case, Book went straight to his boss for help, which is normal police procedure for him ("old skills"). And his cop instinct betrays him. His intuition now takes him where he had gone earlier in the story—back to his sister Elaine's house. He now knows full well that the witness and his pretty mother are in grave danger. He gets the only person he knows he can trust—his partner Carter—to cover his trail (old skill) and relies solely on his well-honed policeman instinct to protect the material witness. Right now, it's his only ace in the hole.

The scene where Book arrives at Elaine's house to rescue Rachel and Samuel was moved to take place several scenes sooner than written in the original screenplay. And the scenes of Schaeffer's and McPhee's arrival at Elaine's house were moved all the way from pages 57–58 to take place earlier in the story around page 43.

So Book takes Rachel and Samuel to where he knows they will be safe now: their Amish home. He has full intent to go back and fight this battle as a tough, honest cop would (old skill). The only problem is he slips into unconsciousness caused by the gunshot wound. At the moment that he realizes he's not going to make it back to Philadelphia, you might say the protagonist experienced "First Character Growth" in the story. In general structure theory, this is the realization that it's not going to be so easy to get back to the old life where things are so much more familiar and well-honed skills are much more useful. This defining scene was set up or foreshadowed in the underground garage when McPhee shot Book.

The Pages 31–45 Structure in the screenplay actually runs from pages 36–47. Normally, the first of four fifteen-page "mini-dramas," the on-screen running time is very close to fifteen minutes and—to this point—the total running time for the entire film is around forty-five minutes. Considering the average of one page equals one minute, this is near the perfect pacing of classic screenplay structure. The action scene in the underground garage runs longer than the written pages and so does the arrival scene at the Lapp Farm.

Now the protagonist, John Book, has no choice but to remain at the Lapp Farm—he's unconscious . . . *Pages 46–60:* protagonist starts to get into big trouble. By page 60, reaches the "point of no return" in pursuit of goal. The protagonist now leaves behind the old situation and is fully committed to the new situation. Protagonist encounters second major obstacle bigger, more serious than the first and overcomes it.

Rachel's silent admiration of John Book is suddenly broken by Eli's arrival. He wants to know if the "English" is dead. Together, they take Book back to the farmhouse. Eli wants the cop's service pistol out of the house but Rachel puts it and his clothes in a chest. The local Amish doctor treats Book's wounds but Rachel won't let them take him to a hospital. Eli is concerned that if Book dies, they will have to deal with the English law. Rachel appeals to Eli's sense of humanity.

Book curses bitterly in his feverish unconsciousness as Rachel looks on. She's become his angel of mercy.

Meanwhile, Schaeffer calls the local Lancaster County Sheriff searching for Rachel Lapp, but he has no address. He learns that Lapp is a common name much like Smith and Jones, causing Schaeffer to lose his patience. The city cop insists that the rural sheriff use the telephone to canvass the area and find Rachel Lapp. But Schaeffer learns that the Amish don't have telephones . . . or televisions or radios or electricity for that matter.

Back at the Lapp farm, Book awakens to a group of Amish men who stand around him as if posing for an Old Dutch painting. Book learns that these men are the local leaders and that he's been out of it for two entire days. Book decides he must leave immediately . . . but quickly discovers he's still too weak.

Later while Book sleeps, young Samuel enters with a fresh bed pan. He makes sure the cop is asleep before opening the chest and taking out the .38-caliber service revolver. Book comes to and takes the gun from the boy. He unloads it, then explains how the deadly weapon works . . . even let's Samuel hold it. They connect at that moment as Book gives the boy a lesson on how to handle a gun. Rachel angrily interrupts the warm exchange and blesses out John Book for teaching her son about violence! Book insists that while he's staying at the farmhouse, Rachel put the gun somewhere the boy can't find it.

Later, Eli gives Samuel a talk about guns and violence . . . quoting the Bible in the process. It's a touching scene as the elder passes on his wisdom to the child. Meanwhile, Rachel enters to see

Book reading Amish and farming magazines to pass the time. They share a light moment as she gives him her dead husband's black clothes that do not fit well. Book's a larger man so it's not a good fit. Book wants to get to a telephone so he joins Eli on his way into town. Book insists on taking his gun with him and has to fish the bullets out of a tin of flour.

At the general store, Book calls Carter, his partner. Book tells him he's coming in, but Carter says it's too hot. Carter warns Book not to do anything stupid or Schaeffer will surely have his ass.

Book hangs up the telephone, resigned to the wait . . .

Pages 46–60 Analysis: The second of four fifteen-minute mini-dramas, only one scene is cut from the screenplay in the film:

1. A scene where the elders tell Rachel to get Book back to his own people as soon as possible.

In classic screenplay structure theory, this is the point in the story when the protagonist realizes that getting back to his or her old life is not going to be easy and those old skills do not work as well in reaching his or her goal in the story. The interesting thing about the story at this point is that the subplot that was firmly established in Act One is now moving to the foreground of the film. We are subtly aware that the "police action drama" is going on off-camera while our protagonist licks his wounds in order to get back into the fray. It is the impending doom that all hell could break loose at any moment that keeps the story's subplot tense. The story now concentrates on the Book-Rachel-Samuel character triangle. The theme of violence is explored as the protagonist throws off the normal routine of the Amish family. This is indeed new territory for everyone involved. John Book is firmly established as a "fish out of water."

To help emphasize the new situation more, the screenwriters put Book in strange clothes and took away his gun. But as soon as he's able, he reaches back into his old life by calling his partner Carter for help. Learning of Schaeffer's intense search for him, the protagonist realizes he can never go back to his old life. Too much water under the bridge for that to happen . . . he's at the point of no return . . .

At Pages 46–60 Structure, the film's total running time is around fifty-six minutes. This portion of the story covers pages 47–67 in the screenplay. This is the First Half of Act Two. The overall effect is that the protagonist is "gaining ground" in the story.

Pages 61–75: by page 75, things become unbearable for protagonist as a new, larger obstacle looms. It looks as if all is lost. The protagonist wants to give up, but something happens that changes everything and it's something needed all along: a new, better, more urgent goal to pursue.

Book works on his sister's Volkswagen, discovers that the battery has gone flat. Eli watches him disapprovingly. Eli suggests that if Book's well enough to fix his car, he's well enough to do some work around the farm. There's a humorous moment when Eli asks Book if he's ever milked a cow. Book doesn't quite understand the word *milking* and Eli asks if he knows what a cow is. Book says he's seen pictures.

Eli wakes up a blurry-eyed Book at 4:30 a.m. the next morning. In the barn, Book struggles to get milk from the cow's udders. Eli tries to coach him and then shows him how to do it. Book still can't get out the milk. Eli asks him if he's ever handled a teat before. Book says not one that big. Eli gets the joke and cackles. This light moment bonds these men and Book realizes he's made a connection.

As daylight approaches, Book is taken by its beauty. He eats a hearty breakfast with Rachel, Samuel, and Eli . . . just like one big happy family. Afterwards, as Book collects the pieces of the birdhouse he destroyed, Hochleitner arrives. He announces he's come to see Rachel and the two men suddenly become competitive, almost measuring each other for size. As the Amish suitor sits sipping lemonade with Rachel, a wave of jealousy sweeps Book.

In the carpentry shop, Book works on repairing the birdhouse to stay busy. After her admirer leaves, Rachel joins him, surprised by his woodworking skills. She wonders why he's a cop instead of something more useful . . . like a carpenter. This is a discussion in which they'll never find agreement.

That night, Book resumes his effort to repair the car. Rachel wanders in, curious about what he's doing. He makes a right connection and the radio comes on. Rock and roll fills the quiet barn. It's a song that Book knows the words to, so he sings the lyrics. He grabs Rachel and forces her to dance with him. She easily gives in and is thoroughly amused by Book's rare charm. There's a moment between them that a kiss could easily be the next move . . . but Book chooses not to. With Rachel uncharacteristically laughing in his arms, twirling around the hay-covered floor of the barn to Sam Cook's soulful 1960s tune—Eli angrily interrupts the "immoral" behavior. Book tries to explain to Eli that this is not Rachel's fault. But Eli's face is so twisted with anger that Book leaves them. He knows this is not his fight.

Eli all but threatens Rachel with the fact that she could be shunned by the elders. We learn her behavior with Book has become the gossip of the community and very upsetting for many. But Rachel, despite being shaken by his lecture, stands up to Eli.

Meanwhile, Schaeffer sits with Carter in his office. With a beguiling smile, he beseeches Carter to talk to John Book—convince him to come back. We learn that Schaeffer and Book were once partners and they both laugh at the thought of Book at an Amish prayer meeting. Schaeffer compares the police with the Amish as being a cult with our own rules.

By the expression on Carter's face . . . we know he knows he's in deep trouble . . .

Pages 61–75 Analysis: The third fifteen-minute mini-drama has only one short scene cut from the screenplay:

1. A dinner scene with Book, Eli, and Rachel, as they talk about an upcoming barn raising.

In screenplay structure theory, this is the point in the story when the protagonist—having realized he or she can never go back to the old life—must figure out new ways to accomplish his or her goal in the story. While Book continues to work on fixing the car, he becomes distracted by his host. Though he knows he's simply buying time in order to get himself back into action, Rachel's charm totally disarms him. The major complication becomes falling in love with her, this "idyllic" family lifestyle, and his affection toward Eli . . . and he may well lose it all if Schaeffer finds them.

Suddenly, he can see it's going to be hard to leave when the time comes. Rachel becomes a new "obstacle" to him pursuing the goal at hand of stopping Schaeffer before the dirty cop can get to him and the boy witness. But then Schaeffer has not laid down either. In the meeting between him and Book's partner, we realize something is amiss and it probably isn't good news for Carter or for Book . . .

John Book is shaken back to reality when Eli's wrath comes down on Rachel. He realizes what he's doing is not working. He's getting nowhere being stuck on this farm.

Here, the upcoming pages 61–75 "all is lost" structure milestone for the protagonist is cleverly cloaked from him but foreshadowed to us—the audience. We know that Carter is in trouble even though Book does not. This is excellent screenwriting technique that bends the rule of classic structure in order to create suspense. The moment of Rachel being chewed out by Eli forebodes a certain "dark moment" to Book . . . a sense that he can't have this woman (the subplot) even though he knows he's falling in love with her.

Again, the subplot continues in the forefront of the film while the main plot is being visited at each "structure milestone." The effect is to remind us, the audience, of the impending doom that is about to come crashing down on the protagonist.

At Pages 61–75 Structure, the total film running time is about seventy-one minutes and this portion of the story covers pages 67–78 in the screenplay. This is very close to the pacing of classic structure.

Pages 76–90: by page 90, protagonist's back is against the wall, must tackle a new main obstacle with renewed zest. The new challenge is the result of overcoming first obstacle of the new goal and an antagonist or villain who becomes extremely proactive. Protagonist has no choice but to go for broke.

It is early morning in Amish country. A caravan of buggies arrives at a spacious farm. A montage of a barn raising unfolds and prominently features John Book working. Hochleitner is there and is very friendly to Book even though he knows Book is his competition for Rachel's affections. But by Hochleitner's demeanor, we know he sees Book more as a minor distraction than a permanent threat. A sequence of beauty shots and swelling music unfolds the full day of hard work it takes to build a barn. The men work while the women supply cool glasses of lemonade. Young Samuel and the other kids appear to be carpenters in training. At noon, the women have prepared a hearty meal and quietly gossip about the stranger's relationship with Rachel. The construction resumes and at a critical point in the construction, Hochleitner helps Book, thoroughly disarming the tough cop and earning some respect in the process. Finally, the barn is finished as the sun gently sets on the distant horizon . . .

After a hard day of labor, Rachel cleans up in the farm's washroom. As she pours hot water in the basin, she sees a reflection of Book in the copper finish of a pan. Book stands at the doorway, transfixed by Rachel—bare from the waist up—her back to him. Rachel hesitates and, in a solemn moment of decision, slowly turns without shame to face Book. Her milky white breasts are now in full view for Book to admire. Their eyes meet. Book wants to go to her but can't make himself do so. Then Rachel drops her eyes to the floor, covers herself, and looks away in disappointment.

Book sits alone in the gloom of his room, lost in deep regret . . .

At dawn, Book approaches Rachel as she feeds the chickens. He tells Rachel that if they had made love the night before, he'd have to stay or she'd have to leave. Rachel can't face him . . .

Book and Eli are at the country store as several rowdy young men harass the Amish with vulgar slurs. One tourist wants to take a picture of Book. He stuns the woman by telling her he'll rip her bra off if she does.

Book calls the police station, asks for Carter. He's abruptly transferred. A soothing voice asks if he's a member of the family. Book learns the night before that Carter was killed in the line of duty. Book hangs up, utterly stunned by this news. He now calls Schaeffer's home. Schaeffer tells Book he likes his style by calling him at home so he can't run a trace. There's some fear on the deputy chief's face as he tries to convince Book to come in out of the cold. Book loses his temper and threatens Schaeffer's life—revealing he's correctly deduced that Carter has been killed by his order. Book slams down the phone, barely able to control his inflamed temper.

Pages 76–90 Analysis: In the last of the four fifteen-minute mini-dramas, two scenes were cut from the screenplay:

1. Carter getting beaten and tortured by McPhee and other dirty cops in a huge warehouse.
2. An early evening bonding scene between Book and Samuel.

In classic screenplay structure theory, this is the point in the story when the protagonist—having experienced a sense of all is lost or a dark moment—wants to give up and just walk away from the story. But the only problem is that the antagonist or villain simply won't let that happen. He or she, in effect, puts the protagonist on the defensive . . . on the run . . . eventually pushing his or her "back against the wall."

While Book spends his time building a barn, the villains take away his only hope of reaching his goal by killing his partner. He's all but abandoned his original goal. But, of course, the villains have not! Of course, he doesn't know that yet, but we know something is up. The subplot continues to drive the film as the story finishes the development of the character triangle involving Book, Rachel, and Samuel. Eli and Hochleitner, two other pivotal characters (who rotate with Samuel on the third point of the triangle) are also developed in their relationship with the protagonist.

Book is confronted with a decision when Rachel shows bare breasts to him. He's been running away from making this decision but now it stares him in the face, no pun intended. He chooses not to make love to the Amish woman—a moment of truth for both protagonist and antagonist in the subplot of the story.

Book now knows he must get out of there and take care of Schaeffer and his goons before they do the same to him. This is the protagonist's discovery of the "key thing"—the thing he needed all along to solve his problem. He gets back on track to his original goal. He goes to the general store to call for help . . . only to get the full force of the "all is lost and dark moment" of the main story—Carter's dead. With his back against the wall, he now knows there's only one solution—confront the true antagonist. So he calls Schaeffer and tells him he's coming to get him.

The total running time at the end of the Pages 76–90 Structure is about eighty-six minutes and covers pages 78–86 in the screenplay. This is excellent classic screenplay pacing.

This is the end of the Second Half of Act Two. The overall effect is that the protagonist is "losing ground" in the story. Notice that each of the fifteen-minute dramas had a beginning, a middle, and an end—each with a climax and a purpose. The love story became the driving force in Act Two while the action-police-crime became structure linchpins to punctuate each of the four mini-dramas. The "molding" of the screenplay's structure at times bends classic structure in order to maintain the protagonist's movement through the story in an organic or natural way. There is a definite "character arc" to John Book in this middle one hour of the story. And the entire one hour (every scene in fact) is fraught with one "confrontation" after another. That is really the key to writing good drama. The flow of the unfolding drama first gets the audience behind John Book and Rachel, rooting for them to escape the villain and become a couple. Then the story turns at midpoint as it all starts to unravel for them.

If you notice in your copy of the screenplay, all the scenes cut from it are "expository" in nature. They contained information that was obvious in other scenes. These scenes often stay in a screenplay until post-production because it's needed to understand a story while reading it. The translation to the screen often renders these scenes unnecessary, and they hit the cutting room floor.

Pages 91–95: start protagonist's journey to getting the golden ring. Wrap up subplot while building to climax: restate the central question of the story and protagonist's commitment to the new life. Revisit what happened between pages 31–45.

Thoroughly distracted, John Book heads back to the buggy. He witnesses the rowdy young men as they harass Hochleitner who simply takes it in silence. Eli can see Book's anger bubble to the top, warns him that this happens all the time. He tells Book that it's not his way of settling a dispute. The rowdy gets into Book's face with more of the same. Book warns the man that he's making a mistake while Hochleitner insists that everything is okay. The man knocks Book's hat off his head, stomps on it, picks it up, crumples it, and then puts it back on Book's head. A dramatic pause, then Book explodes—the young man never knows what hits him! Book takes out another youth with a vicious punch to the face. The tourists look on in sheer shock as Hochleitner explains with a wry smirk that Book is his cousin from Ohio. As the buggies leave carrying Book, Eli, Rachel, and Hochleitner, a local man calls out that this won't help the tourist trade . . . and explains what happened to a curious local police officer who arrives at the scene.

Pages 91–95 Analysis: In classic screenplay structure theory, this is the point in the story where the protagonist normally gives pause to take stock in where he or she has come and where he or she must go to reach the goal of the story. That's exactly what John Book does after receiving the news of his partner's death. While this moment was foreshadowed earlier in the story, the full force of the story's "all is lost and dark moment" hits him hard here.

John Book has his back against the wall. He knows it, too. So, when confronted by the hoodlums at the general store, he can no longer allow his peaceful recline to this situation to continue. The decision to use force instead of backing down from the rowdy young punk clearly tells us that this character is more determined than ever to rid the world of such people. And he's willing to do it in any way necessary—including force. In fact, one might say he wasn't hitting the hoodlum but symbolically smashing Schaeffer in the face. In the screenplay, the writer actually indicates that Book is taking out his anger with Schaeffer on the young man.

His action also shows his new friends—Rachel, Eli, and Hochleitner—that there is, indeed, a place in the world for men like John Book . . . if only to keep these insensitive people at arm's length from the Amish culture and preserve their freedom of movement. But the irony is vivid when the local man shows his concern that the tourist trade might be hurt by Book's violent response. In other words, he expects everybody else but the Amish to be violent.

Book's "fatal flaw" of using force also helps Rachel to recommit to her Amish lifestyle and realize that Hochleitner has more of a place in her life than this Philadelphia policeman.

At this point, the film's total running time is about eighty-nine minutes and covers pages 86–89 in the screenplay. Despite the scene cuts and revisions from the original screenplay, the serendipitous process of writing, producing, directing, and editing a film keeps the structure on classic pace.

Pages 96–Ending: build to the climax of the main story: the protagonist gets the golden ring, but it's not exactly what was expected, it's something else entirely . . . more than expected.

After returning from the country store, Rachel encounters Samuel in the kitchen playing with a wooden toy given to him by Book. Out of the window, Rachel sees Book and Eli working on the birdhouse . . . and she knows full well that Book is about to leave the farm and her behind.

Later, Rachel asks Eli if Book is leaving. Eli admits he's leaving the next day. She's hurt, near panic, wants to know why. Eli explains that Book is going back to his world because he doesn't belong in theirs.

As Book finishes erecting the repaired birdhouse, Rachel confronts him. There's no words passed between them. None necessary, it seems. With the sun dipping below the horizon, Book and Rachel embrace as if their very lives depended on doing so . . . they kiss passionately.

Dawn the next day, McPhee, Schaeffer, and another Henchman arrive. They break into the house, terrorize Rachel and demand to know where they can find Book. McPhee slaps Eli around when he tries to warn Book.

Book sees McPhee and Eli, bolts from the house to the barn. On the way, he grabs Samuel and tells him to go to Hochleitner and stay there. Samuel is concerned that Book may get killed, insists that Book get his gun. But Book sends him on his way.

McPhee and the third Henchman, fully armed, invade the barn with intent to kill. Schaeffer watches Eli and Rachel in the kitchen where he can also watch the barn.

Book can't get the old car started. But the Henchman gives chase, firing his shotgun. Book escapes through a cattle pen and through a trap door at the top of an empty grain silo. Waiting for the right moment, Book waits for the Henchman to enter the silo then unleashes a rainstorm of raw grain on the dirty cop . . . Gunfire misses Book as the grain buries the man alive.

The gunfire alerts Schaeffer. Eli and Rachel hold their breaths as Schaeffer leaves the kitchen with concern.

McPhee enters the barn, gun at the ready . . . stalking for his prey. Book opens the trap door to the silo and struggles to get the Henchman's shotgun that's buried in grain. He gets it free, checks the breech and it is empty! He goes through the dead man's pockets for shells. He slams them into the shotgun just in time to raise it at the approaching enemy. It's like an Old West quick draw contest as Book blasts McPhee to kingdom come . . . leaving a bloody spot on the barn wall as the dead cop slides to the hay-covered floor.

Schaeffer levels his gun on Book, demands for him to drop the shotgun. At that moment, Samuel rings a community bell to alert the neighborhood to the trouble. Schaeffer puts the gun to Rachel's head as—on the near horizon—a group of Amish men approach with a determined gait.

Schaeffer identifies himself a police officer as he's surrounded by Hochleitner and his band of men. He threatens to kill the group if they interfere. Book talks Schaeffer into giving up and peacefully takes the gun away from Schaeffer . . . who realizes he's defeated.

Pages 96–Ending Analysis: There was one minor cut from the screenplay to the screen:

1. Samuel and Rachel getting the gun to help Book during the climax.

In classic structure theory, this is the part of the story when the protagonist, after realizing the only solution to his or her problem is to literally face the person creating the problem, does just that—confronts the villain (the true antagonist) of the story. Even though Schaeffer and McPhee came after Book, he was in the process of leaving the Lapp farm and going after them. He was fully prepared to use whatever force necessary to win at this point. His first concern was to protect the witness, Samuel, and the kid's family. He successfully used violence to take out one of the Henchman but not with a gun. He used grain instead. He also used the barn and cows to his advantage as the Henchman gave chase.

Ultimately, Book had to rely on the use of a gun to kill McPhee. He had no choice and it clearly made him feel remorseful. So much so, that when confronted by Schaeffer, he chose not to use gun violence but to appeal to a peaceful resolve. John Book had clearly been affected by his experience among the Amish, though it's clear at the end that he's still very much in touch with being a police officer.

This portion of the screenplay covered pages 89–101.

Ending: wrap-up of main story illustrating the growth of the protagonist; hint: people don't change, they grow. Tie up loose ends.

As the Lancaster County police take Schaeffer into custody, paramedics take care of the dead bodies. There are no Amish around this mess as Book talks to uniformed police officers. Smoking a cigarette, back in his own city clothes, and laughing with his fellow officers, it's clear that Book is back in his true element.

Before departing, Book sits with Samuel in a field of grain. The boy realizes this man is going away forever, and he's very disappointed. Somehow, we know this youngster understands Book better than anyone else.

Book goes to Rachel and lingers with her at the open farmhouse door. There are no words here as their eyes search each other's. Behind Rachel is the gloominess of the farmhouse that has no electricity or running water. Behind Book are the open, verdant sun-drenched fields. They both want to say something to somehow explain their feelings for each other. But, in the end, no words are spoken as Book nods and leaves her at the door.

Eli tells Book he should be careful among the English as Book heads for the Volkswagen. The two men exchange glances of mutual respect.

As Book's car drives away, Hochleitner approaches with a bounce in his step and offers the briefest tip of his Amish hat, bidding John Book good-bye . . .

The End

The Ending Analysis: The "crime and punishment" loose ends are wrapped up in a single page when the local police take Schaeffer into custody. The audience knows this man will get his just punishment. All important relationships established with the protagonist are also wrapped up. Eli bids Book good-bye with the very same warning that he'd given Rachel at the train station when she began her odyssey into the world outside of Amish country. Samuel said good-bye to Book, showing his respect and—in some regard—gives us a sense that he now is better equipped to venture out among the modern world than his elders.

Then there's Rachel . . . a love that bloomed yet can never be requited . . . two worlds apart that can never co-exist. A bittersweet ending as both people realize they're the better for having met if only briefly . . .

The screenplay runs a total of 102 pages.

In many ways, the screenplay for *Witness* breaks classic structure rules while still paying homage to them and not allowing the page count to drive the writing. The character milestones of structure are the focus of this screenplay, not the number of pages it takes to get to each milestone. That means that the screenwriters clearly understood the importance of character to this story rather than the number of scenes. This is always a tricky part of screenwriting. On one hand, you have to use up a certain amount of time. But on the other, you can't let the clock dictate how the story will flow. It comes down to a delicate balancing act.

The screenwriters used "theme" as the glue to hold this story together. If you were to really look over the script, you'll find that overall there's very little dialogue in this screenplay; and hardly any exposition. The writers let the character's behavior carry the story. It is the "What happens next?" approach to storytelling that makes this film work so well. But most important, the screenwriters clearly understand the emotional appeal of this story. The basic premise is totally depended on the protagonist maintaining the safety of a small, likable, innocent child and his attractive mother . . .

Glossary of Screenwriting Terminology

Academy of Motion Pictures Arts and Sciences: a professional honorary organization whose goals are to advance the arts and sciences of motion pictures; foster cooperation among creative leaders for cultural, educational, and technological progress; recognize outstanding achievements; cooperate on technical research and improvement of methods and equipment; provide a common forum and meeting ground for various branches and crafts; represent the viewpoint of actual creators of the motion picture; and foster educational activities between the professional community and the public-at-large. The Academy's field of activity does not include economic, labor, or political matters.

Academy of Television Arts and Sciences: Membership is open to those persons who are or who have been actively engaged in activities related to the production or distribution of audio-visual works for national exhibition by means of telecommunications in twenty-seven peer groups.

Act: a measure of dramatic structure, which is a collection of sequences in a screenplay, teleplay, or film.

Act Break: the dramatic point in a teleplay that marks the end of an act before going to commercials.

Action-Description: an element of screenplay page format that describes what the audience sees on the screen.

Act One Metaphor: A device, either visual or in dialogue, that symbolizes theme in a screenplay, teleplay, or film.

Agent: a person who represents talent, that is, writers, who can legally negotiate employment.

All Is Lost: the point in classic screenplay structure where the protagonist arrives at his or her lowest point because the obvious solution to the story's problem is removed by the story's antagonist.

Antagonist: the dramatic role in a story whose primary purpose is to oppose the main character, the protagonist.

Arc: the growth or change in a character measured from the start to the finish of a story, as in *character arc*; also refers to how a story progresses from start to finish, as in *story arc*.

Area: subject from which theme and/or humor is extracted in a screenplay or teleplay's scene or sequence.

Associate Producer: a position that entails working for the producer and consists of managing the detail work assigned before, during, and after production.

Back against the Wall: the point in classic screenplay structure where the protagonist has only one choice: to try to solve the story's problem in the climax; marks the second plot point in feature film structure.

Back-Door Pilot: a television movie that is also the prototype for a weekly television series, usually a one-hour drama; sometimes the prototype for a series of movies on a network.

Back Story: events that took place in characters' lives before the story began.

Beats: major sequences in a story.

Beat Sheet: a document that outlines the major sequences, primarily in a television episode, but sometimes used for feature film scene outline development.

b.g.: abbreviation for background; appears in lowercase in the body of an action-description.

Board, the: the daily production schedule for a television episode, movie, or feature film.

Bottle Story: nickname for the storytelling technique that puts the characters of a television series into a small number of sets or locations in order to take them out of the series normal routine.

Breakdown Writer: the job that creates scene outlines from stories to be written for episodes on daytime drama.

Central Question: the *physical* and *metaphysical* thematic questions that the protagonist endeavors to answer by solving the problem in a story.

Classic Structure: the approach to storytelling that utilizes three acts; based on Aristotle's *Poetics* written in 350 B.C.

Climax: the final confrontation in Act Three between the story's protagonist and antagonist or villain.

Co-executive Producer: essentially an executive producer in training in television; also called a *showrunner*; in film, usually someone who contributes in an important way to get a film sold and produced, often involves acquiring finances.

Conflict: the result of characters in opposition in a scene or story.

Context: one particular scene's relationship to one or more scenes that come before or after.

Continuing Storylines: narratives in a television series that take more than one episode to resolve.

Co-producer: in television, essentially a producer in training primarily associated with post-production; in film, the job of co-coordinating the above-the-line details of production; often used as an "honorary" title for writers.

Co-production: two or more companies sharing financial liability and potential profits of a television or film project.

Dark Moment: the dramatic point in classic structure when the protagonist loses an emotional relationship with a likable key pivotal character in the story.

Daytime Drama: a soap opera.

Deficit: the lack of funding assumed by a licensee who sells a television series or movie to a network.

Demographic: the characteristics of a particular audience group pursued by television advertisers.

Denouement: the winding down of a story after its climax, which wraps up all major relationships with the protagonist.

Development: the process of bringing a screenplay or television idea to the screen at a studio, production company, or network.

Director: the person responsible for the actors' performance and executing all aspects of production and post-production.

Double Climax: a second final confrontation in Act Three; usually used in thrillers and sci-fi film and television.

Dramatic Action: the decision-making process of a character that moves him or her from one point in a story to the next.

Emotional Climax: the final confrontation between the protagonist and antagonist or villain that involves solving the inner conflicts between them.

Entertainment Attorney: a person with a law degree who engages in the legal affairs of the entertainment industry; has the ability to negotiate contracts.

Epilogue: a part of story structure that concludes unresolved issues.

Episode: a complete unit of storytelling in a television series; usually daily or weekly.

Episode Arc: the progression of storylines over the course of one episode of a television series.

Executive Producer: the top manager of a television series, sometimes called a *showrunner*; in film, usually someone who brings important talent or significant financing to a project.

Executive Story Editor: a writer who supervises staff story editors and works directly for producers.

Exposition: the telling of events in a story or characters' past that have significant context to present events.

External Conflict: the physical opposition characters experience from other characters' efforts to achieve their goals in a story.

Fade In: the traditional way to start a screenplay; denotes the screen slowly making a transition from black to an image.

Fade Out: the traditional way to end a screenplay; denotes the screen slowly making a transition from an image to black.

Fatal Flaw: a term that refers to a character's primary weakness that makes him or her human and elicits sympathy from the audience.

f.g.: abbreviation for foreground; lowercase when used in an action-description.

First Character Growth: the point in classic screenplay structure when the protagonist realizes that solving the problem-predicament in the story will not be easy; occurs at structure page 45 of a feature film screenplay.

First Plot Point: the first major turning point in classic structure, which marks the end of Act One.

Fish Out of Water: a term used to describe a character moving out of their normal existence or routine, usually the story's protagonist.

Flashback: a term for the parallel narrative technique used in film or television to take the audience to a past incident or story.

Foreshadow: a clue or event that portends a future incident in a story.

Franchise: the general setting for a television series, for example, law, police, the family unit.

Freelance Writer: a writer who is not employed full-time by a television series, studio, or production company and works on a project-to-project basis.

French Scene: a theater term that describes a scene within a scene.

Genre: a type of narrative with identifiable and distinct dramatic elements to its storytelling.

Headwriter: a writer who supervises all staff writers, usually on a daytime drama.

High Concept Premise: a story idea whose situation is more important to the story or plot than the characters.

Hook: a scene or sequence that grabs the audience's attention and promises a certain genre of storytelling.

Improvised Series: a style of television writing that relies on ad-lib dialogue.

Inciting Incident: the event, whether past, present, or future in a story that sets into motion the protagonist's problem.

Intercut: the direction a writer gives in a screenplay or teleplay to designate that shots from two or more separate scenes should be edited together in post-production; primarily used for telephone conversations.

Intercutting: a style of writing that alternates between two or more scenes on a collision course building toward a climatic event; the use of mini-sluglines is essential.

Internal Conflict: the emotional turmoil a character experiences within himself or herself in the course of the story.

Key Thing: the information the protagonist needs to solve the problem in the story, revealed near the end of Act Two in classic structure.

Licensing Fee: the amount of money paid to the owner of a creative property to exploit it for profit, for example, television series or movie.

Linear Story: a narrative that starts at the beginning and unfolds in chronological order.

Line Producer: the person responsible for all the technical aspects of a film or television production.

Location Manager: the person responsible for finding and securing sets not constructed on a soundstage for production of a film or television series.

Lo-high Concept: a drama (which is generally not considered a popular genre) that has a situation that is patently more important to the story than the characters.

Made For: a television movie specially developed for distribution on pay cable networks.

Main Plot: the events created in a story by the protagonist as he or she pursues solving a problem, generally in the "public" realm of the story, for example, on the job.

Manager: someone who guides writers' or actors' careers but does not have the legal right to negotiate contracts or employment.

Members Basic Agreement: the Writers Guild of America's working rules.

Metaphor: one kind of object or idea represents a certain meaning in place of different object or idea.

Metaphysical Central Question: the intangible goal the protagonist pursues in the story; the universal truth.

Midpoint Crisis: an event that happens halfway through a story that provokes the protagonist to act on solving the story's problem prematurely.

Mini-Climax: a dramatic confrontation between the protagonist and antagonist in a sequence that builds to the larger final confrontation.

Mini-Drama: a sequence or series of sequences that tell a story within a story in classic structure.

Mini-Goal: an important short-range objective the protagonist needs to accomplish in order to solve the larger problem in the story.

Mini-Series: a limited television series, usually four hours, but sometimes up to twelve hours, shown over a short period of time.

Mini-Slugline: an abbreviated scene heading without the designations of INT. or EXT. or DAY or NIGHT.

Mnemonic Device: a word or phrase that is repeated in dialogue so that the audience will remember it as important to a story's theme; usually the meaning begins with a negative connotation and finishes with a positive meaning.

Money: slang term for the star of a television series and/or the series regulars.

Moral Dilemma: the choice between two equally distasteful options that involves right and wrong.

Motivation: the dramatic reason for which a character acts in a story; what a character wants in a scene; sometimes called *intention*.

Movie of the Week: a movie developed specifically to be broadcast on commercial television.

Multiple Storylines: several different stories running simultaneously in a television episode or feature film.

Narrative: another term for story—the wants, needs, and desires upon which the protagonist must act to reach a goal, usually involved with solving a specific problem.

Nonlinear Story: a narrative that is not told in chronological order.

Non Sequitur: in dialogue, the illogical progression of a conversation between characters; matching a specific visual situation with improbable dialogue.

Obstacle: an impediment to a character's goal in a story.

OFF: a popular reader-friendly term used in scripts to indicate an important shot for the reader of a screenplay or teleplay, for example, OFF Jack's grin.

ON: a popular reader-friendly term used in scripts to indicate an important shot to the reader of the screenplay or teleplay, for example, ON Jack's grin.

Opening Sequence: a series of scenes designed to promise the audience a certain genre and theme and portends the story's problem.

O.S. or o.s.: abbreviation for offscreen; written in all caps and enclosed in parentheses if next to a character's name over dialogue; written in lowercase if within an action-description.

Pacing: measured increments of time at which a screen story unfolds.

Parallel Narrative: the style of storytelling that weaves together more than one story or plot.

Parenthetical: an element in the format of a screenplay that gives emotional or physical direction for a character's dialogue.

Payoff: to provide a dramatic conclusion to a story element presented earlier (a setup).

Physical Central Question: the tangible goal the protagonist pursues in the story.

Physical Climax: the event where the protagonist either succeeds or fails at solving the external conflict (as opposed to the inner conflict) in the story.

Pilot: the prototype episode for a television series.

Pitch: the verbal articulation of an idea or story to an agent, producer, or executive in a meeting whether formal or informal.

Pivotal Character: a supporting character who has a significant impact on the outcome of a story.

Plot: the events in a story generated primarily by the protagonist's pursuit of a goal in a story.

Plot Reversal: the dramatic turn of events in a story that provides a setback to the protagonist's goal.

Point of Attack: the event that sets into motion the start of a story.

Point of No Return: the point in classic screenplay structure when the protagonist has no choice but to try to solve the problem in the story prematurely (see Midpoint Crisis).

Point of View: the eyes through which a story is told, usually the protagonist's, sometimes the antagonist's; written in the script as POV when denoting visuals seen through the eyes of a character(s).

Post-production: the technical process of combining picture, sound, and special effects of a film after principal photography is completed.

Premise: the focused idea, usually one or two sentences, which can be expanded into a story for a feature film or for a television storyline.

Prep: the process of planning and organizing the necessary elements prior to shooting a film or television episode.

Producer: the primary manager of a film or television project, generally from a creative perspective.

Production: the process of shooting a film or television episode.

Prologue: a scene or sequence that sets the stage for the telling of a story.

Protagonist: the main character in a story through whose eyes a story is told.

Query Letter: a document seeking to create interest in a creative work, generally one page sent to artist representatives.

Reality Television: unscripted programs using everyday people as the talent.

Recommit to Original Goal: the point in classic screenplay structure just after the Second Plot Point when the protagonist regroups and starts to pursue the final confrontation with the antagonist.

Recurring Characters: characters who do not appear in every episode of a television series but appear often enough to be considered a regular member of the cast.

Repurposing: the broadcasting of a network's television series or specials on a different network; usually both networks are owned by the same parent company.

Rising Action: the unrelenting escalation of the stakes for the protagonist in a story.

Runner: not a story or plot but the exploration of relationships between two or more characters in a feature film story or television storyline.

Running Dialogue: a phrase that refers to a character's offhanded remarks that reveal his or her values, beliefs, and attitudes toward life or a specific situation.

Scene: a series of shots that takes place in one set.

Scene Heading: a line in a screenplay or teleplay that designates where action takes place; written in all caps.

Scene Outline: a planning document that determines the exact locations and dramatic content of each location in a screenplay yet to be written.

Season Arc: the overall progress of character relationships within a television series, usually over twenty-two episodes.

Second Plot Point: the event in a story when the protagonist makes a transition from a series of confrontations to the story's resolution; marks the end of Act Two.

Sense of Urgency: a series of deadlines that motivate the protagonist to take actions to solve the problem in the story.

Sequence: a series of scenes that tell a story within a story in a feature film screenplay or television episode.

Series Arc: the overall progress of character relationships within a television series, generally over one hundred episodes (five years) but can be longer.

Series Bible: the document that sets the rules of a television series so that writers, producers, directors, and executives agree on its content and direction.

Series Concept: a document that explains the format of a television series in terms of its premise, franchise, regular characters, and sample episode loglines.
Series Franchise: the setting or world in which a television series takes place, for example, crime scene investigation.
Series Premise: the underlying theme that is explored in each episode over the run of a television series, for example, "the truth is out there."
Series Regulars: the cast of characters who appear in each episode of a television series.
Service the Money: to get all the series regulars (the stars) involved in storylines in an episode.
Setting: the place in which a scene or story takes place; the world that is explored in a story.
Setup: a clue that motivates the audience to wonder "what's going to happen with that?"
SFX: abbreviation used in a screenplay or teleplay to denote a sound effect
Shot: a single image photographed with a film or video camera.
Showrunner: nickname for the producer who manages the day-to-day operations of a television series.
Sitcoms: slang for "situation comedies," which are series that are generally based on a specific state of affairs in which the characters find themselves.
Slugline: nickname for a scene heading.
Sotto: a stage whisper where the audience can hear the dialogue but the other characters in the scene can't.
Spec: a script written on speculation (unpaid).
Spin-off: nickname for creating a new series based on one or more characters from a particular television series.
Spine: another term for story—the wants, needs, and desires upon which the protagonist must act to reach a goal, usually involved with solving a specific problem.
Staff Writer: a screenwriter who is employed full-time writing for a television series.
Story: the wants, needs, and desires that the protagonist must act upon to reach a goal, usually involved with solving a specific problem.
Story Editor: a screenwriter employed full-time who is primarily responsible for maintaining story and character continuity over the course of a season of a television series.
Story Structure: the manner in which a plot unfolds as the protagonist acts to solve the problem in the story.
Structure Milestone: a significant turning point in the story as the protagonist pursues a solution to the problem in the story.
Subplot: the emotional relationship between the protagonist and the antagonist in his or her private life that primarily explores the theme of a feature film.
Subtext: the undercurrent of theme in a scene or sequence; what a scene of sequence is really about.
Supervising Producer: the producer who oversees the staff of a television series; in training to become a co-executive producer.
Suspension of Disbelief: creating a situation in a story the audience can accept though it may be improbable in reality.
Synopsis: a short narrative description of a story or plot for screenplay or teleplay that has already been written.
Tag: an ending scene or sequence that concludes a television episode; also called *epilogue*.

Talky: dialogue between characters that is directed more to the reader or audience for informational purposes than to the characters involved in the conversation.

Teaser: a *prologue*; a scene or sequence that sets a story into motion.

Theme: the universal reason for telling a story; the story's meaning.

Tragic Character: a likable pivotal character who often speaks for the audience and generally dies in the story.

Treatment: a planning document used as a step in the process of a broadly developing story to be executed into a screenplay or teleplay; usually the basis for scene outline development.

Twist: an unexpected gain or loss by a story's protagonist; a surprise ending.

Unity of Opposites: the concept that a story's protagonist and antagonist cannot get what each wants in the story without defeating the other; "someone must lose."

Unlikely Hero: an unlikable pivotal character who, in the end, saves the day for the protagonist.

Villain: the "true" antagonist in a story, often cloaked in the story until revealed by the events of the story.

Visual Motif: a recurring object or image that represents a story's theme.

V.O. or v.o.: abbreviation for voice-over; written in all caps next to character's name over dialogue; use lowercase within an action-description.

Writers Guild of America: a labor organization representing writers in the motion picture, broadcast, cable, interactive, and new media industries, made up of Writers Guild of America, West (Los Angeles) and East (New York).

Index

About the Author

Stephen V. Duncan is currently a tenured associate professor of screenwriting at the Loyola Marymount University's School of Film and Television in Los Angeles, Calif. His credits include co-creator and executive consultant of the award-winning, critically acclaimed CBS-TV one-hour Vietnam War series *Tour of Duty*, writer-producer of the touted ABC-TV one-hour action series *A Man Called Hawk*, and the co-writer of the highly praised Turner Network Television original movie *The Court-Martial of Jackie Robinson*.

Duncan has developed and written projects for Warner Bros., New World Television, vonZerneck-Sertner Films, Spelling Television, Columbia Television, NBC Productions, Republic Pictures, and Tri-Star Pictures. He's an award-winning writer-producer-director of industrial and informational film and video, having received numerous Gold and Silver Angel Awards from the International Television Association.

Duncan graduated cum laude with a bachelor of science degree in art design from North Carolina A&T State University and holds a master of arts degree in communication arts: television and film from Loyola Marymount University.